FAMILY ISSUES IN CURRENT GERONTOLOGY

FAMILY ISSUES
IN CURRENT
GERONTOLOGY

Sponsored by
THE GERONTOLOGICAL SOCIETY
OF AMERICA

Lillian E. Troll, Editor

SPRINGER PUBLISHING COMPANY
New York

Copyright © 1986 by the Gerontological Society of America

Springer Publishing Company, Inc.
536 Broadway
New York, NY 10012

86 87 88 89 90 / 5 4 3 2 1

Library of Congress Cataloging-in-Publication Data

Family issues in current gerontology.

  "Second volume of Current Gerontology"—Foreword.
  Reprints of articles from the Journal of Gerontology, and The Gerontologist.
  Includes bibliographies and index.
  1. Aged—United States—Family relationships. 2. Aged—Care and hygiene—United States.   I. Troll, Lillian E.   II. Gerontological Society of America. III. Journal of Gerontology. IV. Gerontologist. [DNLM: 1. Family. 2. Geriatrics. 3. Interpersonal Relations.   WT 30 F1985]
HQ1064.U5F275   1986   306.8'7   86-600307
ISBN 0-8261-5561-8 (pbk.)

Printed in the United States of America

Contents

VI Kinship Networks

VII Childlessness and Divorce

Contributors

Greg Arling, Ph.D.
Director
Virginia Center on Aging
Virginia Commonwealth University
Richmond, Virginia

Maxine P. Atkinson, Ph.D.
Department of Sociology and Anthropology
North Carolina State University
Raleigh, North Carolina and
Postdoctoral Fellow
Center for the Study of Aging and
Human Development
Duke University Medical Center
Durham, North Carolina

Elizabeth A. Bankoff, Ph.D.
Department of Behavioral Sciences
The University of Chicago
Chicago, Illinois

Linda J. Beckman, Ph.D.
Department of Psychiatry
School of Medicine
University of California at Los
Angeles

James N. Breckenridge, Ph.D.
Center for the Study of
Psychotherapy and Aging
Palo Alto Veterans Administration
Medical Center
Palo Alto, California

Elaine M. Brody
Philadelphia Geriatric Center
Philadelphia, Pennsylvania

Marjorie H. Cantor, M.A.
Brookdale Professor of Gerontology
Graduate School of Social Service
and the Third Age Center
Fordham University
New York, New York

Robert J. Caslyn, Ph.D.
Assistant Professor of Psychology
University of Missouri—St. Louis

Donald J. Catalano, M.S.W., M.P.H.
Medical Anthropology Program
University of California, San
Francisco

Victor G. Cicirelli, Ph.D.
Department of Psychological
Services
Purdue University
West Lafayette, Indiana

Gary T. Deimling, Ph.D.
The Margaret Blenkner Research
Center
The Benjamin Rose Institute
Cleveland, Ohio

Gerda G. Fillenbaum, Ph.D.
Center for the Study of Aging and
    Human Development
Duke University Medical Center
Durham, North Carolina

Dolores Gallagher, Ph.D.
Geriatric Research, Education, and
    Clinical Center
Center for the Study of
    Psychotherapy and Aging
Palo Alto Veterans Administration
    Medical Center
Palo Alto, California

Judith Gonyea, Ph.D.
Pacific Northwest Long Term Care
    Center
University of Washington
Seattle, Washington

Carole K. Holahan, Ph.D.
Measurement and Evaluation
    Center
University of Texas at Austin

Nancy Hooyman, Ph.D.
School of Social Work
University of Washington
Seattle, Washington

Betsy Bosak Houser, Ed.D.
Department of Psychiatry
School of Medicine
University of California at Los
    Angeles

Colleen Leahy Johnson, Ph.D.
Medical Anthropology Program
University of California, San
    Francisco

Vira R. Kivett, Ph.D.
School of Home Economics
Department of Child Development
    and Family Relations
University of North Carolina
Greensboro, North Carolina and
North Carolina Agricultural
    Research Service
North Carolina State University
Raleigh, North Carolina

William J. McAuley, Ph.D.
Associate Director for Research and
    Policy Analysis
Virginia Center on Aging
Virginia Commonwealth University
Richmond, Virginia

Charles H. Mindel, Ph.D.
Graduate School of Social Work
University of Texas at Arlington

Jim Mitchell, Ph.D.
Department of Sociology,
    Anthropology, and Economics
East Carolina University
Greenville, North Carolina

Rhonda Montgomery, Ph.D.
Pacific Northwest Long Term Care
    Center
University of Washington
Seattle, Washington

Elizabeth Mutran
Department of Sociology
University of Iowa
Iowa City, Iowa

Mary Anne P. Myers
Department of Sociology
University of North Carolina
Chapel Hill, North Carolina

Corinne N. Nydegger, Ph.D.
Medical Anthropology Program
University of California, San
Francisco

James Peterson, Ph.D.
University of Southern California
Los Angeles, California

S. Walter Poulshock, Ph.D.
The Margaret Blenkner Research
Center
The Benjamin Rose Institute
Cleveland, Ohio

Jasper C. Register, Ph.D.
Associate Professor
Department of Sociology,
Anthropology, and
Economics
East Carolina University
Greenville, North Carolina

Ethel Shanas, Ph.D.
Department of Sociology
University of Illinois at Chicago

Larry W. Thompson, Ph.D.
Center for the Study of
Psychotherapy and Aging
Palo Alto Veterans Administration
Medical Center
Palo Alto, California

Peter Uhlenberg
Associate Professor
Department of Sociology
University of North Carolina
Chapel Hill, North Carolina

Laurence M. Wallman, M.A.
Center for the Study of Aging and
Human Development
Duke University Medical Center
Durham, North Carolina

Jonathan L. York, M.A.
Director
Older Adult Services
St. Lawrence Hospital CMHC
Lansing, Michigan

Foreword

This is the second volume of *Current Gerontology*, a monograph series taken from the two journals of the Gerontological Society of America, *The Journal of Gerontology* and *The Gerontologist*. Each volume in the series focuses on a single issue area of current concern in gerontology and provides a rich collection of facts, concepts, and controversies. The series extends the usefulness of GSA journal articles by presenting them in a thematic form that can be used in education and training programs and that can reach various types of readers who may not regularly read the Society's journals.

Family issues was selected as the theme for this second volume because many recent articles in Society journals deal with these issues, and interest in family aspects of gerontology extends well beyond the boundaries of the membership of the Gerontological Society of America.

Dr. Lillian Troll, one of our foremost scholars in family gerontology, was selected by the Editorial Committee to edit this volume. She was asked to select an array of articles and provide brief editorial introductions. Instead, she chose to extensively review the literature in each of the topic areas and provide a much more integrated context for the articles than is typical of books of readings. Indeed, with her introductory materials, *Family Issues in Current Gerontology* is essentially an up-to-date text with readings. As such, it will be a welcome addition to the field.

Robert C. Atchley
Editor-in-Chief
Current Gerontology

Introduction

Most older people have family connections. They have husbands or wives, children and grandchildren, sisters and brothers, cousins, nieces, and nephews. They also have multiple in-laws. Many have ex-in-laws and multiple stepchildren and stepgrandchildren. Most have family contacts. They live with or near other family members. They visit them, exchange letters with them, and speak with them on the telephone. They help them and are helped by them, both with money and services. They care for them or are cared for by them as need arises. And they have a variety of strong feelings for them: love, hate, friendship, loyalty, obligation, security.

This volume, a publication of the Gerontological Society of America, contains reprints of 20 articles from its two journals: *The Journal of Gerontology* and *The Gerontologist*. These articles were selected because they seem to be the most significant ones published during the past few years. Other relevant and important articles have appeared in other journals, notably the *Journal of Marriage and the Family*. They will be discussed here in connection with the topics covered. Also, the information in the articles included in this volume will be placed within the context of earlier work and theory.

This volume has been divided on an a priori basis into several parts. This division is not equal in content because some of the areas have received more attention than others over a longer period of time than others, and there are reasons why this is so. Also, some of the articles deal with more than one topic. It is strategic to place such multitopic articles in the part where they are first appropriate and then refer back to them in later sections.

Each part, therefore, will be introduced by an overview or comments that present what I perceive as the major question in that area and the relevant theory and past empirical work in that area, as well as references to concurrent articles in other journals.

The first part deals with changes in marital relations over time. Its focus is the dyad, the married couple. Part II, dealing with widowhood, changes its focus to the individual, the survivor of a couple or dyad. Part III turns to dyads again, to the parent–child relationship in old age. Part IV moves to a somewhat larger cast of characters, the quantity and sometimes the correlates of caregiving. Part V is similar and deals with living arrangements. Since the Gerontological Society of America has already published a volume on caregiving in more institutionalized or applied settings (*Current Gerontology: Long Term Care*, edited by Sheldon Tobin), this volume will attend largely to the noninstitutional, home, and community settings. The last two parts, VI and VII, cover particular issues and relationships of older people— siblings, grandchildren, networks, and family systems in Part VI and the effects of childlessness and divorce in Part VII.

Several reviews or collections of readings on families of older people are recommended for anyone interested in further pursuit of this topic. Aside from the host of current textbooks on aging in general and empirical research reports and handbooks, these include Shanas and Streib (1965), Troll, Miller, and Atchley (1979), Troll (1982a), Brubaker (1983), and Bengtson and Robertson (1985).

Part I

Marriage

In the Western world—Canada and the United States and Western Europe—very few people now labeled "old" (usually meaning over 60 or 65 years of age) have never been married. In fact, research on never-married older people is practically nonexistent because there are so few to study (see Huyck & Hoyer, 1982; Skolnick, 1981; Troll, Miller, & Atchley, 1979).[1] Less than 5% of older Americans are potential subjects. On the other hand, many older people are not married currently, at least to their first spouses, particularly at very old ages. Skolnick's longitudinal study members, who are "advantaged" and only middle-aged rather than old, represent a high point of marital stability in that 75% of them are still married to their first spouses, after at least 20 years. Another way to put it is that the chances of couples who married in the 1930s and 1940s reaching their golden wedding anniversaries are less than 5%. In spite of increased life expectancy, no more couples reach this marker nowadays than did a century ago. The difference is that before 1974 marriages ended with death; after 1974 they ended with divorce more often than death (Glick, 1980). At the end of the 19th century, the average length of marriage at the time one spouse died was about 28 years; in the late 1970s it was over 43 years (Goldman & Lord, 1983).

What might we want to know about couples in the later years of life? There are at least six major questions we might ask.

1. What is the quality of marriage in old age? Does the way husbands and wives feel about each other change systematically over time?

[1]References cited in part introductions have been combined into one list, to be found at the end of the volume, pages 362–372.

2. What about sex in old age?

3. What about patterns of division of labor? Do patterns once established persist, or do they change with particular events like retirement?

4. What about caregiving? Is the quality of care to sick old people better or worse if the caregiver is a spouse rather than a child or an institution?

5. What are the effects, in general, of parenting, of the "emptying of the nest," of retirement from the labor force, of financial changes, of changes in residence, or of illness on the marital relationship?

6. Are there major differences associated with socioeconomic status, race, or ethnicity?

Clearly, some of these questions overlap. Some ask about what is and others focus more on possible causes of what is. Each will now be considered briefly.

QUALITY OF MARRIAGE

While some define a good marriage as one that lasts, most research suggests that otherwise "good" marriages can end in divorce (or death), and "bad" marriages can last for more than 50 years (Troll, Miller, & Atchley, 1979). Regardless, it is possible to study only those marriages that last.

Marital quality is judged and measured in different ways. The most common is "marital satisfaction." Respondents are sometimes asked directly, "How satisfied are you with your marriage (or your spouse)?" or "If you had it to do over, would you still marry your present spouse?" Obviously, these are evaluations of the individuals, not of the relationship.

Over and above the problems of comparing different meanings of marital satisfaction or adjustment are the problems of getting couple scores from individuals' reports. What about couples in which the wife's report differs from her husband's, as is frequently the case? If the couple's marriage is really two marriages, his and hers (Bernard, 1973), whose satisfaction should we consider?

The most desirable way of finding out about the quality or dynamics of a relationship like that of a married couple would be to consider the couple as the unit that we study, to measure their relationship directly instead of getting each member's perception of the relationship. This is a more difficult task than asking people questions, even if you try to combine their answers, and so it has almost never been done, particularly in the research on older marriages. An example of this technique is the study of communication patterns by Raush, Barry, Hertel, and Swain (1974). Skolnick (1981), by using ratings by observers in addition to self-reports by marital partners, comes closer to this goal than most investigators.

Based on individuals' reports, then, much of the evidence has suggested that marital satisfaction starts decreasing almost immediately after marriage, particularly for couples who become parents. There is also some evidence that satisfaction goes up again after the children leave home and the couple is alone together again, but then many of the more dissatisfied couples may have divorced by the time their children are grown (although divorce is most prevalent in the first months and years of marriage, as will be noted in a later section).

One California study points to a possible reason for some of the lack of consistency in findings in this area. Gilford and Bengtson (1979) showed different developmental patterns for positive marital feelings and negative ones. Unfortunately, their data are not longitudinal (following the same couples over time) but, rather, compare three generations of adults. Among the members of the young-adult generation—the grandchildren—*both* positive and negative feelings are high. There is at this time of life what one might call a lot of "heat," both love and hate, fighting and sex. This kind of bivalent interaction in youth had earlier been described by Feldman (1964) and may reflect the extreme nature of youthful emotion (Lowenthal, Thurnher, & Chiriboga, 1975). The members of the middle generation, the parents of the young adults, report much less positive interaction than does the youngest generation—in fact, the lowest of all three generations—but also much less negative feelings. They neither fight as much nor love as much. The oldest generation, the grandparents, about the primary ages of concern of this volume, have the lowest amount of negative sentiment but more positive attitudes toward their spouses than do the members of the middle generation, their children. Thus, if we could extrapolate a process over time from these cross-sectional data, we might conclude that there is a steady decline in negative feelings combined with a curvilinear pattern of positive feelings—perhaps more positive after the children leave home.

The first reprint included in this volume, Holahan's (1984) comparison of the marital satisfaction and attitudes of older people (not couples, unfortunately) who had been studied over a 40-year period (longitudinal data) with that of a matched sample of young married people (cohort comparison) is of particular interest. One of her findings is that even though the older women's marital satisfaction decreased over time, it was still higher than that of the younger, more recently married women.

The older men, on the other hand, showed no change in satisfaction over time. They were also more satisfied with their marriages than were the younger men. These findings suggest a triple process. First, there are sex differences. Older men are more satisfied than older women. Second, there are length of marriage differences, but for women only. Third, there are historical differences. People who got married in 1940 say they are more satisfied than those who got married in 1970.

Note that this study looks at the responses of individuals, not couples. It also includes remarried as well as still married people. It is likely that many of the men are talking about newer spouses than the women are. The dropout rate of subjects was not because of divorce but rather because of death and other causes of sample attrition.

Two other longitudinal studies, each covering a shorter duration of marriage than did Holahan's study (40 years), show conflicting data. Pineo (1961) surveyed 400 couples who had been married up to 20 years and who had originally been part of a study of 1,000 engaged couples studied by Burgess and Wallin (1953). Pineo found substantial "disenchantment" over time. There were significant declines in "marital adjustment," "love," "permanence," and "consensus" reported by both husbands and wives. There were also less sharing of interests and activities and lowered frequency of sexual intercourse. Incidentally, husbands and wives agreed only moderately—a correlation of .42 on all measures combined and .36 on marital satisfaction.

Pineo (1961) concluded that there had been a progressive "loss of fit" between partners over the years. It is unfortunate that these couples have not been reinterviewed. Their children were just entering their teens, for the most part, and it would be interesting to know whether the negative process continued or became reversed after the children grew up and left home, as some cross-sectional data suggest (e.g., Feldman, 1964; Gilford & Bengtson, 1979).

Skolnik's (1981) analysis of the last follow-up of the Berkeley longitudinal sample is based on a much smaller number of subjects than Pineo's, more comparable to Holahan's. However, she was able to include more qualitative data and to look at the couple as a unit. She was also able to compare the middle-aged information with the same people's premarital, even childhood personality data, at least for the one of the spouses (88 women and 83 men) who had been in the longitudinal study.

Skolnick (1981) stresses the diversity of change patterns over time. She is also more optimistic than most other writers. The low incidence of divorce in this sample—only 25% after 16 to 18 years—reflects its high socioeconomic status. The 82 enduring marriages showed no evidence of universal decline in marital quality, as Pineo (1961) found, at least from the birth of the first child (no "honeymoon"-time interviews are available). Also, as in these other studies, few of the couples are in the "empty nest" phase of marriage, and we can only hope that the next follow-up may answer questions about the effect of departure of children from the scene. Some marriages got better and some got worse—obviously, those couples who divorced should be added to the getting-worse group. Sixty-three percent of the marriages improved and 14% deteriorated (in the opinion of the one spouse who reported). It was Skolnick's "overwhelming impression" that changes were primarily due to situational factors such as money, demands of children, in-laws, grandparental relations, or health.

The strongest correlate of marital satisfaction was, almost redundantly, affectionate and enjoyable personal relations. These "good" marriages, however, varied in other characteristics, like togetherness and the kinds of marriages their parents had. They tended to accept conflict as a normal part of married life and they also tended to be homogamous in personality. It is important to remember, though, that the marriage which is reported as good by one partner might not be considered as good by the other; the correlation between husbands' and wives' ratings of marital satisfaction was only .31 (even lower than what Pineo's respondents had). Where husbands and wives differed widely, the husbands tended to be more satisfied than their wives. Men's satisfaction with their marriage reflected their general satisfaction with life—with their career success, for example—while women's was less linked to factors extrinsic to the marriage.

So far, we have no longitudinal data on couples after their children leave home. Only a few studies have looked at marital relations of older couples (Atchley & Miller, 1983; Brubaker & Hennon, 1982; Parron, 1979; Swenson, Eskew, & Kohlhepp, 1981). The New Jersey golden wedding couples interviewed by Parron were, with few exceptions, "remarkably close." In fact, they described their past relationship as having "always been close." Rather than "his" and "hers" marriages, they were now seen as "theirs." They were committed to making their marriages work, they needed each other "more than ever," and they put their partners ahead of all other people.

Swenson and his colleagues (1981) pursued a more theoretically ambitious goal, comparing couples at different stages of the "family life cycle" on two marital relationship scales—expression of love and extent of marital problems—and on an "ego-development" scale. Their developmental findings parallel those of Gilford and Bengtson (1979) mentioned earlier, with progressively less expression of love associated with the longer marriages. (These are also cross-sectional data). Marital problems peaked among those couples involved in raising children, higher then than that found in the beginning of marriage or later on. The relation of these trends to ego development is particularly intriguing, suggesting an explanation for some of the conflicting findings about a rise in marital satisfaction post-childrearing. Two levels of ego development were considered: "conformist," involving stereotyped ways of looking at their spouse, and "post-conformist," involving openness to seeing each other in less role-stereotyped ways. The conformist couples showed a decrease in expression of love after the childrearing phase, but the post-conformist couples actually reported more love in the later years than earlier. Sadly, most couples tend to be conformist, and since most research reports present only averages, the prevailing findings would suggest declines in marital satisfaction over the years. Stereotyped ways of viewing their spouse would lead to gradual loss of "true" interactions. Perhaps both the Berkeley sample studied by Skolnik (1981) and the couples interviewed by Parron (1979) were preponderantly post-conformist, developing in complexity over their lives, becoming less role-stereotyped, and thus able to revise their attitudes and behaviors to adapt to changes in their partners and in their circumstances.

Another aspect of the relationship between marital matching and personality development concerns lack of symmetry in the development of the two individuals concerned. Troll (1985b) suggests that continued maintenance of "fit," to use Pineo's term, can be obtained only if both husband and wife do not change over the years or if they change the same way.

LOVE AND SEX

One often-mentioned finding about love is its change over time. Cuber and Harroff (1963) described five kinds of love found among their sample of "significant Americans": conflict-habituated, devitalized, passive/congenial, vital, and total. The older respondents reported more devitalized and passive/congenial than the younger ones. Reedy (1977) found six different aspects of love among happily married couples. Younger couples ranked physical love—sex—highest; older couples, emotional security and loyalty. Troll (1982a) makes a distinction between attraction and attachment. Attraction is high in the beginning of a relationship, but, deriving from novelty, it must fade over time, being replaced by attachment or close psychological bonding. Sternberg (1985) synthesized earlier work by hypothesizing three components of love: passion, intimacy, and commitment. Passion is what he terms a "salient" component; it is also ephemeral. Intimacy or friendship lasts longer, is more salient than commitment, and is more subject to conscious control. Commitment is the most stable component over time, and easily subject to conscious control. It is characteristic of long-term relationships.

Apparently, satisfaction with marriage and the quality of marital relations are independent of passionate love and sex, particularly in later life. Swenson and his colleagues (1981), as noted above, and Skolnik (1981) show that love can remain throughout the life of a marriage, but that it would be defined differently at different times.

Sexual love is often seen as primary in early marriage but incidental to later marriage. However, we should not assume that sex is either irrelevant or impossible in later life. A number of writers and investigators of the 1970s pointed to the continued potential for sexual enjoyment throughout life (e.g., Masters & Johnson, 1966). Some women, for example, report an upswing of sexual enjoyment after menopause, and men who are impotent can be helped to reverse their condition.

Following this set of findings, many practitioners believed that it was desirable to encourage physical sex among all older people, that it was vital to physical and mental health. An article by Thomas (1982) points to some of the absurdities of this "movement." He argues that sex is for enjoyment (and procreation, of course) but should not be considered an "essential vitamin."

HOUSEHOLD DIVISION OF LABOR

Do older husbands and wives share housework more than they did when they were younger? Does retirement make a difference? Does retirement of husbands make more difference than retirement of wives? Research has looked at development of personality differentiation between men and women, at normative attitudes toward division of family responsibilities, and at actual behavior. Part of the mission of the women's movement was equality in all the work of marriage: in household tasks, in earning a living, in child care. How well has this mission succeeded?

First, with regard to sex-role orientation, Gutmann (1975) argues that the demands of parenthood shape personality, encouraging women to heighten their expressive and men their instrumental natures—to use the dichotomy suggested earlier by Parsons (1955). After the "emptying of the nest," then, in middle age, men would again become less instrumental, more nurturant, and women more assertive.

Twenty years ago, Lipman (1961) found that a majority of his sample of men and women over 60 years of age believed that household tasks should be shared, with more women believing this than men. More recently, a few investigators have reported no difference in beliefs about instrumental activity differences between young and early-middle-aged respondents, but greater endorsement of expressive functions by middle-aged respondents (Fengler, 1973; Scanzoni, 1975; Thurnher, 1976).

Holahan's (1984) longitudinal study, the first article in this volume, not only looked at marital satisfaction, but also at attitudes about sharing household work. Her data are consistent with previous findings. The attitudes toward sharing on the part of her women subjects became more egalitarian over time, consistent with previous reports, and were more egalitarian than those of the male subjects, also consistent with Lipman's (1961) findings; but they still were more traditional than those of younger women today. The older men's attitude change, however, may be more a matter of development over life than of societal change, since they espoused more egalitarian values in their older ages than the younger men did. Thus, older couples today approve of sharing household work more than they did when they were young but not more than younger couples of today do.

A review of the research before and during the 1970s concludes that retired couples, who are often assumed to be readier to share household work, do "a great deal of sharing . . . but not . . . upon sex-stereotyped lines" (Troll, Miller, & Atchley, 1979, p. 61). Even in an era of high sex stereotyping, Lipman (1961) found that "many retired husbands worked together with their wives on chores that required little specialized skill and knowledge, such as washing dishes and shopping for groceries." When Ballweg (1967) compared retired husbands with employed husbands of the same age, they were not more likely to share activities as a whole but rather to assume responsibility for a few tasks already socially defined as "masculine."

A more recent Canadian study (Keating & Cole, 1980) states that "after a post-retirement period of increased sharing, most couples reverted to their pre-retirement division of roles." In general, older couples, even retired couples, do not change their patterns of household work as much as one might expect, or as much as they—at least the wives—expect (Albrecht, Bahr, & Chadwick, 1979). This is particularly true for working class couples, who are more likely to see providing money and goods as a man's job and housekeeping as a woman's. While Albrecht and his colleagues found greater acceptance for sharing of the provider role among younger couples, even they— the younger couples—saw child care, kinship maintenance, and housekeeping as women's work.

As more women enter the population of the retired, it becomes appropriate to see how their retirement affects marital division of labor. Two studies (Brubaker & Hennon, 1982; Szinovacz, 1980) found traditional patterns persisting just as they do after the retirement of husbands. Employment of wives among younger couples, incidentally, has not been shown to alter such traditional divisions of household tasks (see Troll, Miller, & Atchley, 1979, for a review). Employed mothers have been found to do about five times more housework than their husbands (Walker, 1970). Szinovacz noted a variety of patterns after wives' retirement, including some families in which husbands increased their household work. However, the common idea that women find retirement easier than men because they always have their home activities to keep them involved does not seem to hold true. At least, they have usually had the home activities all along; there is no change.

CAREGIVING

This is just a brief note here, because the general topic of caregiving is presented in a later section. There is a sharp sex division in who takes care of old people when they are sick that is not too different from what exists at younger ages. Because of the fact that, at least among people now old, husbands are older than their wives, women have a longer life expectancy, and men are more likely to remarry than are women, most older men, when they are sick, are cared for by a wife and most older women by a daughter. The article by Johnson and Catalano (1983) is included in this volume because of its information about the difference in spousal caregiving from that by children or professionals. When a spouse (usually a wife, remember) takes care of a person released from an acute-care hospital, the services she renders tend to be more lasting and more comprehensive. Note that only 4% of the people followed in the study who were taken care of by a spouse landed back in the hospital or in a long-term care institution during the 8 months following, compared with 20% of the unmarried. Several factors may operate here.

In the cohort now old, commitment to a spouse is still predominantly "for better or for worse." Further, the commitment becomes a joint one. Observers have noted that older couples become interdependent at the end of life, nursing each other and dividing up household chores on the basis of ability. Clark and Anderson (1967) use the term "symbiotic" to describe this kind of relationship. Johnson (1985b) noted that in over three-quarters of the couples in which one spouse took care of the other, the caretaking member was also likely to be in poor health. Because in most of these cases both husband and wife did what they could, their expressed marital satisfaction was high—but, Johnson adds, they showed little emotion in their relationship. There seem to be sex differences. The caretaking wives said they were burdened more than did the caretaking husbands. The women were likely to do most of the work themselves, while the men were more likely to use community help. Thus, the women were more likely to be confined to their homes. Zarit, Reever, and Bach-Peterson (1980) found that burdens were felt to be lighter by those caretakers (spouses or daughters) who get more visits from relatives and friends, that in fact feeling burdened was not related to the severity of the illness but to the social support.

Finally, it is possible that the close bodily intimacy of tending a sick person may be more comfortable for a spouse than for a child. After all, marriage is supposed to involve physical intimacy, while parents and children are supposed to avoid it, at least after adulthood, in our culture.

EFFECTS OF MAJOR LIFE EVENTS

For couples, three major life events in the later years are departure of children from the home (empty nest), retirement, and major illness. Earlier views of these events tended to perceive them as creating switching points or crisis points in the lives affected, but the bulk of research evidence forces us to conclude that such changes in circumstances are better viewed as processes, preceded by anticipation, preparation, and rehearsal and followed by gradual adaptation. There is little evidence for abrupt transitions.

Much has been said about the beneficial effect of the empty nest upon marital quality, and this has been discussed in the answer to Question 1 above. As noted there, research like that of Swenson et al. (1981) has not found immediate improvement of marital quality. In fact, expression of love is usually even lower among couples in this "stage" than among those whose children are still at home. If there is any improvement related to departure of children, even to the economic consequences of their absence, and not just to differences between the cohort of those now past childrearing and those still raising children, such changes take a long time to happen and seem to occur only for couples of post-conformist ego development. That is, couples ready to see changes in their partners, couples who are open to new information, can grow toward more satisfactory relationships, but not couples who follow the same set of interactions "stamped in" by 20 years of living together. It is individual personality attributes of the partners, not the event itself, that is causal. Finally, as noted earlier, it depends on which aspect of the relationship one is examining: positive or negative feelings, for example.

There is more popular endorsement for the effect on marriage of retirement than for the effect of the empty nest, but as both Atchley and Miller (1983) and Keating and Cole (1980) report, findings are ambiguous, at best. Atchley and Miller conclude from longitudinal data that retirement "has no measurable effect on the quality of couples' lives." Keating and Cole's women respondents complained of decreased personal freedom and too much togetherness. On the other hand, they also said that the pleasure in the company of their husband and the feeling of being needed offset their loss of personal freedom. They apparently felt they had to do more organizing of their husbands' lives, but their husbands were not altogether pleased by this added control. And then, as noted, Swenson and his colleagues (1981) found improvement in the quality of marriage for some. But even these investigators found no change in household division of labor.

There is a suggestion that caring for a sick spouse in later life is often associated with an intensification of interactions, with a tightening of bonding and exclusion of everyone but the spouse (Johnson, 1985b). On the other hand, Zarit and his colleagues (1980) and others found no differences between daughters and wives in admissions of feeling burdened by caretaking. Johnson does conclude that "illness has been found to have far more impact than retirement on marital satisfaction."

SOCIAL GROUP DIFFERENCES

A major difference that social-group membership contributes to couple relations is in the number of couples itself. In relatively disadvantaged groups (lower in socioeconomic status, black and Hispanic, recent immigrants, etc.), a smaller percentage ever got married, and there is more separation, divorce, and lower age of widowhood than in more advantaged groups. Partly for these reasons, and also to control for variation in non-central variables, most research on couples has been with white, middle-class samples (see Mindel, 1983). However, by deducing from other data, such as Skolnick's (1981) report that fluctuations in marital quality are associated with financial ups and downs, it would not be unwarranted to state that marital quality in disadvantaged groups would be lower than in advantaged groups.

1

Marital Attitudes over 40 Years: A Longitudinal and Cohort Analysis*

Carole K. Holahan

In recent years researchers have become increasingly aware of the influence of the biosocial and historical context on human development (Baltes et al., 1980). Significant cohort differences have been reported, for example, in the study of intelligence (e.g., Schaie, 1979), as well as in the study of socialization and personality (e.g., Elder, 1979; Woodruff & Birren, 1972). The accumulation of evidence concerning cohort influences has led to greater caution in the interpretation of cross-sectional research results. In cross-sectional studies, aging and cohort are inherently confounded, and Schaie (1979) has strongly advocated the use of sequential research designs to prevent possible erroneous interpretations. Although resources for a complete sequential design are rarely available, it is possible to gain greater understanding of life cycle change by employing multiple

*Journal of Gerontology, 39 (1) (1984), 49–57.

This research was supported by National Institute on Aging grant AG01015 to Robert R. Sears, Stanford University. The author is grateful to Robert R. Sears and Pauline S. Sears for their many helpful suggestions throughout the conduct of this project. Thanks are due to Janet T. Spence for her thoughtful comments on an earlier draft of this manuscript. Thanks are also due to Lee Olsen and David Kaku for their assistance in coding. This research was conducted in part while the author was a Visiting Scholar at the Center for Research on Women, Stanford University.

research strategies (e.g., Woodruff & Birren, 1972). Most of the previous work of this kind, however, has involved personality and cognitive variables.

The present study was undertaken to investigate change in adulthood in the attitudinal realm—specifically, changes in *marital attitudes* from a developmental and historical perspective utilizing longitudinal and cohort comparisons. The study focused on attitudes related to egalitarianism in marriage and to marital satisfaction and examined these attitudes in light of the dramatic sociocultural change in the last 40 years in the social roles of women and men. To accomplish this goal, two studies were conducted. The first consisted of a longitudinal analysis of changes in attitudes of a sample of individuals from the Terman Study of the Gifted from 1940, when they were approximately 30 years old, to 1981, when they had reached the age of 70. To aid in the interpretation of this 40 year comparison of the Terman subjects, a cohort comparison was carried out in which their responses in 1940 at the age of 30 were compared with those of a contemporary sample of 30-year-old adults.

In investigating change in marital attitudes in adulthood, previous work relating to attitude change more generally over the life span must be considered. According to Glenn (1980), it is widely believed that individuals become more conservative in their attitudes throughout adulthood. This belief is reinforced by the results of cross-sectional analyses of attitude data. For example, middle-aged and older adults have been shown to be moderately more conservative on economic and political issues and substantially more conservative on moral issues than adults under age 30. Glenn, however, in summarizing the research in this area, found little evidence to support the notion that conservatism increases with age in adulthood. Both individuals and cohorts appear to have become more liberal during the last several decades (e.g., Cutler & Kaufman, 1975; Greeley & Spaeth, 1970). Accumulated evidence (e.g., Carlsson & Karlsson, 1970) supports, instead, what has come to be known as the aging–stability hypothesis. According to Glenn's statement of this hypothesis, the general change proneness of cohorts declines approximately linearly after young adulthood. Thus, younger cohorts are predicted to change to a greater extent than older cohorts in response to a particular influence for change, producing age differences in attitudes.

The unique status of the Terman subjects in the history of psychological research provides a compelling rationale for their continued study. In 1922 Lewis Terman began his study of high-IQ children in urban California. These individuals have now been followed for over

60 years (Burkes et al., 1930; Holahan, 1981; Oden, 1968; P. Sears, 1979; P. Sears & Barbee, 1977; R. Sears, 1977; Terman et al., 1925; Terman & Oden, 1947), and now provide the most complete record presently available of the human life cycle from childhood to old age. In addition, their selection on the basis of high intellectual ability allows us to examine human development within the context of maximum intellectual potential. Moreover, the Terman subjects experienced a set of dramatic historical events in their lifetime, presenting the opportunity for the study of the effects of major sociocultural change.

The Terman sample reached young adulthood at a period of major economic and political insecurity. When the Great Depression reached its most severe level in 1932 and 1933, most of the Terman subjects who had attended college had recently completed their undergraduate education. From the 1930s to the 1940s, the pressures of the Depression reinforced traditional roles for men and women (Chafe, 1972). Thus, the prevailing social structures during the Terman sample's youth reflected relatively restricted gender roles, with women's chief involvement in the home and men's chief involvement in the area of work.

Although women entered the labor force in large numbers during World War II, its conclusion was accompanied by a return to traditional roles. Women's participation in higher education relative to men's declined sharply in the 1940s but increased in the late 1950s and continued to grow in the 1960s and 1970s. The increase in women's educational involvement has been accompanied by a significant rise in the rate of women's employment, particularly for married women, although women have yet to reach a level of occupational attainment equal to that of men (Stromberg & Harkess, 1978). There is a general agreement, however, that women's roles are changing, and current investigators have suggested that these changes have been accompanied by changes in societal roles for men as well (e.g., Pleck, 1979).

In view of the significant role changes for women and men over the last 40 years, the use of a time-lag approach in the present investigation in addition to longitudinal measurement adds considerably to the potential information to be obtained from the study. The availability of the cohort results provides the opportunity for assessing differences in the historical contexts in which the longitudinal measures were obtained. It is important to note, however, that the addition of the time-lag comparison alone will not allow for the separation of history-graded and aging effects; more complex designs would be necessary to unravel the complex interrelationships of aging and cohort. The relative consistency or inconsistency of the longitudinal and time-lag comparisons, however, does provide a basis for the generation of hypotheses concerning the contribution of aging and historical influences to attitude change over the life span.

METHOD

Participants and Procedure

Terman Sample

The archives of the Terman Study of the Gifted were searched for all participants who graduated from Stanford University or the University of California, Berkeley, who responded to the 1940 questionnaire, who were married at the time of their response to the 1940 survey, and were between the ages of 26 and 37 in 1940. This search yielded 71 men and 73 women. The mean age of the men was 30.8 (SD = 2.67) and of the women was 29.97 (SD = 2.44). Men's college graduation dates ranged from 1925 to 1935 (median = 1930). Women graduated from 1922 to 1939 (median = 1930).

In the spring of 1981 a questionnaire consisting of a subset of items used by Terman in his 1940 follow-up was mailed to all participants in this subsample who were believed to be living and had not previously withdrawn from the study. Forty-eight questionnaires were returned from the men, and 54 from the women. Of the original 71 male participants, 17 were deceased in 1981, and two had withdrawn from the study. Of the original female participants, eight were deceased in 1981, and two had withdrawn from the study. Thus, 96% of male participants and 87% of female participants who are believed to have received questionnaires returned them.

Contemporary Sample

A random sample of Stanford University alumni from the graduation years of 1968 to 1972 was selected from university files. A questionnaire consisting of a subset of items used by Terman in his 1940 follow-up was mailed to this sample in August, 1979. Participants' responses to the questionnaire were anonymous. Questionnaires were mailed to 380 women and 429 men. Discounting those questionnaires that were returned by the post office as nondeliverable, the overall return rate for the mailing was approximately 30%. Whereas accurate information concerning marital status was unavailable for many of the graduates, both single and married individuals were included in the mailing. Due to the lack of information concerning both the accuracy of the alumni file address list and the proportion of married graduates in the mailing, the 30% estimate on the return rate may be assumed to be conservative for married participants. Restricting the study to married respondents resulted in 87 usable questionnaires for women and 74 usable questionnaires for men. The mean age for men was 30.8 (SD = 1.44) and for women was 30.8 (SD = 1.56). The mean graduation year for both men and women was 1969.

The contemporary sample of Stanford alumni was chosen as a comparison group in order to provide a suitable match for Terman subjects with equivalent educational backgrounds. Although the contemporary sample was probably not as intellectually select as the Terman subsample, Stanford SAT data show median scores for these graduation classes to have been from 1.5 to 2 standard deviations above the mean for national norms. Because there is no evidence that IQ has a strong relationship to attitudes and values concerning marriage, it is believed that the two samples were sufficiently matched in intellectual ability to control for any relationship between IQ and marital attitudes. Similarities in socialization and educational experiences were seen as more relevant to the variables of interest in this study. The similarity in socioeconomic status for the two groups is underscored by the fact that no significant difference was found in an analysis of occupational ratings for the two cohorts of men measured at age 30.

Measures

Marital Status

Information regarding marital status was obtained for the Terman sample in 1940 and 1981 and for the contemporary sample.

Views About the Ideal Marriage

Nine items were used to measure participants' attitudes toward marriage. Each item was scored on a 5-point scale ranging from 1 (decidedly not desirable) to 5 (very essential). The items included: (a) the husband should be some years older than the wife; (b) the husband should "wear the pants"; (c) husband and wife, if congenial, should take their vacations together; (d) the wife should have money of her own, or should earn her own living by paid employment, and not be financially dependent upon her husband; (e) the wife should be allowed a definite budget for the household and for her personal expenditures; (f) the wife should be kept fully informed of the family finances and of her husband's business; (g) the father should take an active interest in the discipline and training of the children; (h) the husband and wife should frequently express their love for each other in words; and (i) the same standard of sexual morality should apply to both husband and wife.

These items were drawn from a broad test of marital aptitude administered to the Terman sample (Terman & Oden, 1947). They were selected for the present study on the basis of their face validity in yielding information concerning the changing roles of women and men. Test-retest reliabilities over a 2-week period for these items with a contemporary sample of graduate students from the University of Texas at Austin ($N = 35$) calculated by percentage of agreement showed a median reliability of .80, ranging from .59 to 1.00. Additional information available on the questionnaire allowed the establishment of concurrent validity for two of the items. The difference between the husband's and wife's ages was correlated across cohorts with the item concerning the view that the husband should be some years older than the wife ($r = .37$ for men, and $r = .38$ for women, $p < .01$). In addition, the item concerning the view that the wife should work or have money of her own was positively correlated with the number of years worked regularly by the Terman women after marriage ($r = .45$, $p < .05$) and with the number of years the Terman men reported their wives having worked ($r = .48$, $p < .05$).

Marital Satisfaction

The Terman sample in 1940 and contemporary sample responded to questions concerning their present marriage. The Terman sample in 1981 was asked to respond in terms of their present or most recent marriage, because a number of the participants were no longer married.

Participants were asked to rate the frequency of regret of their marriage on a scale ranging from 1 (never) to 4 (frequently). In addition, they were asked if they had ever seriously contemplated separation or divorce. Test–retest reliabilities over a 2-week period for these items with a contemporary sample of married graduate students from the University of Texas at Austin ($N = 20$) calculated by percentage of agreement were .90, 1.00, and .85, respectively.

Seven items were used to construct a marital satisfaction scale. Each item was scored from 1 (untrue) to 4 (completely true). The items included the following: (a) Whenever I have any unexpected leisure I always prefer to spend it with my spouse; (b) When I get money unexpectedly my first thought is how can I use it for my spouse's pleasure; (c) When my spouse and I are alone together we are almost continuously gay and delighted with each other; (d) My spouse never does or says anything that either irritates or bores me in the slightest; (e) My spouse's personality is so completely satisfactory that there is no one else in the world with whom I could be as happy as I am with my spouse; (f) If my spouse were to die; I would prefer to die also, provided I were not prevented by family responsibilities or religion. The seven items were summed and averaged to compute a total marital satisfaction score. The Cronbach alphas for this scale for the Terman sample in 1940, the contemporary sample, and the Terman sample in 1981 ranged from .79 to .87. The test–retest reliability correlation coefficient over a 2-week period for a contemporary sample of married subjects ($N = 20$) was .83.

In addition, participants were asked how happy their marriage has been on a single item scored on a 7-point scale. The scale ranged from (1) extremely unhappy to (7) extraordinarily happy, with intermediate options representing degree of happiness compared with the average marriage. Test–retest reliability over a 2-week period for this item for a contemporary married sample calculated by percentage of agreement was .89.

All of the items concerning marital satisfaction and happiness were drawn from a larger test of marital happiness constructed by Terman in 1940. Terman and Oden (1947) reported that all single items on the marital happiness test were examined for their ability to discriminate between high and low scorers on the total test. The marital happiness test developed by Terman was found to predict marital success or failure 6 years later.

RESULTS

Longitudinal Comparisons

Views of the Ideal Marriage

Planned orthogonal comparisons were used to test changes in views of the ideal marriage for the Terman men and women separately over the last 40 years. Sex differences in these attitudes were also of interest and were tested using the same procedure.

Longitudinal comparisons indicated that the Terman subjects have become more egalitarian in their attitudes toward role relationships in marriage over time, with greater change occurring for women. For women, there was a significant change on the item concerning the advisability of the husband being older than the wife and a trend ($p <$ .10) on the item concerning the adherence to the same standard of sexual morality for both husband and wife, with less endorsement of age differences between spouses and greater endorsement of equality in sexual standards observed in aging. (See Table 1.1 for means and significant levels). Both the Terman men and women showed a declining emphasis on the husband's dominance in marriage as they aged as determined by the item concerning the husband wearing the pants in the family.

Despite longitudinal changes in the direction of greater egalitarianism, sex differences were found on two of these items. Men were in greater agreement that the man should wear the pants in the family, t (95) = 2.18, $p <$ .05. An examination of the means shows that although the men's and women's ratings were approximately similar in 1940, the women's ratings were lower than the men's in 1981, reflecting their greater change in this attitude. The view that the same standard of sexual morality should apply also showed a significant sex difference t (99) = 2.04, $p <$ 0.5, with women's ratings higher.

The analysis of items concerning family finances showed changes in attitudes toward the handling of these matters for the Terman subjects as they aged. Both men and women showed a change toward greater agreement that the wife should be financially independent of the husband (see Table 1.1 for means and significant levels). In addition, both men and women at age 70 showed less agreement with the attitude that the wife should be allowed a definite budget for the household, reflecting changing customs in the management of household finances. Sex differences were maintained on these items, however, with women showing greater agreement with financial independence for women, t (98) = 3.02, $p <$ .01, and with the view that the wife be allowed a definite budget of her own, t (98) = 3.53, $p <$ .001. In addition, there was a significant sex comparison on the item concerning the wife's being fully informed of the family finances, t (98) = 4.40, $p <$ .001, with women endorsing this attitude more highly.

One item showed a change in men's emotional involvement in marriage as they aged, with the Terman men at age 70 showing greater agreement with the view that husband and wife should frequently express love in words than they had at age 30 (Table 1.1). There was a significant overall sex difference on this item, t (99) = 3.57, $p <$ .001, with women's ratings higher.

Table 1.1 Means and Results of Planned Comparisons of Views of the Ideal Marriage for the Terman Subjects in 1940 and 1981

Items	Men (n = 48)					Women (n = 54)				
	1940		1981			1940		1981		
	M	SD	M	SD	t	M	SD	M	SD	t
The husband should be older than the wife	3.25	.57	3.15	.51	1.38	3.28	.53	3.08	.27	2.87
The husband should "wear the pants"	3.47	.83	3.06	.89	3.18**	3.40	.86	2.46	.91	7.63***
The wife should be financially independent	2.40	.80	3.00	.66	4.76***	2.70	.72	3.41	.72	6.09***
The wife should be informed of finances	4.38	.71	4.47	.58	<1	4.79	.41	4.75	.43	<1
The wife should be allowed a definite budget	3.75	1.04	3.42	1.09	2.29*	4.40	.82	3.96	.99	3.17**
The same standard of sexual morality should apply	4.52	.74	4.58	.74	<1	4.64	.56	4.85	.36	1.95
The father should take an active interest in the training of children	4.70	.51	4.83	.38	1.64	4.89	.32	4.83	.42	<1
The husband and wife should express their love in words	3.89	.88	4.23	.91	2.73**	4.43	.69	4.62	.63	1.02
Husband and wife should vacation together	4.17	.61	4.15	.87	<1	4.12	.58	4.19	.65	<1

*p < .05; **p < .01; ***p < .001.

Marital Satisfaction

Planned orthogonal comparisons were used to test separately the changes in marital satisfaction for the Terman men and women over the last 40 years and to test for sex differences in regard to regret of marriage, the 7-item marital satisfaction scale, and the single item concerning happiness compared to the average marriage. Whereas subjects were asked to respond to these items in terms of their present or most recent marriage, the entire 1981 sample was used in the analysis. For women, there was a significant difference in marital satisfaction and happiness as measured in 1940 and 1981 for both the 7-item marital satisfaction scale, t (94) = 3.00, $p < .001$, and the single-item measure of marital happiness, t (97) = 3.48, $p < .001$, with less satisfaction in aging. There were no significant differences across the two time periods for the men in the sample nor were there significant sex differences. Because a number of the subjects were no longer married as a result of widowhood or divorce, these analyses were repeated including only those individuals who were married at the time of the 1981 survey. No significant results emerged from these analyses.

Cohort Comparisons

Views of the Ideal Marriage

Planned orthogonal comparisons were used to test separately the differences in views of the ideal marriage for the Terman subjects in 1940 and contemporary 30-year-old adults. Sex differences in these attitudes were also tested using the same procedure.

There were indications that the contemporary women are more egalitarian in their attitudes toward role relationships in marriage than were the Terman women. Contemporary women agreed less with the view that the husband should be older than the wife and were also significantly less likely to believe that the husband should wear the pants in the family (see Table 1.2 for means and significance levels). A strong overall sex difference was found on the item concerning the husband wearing the pants in the family, t (299) = 3.58, $p < .001$. It is interesting to note that although the means for men and women were almost identical in 1940, contemporary women differed from the earlier cohort, but contemporary men did not, reflecting the significant attitude change for women between the two time periods. The item concerning the adherence to the same standard of sexual morality for husband and wife showed evidence for en-

Table 1.2 Means and Results of Planned Comparisons of Views of the Ideal Marriage for the Terman Subjects in 1940 and for Contemporary 30-Year-Olds

	Men					Women				
	Terman (n = 71)		Contemporary (n = 74)			Terman (n = 73)		Contemporary (n = 87)		
Items	M	SD	M	SD	t	M	SD	M	SD	t
The husband should be older than the wife	3.24	.60	3.12	.40	1.46	3.31	.52	3.11	.44	2.56*
The husband should "wear the pants"	3.45	.81	3.36	.82	<1	3.40	.93	2.62	1.18	5.10***
The wife should be financially independent	2.37	.80	3.61	.74	9.72***	2.68	.77	3.59	.77	7.43***
The wife should be informed of finances	4.38	.68	4.57	.58	2.11*	4.81	.40	4.77	.48	<1
The wife should be allowed a definite budget	3.76	1.06	3.67	1.16	<1	4.36	.81	3.44	1.34	5.11***
The same standard of sexual morality should apply	4.58	.73	4.72	.54	1.51	4.71	.52	4.83	.44	1.34
The father should take an active interest in the training of children	4.73	.48	4.95	.23	3.87***	4.89	.32	4.92	.31	<1
The husband and wife should express their love in words	4.11	.85	4.64	.56	4.66***	4.44	.69	4.61	.62	1.55
Husband and wife should vacation together	4.23	.61	4.54	.50	3.06***	4.14	.59	4.28	.70	2.37*

*$p < .05$; **$p < .01$; ***$p < .001$.

during sex differences, with women's ratings higher than men's, t (300) = 1.86, $p < .10$.

Analyses of items concerning family finances suggest changes in this area over the last 40 years. Both men and women endorsed financial independence for women to a greater degree in 1979 (see Table 1.2 for means and significance levels). Contemporary men were also more highly in favor of women being informed of family finances, but the comparison for women was nonsignificant, with women at both time periods expressing a high level of agreement. The item concerning the wife being allowed a budget of her own points to another change in the customs and attitudes concerning the management of family finances. Contemporary women expressed less agreement with this item than the Terman women, with several of them objecting to the word "allowed" in the item, although no difference was found between the means for men at the two time periods. An overall sex difference was observed on the item concerning the wife being fully informed of the family finances, however, t (299) = 5.05, $p < .001$, suggesting some enduring sex differences in attitudes concerning the distribution of financial responsibility and power in marriage.

The results for three items suggest a greater interest in the relationship aspects of marriage in contemporary adults, especially for men. Contemporary men endorsed the father taking an active role in childrearing as well as emotional expressiveness in marriage to a greater extent than did the Terman men (Table 1.2). No differences were observed for women on these two items across the two time periods, with women consistently endorsing these attitudes at a high level. Women, however, were in overall greater agreement with verbal expressiveness in marriage than men, t (300) = 1.90, $p < .10$. Although the means on this item differed for men and women in 1940, they were virtually identical in 1979. Both men and women endorsed joint vacationing to a greater degree in the contemporary sample. There was a significant sex difference on this item, t (298) = 2.49, $p < .05$, with men's ratings higher.

Marital Satisfaction

Planned orthogonal comparisons were used to test separately the differences in marital satisfaction for the Terman subjects in 1940 and for contemporary 30-year-old adults, for the items concerning regret of marriage, the 7-item marital satisfaction scale, and the item concerning happiness compared to the average marriage. Contemporary women expressed more regret concerning their marriage, t (298) = 2.49, $p < .05$, and less satisfaction on the 7-item marital satisfaction scale than did the Terman women, t (300) = 4.67, $p < .001$. Contemporary men also expressed less satisfaction on the marital satisfaction scale than did the Terman men, t (298) = 254, $p < .05$.

Contemplation of divorce or separation was tested separately for men and women using chi-square analyses. More contemporary women had contemplated divorce than the Terman women, χ^2 = (1) 8.28, $p < .01$. No significant differences were found on these two variables for the two cohorts of men.

DISCUSSION

Despite prevailing popular beliefs of increasing conservatism with age, the results of the present study suggest that significant change in the direction of increased egalitarianism has occurred in marital attitudes for the Terman subjects over the more than 40 years from 1940 to 1981. This was particularly true for the Terman women in regard to role relationships in marriage (i.e., decreasing beliefs that husbands should be older than wives and that husbands should wear the pants in the family). The Terman women in the older years also believed more strongly in the same standard of sexual morality for husband and wife. Furthermore, results concerning attitudes in regard to the management of money are consistent with changes in women's societal roles. Both the Terman men and women in their 70s expressed greater agreement than they had in their 30s with the view that the wife should work or have independent income. Concomitant changes in attitudes regarding the household management of money were observed in regard to the wife being allowed a definite budget of her own, a custom that would more likely hold in a time of complete financial dependence of wives on husbands. Both the Terman men and women were less likely to agree with this attitude as they aged. Their change in attitude, however, was not nearly so dramatic as the cohort difference for women. Several of the contemporary women, in fact, commented on the use of the word "allowed" in the question, itself a sign of changing mores.

Despite observed longitudinal changes in an egalitarian direction, evidence for enduring sex differences in some areas is apparent. This was notably true concerning the wife's being fully informed of the family finances; a strong sex effect was found in both the cohort and longitudinal comparisons, with women favoring this view more than men. A consistent, though weaker difference was found concerning adherence to the same standard of sexual morality by both husband and wife in both the cohort and longitudinal comparisons, with women endorsing this view more highly. In addition, there was a significant sex difference concerning the wife's being allowed a budget of her own in the longitudinal comparisons. The Terman women consistently endorsed this attitude to a greater extent than the Terman men, reflecting the maintenance of their own interests in marriages taking place at a more traditional time.

There was striking evidence that contemporary men are more involved in family life, as evidenced by the cohort analyses concerning expressing love in words, the father participating in the disciplining of children, and husbands and wives taking vacations together. These results are in line with Bernard's (1981, p. 10) suggestion that for men, the traditional role of the good provider is now accompanied by two new demands: "(a) more intimacy, expressivity, and nurturance . . . and (b) more sharing of household responsibilities and child care." These results are also in accord with those of Pleck (1979) in suggesting significant movement in the direction of greater family participation for men. This change is echoed in the longitudinal comparison for men on the item concerning expressing love in words. Women were already relatively high on this item but did show some evidence for change. Overall sex differences on this item, however, are stronger for the Terman longitudinal comparison than for the cohort comparison, and it is interesting to note that the endorsement of this attitude by contemporary men and women was almost identical.

When marital satisfaction was examined across cohorts, there was evidence for lower marital satisfaction for contemporary men and women. This result is in accord with the increase in reported marital problems from 1957 to 1976 noted by Veroff et al. (1981), and is consistent with other data reported by Veroff et al. concerning an increasing awareness of the relationship aspects of marriage. Increased egalitarianism in marriage is apparently accompanied by greater strains than more traditional patterns, where less negotiation is required for smooth marital functioning. It is interesting to note, however, that no difference in the measure of happiness compared with the average marriage was observed in the present study and that Veroff et al. reported an increase over the years on their measure of marital happiness.

The longitudinal analyses of satisfaction in present or most recent marriage reflected the historical comparison for women when all of the Terman women responding in 1981 were included in the analysis. When only married women were included, no decline in marital satisfaction was found. Perhaps the difficulties of aging and the possibility of widowhood restrain the expression of marital dissatisfactions for married women in their 70s. Alternatively, it is possible that women who have remained married into their 70s are expressing a genuine satisfaction with their marriage at this time.

Several results in this study suggest the possibility of developmental change in role behavior in adulthood. Although the Terman men showed a change in a more egalitarian direction concerning the husband wearing the pants in the family, there was no difference between contemporary men and the Terman men when they were 30. This is one of the few instances where the longitudinal comparison was more dramatic than the time-lag comparison. This result suggests that men may adhere more strongly to traditional sex roles related to dominance in young adulthood than in the later years of marriage. In addition, the longitudinal results for women covering this attitude, and age differences between spouses, are in accord with changes in the direction of greater masculine role behavior for women. These results are congruent with the crosscultural work of Gutmann (1977) in regard to developmental gender shifts. Gutmann found evidence for changes in the behavior of both men and women across the adult life span such that women demonstrate increasing dominance and independence with age and men demonstrate less aggression and increasing dependence and affiliation with age. He bases his theory on responses to the developmental crises and imperatives of adulthood, particularly parenthood, which place subtle demands on the kinds of behavior that men and women exhibit at different stages in the life cycle.

Consistent with the aging–stability hypothesis, cohort differences for men were generally greater than longitudinal changes, and in several instances differences were observed in the cohort comparisons but not in the longitudinal comparisons. For women, in contrast, when longitudinal changes occurred they often matched cohort differences. The Terman women were more responsive to the recent sociocultural changes in gender roles on items directly concerned with independence and equality for women than were the Terman men. The fact that the Terman women at age 70 responded in a manner so consistent with the responses of contemporary younger women is compatible with results reported by Sears and Barbee (1977). They found that many of the lifetime homemakers in the Terman sample reported in their 60s that, if they could make the choice again, they would be more inclined toward some kind of career involvement. These results may have implications for the study of attitude change in later adulthood concerning issues that impact favorably on the lives of other social groups such as minorities that find themselves in a less favored position in society. Perhaps the attitudes of the dominant group change less than those of the non-dominant group in the presence of such sociocultural change.

In summary, the results of the present study indicate that considerable change has occurred in marital attitudes for the Terman subjects over the 40 years from age 30 to 70. These changes are in accord with the trend toward greater sex role equality in our society. Because of the select nature of the Terman and contemporary sample, further research should focus on extending the results of this study to other socioeconomic groups. Although the present study cannot unravel the conceptual confounding of historical time and aging, it does allow for the formulation of hypotheses concerning probable causes of observed longitudinal differences. There were two instances in which longitudinal effects for men were observed in the absence of cohort effects, favoring a life cycle explanation for men on those attitudes. In general, however, when longitudinal changes occurred they were consistent with historical change. A hypothesis of the combined influence of historical change and aging thus appears plausible with sociohistorical change reinforcing developmental changes in aging.

REFERENCES

Baltes, P. B., Cornelius, S. W., & Nesselroade, J. R. Cohort effects in developmental psychology. In J. R. Nesselroade & P. B. Baltes (Eds.), *Longitudinal research in the study of behavior and development*. Academic Press, New York, 1980.

Bernard, J. The good-provider role: Its rise and fall. *American Psychologist*, 1981, *36*, 1–12.

Burkes, B. S., Jensen, D. W., & Terman, L. M. The promise of youth: Follow-up studies of a thousand gifted children. *Genetic studies of genius* (Vol. 3). Stanford University Press, Stanford, CA, 1930.

Carlsson, G., & Karlsson, K. Age cohorts and the generation of generations. *American Sociological Review*, 1970, *35*, 710–718.

Chafe, W. H. *The American woman: Her changing social, economic and political roles, 1920–1970*. Oxford University Press, New York, 1972.

Cutler, S. J., & Kaufman, R. L. Cohort changes in political attitudes: Tolerance of ideological nonconformity. *Public Opinion Quarterly*, 1975, *39*, 63–81.

Elder, G. H. Historical change in life patterns and personality. In P. B. Baltes and O. G. Brim (Eds.), *Life-span development and behavior* (Vol. 2). Academic Press, New York, 1979.

Glenn, N. D. Values, attitudes, and beliefs. In O. G. Brim & J. Kagan (Eds.), *Consistancy and change in human development.* Harvard University Press, Cambridge, MA, 1980.

Greeley, A. M., & Spaeth, J. R. Political change among college alumni. *Sociology of Education,* 1970, *43,* 106–113.

Gutmann, D. The cross-cultural perspective: Notes toward a comparative psychology of aging. In J. E. Birren & K. W. Schaie (Eds.), *Handbook of the psychology of aging.* Van Nostrand Reinhold, New York, 1977.

Holahan, C. K. Lifetime achievement patterns, retirement and life satisfaction of gifted aged women. *Journal of Gerontology,* 1981, *36,* 741–749.

Oden, M. H. The fulfillment of promise: 40-year follow-up of the Terman gifted group. *Genetic Psychology Monographs,* 1968, *77,* 3–93.

Pleck, J. H. Men's family work: Three perspectives and some data. *Family Coordinator,* 1979, *28,* 481–488.

Schaie, K. W. The primary mental abilities in adulthood: An exploration in the development of psychometric intelligence. In P. B. Baltes & O. G. Brim (Eds.), *Life-span development and behavior* (Vol. 2). Academic Press, New York, 1979.

Sears, P. S. The Terman genetic studies of genius, 1922–1972. In National Society for the Study of Education, *The gifted and the talented: Their education and development* (78th Yearbook). University Chicago Press, Chicago, 1979.

Sears, P. S., & Barbee, A. H. Career and life satisfaction among Terman's gifted women. In J. C. Stanley, W. D. George, & C. H. Solano (Eds.), *The gifted and the creative: A fifty-year perspective.* Johns Hopkins Press, Baltimore, 1977.

Sears, R. R. Sources of life satisfaction of the Terman gifted men. *American Psychologist,* 1977, *32,* 119–128.

Stromberg, A. H., & Harkess, S. (Eds.). *Women working: Theories and facts in perspective.* Mayfield, Palo Alto, CA, 1978.

Terman, L. M., assisted by Baldwin, B. T., Bronson, E., Devoss, J. C., Fuller, F., Goodenough, F. L., Kelley, T. L., Lima, M., Marshall, H., Moore, A. H., Raubenheimer, A. S., Ruch, G. M., Willoughby, R. L., Wyman, J. B., & Yates, H. H. *Mental and physical traits of a thousand gifted children. Genetic studies of genius* (Vol. 1). Stanford University Press, Stanford, CA, 1925.

Terman, L. M., & Oden, M. H. *The gifted child grows up. Genetic studies of genius* (Vol. 4). Stanford University Press, Stanford, CA, 1947.

Veroff, J., Douvan, E. R., & Kulka, R. A. *The inner American: A self-portrait from 1957 to 1976.* Basic Books, New York, 1981.

Woodruff, D. S., & Birren, J. E. Age changes and cohort differences in personality. *Developmental Psychology,* 1972, *6,* 252–259.

2

A Longitudinal Study of Family Supports to Impaired Elderly*

Colleen Leahy Johnson
Donald J. Catalano

Although large-scale surveys have documented the strengths of the family as a support system to the elderly (Shanas, 1979b), there is less understanding of what happens to the elderly and their families when supports are needed over time. This paper attempts to add to our understanding of the longitudinal effect of family care when high needs for supports persist on a more permanent basis. Information on family supports was collected at two points in time: several weeks following discharge from a hospital and again an average of 8 months later. Comparisons are made on support variables at these two times and an analysis is presented of those elderly who were functionally impaired over this 8-month period. Since this group had high needs for supports, it is possible to identify the dominant patterns of support to a long-term high-needs group and to describe the adaptive strategies used by the caregivers in order to alleviate the strains and burdens of care.

Recent research in social gerontology counters the "myth of family abandonment" by documenting through survey research the frequent contact elderly have with family members and the high incidence of family supports to disabled elderly (Shanas, 1979a, 1979b).

*The Gerontologist, 23 (6) (1983), 612–618.

Revision of a paper presented at the 35th Annual Scientific Meeting of the Gerontological Society of America, Boston, November 1982. This research was funded by NIMH Grant No. MH31907. The authors wish to thank Barbara Barer for her contributions to this study.

These surveys report high potentials, but descriptive studies find high levels of strain in the family and perhaps a "wearing down" or erosion of family supports either because of the high level of stress generated or because of the competing commitments of family members (Brody, 1981; Cantor, 1980; Eggert et al., 1977; Johnson, 1983). These latter reports are more consistent with demographic trends which indicate that realistic impediments to long-term family supports exist in terms of the numbers and availability of relatives (Brody, 1981; Treas, 1977, 1981).

Although those supports from individual family members are usually referred to under the rubric of "family caregiving," upon closer examination one finds that the support is extended most often by one family member at a time. In serial order, the spouse functions as the primary caregiver; in the absence of the spouse, a child assumes the role; and in the absence of offspring, another member is responsible (Johnson, 1983). Shanas (1979b) has identified this phenomenon as the "principle of substitution," inferring that any one person is sufficient to meet the needs of the older person.

Studies using a variety of objective measures of family contact and aid agree with this conclusion. However, the primary caregivers are typically age peers (Cantor, 1980). These individuals usually fulfill the role with little assistance from others even though they may suffer themselves from age-related physical, financial, and social limitations (Crossman et al., 1981; Fengler & Goodrich, 1979; Johnson, 1983). Adult children usually remain in contact, but they provide less care to a married parent than to a widowed parent (Johnson, 1983). Usually children have realistic impediments which prevent day-to-day care of the dependent parent. Cicirelli (1981) found that offspring actually provide few services, although they exhibit "filial anxiety" in reaction to the possibility of assuming responsibilities. Childless and unmarried older people may turn to siblings or more distant relatives such as nieces, nephews, or cousins, but these relatives rarely provide a high level of care (Johnson & Catalano, 1981). Instead they usually function as intermediaries in obtaining needed community services for the patient.

In summary, impaired older people usually have at least one family member to call upon for assistance. A spouse provides the most comprehensive care, and a child, although dedicated, is likely to have competing commitments. When older persons must rely on a more distant relative, supports are more perfunctory. When they must rely solely on an age peer, there is a risk of decreased supports because of the potential health problems of the caregiver.

Most of these studies report stress and conflict in situations demanding day-to-day care. Not surprisingly, the degree of reported stress varies directly with the extent of the support provided (Cicerelli, 1981). Given these less optimistic findings on the viability of family supports, it appears that different kinship relationships perform different functions and, ideally, the care of an impaired older relative would be better shared among a group of people. In any case, the family caregiver apparently needs a backup system if strain is to be avoided. Litwak (1980) suggests that specific functions can be performed by the most appropriate category of primary relationship in conjunction with the formal support system. Under this model of shared functioning, the primary concern becomes the degree to which individual older people can mobilize a group of relatives and formal providers who are allocated specific tasks.

Another major question centers on whether reports of contact and aid, indicators that are typically used to evaluate support systems (Schaefer et al., 1981), actually determine the extent to which these activities meet expressive as well as instrumental needs. Additionally, measures of contact and aid do not provide much understanding of the processes by which social supports are associated with improved physical and mental health. Since the incidence of contact has been assumed to provide the positive benefits of support, little consideration has been given to the possibility that caregiving produces conflict in the relationship or imposes other costs on the individuals involved. It has been rare for researchers to consider the family as a source of conflict and stress as well as a source of assistance (Croog, 1970; Schaefer et al., 1981). Certainly the potential for conflict and strain are more likely when family supports are required over a long period of time.

Research on family supports to older psychiatric patients, for example, documents the conflicts, stress and burdens of caregiving (Berezin, 1970; Cath, 1972). The extent to which these findings result from use of clinical populations is difficult to determine since stress is also reported with community samples (Cantor, 1980). While clinical interpretations tend to portray the darker side of relationships, they can also indicate the more dynamic qualities which affect adaptation over time to the burdens of care. For example, longstanding interpersonal problems can reappear in the process (Savitsky and Sharkey, 1973), and the mental health of the caregiver may be adversely affected (Sainsbury & Grad de Alarcon, 1970). The development of hypochondriasis has also been found among older women who care for their disabled spouses (Busse, 1976).

This paper provides objective data on contact and aid to older people over an 8-month period; it also provides an analysis of the more subjective factors influencing the quality of these supports. Social support is defined more broadly here to include not only tangible help and social contact but relationship variables which are also viewed as influencing the quality of the supports. We assume that the initial aid extended upon discharge from the hospital necessitates readjustments in relationships which are only temporary if the patient's functioning is restored to the level of the pre-hospital period. If the period of dependency is prolonged, however, one can predict that the dyadic relationship becomes redefined because of the long-term demands placed on it. Thus, it is this latter subgroup which can provide understanding of family supports over time.

SAMPLE CHARACTERISTICS

The research was conducted with a sample of 167 families in the San Francisco Bay Area between 1978 and 1981. Respondents were selected from lists of patients aged 65 years and over in two acute care hospitals, all of whom had at least one family member in the area. At selected intervals, consecutive admissions who met the selection criteria were contacted. The first set of interviews took place 2 to 4 weeks from discharge from the hospital, and 115 of these 167 were interviewed 8 months later. Lost to the follow-up interviews were 32 elderly who had died, 17 patients or family members who refused to be interviewed, and 33 who could not be located. The sample at Time 2, 68% of the original group, was similar demographically and in family characteristics to the original sample, so the description of the sample reported below describes those at the first contact.

Both structured and unstructured data were collected. The unstructured data were coded by two individuals and an 80% agreement was achieved. In 17% of the cases, the patient alone participated in the interview, and in 30% the patient and a family member were interviewed together; in the remaining 53% the family member alone provided the data. Patients who wanted to be interviewed alone rather than referring us to a family member in general had a higher level of functioning than those for whom a family member was interviewed alone. Correspondingly, this group received fewer family supports. In order to analyze these combined effects, an analysis of variance was performed to examine the effects of the level of functioning (OARS Activities of Daily Living) by who reported on specific variables. In all variables reported here, the level of functioning accounted for significantly more variation than the category of respondent.

The mean age of the post-hospitalized individuals was 74.5 with 43% 75 years of age and over. Fifty-five percent of the patients were female. Of the 49% who were married, 66% were male and 33% female. Females predominated as caregivers, comprising two-thirds of the spouse caregivers and 59% of the offspring caregivers. In regard to household status of the patients, 27% lived alone, 55% lived with an age peer (49% with a spouse and 6% with a sibling), 5% lived with their children in a three-generation household, and 13% lived with children in a two-generation household. After hospitalization 28% of the patients changed these arrangements, with 17% entering a nursing home and 11% moving in with a family member. Most of the elderly had been long-term residents of the Bay Area; only 11% had moved there in the past 10 years, while one-half had occupied their residence for at least 10 years.

In order to control for variation on the basis of ethnic and religious background, sample selection was confined to white Catholics and Protestants of European origin. Twenty percent were foreign born and 47% were Catholic. In education, the sample was evenly distributed, but almost two-thirds of the major wage earners had worked in either skilled or unskilled jobs. Economically 69% reported no financial problems and only 21 were using Medicaid benefits.

Of those with children, the mean number of living children was 2.5; 28 respondents had no children. Only 16% of those with children had no child in the area. Because selection criteria excluded minority groups and the participants were confined to those with relatives in the area, these elderly enjoyed a more favored position than is generally found (Shanas, 1979a). However, this group was quite impaired; only 19% could perform all of the items on the Activities of Daily Living scale without help; 22% were limited in three or fewer activities, another 22% were moderately impaired and unable to perform at least four items and 36% were severely impaired and required round-the-clock care.

FAMILY SUPPORTS EIGHT MONTHS AFTER HOSPITALIZATION

As noted above, the overall findings of this research report that few elderly are abandoned by their families, although most are cared for by a primary caregiver rather than a family as a unit (Johnson, 1983). Although a high level of strain was reported, particularly by children who were caregivers, few of these elderly had their needs go unmet. A family member provided most of the care with little help from formal supports. Given the high level of functional impairment and the fact that only 17% of the respondents were institutionalized, the viability of the family support system is validated. Since there is little depth in the family support system in terms of numbers of potential supporters, however, it is useful to examine how it bears up over time.

Among the more important changes over time is the somewhat improved physical status of the group as a whole. This finding can be explained in part by the attrition rates resulting from the deaths of the more impaired patients. Thus, what remained was a somewhat different group whose physical condition was likely to be stabilized. Using the OARS Activities of Daily Living to measure functional ability, we found no significant differences in the mean level of functioning between Time 1 and Time 2. With regard to specific tasks, only one activity level had significantly changed: there was an increase in the number of patients who were ambulatory outside the home ($t = 3.73$, $p \leq .0003$). Since this factor is critical for independent living, improvement indicates that more former patients were capable of caring for themselves.

Of the 115 respondents contacted after 8 months, 22% had been rehospitalized at least once and 9% had been hospitalized more than once. Other factors remained relatively stable over this time period. At Time 2, 78% remained in their same living environment. Of the 24 patients who had moved, 17 had moved to more supportive housing (three to institutions and eight to homes of family members). Among the caregivers, children reported no significant events that had occurred which affected their capacity to provide supports (e.g., changes in employment, marital or parental status, health status). However, 17% of the spouse caregivers reported that their own health had declined in the intervening 8 months.

Although the functional status of the patients and the availability of the family remained much the same, the frequency of contact with members of the family decreased significantly for the sample as a whole (Table 2.1). Almost three-quarters of the children maintained weekly contact with their parent, but 10% had decreased their visits. The same drop in contact was found among relatives, with only 19% having weekly contact. Contact with friends remained stable during this time period with almost two-thirds having at least weekly visits.

Table 2.1. Comparison of Support Variables at Discharge from
Hospital and Eight Months Later
(n = 115)

Support Variable	Time 1 Post-discharge %	Time 2 8 months later %	χ^2	p
Social Contact[a]	83	73	93.966	.0001
(weekly or more often)	29	19	78.749	.002
Children	61	63	2.15	n.s.
Relatives				
Friends				
Use of physician or social worker	55	34	23.995	.0001
Use of homemaker services	21	19	2.099	n.s.
High strain reported[b]	43	35	21.36	.001
Patients with low morale[b]	27	38	20.756	.001
Patients reported to be lonely	17	34	28.158	.0001

[a]Since all married patients had daily contact with a spouse, this frequency is not reported in the table.
[b]Measures of strain and morale were derived from a series of open-ended questions on the respondents' mood and outlook and their reports on the effect that the illness and need for caregiving had on daily life. These responses were coded by two individuals with an 80% interrater agreement.

The use of two types of formal supports is reported here: consultation with a physician or social worker for advice on the care of the patient and use of homemaker services. It is apparent that reliance on those professionals who were active at the time of hospitalization declined significantly with the break in the linkage to the acute care system (Table 2.1), but the proportion using homemaker services remained much the same.

As Table 2.1 also indicates, the general stabilization of the support system and the slight improvement in the functional status of the patients after 8 months were not accompanied by a general improvement in the patient's mental health. Significantly more patients had problems with low morale and over one-third were reported to be lonely, a proportion which was twice as large at Time 2 as at Time 1.

These changes in patient characteristics and family supports between Time 1 and Time 2 indicate that the event of hospitalization was most likely to activate the family support system as children and relatives increased their contacts and supports to the patient. With a stabilization or improvement in the patient's health and functional status after 8 months, these social contacts declined and old patterns of interaction resumed. Thus, one byproduct of improved health was increased social isolation for the older person, and this change was found to be associated with the decline in his or her morale. Since a significant inverse relationship was found between the patient's morale and the numbers of relatives available (r = −.1889, < .05), it appears that, despite improved functional status, the shrinkage of the social environment has an adverse effect on the older individual.

The data indicate that family members do provide needed help to the older patient, particularly following the crisis of hospitalization. These relatives can be described as a storehouse of resources, available when needed, but after the crisis has passed former patterns of interaction are re-established. It is possible that relatives other than children are "intimate at a distance" under normal conditions (Rosenmayr & Kockeis, 1963), and as a consequence the contact after hospitalization is not sustained over time. Relationships with friends fluctuate and are probably situationally defined (Table 2.1). Since the decline in social contact with family members is apparently not compensated by an increase in sociability with friends, the patient becomes more isolated, a phenomenon associated with lowered morale in old age (Liang et al., 1980).

THE HIGH NEEDS GROUP AT TIME 2

Because some patients became more functionally independent during the time period of the research, they obviously were less likely to impose strain on the family. In order to control for this variation, the patient's status was categorized by the level of functioning at the follow-up interview. Using the descriptive reports from the respondents, we determined that those who could not function in two or more activities without help would need frequent supports from others. Using this criterion, two groups were identified for comparative purposes: the Independent, who had adequate functioning in 11 to 13 activities at Time 2 (*n* = 43, 39%) and the Dependent, who needed help in more than two activities at Time 2 (*n* = 72, 61%).

In an examination of the 72 patients who were dependent at Time 2, it is first important to note that no sharp increase in institutionalization occurred; the proportion remained the same at 21%, although three individuals left a nursing home and three entered one. However, at the follow-up contact the Dependent were significantly higher users of formal supports; almost one-third used a physician or social worker for advice and almost one-quarter used homemaker services.

This proportion is only slightly larger than that for the entire sample as a whole at Time 1. On the whole, those who improved in status did not continue to use formal supports, and only two reported that they needed some supports that they were not receiving. In contrast, among the Dependent, 17% reported that they needed some supports that were lacking.

In regard to the social network, the high needs of the patients obviously required frequent contact with others, so measures of social contact in Table 2.2 are confined to those contacts taking place daily or several times a week. This group of long-term impaired elderly had one advantage; they had more frequent contact with their children than the healthier group. Presumably, these children continued to respond to the high needs of the parent. Yet, the more impaired patients experienced the same decline in contact with other relatives found in the entire sample. The greatest contrast between the groups appeared in contact with friends; friends are notably less likely to be in contact with the more functionally impaired, a finding which suggests that these relationships are difficult to sustain when one is dependent over time. Given the overall decline in social contacts, it is

Table 2.2. Comparisons of Patients' Level of Dependence at Time 2 by Social Support Variables (n = 115)

Support Variable	Independent (n = 43) %	Dependent (n = 72) %	Kendall's Tau B	p
Social Contact[a]				
(daily or several times a week)				
Children	53	81	−.1725	.03
Relatives	21	21	−.09007	n.s.
Friends	57	25	.2538	.0009
			χ^2	p
Changes in family supports				
Increased	5	21		
The same	45	42		
Decreased	50	37	11.833	n.s.
Use of physician or social worker	7	31	18.362	.0004
Use of homemaker services	12	23	2.085	.30

[a]Since all married patients had daily contact with a spouse, this frequency is not reported in the table.

apparent that the older person and probably the spouse or child who is the caregiver experience more social isolation.

The change in family supports was evaluated by examining the open-ended discussions with caregivers. Using this measure, it was found that during the eight-month period the level of family supports remained the same for 42% of the Dependent group, a proportion similar to that found for the Independent group (Table 2.2). Whereas 21% of the caregivers had increased their supports to this high-needs group at Time 2, considerably more—37%—had decreased them. This decrease is compared to the 50% decrease in the Independent group, an understandable decline. However, one can tentatively suggest that attrition takes place in family supports irrespective of the status of the patient.

Although sample size is too small to break down further in tabular form, several trends in this data are worth noting. First, almost half of those who maintained the same level of care provided only per-functory care to the patient in the first place. Furthermore, only two of these 27 caregivers increased their supports to the patient at Time 2. Thus, it seems more difficult for one to increase one's care for an older dependent person if some time has elapsed during which other solutions were found.

Second, the spouse as caregiver is a more stable arrangement over time except in those cases where the spouse's health also declines. A spouse is more likely than a child to provide more comprehensive care over time with a minimum of stress or ambivalence. Of all those in the sample who continued to provide the same level of care or increase it, 62% were spouses and 27% were children. Children, however, are more likely to turn to formal supports or seek other family members to assist them. (The significance of the spouse as caregiver is such that it requires a separate, more detailed analysis which will be reported at a later date.)

Turning now to the dimensions of social supports not usually tapped by researchers, correlations were used to identify significant associations between the patients' functional status and measures of the patients' mood and outlook, the conflict they have with their families and the strain experienced by the caregivers. Table 2.3 indicates a cluster of factors that may have an adverse effect on social support systems when they must function over time. The mood and outlook of more impaired patients were significantly less optimistic than those of the Independent group. The Dependent group reported more economic problems, which suggests a source of vulnerability in long-term chronic conditions. Conflict among family members was

Table 2.3 Comparisons of Patients' Level of Dependence at Time 2 by
Relationship Variables (n = 115)

Relationship Variable	Independent %	Dependent %	Kendall's Tau B	p
Patients with poor outlook	20	52	.2109	.009
Economic problems	32	59	.2661	.0008
Caregiver strain	11	48	.2045	.009
Conflict between patient and caregiver	14	24	.1675	.05
Caregiver's mood and outlook worse	62	46	.1924	.02

also higher in the Dependent group, and the caregivers of the more
impaired patients experienced significantly more strain. Finally,
somewhat to our surprise, the caregivers of the more impaired were
less likely to have problems with their own mood and outlook.

Since this finding is not consistent with the negative events taking
place, the interviews with these caregivers with improved morale
were examined in order to identify the source of this positive finding.
Of the 24 caregivers whose morale had improved, 67% were using
some type of formal supports, a much higher proportion than for the
entire sample. Thus, in view of the continued demands upon the
caregiver resulting from the long-term dependence of an older family
member, there is a tendency to turn to various forms of formal
support, probably as a means of ameliorating the increasing strain
and conflict imposed by the situation.

ADAPTIVE MECHANISMS TO BURDENS OF CARE

Given a potentially high-stress situation and the prolonged dependency of the patient, one can predict changes in the patient's
status, his or her relationship to the caregiver, and the status of the
caregiver. In order to identify these and other patterns, an examination was made of not only the objective measures reported in the
tables but also the more subjective changes taking place in the support system as they were revealed in open-ended data. With this
procedure, two broad categories of adaptive mechanisms were discernible which suggest how relationships become redefined in a
manner which ultimately affects the social support system.

Distancing Techniques

In geriatric medicine, the "cascade effect" is sometimes used to describe a combination of disease conditions and iatrogenic factors that cause a downward spiral of the patient's physical status. For example, a minor ailment might immobilize the individual and, if prolonged, lead to pneumonia, pressure sores, and increasingly serious conditions. As these problems interact and become compounded, the decline can become irreversible and it is difficult to restore the patient to normal functioning.

It would seem that a similar process can potentially affect the social situation of some patients when one singles out significant correlations between the patient's long-term functional status and the variables in the social support system. This cascade effect begins with the patient's status, where the long-term dependency leads to a deterioration in the patient's outlook which, in turn, affects his or her relationship with the primary caregiver. As more expectations are placed on the relationship, the caregiver finds the responsibilities more difficult to tolerate. This situation is probably compounded by the increased social isolation that the dyad experiences. In the end, the situation becomes increasingly difficult to tolerate, but not only because of the constraints inherent in the patient's physical and mental status but also because of the negative valences developing in the relationship itself.

Establishing greater physical distance is one option taken by approximately one-third of the sample, most of whom were children. With some older individuals experiencing long-term impairment, as their psychological resources deteriorate, they become depressed and irritable. Since contacts with friends decline, these persons become more dependent upon their families. Because of their increased dissatisfaction with the support system and the greater demands they place upon the relationship with the caregiver, conflict between them and the caregiver increases, a factor which frequently has a "ripple effect" to other relationships in the family. A daughter's husband and children might complain about her distractions in caring for a parent. The caregivers are also likely to become more isolated from their usual social activities. As the dyadic relationship deteriorates in quality due to changes in both the patient and caregiver, the possibility of alternatives becomes an acceptable means for the caregiver to establish greater distance from the patient.

Establishing psychological distance while maintaining physical proximity is also apparent in some parent-child interactions. When the caregiving imposes high emotional costs, daughters particularly are prone to experience guilt and resentment. These problems become intensified in some ethnic groups which impose sanctions on children who seek nonfamily alternatives. Many individuals in such a situation, however, find means to establish psychological distance from the parent without resorting to institutionalization. They might enter psychotherapy in order to work through old relational conflicts and, in the process, establish autonomy from the parent. In some cases, defenses are built up by systems of rationalization; e.g., "I have done all I can." Although the outcome in some cases can be institutionalization, these psychological supports to the caregivers also can enable them to continue to meet the instrumental needs of disabled parents with minimal emotional commitment.

Some caregivers establish more distance from the patient through *enlarging the family network* to include others in the day-to-day care of the patient. A daughter caring for her widowed mother may seek the help of a sister or a wife might find assistance from her children. Sometimes the diagnosis of a terminal illness elicits more supports from children on a temporary basis. The option was used by approximately 12% of the sample, and the outcomes were generally positive. Less stress was reported and the morale of the caregiver usually improved.

Enmeshing Techniques

These techniques are in direct contrast to the distancing techniques described above. As the dependency of the patient persists, the relationship with the caregiver intensifies often to the exclusion of other relationships. For example, the adaptive pattern of *social regression* is found among older married couples, particularly the childless or those whose children live at some distance (Johnson & Catalano, 1981). As the needs of the frailer spouse increase, the couple increasingly withdraws from previous social involvements, and, like many elderly with high impairment, the partners become isolated from relatives and friends. The healthier spouse is forced to reduce his or her contacts outside the home because no one is available to substitute in caregiving. As a consequence, the couple becomes more interdependent as the partners are increasingly forced to turn to each other for the satisfaction of both emotional and instrumental needs.

Unlike Slater's description of social regression (1963), however, these dyads have few mechanisms available to reverse the situation, usually because of their abbreviated social networks. As needs increase, the interdependence intensifies and the social regression also increases. The risks in this arrangement are primarily traced to the health of the caregiver; if it deteriorates, the situation becomes precarious. Only in the event of rehospitalization might health professionals have the opportunity to intervene to strengthen the support system.

Another mechanism of adaptation is *role entrenchment,* a process in which caregiving is accepted as a permanent, full-time role that takes precedence over other social roles. The caregiver redefines the exchange relationship to exclude some tangible benefits and instead anticipates altruistic rewards which enhance his or her self-esteem and sense of competence. Moreover, the role is viewed as replacing major role losses already experienced, so it is seen as giving new meaning to life. It also permits one to shed auxiliary and perhaps unwanted roles in order to invest one's energies in the patient. As a result, caregiving becomes a way of life chosen to the exclusion of other interests and activities.

This entrenchment technique is used by both spouses and children. For spouses, the redefinition of the role and the total commitment to it can function to replenish the role system which has faced the normal attritions of the aging process (Johnson, 1983). For children, intensifying the role of caring for a parent can be a substitute for a failed marriage, widowhood, or an erratic employment history. It can also be used as a rationalization for an already delayed independence from parents. Moving home and assuming full-time care can solve the child's own economic problems or other difficulties in the assumption of full adult status.

SUMMARY AND CONCLUSIONS

In summary, no unitary trends appear in the efficacy of family supports to the elderly as their dependency needs persist over time. An assessment of 115 older people upon discharge from the hospital and again 8 months later found that the condition of the surviving group as a whole either improved or stabilized. Few dramatic events occurred which decreased the potentials of the social networks, although with less need for supports, both informal and formal supports declined. The average older person was able to function independently, but he or she experienced more loneliness and discontent, a factor which is probably associated with increased social isolation.

In order to identify potential problems in family supports, a secondary analysis was made of those patients with high needs at Time 2 (61% of the sample). For this group, the rate of institutionalization remained constant, although some increase occurred in the use of formal supports. In comparison to the improved group, these high-needs patients had more contact with their children but less contact with friends and relatives. Also, more than a third of the family caregivers decreased their supports to the patient. Those individuals who withdrew some supports were more likely to be children or other relatives and were rarely husbands or wives.

Significant associations suggest that changes take place over time that alter the relationship between the patient and caregiver. With the persistence of poor health and dependence upon others, the patient's mood and satisfaction with social supports decline, and the relationship with the caregiver, in turn, becomes characterized by more conflict. The caregivers experience more strain and seek formal supports or help from other family members. On the whole, the morale of these caregivers improves. We have used the analogy of the "cascade effect" to hypothesize a chain of events in which the family decreases its caregiving and transfers some of the caregiving functions to others.

Since many of the data were descriptive, the adaptive, tension-reducing mechanisms on the part of the caregiver could be identified. Of the two broad types found, one is labeled *distancing techniques,* in which the caregiver, usually a child, decreases supports by establishing greater physical or psychological distance. In the second mechanism, *enmeshing techniques,* used primarily by spouses, the process works to increase the interdependence in the dyad. Some marital dyads experience social regression as they become more socially isolated and retreat into the dyad itself. In other situations, the caregiver's role becomes more firmly entrenched and comes to dominate his or her life to the exclusion of other competing roles.

These findings suggest that family supports play a major role in maintaining dependent older people in the community. Points of strain arise, however, as needs for supports persist over time. Children with their competing commitments and spouses with their own health risks, in combination with the increased social isolation of the patient and caregiver, can make the long-term care of an older person vulnerable. If these problems are identified as they differentially affect various categories of relatives and if supplemental supports are made readily available, the breakdown in family supports could possibly be forestalled.

REFERENCES

Berezin, M. The psychiatrist and the geriatric patient: Partial grief in family members and others who care for the elderly patient. *Journal of Geriatric Psychiatry*, 1970, *4*, 53–64.

Brody, E. M. "Women in the middle" and family help to older people. *The Gerontologist*, 1981, *21*, 471–482.

Busse, E. W. Hypochondriasis in the elderly: A reaction to social stress. *Journal of the American Geriatrics Society*, 1976, *24*, 145–149.

Cantor, M. *Caring for the frail elderly*. Paper presented at the 33rd Annual Scientific Meeting of the Gerontological Society of America, San Diego, 1980.

Cath, S. The institutionalization of a parent: A nadir of life. *Journal of Geriatric Psychiatry*, 1972, *5*, 25–46.

Cicirelli, V. G. *Helping elderly parents*. Auburn House, Boston, 1981.

Croog, S. H. The family as a source of stress. In S. Levine & N. A. Scotch (Eds.), *Social stress*. Aldine, Chicago, 1970.

Crossman, L., London, C., & Barry, C. Older women caring for disabled spouses: A model for supportive services. *The Gerontologist*, 1981, *21*, 464–470.

Eggert, G. M., Granger, C. V., Morris, R., & Pendleton, S. F. Caring for the patient with a long-term disability. *Geriatrics*, 1977, *32*, 102–114.

Fengler, A. P., & Goodrich, N. Wives of elderly disabled men: The hidden patients. *The Gerontologist*, 1979, *19*, 175–183.

Johnson, C. L., Dyadic family relations and social support. *The Gerontologist*, 1983, *23*, 377–383.

Johnson, C. L., & Catalano, D. J. Childless elderly and their family supports. *The Gerontologist*, 1981, *21*, 610–618.

Liang, J., Dvorkin, L., Kahana, E., & Mazian, F. Social integration and morale: A re-examination. *Journal of Gerontology*, 1980, *35*, 746–757.

Litwak, E. Research patterns in the health of the elderly. In E. Borgatta & N. McClusky (Eds.), *Aging and society*. Sage, Beverly Hills, 1980.

Rosenmayr, L., & Kockeis, E. Propositions for a sociological theory of aging and the family. *International Social Science Journal*, 1963, *15*, 410–426.

Sainsbury, P., & Grad de Alarcon, J. The psychiatrist and the geriatric patient: The effects of community care of the family of the geriatric patient. *Journal of Geriatric Psychiatry*, 1970, *1*, 23–41.

Savitsky, E., & Sharkey, H. The geriatric patient and his family: Study of family interaction in the aged. *Journal of Geriatric Psychiatry*, 1973, *5*, 3–19.

Schaefer, C., Coyne, J. C., & Lazarus, R. S. The health-related functions of social supports. *Journal of Behavioral Medicine*, 1981, *4*, 381–406.

Shanas, E. The family as a social support system in old age. *The Gerontologist*, 1979, *19*, 169–175. (a)

Shanas, E. Social myth as hypothesis: The case of the family relations of old people. *The Gerontologist*, 1979, *19*, 3–9. (b)

Slater, P. E. On social regression. *American Sociological Review*, 1963, *28*, 339–364.

Treas, J. Family support systems for the aged: Some social and demographic considerations. *The Gerontologist*, 1977, *17*, 486–491.

Treas, J. The great American fertility debate: Generational balance and support of the aged. *The Gerontologist*, 1981, *21*, 98–103.

Part II

Widowhood

Older widows can be compared, on the one hand, with older people who are still married and, on the other hand, with older single people who have either never married or have divorced. Higher death rates and higher remarriage rates among men result in there being five older widows to every older widower. The median age at widowhood is 68 for women and 71 for men (Lopata, 1979). By the age of 75, 70% of women are widows but only 39% of men are (U.S. Bureau of the Census, 1982). Men whose wives die are much less likely to remain in the category of widower than women whose husbands die are to be called or counted as widows. Only 5% of women who are widowed after 55 ever remarry (Cleveland & Gianturcco, 1976).

Three general issues pervade the literature on widowhood:

1. Mortality rates of the surviving spouse.
2. Physical and mental symptoms accompanying grief.
3. Family supports and loneliness.

Reviews of the literature (Troll, 1982a; Troll, Miller, & Atchley, 1979) show the importance of sex differences in all three areas. A number of studies have looked at vital statistics, following the earlier reports of Young, Benjamin, and Wallis (1963) and Parkes, Benjamin, and Fitzgerald (1969) that surviving spouses had a heightened risk of dying themselves in the first years of widowhood. So far, incidentally, this literature has not tried to correlate heightened death rates among surviving spouses with the extent of caregiving provided prior to the death. At any rate, most of this research shows that widowers are more likely to die than widows. This sex difference probably reflects differential mortality rates by sex rather than any greater vulnerability to loss of a spouse on the part of men. Since then, a Johns Hopkins study (Helsing & Szklo, 1981) found no significant differences in mortality rates between widows and still-married women, and higher death rates for men only between the ages of 65 and 74, and then not in the first 6 months of widowhood.

Foster, Klinger-Vertabedian, and Wispe (1984) found that men who had been married to a wife older than they have a higher death rate than men who had been married to a wife younger than they. Gallagher, Breckenridge, Thompson and Peterson (1983) and Thompson and Walker (1984) found that not only are physical and mental symptoms associated with grief, but they are more frequent among women than among men. Since this sex difference exists in most epidemiological studies on mental health, not only those on widowhood, it may show women's general tendency to report more problems than men do, perhaps because they are less inhibited in this respect rather than because they have greater grief reactions. At any rate, as Gallagher et al. concluded, the emotions of grief should not be considered psychopathology.

Lopata (1979), one of the earliest to study widows and their family supports, notes increased contact with children, siblings, and in-laws, although they do not remain on the scene long. If we look particularly at older widows and at behavior over time, though, as Morgan (1984) did when she analyzed the data from the Longitudinal Retirement History Study, we find that earlier, pre-widowhood family interaction is strongly associated with later family contact after widowhood. Again, since women have more family interactions than men altogether, it is understandable that they continue to have more when they are widowed. Adams (1968b) had earlier reported that adult sons distanced themselves from widowed mothers. The article reprinted here by Bankoff (1983a) shows that the people who are most comforting to recent widows are, in fact, their own mothers (many of whom are presumably also widows). The fact that such help is most important, although not necessarily most frequent, suggests the significance of nurturance and empathy, at least in the acute phase of grief.

Most research has looked at widows in aggregate rather than at the process of becoming a widow, the temporal progression of the adaptation process. Combining all widows regardless of the length of time since the death of their spouses obscures the effects of this process. Bereavement and grief are probably the salient issues in the early months and years of widowhood; other issues, like loneliness and need, may become more salient as time goes on. In a second article, Bankoff (1983b) divided widows who had turned to support groups for help into those in a crisis–loss phase (still acutely grieving) and those in a transition phase, she found that the alternative-help systems they had turned to did not do much for the acutely grieving widows but did help the transitional women. Note that in Bankoff's (1983a) article in this volume she mentioned that it was their mothers who helped the early widows most.

Investigations of women who have been widowed over a period of time (Blau, 1961; Lopata, 1973, 1979) suggest that many older widows quickly grow used to living alone and even prefer to do so. Although they miss their husbands both as persons and as partners in many activities, they become involved in a social life with friends, particularly if they live in an area with a high concentration of widows. In fact, Atchley, Pignatiello, and Shaw (1975) found that older widows had higher rates of social interaction outside their households than did older married women, and Arling (1976) found that such friendship ties were related to higher morale more than exclusive family ties were. Men tend to have fewer close, intimate friends than do women (Troll, 1982a). Their wives are usually their "best friends," so the initial reaction of grief may be even stronger for men than for women (Berardo, 1970). Most of them remarry soon, however.

The lives of middle-class women are more likely to be disrupted by widowhood than those of working-class women (Troll, Miller, & Atchley, 1979). They are more likely to have seen themselves as part of a husband–wife team. On the other hand, middle-class women also have more social options, more nonfamily friends, and more organizational activity, not to mention more resources in general.

Finally, poverty may be the most critical problem for older widows, a majority of whom are below the poverty line (Troll & Seltzer, 1985), partly because women's work (whether in or out of the home) pays less than men's and partly because financial planning on the part of husbands or couples usually does not

3

Effects of Bereavement on Self-Perceptions of Physical Health in Elderly Widows and Widowers*

Larry W. Thompson
James N. Breckenridge
Dolores Gallagher
James Peterson

Despite the consensus among health professionals regarding the stressful nature of bereavement (e.g., Holmes & Rahe, 1967), the data on physical health indices in adults over age 60 are limited and provide conflicting results. Gerber et al. (1975), for example, found an increase in medical problems among widowers 6 months after the death of their spouse, although Heyman and Gianturco (1973) failed to uncover pre- and post-loss differences for either sex on scores for health and hypochondriacal ratings in a prospective, longitudinal study of elderly adults. Clayton (1982) also observed no significant bereaved/control differences in health ratings or the reported number of physical symptoms, physician visits, and hospitalizations during a 1-year interval; this study included elderly participants, but does not report age-specific data. Findings on mortality during the early stages of bereavement have also been inconsistent. Epstein et al. (1975)

Journal of Gerontology, 39 (3) (1984), 309–314.
This research was supported by a National Institute on Aging grant (AGO1959–04).

reported higher mortality rates for widows and widowers than married persons, although Clayton (1982), in a recent review, concluded that there was no increase in mortality for women during the first year. Helsing and Szklo (1981) also reported a higher risk only for widowers from age 55 to 74, but even in this instance the risk was not greater for older widowers during the first 6 months after bereavement, as had been suggested by earlier reports (e.g., Parkes et al., 1969; Young et al., 1963).

Thus, although much has been learned regarding the link between stressful life events and physical well-being (Eisdorfer & Wilkie, 1977; Tessler & Mechanic, 1978), the extent to which older men and women are likely to suffer deteriorating health as a consequence of the loss of their spouse is uncertain. Interpretation of the apparent conflicts within this literature is hindered by a number of methodological concerns. For example, Stroebe and Stroebe (1983) have pointed out that sample sizes and sample selection procedures have varied greatly across reports. Both elderly adults in general and men in particular have been underrepresented in widowhood studies. Although economic circumstances may be important moderators of the impact of bereavement on elderly adults (Atchley, 1975; Balkwell, 1981), few studies have examined the differential effects of socioeconomic status. Further, few studies have employed a multivariate approach to data analysis. Consequently, complex interactions among age, sex, and sociodemographic factors have not been explored fully.

This paper reports data on self-perceptions of physical health status of participants approximately 2 months after their spouse's death. It is one of a series of reports in an ongoing longitudinal investigation of the impact of bereavement on elderly men and women over a 30-month period.

METHOD

Participants

The present sample includes 212 bereaved adults (113 women and 99 men) and 162 comparison control participants (78 women and 84 men) between the ages of 55 and 83. Table 3.1 provides a description of sociodemographic factors for bereaved and control men and women.

These variables were used as covariates for the analysis of physical health indicators. To reduce the number of covariates employed, a

Table 3.1 Means and Standard Deviations of Sociodemographic Variables by Group and Sex

Variable		Bereaved		Controls	
		Men (*n* = 99)	Women (*n* = 113)	Men (*n* = 84)	Women (*n* = 78)
Age	M	69.91	66.71	71.33	69.03
	SD	8.31	7.08	7.94	7.00
Number years mar-ried	M	40.22	37.30	38.22	37.21
	SD	12.30	13.65	14.34	13.08
Present income[a]	M	2.75	3.55	2.82	2.83
	SD	1.30	1.41	1.14	1.17
Lifetime occupation[b]	M	2.27	3.62	2.91	3.65
	SD	1.21	1.93	1.42	1.84
Education[c]	M	4.46	4.40	4.37	4.10
	SD	1.91	1.69	2.19	1.90
Spouse's occupation[b]	M	4.40	2.43	3.99	2.53
	SD	1.91	1.31	1.90	1.41
Spouse's education[c]	M	3.74	4.29	3.82	4.39
	SD	1.73	2.10	2.14	2.11

[a]Income was grouped by categories (1 ≥ $30,000; 6 < $5,000);
[b]occupation was coded 1 = professional/managerial, 5 = unskilled laborer;
[c]education was coded 1 = < 8 years, 9 = advanced degree.

principal components analysis was performed on the seven background variables. Four component scores were utilized in the present paper: (a) longevity (age and years married), (b) subject's socioeconomic status (SES), (c) spouse's SES, and (d) current income. Details of this analysis, the sampling procedures employed, and between-groups comparison of sociodemographic variables are reported elsewhere (Gallagher et al., 1983). Briefly, these two groups comprised Caucasians, most of whom (80%) had some high school education and many of whom had completed college or beyond. Relatively few (4 to 10%) were unskilled laborers, and a sizable number (17 to 34%) were in professional or managerial fields. Income ranged from $10,000 to $30,000 for half the men and 40% of the women. Less than 10% of the men had incomes below $5,000. A greater number of women (12 to 28%) had incomes this low, but their spouses' occupation suggested that their income earlier in life had been substantially higher. Bereaved adults' participation was solicited by mail; names and addresses were obtained from a search of death certificates from the Los Angeles County Department of Health. The comparison sample was recruited from senior centers, residential facilities, and the Emeriti Center mailing list of the University of Southern California.

Procedure

A structured interview was carried out with participants in their homes, unless they requested to come to the research center. The interviews reviewed religious beliefs and practices, coping strategies employed in response to spousal loss, prior stressful life events, utilization of social supports, upheaval in routines of daily living, and self-perceptions of psychological and physical health status. Comparable interviews, with appropriate modifications in wording, were conducted with the comparison participants. (Copies of these interviews are available on request.)

Measures

Participants were asked how often they had seen a physician and how frequently they had been hospitalized during the past 2 months. They reported any health problems during that period and indicated when each disorder had begun. All medications, including prescription and over-the-counter drugs used during that period, were identified; both the approximate date when medications were begun or dosages changed was determined. In addition, participants rated their current health status and their health compared with others their age on 7-point anchored scales. Previous research has indicated that elderly adults' self-ratings of health are positively correlated with physicians' ratings of health status (LaRue et al., 1979) and that perceived health significantly predicts future mortality even after controlling for age, SES, and objective physical health (Mossey & Shapiro, 1982).

Finally, reported health problems were coded by the organ system affected, and a global severity score, following the procedure outlined in Wyler et al. (1968), was created for combined new and worsened illnesses of each person. Weights were assigned to each illness based on Wyler's rankings; he found these rankings to have high concordance with physician judgments (reported Spearman's rho = .94). Because participants differed in the absolute number of new or worsened illnesses, the mean of their severity ratings was employed as an index of the seriousness of participant health problems.

RESULTS

Physician and Hospital Visits

The distribution of physician visits was remarkably similar between groups; 52.66% of the bereaved and 51.66% of the control participants reported one or more doctor visits within the 2-month interval, Mann-Whitney U, $z = -.3427$, $p < .73$. A comparison of sexes for the total sample also did not approach significance, Mann-Whitney U, $z = -1.2724$, $p < .20$. Only 5 of the bereaved and 3 of the comparison control participants reported having been hospitalized during this 2-month period. Four of the hospitalized bereaved were women, and all 3 of the hospitalized control participants were men.

New and Worsened Illnesses

Table 3.2 displays the number of illnesses reported by men and women of each group according to disease type. The bereaved reported more illnesses than control participants (68% vs. 32%), and women more than men (64% vs. 36%). The majority of new or worsened disorders reported by the bereaved were those affecting cardiovascular, gastrointestinal, musculoskeletal, and ear-eye-nose-throat systems. Of those bereaved participants reporting mental health problems, 4 described their disorder as depression, 3 as anxiety or "nerves," 9 as sleep disorders, and 3 as unspecified difficulties. Only 2 control participants reported (unspecified) emotional disorders.

Because the distribution of reported illnesses was highly skewed, this variable was treated as dichotomous (i.e., presence or absence of new and/or worsened disorders). A multiple logistic regression of this variable on bereavement status, sex, and the four indicators of sociodemographic status was performed (Haberman, 1974). With both sex and sociodemographic background controlled, the odds of illness among the bereaved were estimated to be 1.40 times the risk for the comparison control participants, χ^2 (1) = 8.36, $p < .004$. No significant interactions between bereavement status and the other

Table 3.2. Classification of New and Worsened Illnesses Reported by
             Men and Women in the Bereaved and Comparison Control
             Groups

Illness type	Bereaved		Controls	
	Men	Women	Men	Women
Central nervous system	2	2	0	2
Cardiovascular	8	12	4	0
Respiratory	1	1	0	5
Blood disorder	1	3	1	1
Gastrointestinal	3	10	1	1
Endocrine	4	4	0	1
Musculoskeletal	7	15	2	8
Urinary	1	3	0	2
Mental health	9	9	0	1
Trauma	2	1	0	1
Eye, ear, nose and throat	4	10	6	4
Other	2	2	0	2
Total number of illnesses	44	72	13	28
N reporting illnesses	28	51	14	23

independent variables were observed (ps from .24 to .75). The odds of
a new or worsened illness were 1.43 times greater for women than for
men, $\chi^2 (1) = 9.83$, $p < .002$, irrespective of marital status. In addition,
a significant interaction between sex and reported income, $\chi^2 (1) =$
4.95, $p < .03$, was observed, indicating a greater likelihood of illness
for women in lower income brackets. Using Hosmer's goodness-of-fit
index (Hosmer & Lemeshow, 1980), the final regression equation
with all background variables and the Sex × Income interaction term
adequately fit the data, $\chi^2 (8) = 3.92$, $p < .86$.

New or Increased Medication Use

Of those reporting new or increased medication use, 77.55% were
bereaved (23 women and 15 men). A logistic regression of new
medication use (i.e., presence or absence of new or increased usage)
revealed a significant effect for bereavement, $\chi^2 (1) = 10.26$, $p < .001$.
Statistically controlling for sociodemographic factors and sex, the
odds of reporting new and/or increased medication were 1.73 times

greater for the bereaved. Sex could not account significantly for medication use, χ^2 (1) = .661, p < .43, nor was the effect of bereavement found to depend significantly on sex, χ^2 (1) = 1.44, p < .23. Similarly, none of the sociodemographic variables were related significantly to medication use nor were significant interactions observed between these variables and sex or bereavement status. Using the Hosmer index, the equation for medication use adequately fit the data, χ^2 (6) = 10.73, p < .10. Table 3.3 presents the results of the logistic regressions for both medication usage and physical illnesses.

Health and Illness Severity Ratings

Table 3.4 gives the means and standard deviations for bereaved and control participants on three health indices. A Group × Sex multivariate analysis of variance, following Applebaum and Cramer's (1974) approach to uneven cell sizes, revealed a significant main effect for group, F (3, 365) = 3.66, p < .01, canonical R = .171. Neither the effects for sex, F (3, 365) = .407, p < .75, nor for the Group × Sex interaction, F (3, 365) × .566, p < .63, approached significance. Mean scores on each of the three health ratings indicated significantly worse reported health for bereaved compared with the comparison

Table 3.3. Results of Multiple Logistic Regressions of Reported New or Worsened Illnesses and Reported New or Increased Medication Use

	Response Variable			
	Illnesses		Medication use	
Predictors	Coefficient	Z^c	Coefficient	Z^c
Group[a]	−.313	−2.587	−.547	−3.002
Sex[b]	.328	2.379	.145	.779
Group × sex	.016	.133	.232	1.165
Background scores				
Longevity	.129	1.000	.117	.674
SES	.022	.164	−.184	−1.062
Spouse's SES	.016	.132	.032	.194
Income	.095	.741	.130	.776
Income × sex	.287	2.199	—	—
Longevity × group	—	—	.375	1.643

[a]Group coded − 1 = bereaved, + 1 = control;
[b]sex coded − 1 = male, + 1 = female;
[c]Z = logistic coefficient divided by standard error.

Table 3.4. Means and Standard Deviations of Three Physical Health Indices for Bereaved and Control Men and Women

		Bereaved		Controls	
Variable		Men	Women	Men	Women
Perceived health	M	2.74	2.69	.26	2.49
	SD	1.45	1.57	1.40	1.42
Health relative to others	M	2.59	2.63	2.21	2.28
	SD	1.38	1.32	1.23	1.18
Mean severity index	M	35.03	48.93	15.39	20.29
	SD	84.62	117.58	40.87	48.00

control participants: perceived health, $F(1, 367) = 4.88$, $p < .03$, $\omega^2 = .010$; perceived health relative to others the same age, $F(1, 367) = 7.00$, $p < .008$, $w^2 = .016$; and the mean severity of illnesses reported, $F(1, 367) = 7.67$, $p < .006$, $\omega^2 = .108$.

A multivariate analysis of covariance using the four background component scores as covariates was also performed. This procedure assumes that every covariate-dependent variable relationship is identical between groups. The multivariate test of the homogeneity of regression for all four sociodemographic variables was consistent with this assumption, $F(36, 1031.89) = .813$, $p < .78$ (univariate tests, ps from .66 to .90). This analysis yielded a significant main effect for group, $F(3, 361) = 3.53$, $p < .015$, canonical $R = .176$. Neither the main effect for sex, $F(3, 361) = .419$, $p < .74$, nor the Group × Sex interaction, $F(3, 361) = .894$, $p < .44$, reached significance. Taking sociodemographic differences into account, mean scores on each of the health ratings indicated significantly poorer health among the bereaved: perceived health, $F(1, 363) = 4.668$, $p < .03$, $\omega^2 = .010$; perceived relative health, $F(1, 363) = 66.72$, $p < .01$, $\omega^2 = .016$; and mean illness severity rating, $F(1, 363) = 7.60$, $p < .006$, $\omega^2 = .017$.

DISCUSSION

These results are consistent with prior research indicating that conjugal bereavement is a significant stressor that may adversely affect the physical health status of survivors. Our major findings can be summarized as follows: (a) Recently bereaved elderly adults were more likely to report development of a new illness, or worsening of a preexisting condition, than their nonbereaved counterparts. (b) These illnesses were slightly more severe than those reported by the comparison group. (c) The bereaved were more likely to report beginning a new medication or increasing usage of previously taken drugs. (d) The bereaved rated their overall health, and health compared with others their own age, more poorly than the comparison group. (e) There were no significant Group × Sex interactions on any of the statistical tests performed. (f) In general, the effects obtained even after controlling for sociodemographic factors. (g) The bereaved did *not* differ from nonbereaved on number of physician's visits or hospitalizations in the 2-month interval in question. (h) Contrary to prior studies, recently bereaved men did not report greater morbidity than women. In fact, on the only measure where an independent effect for sex was observed (new or worsened illnesses), results were in the opposite direction. Thus, the negative impact of spousal bereavement appears discernible on a number of self-report indices of physical health status as early as 2 months after the loss.

Our findings do not support those of Clayton (1982), Heyman and Gianturco (1973), and Parkes and Brown (1972). As noted earlier, this may reflect sampling differences; neither Clayton nor Parkes focused exclusively on elderly adults, whereas Heyman and Gianturco sampled long-term participants who may have represented elite survivors, as discussed in Schaie (1973).

Absence of greater morbidity in bereaved men compared with women conflicts with the findings of Berardo (1970), who noted more devastating effects for older male survivors of spousal loss. The present results are, however, consistent with the findings of large-scale population studies (i.e., higher scores for women on indices of poor health regardless of marital status, National Center for Health Statistics, 1976). The present findings may have been a function of the close proximity between spousal loss and the assessment of reported health. It may be that those health difficulties that impact bereaved men develop over a longer period of time (Helsing & Szklo, 1981; Stroebe & Stroebe, 1983). Inspection of mortality data for the present sample of bereaved over the first year after loss has revealed comparable findings: Twelve deaths occurred among the bereaved men (13% of that group) compared to only one death among the bereaved women. Two men and no women died among the control participants for the same period. Of the 12 deaths, half occurred between 2 and 6 months after the loss, and the other half between 6 and 12 months. These data suggest that bereaved men are likely to be underestimating their health difficulties at 2 months after the death of their wife.

An additional point concerns the reliance of self-report data in the current study. The validity of such data depends upon the respondent's willingness and ability to answer questions fully and accurately. Although it may be argued that this was a difficult task so soon after spousal loss, it should be noted that collection of self-report data has been the predominant method used to obtain indices of physical health status in virtually all studies of bereavement conducted to date. Its use is supported by the agreement of elderly adults' self-reports with physicians' ratings (LaRue et al., 1979) and significant prediction of subsequent mortality (e.g., Mossey & Shapiro, 1982). Nevertheless, because we are reporting an association between bereavement and perceived health status, caution is necessary when making inferences about actual physical health status.

Finally, sample characteristics must be taken into account when interpreting the data reported here. This was a strictly volunteer sample of community-residing Caucasian older adults who, by and large, were in middle to upper socioeconomic strata. Health perceptions may differ for recently bereaved older persons who are in less advantaged situations or who come from different racial or ethnic backgrounds.

REFERENCES

Appelbaum, M. I., & Cramer, E. M. Some problems in the non-orthogonal analysis of variance. *Psychological Bulletin*, 1974, *81*, 335–343.

Atchley, M. H. Dimensions of widowhood in later life. *Gerontologist*, 1975, *15*, 176–178.

Balkwell, C. Transition to widowhood: A review of the literature. *Family Relations*, 1981, *30*, 117–127.

Berardo, F. M. Survivorship and social isolations: The case of the aged widower. *Family Coordinator*, 1970, *19*, 11–25.

Clayton, P. J. Bereavement. In E. S. Paykel (Ed.), *Handbook of affective disorders*. Guilford Press, New York, 1982.

Eisdorfer, C., & Wilkie, F. Stress, disease, aging, and behavior. In J. E. Birren & K. W. Schaie (Eds.), *Handbook of the psychology of aging*, Van Nostrand Reinhold, New York, 1977.

Epstein, G. E., Weitz, L., Roback, H., & McKee, E. Research on bereavement: A selective and critical review. *Comprehensive Psychiatry*, 1975, *16*, 537–546.

Gallagher, D. E., Breckenridge, J. N., Thompson, L. W., & Peterson, J. Effects of bereavement on indicators of mental health in elderly widows and widowers. *Journal of Gerontology*, 1983, *38*, 565–571.

Gerber, I., Rusalem, R., Hannon, N., Battin, D., & Arkin, A. Anticipatory grief and aged widows. *Journal of Gerontology*, 1975, *30*, 225–239.

Haberman, S. J. *The analysis of frequency data*. University of Chicago Press, Chicago, 1974.

Helsing, K. J., & Szklo, M. Mortality after bereavement. *American Journal of Epidemiology*, 1981, *114*, 41–52.

Heyman, D. K., & Gianturco, D. T. Long-term adaptation by the elderly to bereavement. *Journal of Gerontology*, 1973, *28*, 359–362.

Holmes, T. H., & Rahe, R. H. The social adjustment scale. *Journal of Psychosomatic Medicine*, 1967, *11*, 213–218.

Hosmer, D. W., & Lemeshow, S. Goodness of fit tests for the multiple logistic regression model. *Community Statistics*, 1980, *9*, 1043–1069.

LaRue, A., Bank, L., Jarvik, L., & Hetland, M. Health in old age: How do physicians' ratings and self-ratings compare? *Journal of Gerontology*, 1979, *34*, 687–691.

Mossey, J. M., & Shapiro, E. Self-rated health: A predictor of mortality among the elderly. *American Journal of Public Health*, 1982, *72*, 800–808.

National Center for Health Statistics. Differentials in health characteristics by marital status: United States, 1971–1972. *Vital and Health Statistics*, 1976, Series 10, No. 104.

Parkes, C. M., Benjamin, B., & Fitzgerald, R. G. Broken heart: A statistical study of increased mortality among widowers. *British Medical Journal*, 1969, *1*, 740–743.

Parkes, C. M., & Brown, R. J. Health after bereavement: A controlled study of young Boston widows and widowers. *Psychosomatic Medicine*, 1972, *34*, 444–461.

Schaie, K. W. Methodological problems in descriptive developmental research on adulthood and aging. In J. R. Nesselroade & H. W. Reese (Eds.), *Life-span developmental psychology: Methodological issues*. Academic Press, New York, 1973.

Stroebe, M. S., & Stroebe, W. Who suffers most? Sex differences in health risks of the widowed. *Psychological Bulletin*, 1983, *93*, 279–301.

Tessler, R., & Mechanic, D. Psychological distress and perceived health status. *Journal of Health and Social Behavior*, 1978, *19*, 254–262.

Wyler, A. R., Masuda, M., & Holmes, T. H. Seriousness of illness rating scale. *Journal of Psychosomatic Research*, 1968, *11*, 363–374.

Young, M., Benjamin, B., & Wallis, C. The mortality of widowers. *Lancet*, 1963, *2*, 454–456.

4

Aged Parents and Their Widowed Daughters: A Support Relationship*

Elizabeth A. Bankoff

Do parents play important nurturing and supportive roles for their adult children, particularly during difficult times? Put another way, do middle-aged children need their parents' support when experiencing a life crisis such as death of a spouse? The present study addressed these questions by investigating the role of social support from parents, as well as other family members, friends, and neighbors in enhancing the psychological well-being of recent and still grieving widows.

A growing body of literature suggests that an individual's social network is an important factor mediating adjustment to stressful life events in general (Gourash, 1978) and to death of a spouse in particular. The lack of an intimate relationship was found to be related to depression among the widowed (Lowenthal & Haven, 1968). Living with kin (Bornstein et al., 1973) and living near adult children (Clayton et al., 1972) were found to be negatively correlated with depression among older widows and widowers in their first 5 years of bereavement. Similarly, Parkes (1972) found that widows who see the smallest number of friends and relatives during the first year of

*Journal of Gerontology, 39 (2)(1984), 230–239.

The research reported in this paper was supported with a grant from the National Institute of Mental Health, PHS#5, R01-MH30742. M. A. Lieberman and L. D. Borman were the co-principal investigators.

bereavement have significantly more psychological disturbance than those who see more friends and relatives.

The role of parental support for newly bereaved widows, however, remains unclear. In part, this lack of clarity may reflect an emphasis on the elderly widow in most investigations of widowhood. As a result, questions regarding the role of support for the widowed have focused on support from persons of the same or younger generations. Little consideration has been given to the support role the elderly parent may play for younger widows. This oversight is unfortunate since the average age that widowhood occurs is 56 years (*Information on Aging*, 1981); many new widows have at least one living parent who is a potential source of support.

The lack of clarity regarding the role of parental support for adult children in distress may also reflect the current confusion over the extent to which adult children are psychologically dependent on their parents in general. Lopata (1979) found that few widows reported that their parents were major contributors of emotional support either immediately prior to their husbands' illnesses or 10 years after their deaths. She suggests, therefore, that "children draw away from their emotional dependence on their parents relatively early in adulthood" (1979, p. 235). However, Cohler and Grunebaum (1981) maintain that adult women and their mothers continue to be psychologically dependent on each other. Similarly, Schwartz (1979) argues that a child's psychological dependence on a parent continues until the parent's death. As such, whether or not elderly parents play an important support role for their now widowed daughters remains a question—which this study addresses.

METHOD

Sample

The findings presented here are based on a sample of widows who participated in a nationwide study of alternative help systems at the University of Chicago from 1978 to 1981 (Lieberman & Borman, 1979). To procure the sample, mailing lists of names of widowed people were obtained from two organizations of widowed people, one in Chicago, the other nationwide. The mailing lists were generated by the chapters of these organizations for the purpose of recruiting recently widowed people into the group. Thus, the lists included both names of widowed people who were members and names of those who had been invited to join but did not. A total of 2,798 questionnaires were mailed during the summer of 1979. Fifty percent of those delivered were returned. From these returns, Caucasian women who were widowed 18 months or less and who indicated that they were still grieving ($n = 98$) were selected for the present study. Because the purpose of this study was to explore the role of social support for recent and still grieving widows, respondents who were widowed longer than 18 months or who reported that they were no longer grieving were excluded from further analyses, as were all of the widowers.

Fifty-eight percent of this sample was employed at least part-time. Although 93% were mothers, 45% lived alone. Fifty-four percent had at least one living parent. Fifty-one percent were Catholic, and the remaining 49% were Protestant. Twenty-two percent had earned a bachelor's degree; 10% had not completed high school. The mean age was 52 years—just slightly younger than the national average (*Information on Aging*, 1981), and the average number of years lived in their present community was 27.

Measures

Bradburn's Affect Balance Scale (Bradburn, 1969) was employed as the measure of psychological well-being. This scale includes five items tapping positive feelings experienced in the past few weeks (i.e., have you felt: pleased, excited or interested in something, on top of the world, things were going your way, and proud), and five items tapping negative feelings experienced during the same time (i.e., have you felt: restless, lonely, bored, depressed, and upset). Well-being was calculated by subtracting the total number of negative feelings experienced from the total number of positive feelings experienced: the resulting scores ranged from + 5 (high) to – 5 (low).

Each respondent was asked to report how much of six different types of support they received from each of seven different sets of network associates: parents, in-laws, children, other close relatives, married friends, widowed or otherwise single friends, and neighbors. The six types of support included contact, intimacy, assurance of emergency assistance, emotional support, guidance, and approval of a new lifestyle.

The measures of contact, intimacy, and assurance of emergency assistance had been developed for a study of life events and adaptation in adulthood by Pearlin and Lieberman (Lieberman & Glidewell,

1978). The contact scale indicates how often the widows get together or speak over the phone with each of the seven network associates. The intimacy support scale determines the frequency with which the widows discuss their important personal problems with these network associates. The assurance of emergency assistance support scale measures the extent to which the widows feel they can depend on their network associates for emergency help. Similar scales were developed for this study to measure the amount of emotional support received from each set of network associates, the amount of guidance received, and the amount of approval received for starting to lead an active social life. Each item was answered on a 4-point scale (i.e., never, occasionally, often, or very often). In addition, respondents were able to identify inappropriate items in any of the sets (e.g., questions about children for childless respondents) by checking a fifth option: deceased/not applicable. Support scores for each of the seven sets of network associates were derived by calculating the mean response across all six types of support provided by each particular associate. For example, the summary support score for in-laws represents the average amount of all six types of support provided the widow by her in-laws.

RESULTS

The analytic task was to determine whether or not it makes a difference who is giving the support. This study sought to determine if the support provided by different network associates to these widows related differentially to their psychological well-being. This query focused on the relative importance of parental support for these recent and still grieving widows. Accordingly, the support scores for each of the seven sets of network associates were used in a multiple regression analysis predicting well-being (i.e., Affect Balance scores) for these widows. Support scores for each of the associates were entered into the equation only if the associates were available as support providers. If the widow indicated that a particular associate was not applicable or was deceased, the score for this associate was omitted, using a pairwise deletion technique. Use of this technique allowed for evaluation of only the relevant network. For example, children's support was not evaluated for childless respondents.

The results of this analysis indicate that the source of the support makes a significant difference in terms of its effectiveness for these recent and still grieving widows. As reported in Table 4.1, of the

Table 4.1. Stepwise Multiple Regression of Sources of Support on Indicator of Psychological Well-being

Well-being indicator	Predictor variable	R^2 increment	Unstandardized regression coefficient	Standardized regression coefficient	Overall R^2
Psychological well-being					.16*
	Parental support	.11	1.00	.30	
	Widowed friends support	.05	.63	.22	

Note: All seven predictor variables were available for entry into the equation in single steps from best to worst. Variables were entered, however, only if their calculated *F* value was significant.
*$p \leq .05$

seven potential sources, support from only two—parents and widowed or otherwise single friends—was positively associated with the reported well-being of the widows, net of the other independent variables. Together, the support provided by these two sets of network associates accounted for 16% of the variance in the widows' psychological well-being, $F(98) = 3.66$, $p < .05$. Parental support was the most important, accounting for 11% of the total variance. Moreover, these data reveal that quantity of support does not necessarily predict its effectiveness. Despite the fact that these widows received more support from their children than from their parents (Table 4.2), the former are not effective supporters, although the latter certainly are.

Support from their aged parents appears to be related most crucially to the psychological well-being of these recent and still grieving widows. Parental support assumes a particularly key role for these widows in light of their nonresponsiveness to support from most others. However, what happens when parental support is unavailable? If these widows do not have living parents or if their living parents do not supply much support, does support from other sources compensate for this lack? Can support from other network associates substitute for parental support?

A number of increasingly specific analyses were employed to examine this issue. First, a one-way analysis of variance was used to determine whether differences in psychological well-being exist among the following groups of widows in this sample: those with no living parent ($n = 45$); those who receive relatively little support from their living parents ($n = 19$); those who receive strong parental sup-

Table 4.2. The Average Amount of Support Provided by Each Set of Network Associates

Network associates	N	M	SD
Parents	54	2.64	.70
In-laws	63	2.19	.80
Children	89	3.17	.61
Other close relatives	91	2.58	.85
Married friends	97	2.55	.80
Widowed friends	89	2.64	.81
Neighbors	97	2.19	.81

Note: Levels of support ranged from 1.0 (no support) to 4.0 (strong support).

port (n = 34). A priori contrasts tested the well-being differences between the latter two groups and between the parentless group and the combined groups of widows with living parents. Multiple regression analysis then determined whether the combined support received from the rest of the network significantly affects the well-being of those recent widows who receive little or no parental support. Finally, multiple classification analyses were used to examine the compensating effects of support from each of the other network associates for all three parental support groups—those with no living parent, those with relatively little support from living parents, and those with strong parental support. Through this modified analysis of variance technique, the support from each of the other six sources was introduced as a covariate, allowing assessment of how much such support adjusted the well-being scores for each of the three groups.

The results of the analysis of variance indicate that no significant differences in well-being exist when comparing all three groups of widows. Simply having a living parent or not does not relate to any difference in well-being as indicated by the a priori contrast that tested for differences between parentless widows and all those with living parents. However, whether or not living parents provide strong support was found to be associated with the psychological well-being of these recently widowed women. Those widows who receive little support from living parents have the lowest sense of psychological well-being (M = − .28). In contrast, those with strong parental support fare best (M = .79), $t(94)$ = 2.1, p = .04.

The multiple regression analysis reveals that the combined support from the rest of the social network does not significantly affect the sense of well-being of those widows with little or no parental support.

Finally, the results of the multiple classification analyses suggest that only widowed or otherwise single friends' support has an impact above and beyond the effects of having or not having parental support, $F(95)$ = 5.92, p = .02. These analyses, however, indicate that support received from these friends has no compensating effect on those widows who receive little support from living parents; these friends' support seems only to compensate for lack of parental support if the parents are deceased.

This set of findings indicate that for those recent widows who receive little support from living parents, the support provided by any or all of the other network associates is not able to increase their sense of well-being.

DISCUSSION

It appears that elderly parents play a crucial supportive role for their widowed daughters. These analyses indicate that parents are the single most important source of support gained from the informal social network; parental support is related most strongly to the psychological well-being of these recently widowed women. Not only do those widows with little parental support concomitantly experience a more depressed sense of psychological well-being than their peers with strong parental support, but no other associate's support appears to be able to compensate for weak parental support as long as the parents are still living. Although support from widowed friends seems to enhance the well-being of parentless widows, it has no apparent effect on the well-being of those who receive little support from living parents. The support provided by any or all of the other network associates has no effect on the psychological well-being of those widows receiving relatively little support from living parents. If aged parents are still living but do not help their newly widowed daughters by providing strong parental support, no other network associate's support seems to be able to help in their stead.

Early in the bereavement process grieving individuals tend to withdraw psychologically from the world around them; they are characterized by an unresponsiveness to relationships (Lindemann, 1944; Marris, 1958; Parkes, 1975, 1972). The fact that most of the supports provided were empirically unrelated to the well-being of these widows may be a reflection of the reality of their psychological state of apathy towards the world in general and nonresponsiveness to human relationships in particular. This tendency towards apathy and nonresponsiveness also serves to underscore the potential importance of parental support. When very little seems to make a difference, that which does—in this case, parental support—assumes a more critical role.

The particular importance of parental support can be understood better in the context of previous research into the experience of widowhood. Walker et al. (1977) suggest that during the period of grief soon after the death of a spouse, the most salient need is usually for empathy and strong emotional support. In other words, the widow needs nurturance. She needs to be able to be dependent and to have someone take care of her. In light of the fact that parents are the prototypical providers of nurturance, the unparalleled sources of earlier satisfaction of dependency needs, it becomes understandable why parents become the most salient sources of support during such a difficult time in their child's life. Parents can provide a nondemand-ing private sphere into which the grieving widows can temporarily regress (Berger & Kellner, 1970). Walker et al. (1977) note that close-knit relationships resulting from a history of strong ties (as character-ized by the widow and her parents) are best able to reduce widows' loneliness. Such relationships are also best able to maintain a static social identity that is often coveted by newly bereaved widows (Parkes, 1972).

Although confirming data are not available, it should be borne in mind that in a sample of widows with a mean age of 52 years, parents will typically mean mother. Because the average age of parents in this sample is approximately 75, it is probably safe to assume that a substantial number of the widows have only one parent still living—their mothers, who are widows themselves. In addition to being best able to provide nurturance, these widowed mothers are also able to be empathic with their grieving daughters, having experienced the pain and loss themselves. It may well be, as Silverman (1970) among others has suggested, that widows have a great need for emotional support from people who have gone through the same experience. As one of the widows in this study reported:

> What's helpful? Why people who are in the "same boat." Unless you've been there you just can't understand. And, real understanding, that's what we need. At least, that's what I need.

The middle-aged child and her own mother both now share the same role—widow. Thus, the two generations share similar concerns and interests. Under such circumstances daughters may look to their own mothers for help, for the mother can be an ideal role model (Cohler & Grunebaum, 1981). Such sharing of roles may also explain why support from widowed friends is effective for the parentless widow. Such friends also understand and provide the widow with positive role models.

It is possible that experiencing a life crisis such as conjugal bereave-ment intensifies a child's need for parental support. Caution should be taken with attempts to generalize beyond this set of circumstances. It may be that in the relative calm of everyday life adult children do not have much need for parental support. We do not have data regarding the extent to which these daughters needed or received parental support. We do not have data regarding the extent to which these daughters needed or received parental support prior to their widowhood. However, in the midst of the trauma of recent widowhood, the parent-child relationship that provided a more caring response was the relationship that most helped these grieving daughters. It may be, as Cohler and Grunebaum (1981) argue, that the important issue regarding aged parent-adult child support relationships is not closeness versus distance in everyday life. The important dimension for our future consideration may be "the extent to which adults are able to adapt to situations and events calling for either a more autonomous or a more caring response" (Cohler & Grunebaum, 1981, p. 335).

Aging parents want to continue making a positive contribution to the lives of their children (Arling, 1976; Hirschfield & Dennis, 1979; Hochschild, 1979; Marris, 1958). The present study suggests that they have an important, if not unique, contribution to make. Much emphasis today is placed on the roles adult offspring play in support of their parents. There is little understanding, however, of the viable support role aged parents can play for their adult children. This research suggests that more attention should be given this aspect of the relationship.

REFERENCES

Arling, G. The elderly widow and her family, neighbors and friends. *Journal of Marriage and the Family*, 1976, *38*, 757–768.

Berger, P. L., & Kellner, H. Marriage and the construction of reality. In H. P. Dreitzel (Ed.), *Recent sociology*. MacMillan, London, 1970.

Bornstein, P. E., Clayton, P. J., Halikas, J. A., Maurice, W. L., & Robins, E. The depression of widowhood after thirteen months. *British Journal of Psychiatry*, 1973, *122*, 561–566.

Bradburn, N. *Structure of psychological well-being*. Aldine, Chicago, 1969.

Clayton, P. J., Halikas, J. A., & Maurice, W. L. The depression of widowhood. *British Journal of Psychiatry*, 1972, *120*, 71–77.

Cohler, B. J., & Grunebaum, H. *Mothers, grandmothers, and daughters*. John Wiley, New York, 1981.

Gourash, N. Help seeking: A review of the literature. *American Journal of Community Psychology*, 1978, *6*, 413–423.

Hirschfield, I. S., & Dennis, H. Perspectives. In P. K. Ragan (Ed.), *Aging parents*. The University of Southern California Press, Los Angeles, 1979.

Hochschild, A. Disengagement theory: A critique and a proposal. *American Sociological Review*, 1975, *40*, 553–569.

Aspects of the aging national population. *Information on aging*, October, 1981, No. 23, 6.

Lieberman, M. A., & Borman, L. D. (Eds.) *Self-help groups for coping with crisis*. Jossey-Bass, San Francisco, CA, 1979.

Lieberman, M. A., & Glidewell, J. C. Overview: Special issue on the helping process. *American Journal of Community Psychology*, 1978, *6*, 405–411.

Lindemann, E. Symptomatology and management of acute grief. *American Journal of Psychiatry*, 1944, *101*, 141–148.

Lopata, H. Z. *Women as widows: Support systems.* Elsevier, New York, 1979.

Lowenthal, M. F., & Haven, C. Interaction and adaptation: Intimacy as a critical variable. *American Sociological Review*, 1968, *33*, 20–30.

Marris, P. *Widows and their families.* Routledge and Kegan Paul, London, 1958.

Parkes, C. M. *Bereavement: Studies of grief in adult life.* International Universities Press, New York, 1972.

Parkes, C. M. Unexpected and untimely bereavement: A statistical study of young Boston widows and widowers. In B. S. Schoenberg, I. Gerber, A. Weiner, A. H. Kutcher, D. Peretz, & A. C. Carr (Eds.), *Bereavement: Its psychosocial aspects.* Columbia University Press, New York, 1975.

Schwartz, A. N. Psychological dependency: An emphasis on the later years. In P. K. Ragan (Ed.), *Aging parents.* The University of Southern California Press, Los Angeles, 1979.

Silverman, P. R. The widow as caregiver in a program of preventive intervention with other widows. *Mental Hygiene*, 1970, *54*, 540–547.

Walker, K. N., MacBride, A., & Vachon, M. L. S. Social support networks and the crisis of bereavement. *Social Science and Medicine*, 1977, *2*, 35–41.

Part III

Parent–Adult Child Relations

The myth that parents and their adult children are essentially estranged from each other in today's Western society is so widespread and persistent that it is impossible to convince the general public that it is untrue. Yet most adult children keep in close touch with their parents, live not too far away from them, visit them frequently, or if they live too far away to do that, phone each other and aim for long visits at less frequent intervals. They also help each other in many ways, including caregiving when that is needed. Abandonment of parents in old age is extremely rare, as is "elder abuse."

On the other hand, it is important to note that having children does not increase the happiness of older people, at least in modern times. As noted in Part I, it has long been known that marital satisfaction of parents goes down after the birth of the first child (e.g., Pineo, 1961), is higher for married couples without children than for those with children (Feldman, 1964, 1981), and goes up again, for at least some parents, when their children leave home (Troll, Miller, & Atchley, 1979). More recent comparisons of older people with and without children (Glenn & McLanahan, 1981, 1982; Rempel, 1985), based on large-scale U.S. and Canadian samples, show basically no effect on the happiness of older people of having children. In a few cases, in fact, those with children—particularly fathers—were less happy than nonparents. The only positive benefit of having one or more children was more neighborhood interaction. The childless, Rempel noted, seemed to have found alternative ways of living that served them well, suggesting that it is the quality, not the quantity, of interactions that counts. We are reminded of Lowenthal and Haven's (1968) finding that it is having a confidant, no matter who that person is, that makes for satisfactory survival in old age. The number of children, incidentally, does not seem to make any difference in this respect. Having one child does it.

Numerous surveys of residential proximity between older parents and their children show that the parents prefer to live in their own homes but near their children (Troll, Miller, & Atchley, 1979). The prevailing values in our society are that adults should live in separate households unless they are married couples or parents raising young children. And indeed, less than 10% of parents over the designated "old age" of 65 live with their children, and these tend to be women more often than men, as we would expect from the information on widowhood in the first section of this volume. Many students are surprised by this fact and even more by the finding that almost a quarter of Americans between 18 and 25 years of age live with their parents (Troll, 1985b). Both of these figures fluctuate with economic conditions. When times are good, more adults of all ages move into their own homes. When times are bad, families double and triple up. When people 65 and older do live with a child, that child is likely to be a daughter rather than a son, an unmarried daughter rather than a married one, and it is more often the parent that is the "head of the household" than the child. Finally, these multi-generational households are more likely to be two-generation than three-generation. Only 8% have grandchildren and grandparents living together.

To those who regret the disappearance of the "golden age" of the extended family, a historian (Smith, 1979) has demonstrated that this present percentage of three-generation households is not lower than in 1900 or earlier but, in fact, higher. In 1900, older married people who lived with a child were most likely to live with an unmarried daughter, just as is true now. If they lived with a married child, their grandchildren had already grown up and left. But since far fewer people lived to be old then, the number of three-generation households was more like 3% than 8%. Living arrangements are discussed further in Part V.

Four-fifths of all people now over 65 in the Western world have living children. Of those who do, between 78 and 90% have seen at least one child within the last week and talked with them on the telephone at about the same frequency (Cicirelli, 1983a; Troll, Miller, & Atchley, 1979). The telephone is not a substitute for visiting, incidentally; the same people visit and telephone each other. A 1975 survey of older Americans (Harris & Associates, 1975) found that 87% between the ages of 18 and 64 had seen their children and 48% had seen their parents within the past day. Of those over 65, 55% had seen a child that day and 32% had seen a parent (about 10% of people over 65 have children who are also over 65). A recent survey of family interaction at different ages (Leigh, 1982) reported that such interaction does not vary much with age. Those families who visit a lot have always visited a lot, and those who seldom see each other have almost always been distant. Studies of the effect on family contact of the birth of a baby (Belsky & Rovine, 1984) or of widowhood (Morgan, 1984) also show stability of interaction over time. Temporary rallying to the aid of children or parents at times of crisis are just that—temporary. Morgan found that knowing how much contact parents and their adult children had in 1969 was the best predictor of frequency of visiting 6 years later, even though many of the parents had become widows during that time. Lopata (1973) had earlier reported the transitory nature of relatives' support in a crisis. Some longitudinal Israeli data (Weihl, 1985a) show that only a small proportion of older people claimed not to have seen a child in the week preceding the interview, and this proportion dropped from 19% at the time of the second round of interviews to 12% at the third round, perhaps reflecting an increase in monitoring and helping as parents' needs increased. The kind of rallying around at the time of crises seems to be different from the gradual increase in involvement attendant upon the aging process.

Three articles included in this volume (Brody, 1985; Johnson & Catalano, 1983; Shanas, 1979) present data about the close contact between older parents and their children. They all show that if a spouse is not available to help when help is needed, it is a child who provides the major caregiving. Actually, help is usually a mutual process. The parent generation gives services and more money to their children, and the next generation gives emotional support, household help, and care during illness to their parents. These separate donations can be counted as reciprocal over the lifetime, flowing more toward younger generations at first and shifting toward older generations as circumstances change. Caregiving is discussed further in Part IV.

In the United States there is very little economic support given to older parents by their children; sometimes because the parents are able to manage on Social Security and pensions; sometimes because giving money up the generational ladder is not normative. There are class differences. In the middle class, considerable financial assistance continues to flow from parents to children into advanced old age. In the working class, however, more financial assistance goes from the middle generation to both older and younger generations because the middle generation has usually had more opportunity to accumulate assets than their parents had (Hill, 1965). Using Canadian data, Cheal (1983) looked at "intergenerational family transfers." Several earlier studies had found that gift giving to family members by old people, although not greater than by the middle-aged, was greater than that by young adults and not related to economic wealth. (He did not include the kind of economic transfers provided in wills.) At the same time, older people receive less family economic support than do younger people. Thus, the ratio of money received from children and grandchildren over money given to younger generations declines regularly with age of household heads. While this directional flow of money was linear, gift giving did decline after the age of 65 from its middle years peak, perhaps because getting around and shopping becomes more difficult.

The most salient kind of help, of course, is taking care of parents who become sick and feeble. Shanas (1979) refers to national survey data, Johnson and Catalano (1983) to particular cases of San Francisco people coming out of the hospital, and Brody (1985) to interviews with grandmothers, daughters, and granddaughters about expectations and desires for future care. All show the same patterns. When a spouse is not available, a child (mostly daughter) is the caregiver. Cicirelli (1983b), among others (Bengtson, Olander, & Haddad, 1976), tried to predict which children would actually come when needed. Presumed "feelings of attachment," expressed in "attachment behavior," like living nearby and keeping in touch, are of primary importance in such predictions.

Obviously, choosing to live near each other, to visit and keep in touch, and to help each other in times of need bespeak involvement. But they could also come from feelings of obligation or duty, fear of public censure or shame. A number of investigators have been interested in how much affection, love, or attachment exists between adult children and their parents. To begin with, most research shows that perceived feelings of closeness are independent of actual involvement and care (Troll & Bengtson, 1979). Perhaps we should consider the strength of relationships rather than whether they are positive or negative. People can resent having to bear the burdens of caring for sick old parents, but they never think of not doing so. In fact, where there is strong attachment, we can expect both strong positive and strong negative feelings existing together.

What about their relationships with their children makes older parents feel good? Bengtson and his colleagues (1976) cite a cluster of conditions they label "family solidarity." These include mutual satisfaction with family life, feeling that you belong, together with its accompanying "positive sentiment," and sharing the same values (cf. Johnson & Bursk, 1977; Medley, 1976; Streib, 1965). These are over and above the basic factors of health and money, of course (cf. Edwards & Klemmack, 1973; Johnson, 1978; Palmore & Luikart, 1972). Quinn (1983) put these variables together into a regression analysis to see which did contribute to morale among people over 65. In accord with almost every other study in this field, he found that health was the major contributor to psychological well-being in old age and that quality of parent–child relationships was next in order, but much less important.

There are four different parent–child dyads: mother–son, mother–daughter, father–son, and father–daughter (not counting in-laws and step-parents). Therefore, parent–child relationships can be different depending upon which dyad is involved. Although only a few studies have compared these relationships directly, those studies suggest that the mother–daughter bond is the strongest one throughout life and that families are held together by mother–daughter linkages, at least in the Western world (Troll, Miller, & Atchley, 1979).

From the beginning, apparently, mothers are likely to feel more comfortable with their infant daughters than with their infant sons (Rothbart & Maccoby, 1966). Different reasons have been suggested for this phenomenon. It may be that little girls are more familiar to mothers, more like themselves. It may be that girls, maturing earlier than boys, are easier to handle. It may be that, as Freud (1933) wrote, daughters can identify with their mothers in addition to becoming attached to them, and thus have stronger bonds with them than sons, who can only be attached to them. Chodorow (1978) hypothesizes that this strong connection makes daughters want to become mothers in order to repeat or continue the relationship, just as mothers see themselves over again in their daughters. Whatever the reasons, it has been found that infant boys get better care from their mothers if their fathers are around—just around, not necessarily sharing the feeding and diapering (Lamb & Lamb, 1976). It is as if mothers need a man present to interpret the alien maleness. Further, the Lambs report that early mother–child relationships are more dyadic than father–child relationships, that the mother–child bond is more direct. Unless the father is the primary caretaker, his interactions with his child are embedded in a network of all family relations, and his role is often defined by the mother.

Sex differences are noticeable throughout childhood. As toddlers, girls stick to their mother's knee more than do boys (Shephard-Look, 1982). Later in life, boys and men wander; girls and women stick around. Mothers are more familiar to daughters than to sons and also stricter to daughters. They are also probably less appreciative of daughters—at least they are when the daughters are adults (Hagestad, 1977). Reciprocally, daughters find mothers familiar, and they see them as more demanding and unappreciative (Turner & Huyck, 1982).

Adult daughters are more likely to live close to their mothers, to visit them, and to exchange help with them than are adult sons (Cicirelli, 1983a; Shanas, 1979). Over time, the kind of relationship a mother and her daughter have had tends to persist. Consequently, men are more likely to be in touch with their wife's parents than with their own (Troll, Miller, & Atchley, 1979). A New York City study (Haller, 1982) found that middle-aged mothers and their young-adult daughters were more attached to each other than middle-aged mothers and their young-adult sons.

Only 5% of Indiana parents and their adult children reported any serious conflict (Cicirelli, 1981). Like Hagestad (1984) and Troll (1972), Cicirelli suggests that the low incidence of conflict would be attributed to everybody's careful avoidance of troublesome issues. Hagestad found a "demilitarized zone" in family communications at all age levels.

Could it be that it is the strains of avoiding such open conflict, part of the strains of maintaining such important relationships, that make parents no happier than those having had no children?

Weishaus (1978) analyzed the course of mother–daughter relationships over 40 years, using the Berkeley Guidance Study files. She found generalized stability in the quality of these relationships, underscoring the cross-sectional findings of Cicirelli (1981), Johnson and Bursk (1977), and Baruch and Barnett (1983), among others. A major issue in the area of feelings—remember, not care—is the effect of parents' poor health, which leads to the necessity of providing long-term care. Declining health seems to lead consistently to decline in the good feelings on the part of daughters (e.g., Johnson & Bursk, 1977). In the Berkeley data (Weishaus, 1978) a change in daughters' feelings was noticeable over the decade from when the daughters were aged 30 to the time they were reinterviewed at age 40. Cicirelli (1983a) interprets this as "filial anxiety." Perhaps the threatened ending of a mother's life, signaled by her declining health, arouses anxieties in her children, related to their anticipation of their own mortality. We often gauge how long our own life is likely to run by how long our parents live (Marshall, 1975).

Another possible reason for the deterioration of daughters' feelings in response to mothers' decline is the dislocation of older patterns of helping between them. The article in this volume by Bankoff (1983a) points to the importance of help by mothers to daughters. Baruch and Barnett (1983) and Johnson (1978) also associate decline in parents' health with decline in adult children's good feelings. Baruch and Barnett, who had interviewed Massachusetts middle-aged women, found that the warmth they felt toward their mothers was related to their reports of their mothers' health.

Troll (1983) labeled grandparents "family watchdogs" because, although they prefer to lead their own lives and not become too heavily involved in the lives of their children and grandchildren, they quickly come to their rescue in times of trouble. Glenn and McLanahan's (1981, 1982) findings are also consistent with this hypothesis, perhaps the other side of the same coin. The parent–child relationship is distinguishable by persistence and aid. Children turn first to parents for help when they need it and parents to children. Therefore, being a parent is automatically associated with troubles, which can balance the delight in children's success and happiness.

Do daughters become closer to their mothers after they have themselves become mothers? Research findings are not consistent. Some find that they do (Baruch and Barnett, 1983; Bengtson and Black, 1973; Fischer, 1981). Others, however (Haller, 1982; Walker & Thompson, 1983) find that unmarried young women are closer to their mothers than married and married with children. Fischer, incidentally, found that marriage and motherhood seemed to move young women closer to their own mothers, or at least to having less conflict with them and more conflict with their mothers-in-law, who may be safer targets for hostility.

The marital status of middle-aged mothers, curiously, does not seem to make a difference in their relationships with their young-adult daughters, although it does with their sons (Adams, 1968b). Adams found that sons were less likely to be close to their mothers after the mothers were widowed than when they were still united with the sons' fathers. Adams attributes this strain to conflicts between sons' feelings they should be responsible for their mothers' welfare and mothers' desires to be independent, but another interpretation is also possible. This other explanation derives from the kind of family linkages Lamb and Lamb (1976) distinguished, mother–child dyads being more integral than father–child dyads. Analogous data come from two studies of adults: Hagestad, Smyer, and Steirman (1984) and Nydegger and Mitteness (1982). Hagestad and her colleagues found sex differences in the utilization of family resources following divorce. Most women turned to their kin at this time of crisis and need, but only the men whose parents were living did so. In other words, men's family bonds are contingent, not direct. Nydegger and Mitteness found that the primary cause of strain between middle-aged fathers and their adult children is related to marriage and divorce; in other words, to maintenance of family networks. Cicirelli (1983b; this volume) compared help given aging parents by their children's marital status. Generally, whether they were still married, divorced, or remarried made no difference, at least for daughters. It is not surprising, though, that those children whose marriages had recently been disrupted were more preoccupied with their own problems and less sensitive to the needs of their parents. Yet they did not give markedly less help when that help was needed. The issues of caretaking are considered in the following section.

Exchange theory has been applied to the study of the relation between mother–daughter feelings and their reciprocity of help. Thompson and Walker (1984), for example, compared two sets of mother–daughter dyads, grandmothers and their daughters and these daughters and *their* daughters. For the younger dyad, attachment was greater when reciprocity was high—when both helped each other a lot. In the older dyad, however, where the issues of autonomy and attachment may have been resolved over the years, imbalances in the exchange of help were not associated with lower attachment. Other data have shown that neither exchange of aid nor frequency of interaction between old parents and their children is related to the parents' morale (Lee & Ellithorpe, 1982).

Which brings us, finally, to issues of measurement and conceptualization. A variety of terms for relationships have been used in the literature and repeated here. These include closeness, attachment, good relationships, intergenerational solidarity, intimacy, affective quality, filial anxiety, stress, strain, conflict, guilt, psychological distance, and positive relationships. Some of these terms are probably synonyms (e.g., good relationships and positive feelings). Some include others (e.g., intergenerational solidarity and positive sentiment), and some are undoubtedly different (e.g., attachment and intimacy). What is clearly needed is an analytic approach like that of Sternberg's (1985) for love, alluded to in Part I. An important beginning has been made by Walker and Thompson (1983), who factor-analyzed a variety of mother–daughter relationship items and obtained the following five factors: general intimacy or affection, attachment, disclosure, tension, and worry. (Notice that there is nothing here like shared happiness.)

5

The Family as a Social Support System in Old Age*

Ethel Shanas

The cultures and the subcultures of a society define both the needs of its members and the ways in which these needs are to be met. The changes in cultures which have accompanied industrialization and urbanization have affected the relationships among family members, irrespective of their ages. This is not solely because of changes in the living arrangements of families which often accompany the push to the city that can now be observed in developing societies. It is also because cultural changes have brought an expansion of what come to be defined as needs. As people live longer, are better educated, and desire a higher standard of living their needs become greater. The abilities of the modern family to fulfill the needs of its members, young as well as old, must be evaluated against the background of this expansion of expectations (Rosenmayr, 1977).

In all developed countries, as individual needs both increase and are differently defined, functions which may once have been the unique province of the family become shared functions of the family and bureaucracy, whether the latter be government, industry or the

*The Gerontologist, 19 (2) (1979), 169–174.

Revised version of a paper presented at the 30th Annual Scientific Meeting of the Gerontological Society, San Francisco, CA, Nov. 1977. The 1975 Survey of the Elderly was supported by the U.S. AoA, Grant number 90-A-369, and the U.S. Social Security Admin., Grant number 10-P-57823. Gloria Heinemann had major responsibility for the preparation of the tabular data.

educational system. Old people, like other family members, have been affected by the changes in social structure which have been accelerated in the last several decades. Where the family was once expected to look after the economic needs of its members, industrial societies such as the U.S. now support the nonworking members of society, old as well as young, through intergenerational rather than family transfers of income. Where in the past the family may have had major responsibility for taking care of its sick elderly, specialized health services such as nursing homes and chronic disease hospitals proliferate to care for those aged who are described as sick and frail. Even in the area of emotional support, long considered the primary function of the family, the bureaucracy now provides social workers who are presumed to have those skills necessary not only to serve the young but to assuage the desires of the elderly for meaningful human relationships.

As one considers the shifts in the function of the family of which the above are only a few illustrations, it may come as a surprise that a major finding of social research in aging in all Western countries has been the discovery and demonstration of the important role of the family in old age. Research evidence indicates that family help, particularly in time of illness, exchange of services, and regular visits are common among old people and their children and relatives whether or not these live under a single roof. Old people living under a single roof together with their children and grandchildren are unusual in industrialized societies and are becoming less common in transitional societies. Joint living is not the most important factor governing the relationship between old people and their grown children. Rather, it is the emotional bond between parents and children that is of primary importance. Leopold Rosenmayr and Eva Köckeis, two Austrian sociologists, describe the desired physical relationship of old people and their children as "intimacy at a distance" (1963, 1965). Old people wish to maintain some physical distance from their adult children without being isolated from them. In a 1975 working paper on family health, a Russian scholar reviewing various Soviet studies reports on the physical distance between young couples and their parents. The majority of young couples in the study are reported as wanting to live next door to their parents or in the same district of the city (Grinina, 1975). Mutual assistance continues between young couples and their older parents as families strive "to keep at a distance from one another but not to break off relationships."

In contemporary society, the family persists as a major source of help to the elderly even in those areas where the assistance of outside agencies is undoubtedly necessary and useful. One may mention, for example, family help to the elderly in case of illness and direct family help with income support, both of which persist in spite of the fact that in all industrial countries arrangements have been made for outside agencies to take over much of the health care and income support of the elderly. Rosenmayr has made an interesting comment on why family help patterns may tend to continue despite the presence of other alternative help sources. "Public action to give support to the elderly has the innate danger to classify them as marginal. It is the dialectics of institutionally organized help to a certain group that this group becomes conscious of a certain bereavement; whereas individual and informal help and assistance based on intimacy may avoid this type of consequence . . ." (1975).

The present paper will report research findings on two aspects of the family as a social support system: the first, family care for the elderly in time of illness; the second, family visiting patterns as these are reported by old people in the U.S.

DATA AND METHODS

The data used in this report come from a national survey of the noninstitutionalized population aged 65 and over. The data were collected in the late Winter and early Spring of 1975. The sample used was a national sample employing probability methods to the household level. In surveys such as this every eligible person has a predetermined chance of being selected.

The overall survey response rate for all eligible respondents is somewhere between 76 and 87%. Eligible respondents were located through screening interviews in pre-selected households. A substantial number of persons were never seen by interviewers but were identified by their neighbors as probably being age 65 and over and hence were considered to be eligible for interviewing. Many of these possible respondents, identified by neighbors, were never located by the interviewers even after repeated visits, and therefore their eligibility for the study was not fully determined. If these possibly eligible respondents are included among the total eligible persons located, the overall response rate in the sample is 76%. If the pool of eligible respondents is restricted to those instances in which the interviewers had enough information to identify the potential respondents as white or Black or other races the response rate is good, 87% for whites and 85% for Blacks.

The survey sample interviewed is in good agreement with the age distribution, the racial distribution and the marital status of the total noninstitutionalized population as reported in the U.S. Census. Because of the close agreement between the demographic characteristics of the sample interviewed and the independent reports of the Census, it seems likely that the true response rate in this survey is somewhat closer to the 87% figure than to the 76% figure conservatively reported.[1] For practical purposes we may assume that the chances are 19 in 20 that the true proportion for any variable will be within the range of the estimate reported in this paper, plus and minus the appropriate sampling error.

In interpreting the findings, it should be kept in mind that the sample does not include the institutional population and hence omits a substantial proportion of the very old, those over 85. Ninety-five percent of the elderly are resident in the community, however, and only about 5% are in institutions at any one time.

THE PHYSICAL MOBILITY OF THE ELDERLY LIVING AT HOME

Table 5.1 is a summary statement of the physical mobility of the elderly noninstitutional population of the U.S. About 3% of the total sample eligible for further interviewing were classified as bedfast and 7% as housebound. The bedfast and housebound elderly located, then, were twice the proportion of the elderly resident in institutions at the time of the survey. In the interviewed sample, 7% of those interviewed were bedfast or housebound, and an additional 7% could go outdoors only with difficulty. The chances are about 95 in 100 that the proportion of elderly bedfast and housebound resident in the community is between about 5.5% and the 10% located in the screening sample. The majority of the sick and frail elderly in 1975 were not in institutions or group quarters. They were living in their own homes or in the homes of family members.

Table 5.2 is a comparison, from U.S. Census data, of the marital status of the elderly in institutions for the sick and frail and the elderly living at home. The institutionalized elderly include three times as high a proportion of persons who have never married as are found in the community, and almost twice as high a proportion of widowed persons. These findings are what one would expect. Per-

[1]A detailed statement of sample errors is available from the author.

Table 5.1. Mobility of the Noninstitutional Population Aged 65 and Over: 1975 (Percentage Distribution).

Degree of Mobility	Men	Women	All[c]
Total Sample Located[a]			
Bedfast	2	3	3
Housebound	6	8	7
Ambulatory	92	89	90
Total	100	100	100
Number of cases (weighted) = [b]	(3070)	(4484)	(7660)[c]
Sample Interviewed Only			
Bedfast	2	2	2
Housebound	3	6	5
Ambulatory	95	91	93
Can go outdoors with difficulty	4	8	7
Can go outdoors without difficulty	91	83	86
Total	100	100	100
Number of cases (weighted) = [b]	(2314)	(3441)	(5755)

[a]The percentage of bedfast respondents is based on all bedfast persons located; interviews with proxy respondents were taken for all bedfast persons who could not be interviewed. The percentages of housebound and ambulatory respondents were estimated from their proportions in the sample interviewed and from background data on nonrespondents secured by the interviewers.

[b]The number of cases is weighted by various sampling fractions. The percentage of eligible respondents who answered these questions is 99.98. In subsequent tables, where 98% or more of the eligible respondents have answered the questions, detailed information on nonresponse will not be given in footnotes. The total sample located includes at least 128 cases of questionable eligibility since they may not be aged 65 and over.

[c]Includes 105 weighted cases where sex is not known.

sons without close family are more likely to be institutionalized when they are ill. This includes the very old, who are largely widowed women, as well as the never married. Townsend reporting on a detailed interview study of institutionalized old people in Britain states "Bachelors and widowers affirmed the importance of wives, and childless persons of children. Men and women alike seemed to recognize that the ability to go on living in a normal community was

Table 5.2. Marital Status of Persons Aged 65 and Over in the Population and of Institutionalized Persons Aged 65 and Over in Different Types of Institutions (Percentage Distribution).

Marital Status	Total Population 65 and Over	Type of Institutions				
		Psychiatric Hospital	Residential Homes	Nursing Homes	TB and Chronic Disease	All Institutions
1970[a]						
Never married	6	33	17	16	21	19
Married[b]	54	30	12	12	20	14
Widowed and divorced	40	37	71	72	59	67
Total	100	100	100	100	100	100
Number of cases =	(20,116,000)[c]	(113,043)	(538,499)	(257,308)	(40,260)	(949,110)

[a]Source: U.S. Bureau of the Census, *U.S. Census of the Population: 1970. Subject Reports. Persons in Institutions and Other Group Quarters*, Final Report PC(2)-4E (Washington, DC: USGPO, 1973), Tables 25, 26 and 27.
[b]The legally and the informally separated have been classified as married.
[c]U.S. Bureau of the Census, *Current Population Reports, Marital Status and Living Arrangements*, Series P-20, No. 255 (March, 1973), Table 1.

weakened in old age if there were no relatives of succeeding generations to replace the loss, by death and illness of relatives of the same
or of preceding generations. . . . Family relationships extend into and
merge with the whole community" (1965).

Old persons with few or limited family relationships are prime
candidates for institutionalization when they become sick.

THE CARETAKERS OF THE ELDERLY SICK

Who are the caretakers, the social supports of the sick and frail aged
living in the community? The data in Table 5.3 provide some of the
answers to this question for bedfast persons. Those in Table 5.4
indicate who helps housebound and ambulatory old persons when
they become ill enough to spend time in bed. The bedfast person and
the ambulatory old person ill enough to be in bed both need to have
food brought into the house, they need to have meals prepared, they
need help with housework. The main source of help for bedfast
persons is the husband or wife of the invalid. Men take over traditionally female tasks as necessary, women find the strength to turn
and lift bedfast husbands. Husbands or wives of the elderly bedfast
persons, themselves elderly, are rarely able to manage the care of a
spouse without outside help. Many of them report that they are
assisted by paid helpers, hence the large mention of paid helpers in
Table 5.3. Children, within and outside of the household, are the next
main source of help. The social services are mentioned hardly at all as
providers of home helpers, but there is a possibility that employees of
social service agencies who are being reimbursed by families are
reported as paid helpers.

About one of every four housebound and ambulatory persons
reported that they had been ill in bed during the previous year. Men,
who are more likely than women to be married, are taken care of by
their wives. Two-thirds of the men who had been ill say their wife
took care of them. Women, who are more likely to be widowed, are
taken care of by their children. A child, either in the same household
or outside the household, is mentioned by one-third of the women as
a source of help in illness. About one of every four persons who said
that they had spent one or more days in bed because of sickness had
no help at all. Women, who are more likely than men to live alone,
are from two to three times as likely as men to say that no one helped
them during their illness.

Table 5.3. Proportion Reporting Each Source of Help, Bedfast Persons Aged 65 and Over, by Tasks for which Help is Received: 1975[a]

Source of Help of Bedfast Persons	Task		
	Housework[b]	Meal Preparation[b]	Shopping[b]
Spouse	38	44	30
Child in household	22	26	34
Child outside household	18	10	28
Others in household	2	3	2
Paid helper	20	18	8
Social services	2	3	2
Relative outside household	3	1	8
Nonrelative outside household	3	4	2
No one	11	14	2
Number of cases (weighted) =	(181)	(181)	(181)

[a]Includes bedfast proxy respondents.
[b]Percentages do not sum to 100 since more than one response could be given.

Table 5.4. Proportion Reporting Each Source of Help, Persons Aged 65 and Over Ill in Bed Last Year, by Sex: 1975[a].

	Task								
	Housework[b]			Meal Preparation[b]			Shopping[b]		
Sources of Help	Men	Women	All	Men	Women	All	Men	Women	All
Spouse	66	22	37	71	23	40	62	25	38
Child in household	9	15	12	7	13	11	9	16	14
Child outside household	6	18	14	6	19	14	10	25	20
Others in household	4	5	5	5	5	5	4	5	5
Paid helper	7	9	8	2	3	3	2	2	2
Social services	0	*	*	1	1	1	0	*	*
Relative outside household	2	6	5	2	6	5	3	8	6
Nonrelative outside household	*	4	3	4	9	7	5	12	9
None or self	10	29	23	10	31	24	9	15	13
Number of cases (weighted) =	(501)	(941)	(1442)	(501)	(944)	(1446)	(501)	(941)	(1442)

*Less than 1% after rounding.
[a]Excludes bedfast persons. The proportions of persons ill in bed last year are: total 26, men 22, and women 28.
[b]Percentages do not sum to 100 since more than one response could be given.

Tables 5.5 and 5.6 illustrate a different aspect of the family as a social support system—the visiting patterns of old people and their children. Table 5.5 gives a summary report of when old persons with surviving children last saw one of their children. More than half of these old people saw one of their children either the day they were interviewed or the day before that. Three of every four persons with children saw a child within the week-period preceding their interview. Only about one person in ten had last seen a child more than a month before his interview.

Table 5.6 gives a detailed statement of the family contacts of the elderly. The data for old people with children and old people without children are presented separately. Among persons with children who did not see a child during the previous week, about four of every ten saw a brother or sister or other relatives. The amount of visiting reported among old people and their children and relatives is much greater than one would believe from accounts in the popular press. Only about 13 of every 100 old people with surviving children saw neither a child nor a relative during the week before they were interviewed.

About 21 of every 100 old people have no surviving children. For these persons, there is some evidence that brothers, sisters and other relatives tend to substitute for a child. Old people with no children are more likely than people with children to have seen a sibling or other relative the week before they were interviewed. More than one-half of these people reported such family contacts.

Table 5.5. When Persons Aged 65 and Over with Surviving Children Last Saw a Child, by Sex: 1975 (Percentage Distribution).

When Last Saw Child	Men	Women	All
Today or yesterday[a]	50	54	53
2–7 days ago	23	25	24
8–30 days ago	13	12	12
More than 30 days ago	13	9	11
Total	100	100	100
Number of cases (weighted) =	(1856)	(2696)	(4553)

[a]Includes persons who live in the same household as a child, 17% of men, 19% of women, 18% of total.

Table 5.6. Family Contacts, Persons Aged 65 and Over with Surviving Children Who Did Not See a Child During the Previous Week and Persons Aged 65 and Over with No Children, by Sex: 1975 (Percentage Distribution).

Family Contacts	Men	Women	All
Persons who did not see a child during previous week:			
Saw a sibling or other relative[a] during previous week	35	43	39
Did not see a sibling or other relative during previous week	62	54	58
Have no siblings or other relatives	3	3	3
Total	100	100	100
Number of cases (weighted) =	(493)	(582)	(1075)
Persons who have no living children:			
Saw a sibling or other relative during previous week	44	62	55
Did not see a sibling or other relative during previous week	51	32	39
Have no siblings or other relatives	5	6	5
Total	100	100	100
Number of cases (weighted) =	(456)	(734)	(1190)

[a]Other relatives exclude grandchildren. If these were included the proportion of persons seeing siblings or relatives would be increased by an undetermined amount.

IMPLICATIONS

Data from the 1975 national survey of the noninstitutionalized community aged clearly indicate that the immediate family of the old person, husbands, wives, and children, is the major social support of the elderly in time of illness. The presence of immediate relatives makes it possible for bedfast persons to live outside institutions. Both immediate family and other kin supply the housebound and ambulatory aged with care for occasional illness. The extended family of the old person, children, siblings and other relatives, through face-to-face visits, is the major tie of the elderly to the community. It is not necessary for old people to have many visitors. What is important is that they have regular and concerned visitors. It is this role that is assumed by members of the kin network.

Family help to the elderly in time of illness and family visiting are more than indicators of need on the part of the elderly. Such patterns are indicators of the mutual expectations of each generation of the other. Old people turn first to their families for help, then to neighbors, and finally, to the bureaucratic replacements for families, social workers, ministers, community agencies, and others because they expect families to help in case of need. Family members respond to the needs of the elderly as best they can, either directly or by providing a linkage with bureaucratic institutions. In a conference held some years ago Joep Munnichs, the Dutch psychologist, raised the question of which is easier to change, the family or the bureaucracy? Munnichs argues that it is easier to change bureaucracy (Munnichs, 1977; Shanas & Sussman, 1977). As families become less able to fulfill the helper role vis-à-vis their aged members they will seek to change and modify the bureaucratic system so that it meets the needs of the elderly in a way more satisfying to both old people and their kin.

REFERENCES

Grinina, O. V. Main directions in social hygienic studies of families in the USSR. Unpub. working paper prepared for Study Group on Statistical Indices of Family Health, Geneva, Feb. 17–22, World Health Organization. WHO/HS/Nat. Comm./75–349, 1975, 1–11.

Munnichs, J. M. A. Linkages of old people with their families and bureaucracy in a welfare state, the Netherlands. In E. Shanas & M. B. Sussman, (Eds.), *Family, bureaucracy and the elderly.* Duke Univ. Press, Durham, NC, 1977.

Rosenmayr, L., & Köckeis, E. Propositions for a sociological theory of aging and the family. *International Social Science Journal,* 1963, *15,* 410–426.

Rosenmayr, L., & Köckeis, E. *Umwelt und families alter menschen.* Neuwied and Berlin, 1965.

Rosenmayr, L. The many faces of the family. Paper presented at a meeting of the Intl. Assoc. of Gerontology, Jerusalem, Israel, 1975. (Mimeo)

Rosenmayr, L. The family—a source of hope for the elderly? In E. Shanas & M. B. Sussman (Eds.), *Family, bureaucracy and the elderly.* Duke Univ. Press, Durham, NC, 1977.

Shanas, E., & Sussman, M. B. (Eds.), *Family, bureaucracy and the elderly.* Duke Univ. Press, Durham, NC, 1977.

Townsend, P. The effect of family structure on the likelihood of admission to an institution in old age: The application of a general theory. In E. Shanas & G. F. Streib (Eds.), *Social structure and the family: Generational relations.* Prentice-Hall, Inc., Englewood Cliffs, NJ, 1965.

6

Parent Care as a Normative Family Stress*

Elaine M. Brody

A central theme in Donald Kent's work was the importance of linking research about aging to practice and policy. He wrote:

> "Research, policy and practice are . . . not the same, but . . . they are not unrelated . . . policy that is not informed by knowledge may well be worse than worthless; it may be dangerous" (1972).

The subject of filial behavior in caring for disabled elderly parents is a case in point. The question "What should adult children do for their dependent elderly parents?" illustrates how values determine whether knowledge is used or ignored in shaping policy decisions. Values also influence the filial behavior of millions of people for whom the question is a salient personal issue. Though the topic of parent care excludes important aspects of family help to the old, it ultimately concerns almost all of us who have had, now have, or may in the future have a parent who is elderly, and all of us who have children and hope to grow old ourselves.

The Gerontologist, 25 (1) (1985), 19–29.
Donald P. Kent Memorial Lecture, presented at the 37th Annual Scientific Meeting of The Gerontological Society of America, San Antonio, TX, November 18, 1984. Appreciation is expressed to M. Powell Lawton, Stanley J. Brody, and Peter R. Brody for their helpful comments on an earlier draft of this paper, and to my colleagues at the Philadelphia Geriatric Center—Bernard Liebowitz, M. Powell Lawton, Morton H. Kleban and the late Arthur Waldman—for their support and participation in the research described. This lecture is dedicated to my four granddaughters: Hannah and Jodi Karpman and Jocelyn and Rachel Brody.

This lecture will argue that parent care has become a normative but stressful experience for individuals and families and that its nature, scope, and consequences are not yet fully understood. Some of the extraordinarily complex factors that interact to determine filial behavior will be explored. A hypothesis will be advanced that may account in part for the myth that adult children nowadays do not take care of their elderly parents as they did in the good old days. In the spirit of the Kent Award, I will comment on some of the ways in which social policy responds to knowledge about filial responsibility.

In approaching my task, I acknowledge deep indebtedness to my long time colleagues at the Philadelphia Geriatric Center—Bernard Liebowitz, M. Powell Lawton, Morton Kleban, and the late Arthur Waldman; to Stanley Brody of the University of Pennsylvania; to the NIMH Center on Aging which financed much of our PGC family research; and to the many members of this Society who have produced a vast body of knowledge about the family relationships of older people.

HISTORICAL PERSPECTIVES

Answers to the question "What should adult children do . . . ?" are profoundly influenced by the pervasive myth that adult children nowadays do not take care of their elderly parents as they did in the good old days.

In 1963, this Society and Duke University sponsored a symposium to examine the facts in the case. The conveners felt that the three-generation family required consideration. They agreed that many programs for older people were based on social myths that had persisted because the assumptions on which they were founded had not been scrutinized by scholars. In the same year in which the conference papers were published (Shanas & Streib, 1965), Kent characterized a related myth (that of the idyllic three-generation household of earlier times) as the "illusion of the Golden Past" (Kent, 1965).

Fifteen years later, the assumptions had been further scrutinized and rejected by much additional research. To the bewilderment of many scholars, the myth had survived nonetheless, prompting Shanas (1979a) to call it a Hydra-headed monster (the monster of Greek mythology that could not be killed).

The 1963 Symposium was a significant watershed in the study of intergenerational relations. There was consensus on facts that are now familiar. Rosow called the conference a "bench mark of the final respects paid to the isolated nuclear family before its interment" (Rosow, 1965, p. 341). Studies had produced compelling evidence to the effect that older people are not alienated from their families. On the contrary, it was clear that strong and viable ties exist among the generations. A consistent theme was the responsible behavior of adult children in helping their parents when need be. Important for our present concern, however, was the conferees' acknowledgement that the effects on those caregivers were hardly touched upon (Streib & Shanas, 1965).

At that time, the number of adults 65 years of age or older had increased by 80% in the previous 20 years. But we were not yet fully aware of the second demographic revolution that was occurring—the change in the age structure of the elderly population with increasing proportions of *very* old people.

Less than 400,000 older people were in nursing homes and homes for the aged, a number that would more than double in the next decade. Services and service-supported living arrangements for the noninstitutionalized elderly were virtually non-existent.

Social Security was beginning to take hold in improving the income position of those who were covered, but the income floor was low and incomplete and there was no social insurance against the costs of catastrophic illness in old age. Schorr's classic monograph on the destructive effects of compulsory family economic support of the aged had been published (1960). Yet in most states, the expectation that adult children should provide such support for their parents was still operationalized by harsh LRR (Legally Responsible Relatives) provisions of public assistance programs, imposing severe strains on families (Brody, 1967a).

At the very time that the Symposium was concerned with the *three-generation family*, a cross-national study by Shanas and her colleagues was underway. The data being collected would show that 40% of older people with children had great-grandchildren (Shanas et al., 1968, pp. 140–145). The *four generation family* already had become a common phenomenon.

In those early 1960s, most intergenerational research focused on noninstitutionalized older people. Our view at the Philadelphia Geriatric Center (PGC) was looking outward from the doors of a facility whose limited mandate was to provide long-stay residential care for the "well" aged. We were experiencing increasing pressure to admit a special subgroup of the elderly—those who were mentally and/or physically disabled. Older people with dementia were prominent among them. The PGC set a precedent by making a deliberate decision to admit people with that diagnosis, and signaled its determination to provide them with treatment rather than custodial care by convening the first national conference on Alzheimer's disease and related disorders (Lawton & Lawton, 1965).

A series of studies of the changing characteristics of our applicants and of the experiences that brought them to the institution led at once to their families. We found evidence of the impact on all family members of having a dependent elderly relative (Brody, 1966a, 1966b, 1967b, 1969; Brody & Gummer, 1967) and began to explore the social cost of care to families (Lawton & Brody, 1968).

It became clear that institutionalization of the aged did not reflect "dumping" or abandonment, a conclusion reached by others (e.g., Lowenthal, 1964; Townsend, 1965). Rather, it resulted from the chronic disabilities and dependencies of very old people combined with the absence, loss, or incapacities of caregiving families, and a glaring lack of supportive community services. After prolonged and strenuous efforts to care for their parents, adult children reached their limits of endurance.

Our dependent applicants, whom we described as the "older old," had aging children many of whom were grandparents; three-fourths of those children were in their 50s and 60s (Brody, 1966b). The crushing reality strains they had experienced often were accompanied by emotional family crises which peaked during the admission process (Brody & Spark, 1966; Spark & Brody, 1970). The older people felt abandoned, their children were conflicted and suffered intensely from guilt, and multiple relationship problems erupted to create a searing experience for members of all generations in the family.

PARENT CARE AS A NORMATIVE EXPERIENCE

What had been happening was that *having a dependent elderly parent was becoming a normative experience for individuals and families* and was exceeding the capacities of some of them.

To illustrate—Between 1900 and 1976, the number of people who experienced the death of a parent before the age of 15 dropped from 1 in 4 to 1 in 20, while the number of middle aged couples with two or more living parents increased from 10% to 47% (Uhlenberg, 1980). At the time of the 1963 Symposium, about 25% of people over the age of 45 had a surviving parent, but by the early 1970s, 25% of people in their late 50s had a surviving parent (Murray, 1973). By 1980, 40% of people in their late 50s had a surviving parent as did 20% of those in their early 60s, 10% of those in their late 60s and 3% of those in their 70s (NRTA-AARP, 1981). Ten percent of all people 65 years or older had a child over the age of 65!

Moreover, while the population of older people was increasing, the birthrate was falling, resulting in a marked alteration in the ratio of potential filial caregivers to those in need of care. The odds of being called upon for parent care were increasing radically, and for increasingly older parents and children.

There are no definitive data on the number of people involved in parent care. One of the difficulties in making an estimate is that surveys identify the proportions of older people in need of services but large studies do not gather detailed data from the perspective of all of the various people in the family who are service providers. A problem in collecting data is that more than one child may be helping the same elderly parent, while some may be helping more than one parent or parent-in-law.

Some notion of the dimensions of the situation can be gleaned from various studies, however. For example, estimates of the overall proportion of noninstitutionalized elderly in need of help range from 17% to 40% (see Brody, 1977a for review). For every disabled person who resides in a nursing home, two or more equally impaired elderly live with and are cared for by their families (Comptroller General of the United States, 1977a). Soldo calculates that two and one quarter million women between the ages of 40 and 59 share their households with elderly kin (1980) and over a million households contain an older person in need of assistance with activities of daily living or mobility—an extreme level of caregiving (Myllyluoma & Soldo, 1983). Soldo's figures, though they are not limited to filial care, reflect only intra-household caregiving. An even larger number of people provide help to old people who do not share their households.

Taken together, these and other findings suggest a very conservative estimate that well over 5 million people are involved in parent-care at any given time. But such cross-sectional data do not speak to the lifetime chances of needing to provide parent care—that is, they do not include people who have provided parent care in the past or who will do so in the future as they and their parents age.

Not only do more people now provide parent care than in the past, but there are differences in the nature and duration of the care provided. Gerontologists need no reminder that chronic illnesses have replaced the acute diseases accounting for most deaths early in this century. As a result, our health systems are struggling to make a major shift in emphasis from acute (i.e., temporary) to chronic (i.e., sustained) care (Brody, S., 1973). People are living longer today after the onset of chronic disease and disability (a phenomenon that has been called "The Failures of Success," Gruenberg, 1977); the number of years of active life expectancy decreases with advancing old age (Katz et al., 1983), and few people reach the end of life without experiencing some period of dependency. More years of dependency mean more years during which there must be someone on whom to depend.

It is *long-term parent care* that has become a normative experience— expectable, though usually unexpected.

The phrase *long-term care* emerged to describe the formal system of government and agencies needed to provide the continuum of sustained helping services dictated by chronicity, though attempts to define it were not made until the late 1970s (Brody, 1977; U.S. National Committee on Vital and Health Statistics, 1978). But the family, virtually unnoticed, had invented long-term care well before that phrase was articulated. The family made the shift from episodic, short-term acute care sooner and more flexibly, willingly, and effectively than professionals and the bureaucracy.

The irony of the myth is that *nowadays adult children provide more care and more difficult care to more parents over much longer periods of time than they did in the good old days.* There is also evidence that adult children now provide more emotional support to the elderly than in the past (Bengtson & Treas, 1980; Hareven, 1982).

At a time when there is a call for new roles for aging adults, a major new role that has emerged for Neugarten's young old (Neugarten, 1974) is that of caregiver for the old old. Can our social values come to regard this role as being as satisfying as second careers of work, volunteer activities, or creative pursuits?

RESEARCH ON FILIAL BEHAVIOR

During the 1960s and 1970s, several major research themes developed, producing a literature too immense to be reviewed here. Particularly relevant are the studies of the role of the family (the informal support system) vis-a-vis government and agencies (the formal support system) in helping the disabled aged. That stream of research found that families, not the formal system, provide 80 to 90% of medically related and personal care, household tasks, transportation, and shopping. The family links the old to the formal support system. The family responds in emergencies and provides intermittent acute care. The family shares its home with severely impaired old people who live in the community (Brody, S. et al., 1978), with rates of shared households rising with the advancing age and poor health of the parent(s) (Mindel, 1979; Troll, 1971). It is the dependable family that provides the expressive support—the socialization, concern, affection, and sense of having someone on whom to rely—that is the form of family help most wanted by the old, but that is not usually counted as a service in surveys.

The members of the family who are the principal caregivers were identified as adult daughters (and to some extent daughters-in-law). They are the main helpers to the old who care for their impaired spouses and the main providers of help to the spouse-less majority of very old people. They predominate among those who share their homes when the elderly cannot manage on their own. (See Brody, 1978; Horowitz, 1982; Myllyuoma & Soldo, 1980; Shanas, 1979b; Troll, 1971.)

The prominence of women in the parent care role should not obscure the efforts of men, however. Sons also sustain bonds of affection, perform certain gender-defined tasks, and become the "responsible relatives" for the old who have no daughters or none close by. And some sons-in-law are unsung heroes.

PARENT CARE AS A STRESS

Recently, research on the effects of caregiving has been accelerating. To put the matter in perspective—In the main, having an elderly parent is gratifying and helpful. Older people are a resource to their children, providing many forms of assistance. Most people help their parents willingly when need be and derive satisfaction from doing so. Some adult children negotiate this stage of life without undue strain and experience personal growth during the process. However, when there is an increase in reliance on children to meet a parent's dependency needs, the family homeostasis—whether it is precarious or well-balanced—must shift accordingly. Such shifts have potential for stress, particularly because they augur increasing dependency in the future.

Some people experience financial hardship and some experience declines in their physical health from the arduous tasks of caring for a disabled parent. Certainly, such problems require attention. However, study after study has identified the most pervasive and most severe consequences as being in the realm of emotional strains. A long litany of mental health symptoms such as depression, anxiety, frustration, helplessness, sleeplessness, lowered morale, and emotional exhaustion are related to restrictions on time and freedom, isolation, conflict from the competing demands of various responsibilities, difficulties in setting priorities, and interference with life-style and social and recreational activities (see Archbold, 1978; Cantor, 1983; Danis, 1978; Frankfather et al., 1981; Gurland et al., 1978; Hoenig & Hamilton, 1966; Horowitz, 1982; Robinson & Thurnher, 1979; Sainsbury & Grad de Alercon, 1970).

Though most such research has focused on the "principal caregiver," there are many findings about the effects on the family. The family is affected by interference with its life-style, privacy, socialization, vacations, future plans, and income, and by the diversion of the caregiver's time from other family members and the negative effects on her health.

Emotional support from spouses (Sussman, 1979), siblings (Horowitz, 1982), and other relatives (Zarit et al., 1980), mitigates the caregivers' strains. But when changes in the family homeostasis stimulate interpersonal conflicts, relationships are affected negatively between husbands and wives, among adult siblings, and across the generations.

In short, filial care of the elderly has become normative but stressful, it affects the entire family, and adult children provide more care and affective support than in the good old days. But some aspects of parent care are not well understood as yet: its place in the individual and family life cycle, the inner processes of individuals and families when parent care becomes necessary, and the interaction of values with personal, situational, and environmental factors in determining filial behavior.

IS PARENT CARE A "DEVELOPMENTAL STAGE"?

Parent care, though normative, does not appear in conceptualizations of what happens during the life course of individuals and families.

In a paper given at the 1963 Symposium, Margaret Blenkner made a seminal attempt to conceptualize the inner experience of adult children when parent care becomes necessary. She described the need for the adult child to have the capacity to be depended on by the aging parent and characterized parent care as a developmental stage of life called "filial maturity"—a transitional stage preceding old age. Therapeutic approaches, she urged, should help adult children to meet their parents' dependency needs (rather than to relieve their guilt) and thus to achieve filial maturity (Blenkner, 1965).

Though there are flaws in Blenkner's particular conceptual and therapeutic approach, at the least she issued an implicit challenge to develop appropriate models.

A basic problem with Blenkner's model is that *parent care is not a developmental stage*. Developmental stages are specific to age-linked periods of time while parent care is not.

The "normal" life crises of earlier life usually occur in a somewhat orderly progression as people move serially through more or less well-defined age categories. Those categories are linked to age-specific cognitive, emotional, and physiological developments and capacities. In sharp contrast, the demands of parent care often are incompatible with the adult child's psychological, emotional, and physiological capacities. In fact, the upward trajectory of the increasing demands on aging children often runs counter to the downward trajectory of their declining abilities to meet those demands.

Parent care is not a single "stage" that can be fitted neatly into an orderly sequence of stages in the life course. Among the elderly, age and stage are not the same (Peck, 1968). Young children are "programmed" developmentally for a gradual reduction of dependency, while the dependencies of old age appear with great variability and irregularity, over much wider time spans, and in different sequential patterns. In addition, the timing of the marriages and parenthood of both parent and child influence the ages and stages of adult children when their parents need help. Parent care, therefore, can overlay many different ages and stages in different people and different families, occurring as it does in young adulthood, in middle age, or even in old age. Moreover, since parent care often is a time-extended process (some of the women in our PGC studies had been helping a parent for more than 20 years), it may span several of the caregiver's age periods or stages.

While the largest proportion of parent caring daughters are in their 40s and 50s, as many as one-third are either under 40 or over 60. The caregiver may be a grandmother who is experiencing the decrements of aging or she may have young children at home.

Even when they are in the same age group, the situations of parent-caring children are extraordinarily variable. One woman in middle age may be engaged in adapting to the onset of chronic ailments and disability; another may be running for Vice President.

Health, marital and economic status, living arrangements, geographic distance from the parent, personality, adaptive capacities, and the quality of parent-child relationships vary. The caregiver may or may not be working. Her retirement or that of her spouse may be imminent or already have taken place. Meeting a parent's dependency needs may be concurrent with the "letting go" of one's young adult children. Or, the theoretically empty nest may contain young adult children who have not left it or have returned to it, a phenomenon that has been increasing.

Among the people who called the PGC for help in one typical day were: an exhausted, 70-year-old woman who could no longer go on caring for her disabled, 93-year-old mother; a recently widowed 50 year old who had just completed her education in preparation for a return to work, but found that her mother had Alzheimer's disease and could not be left alone; a couple in their late 60s with three frail parents between them; a divorcee of 57 who was caring for two disabled sons, a 6-year-old grandchild, and an 87-year-old wheelchair bound mother; and a young couple in their early 30s, about to have a first child, who had taken two older people into their home—the wife's terminally ill mother and the confused, incontinent grandmother for whom the mother had been caring.

Such caregivers do not share a single developmental stage of life. A most important consequence of that fact is the absence of behavioral norms for this normative life crisis. Since behavior in different people and families cannot be measured by the same yardstick, there is no simple answer to the question "What should adult children do . . . ?"

THE INNER MEANING OF PARENT CARE: A DIALECTIC OF DEPENDENCE/INDEPENDENCE

At whatever age or stage the need for parent care arises, the dialectic tension of dependence/independence is a central issue. People vary in the extent to which they have the capacity to meet the dependency needs of others, though growth and change are possible.

As an explanation of the processes that occur, role reversal is a superficial concept at best. (See Goldfarb, 1965 for a discussion of the reasons "role reversal" is inaccurate as a description of dependency on one's child from the perspective of the older person.) Being depended on by one's elderly parent and being depended on by one's young child have different inner meanings. When caring for an infant or child, the future holds promise of a gradual reduction in dependency; caring for an impaired older person presages continuing or increasing dependence. Caregivers have very different reactions to manifestations that are normal and will be dealt with developmentally in the child, but are symptomatic of pathology in the elderly adult—incontinence, for example.

The issue of the older person's dependency on adult children has its origin in the dependency of the helpless infant on the young parent. The inevitable shift in the delicate balance of dependence/independence of the elderly parent and adult child reactivates that child's unresolved conflicts about dependency.

Parent care also stimulates anticipation of the final separation from the parent and of one's potential dependence on one's own children as well. If successful adaptation is to be made, not only must the adult child have the capacity to permit the parent to be dependent, but the parent must have the capacity to be appropriately dependent so as to permit the adult child to be dependable.

There is general acceptance of the proposition that the inevitable vestiges of incompletely resolved crises of earlier stages are reprised and qualify the extent to which later crises are resolved. Since personality continues to develop until the end of life, the way in which the filial crisis is negotiated not only depends on the past, but has implications for the future of the caregiver when she becomes old—and indeed, for that of succeeding generations.

Reactions to the need to provide parent care, of course, range along the theoretical spectrum from health to pathology, as do responses to other life crises. Complex parent care situations occur in the context of the individual's and family's personality and history, qualitative relationships, and coping capacities—all of which qualify the ability to achieve and adapt to the new homeostasis that is required. But the best integrated individual and the best functioning family can be shaken to the core when confronted with reality demands that they cannot meet. It cannot be assumed, as the myth would have it, that the family *is* the problem; more often, the family *has* a problem. Interpretation of "filial maturity" to mean that all of the concrete services needed by the old should be provided by adult children (clearly, a distortion of Blenkner's concept), reinforces the myth by implying that they could do so if only they were "emotionally mature."

When interpersonal problems occur, they are not caused by parent care. Rather, the pressures are such that family relationship problems are reactivated or exacerbated (Brody, 1979). The caregiver's spouse or children may compete with the old person for time and attention.

New battles may be fought in the old wars among the siblings. "I do everything for my mother, but my sister/brother is still her favorite." Old loyalties and alliances as well as old rivalries operate.

Given the reality pressures, given the interpersonal and intrapsychic tensions, it is not surprising that the emotional aspects of caregiving have been a consistent theme in research reports. Nor is it surprising that some adult children relinquish tasks of parent care before others think they should. What *is* remarkable is that so many transcend the strains and take so long to reach their limits of endurance.

But to romanticize the family is just as inappropriate as to be judgmental. The romantic view admires those who continue to care for an impaired older person under conditions of such severe strain that there is deprivation and suffering for the entire family. People in such families may be psychologically unable to place the older person in a nursing home, or, as every service worker knows, may be unable to use formal support services that are badly needed. Whatever dynamics are at work—symbiotic ties, the gratification of being the "burden bearer," a fruitless search for parental approval that has never been received, or expiation of guilt for having been the favored child—excessive caregiving may represent not emotional health or heroism or love, but pathology (Brody & Spark, 1966).

Successful resolution of the filial crisis, then, may involve acceptance by adult children of what they can*not* do as well as acceptance of what they can and should do. For their part, successful adaptation to dependency by the elderly involves *their* acceptance of what their adult children cannot do. It is a curious value that encourages others to continue caregiving no matter the personal cost, but ignores the need of some people to be helped to reduce the amount of care they provide.

INTERACTION OF INNER PROCESSES WITH VALUES AND SOCIOECONOMIC TRENDS

Such inner processes interact with values, socioeconomic trends, and other factors in determining behavior.

As the demand for parent care increased dramatically, a broad socioeconomic trend occurred that is associated with changing values. The rapid entry of middle-aged women—the traditional providers of parent care—into the labor force held the potential for affecting their availability for parent care and for increasing the pressures on them and their families.

Betty Friedan's book, which set in motion the women's movement with its changes in values about women's roles, was published in the same year in which the Symposium was held (Friedan, 1963). It was one of a number of factors that were operating to account for women's march to the workplace, not the least of which was that the money was needed. Between 1940 and 1979 the proportion of working married women between the ages of 45 and 54 increased five-fold. At present, 69% of all women between the ages of 35 and 44 are in the work force as are 62% of those between the ages of 45 and 54, and 42% of those in the 55 to 64 age group (U.S. Bureau of Labor Statistics, 1984).

In order to explore the effects of the converging demographic and socioeconomic trends on filial caregiving, our PGC research group surveyed women who were members of families that included three generations of women.[1] We examined possible changes in values about parent care—in attitudes about family care of the aged and filial responsibility, about gender-appropriate roles, and about filial care vis-a-vis help from the formal system. (For methodology and detailed findings see Brody et al., 1982a, 1982b; Brody et al., 1983; Brody et al., 1984a; Lang & Brody, 1983.)

In contradiction to the myth, we found value continuity in that all three generations expressed firm commitment toward filial help for the aged. Value change was apparent in that large majorities of all generations favored equal roles for men and women—in, for example, the sharing of traditionally female roles such as child care and parent care (though each successively younger generation expressed progressively more egalitarian attitudes).

However, there were many findings indicating tension and conflict between the "new" values about women's roles and the "old" values. For example—Despite the general endorsement of feminist views of the roles of men and women, and though two-thirds of the middle generation women were working, they were more likely to expect working daughters than working sons to adjust their work schedules for parent care. But at the same time, a majority of all generations agreed that it is better for a working woman to pay someone to care for her elderly parent than to leave her job to do it herself.

[1]The Dependent Elderly and Women's Changing Roles (AoA, Grant #90-A-1277). "Women in the Middle" and Care of the Dependent Elderly (AoA, Grant #90-AR-2174).

The potentially conflicting values and multiple roles of the middle generation women whom we called the "women in the middle" (Brody, 1981) often led them to have incompatible views. They wanted to be responsible as daughters but not to become dependent on their children in their own old age. Similarly, the granddaughters, at an average age of 23, were the generation most in favor of egalitarian gender roles, but also were the ones most in favor of family care of the aged and the most in favor of grandchildren helping the old—an expression of what we called "grandfilial responsibility." Moreover, those young women expected to work more years than their mothers had expected to work when they were young, but they also expected to marry and have as many children as their mothers had.

Clear statements of these women's values—their "normative expectations [that] serve as guidelines for behavior" (George, 1980)— related to emotional support. Overall, emotional support is what members of all three generations wanted most from their adult children in their own old age. As in other studies, they strongly preferred households separate from their children and did not wish to be financially dependent on them. Family bonds were not equated with economic help, shared households, personal care and instrumental services. But there was variability as well, with preferences differing with the women's lineage position in the family, different situations, social and health status, ethnic backgrounds (Johnsen & Fulcomer, 1984), and according to the specific kind of help needed.

However, the actual behavior of the middle generation women, all of whom had a living elderly mother, demonstrates once again that attitudes and opinions are not always reflected in behavior. Despite their attitudinal acceptance of formal services and their consensus about egalitarian roles, the middle-generation daughters behaved not only in accordance with their unchanged values about family care of the elderly, but in accordance with "traditional" values about women's roles. They were the major source of help to their mothers even though their responsibilities rose steeply as they grew older. In response to the new demography, the older of the daughters (those in their 50s and 60s) provided many more hours of help and did more difficult tasks for their older and more dependent mothers. They also were more likely than the younger daughters to share their households with their mothers—a phenomenon we called the "refilling of the empty nest" (Brody, 1978). In comparison with their elderly mothers when the latter were in their middle years in the good old days, they also provided more emotional support to their elderly parents, provided more emotional and financial support to their own children, and had worked more (Brody et al., 1982b). When faced with competing demands on their time, what these women gave up was their own free time and opportunities for socialization and recreation. Findings such as these led us to be concerned about the mental and physical health of "women in the middle."

CAREGIVING CAREERS

But being in the middle because of parent care is not a single time-limited episode in the life-course, as data from more recent PGC studies[2] show.

In this research we compared working and nonworking women with respect to their parent care behavior and the effects they experience from caregiving. All of the women in the study were married and were acting as principal caregivers for widowed elderly mothers who required varying amounts of help.

Care of a particular parent at a particular time proved to be only one phase of these women's careers in caregiving, caregiving careers that extend well into late middle age and early old age. Almost half of them had helped an elderly father before his death and one-third of them had helped other elderly relatives. Twenty-two percent were currently providing help to another elderly relative as well as to their own mothers—to parents-in-law, grandparents, aunts, cousins, and more distant relations. And two-thirds of them had children living at home, most under 18 years of age and some (about 10%) younger than six. Given the discrepancy in life expectancy for men and women, it is inevitable that many of these women will care for dependent husbands in the future.

To emphasize—*for many women, parent care is not a single time-limited episode in the life course.* Not only can it begin at widely differing ages and be superimposed on more than one of the other individual and family life stages, but dependence/independence issues may be replayed many times. They can be multiple and multi-layered as one's parents and parents-in-law and even grandparents and other elderly relatives require help sequentially or simultaneously. And all of these complex factors operate for the other adult children and their spouses as well, combining to affect parent care in almost infinite variations.

[2]Women, Work, and Care of the Aged: Mental Health Effects (NIMH, Grant #MH35252), and Parent Care, Sibling Relationships, and Mental Health (NIMH, Grant #MH35252-04).

DO WORK AND PARENT CARE COMPETE?

Another finding from the same study speaks directly to the potential competition between work and parent care. It illustrates the subtle interplay of values, reality pressures, personal characteristics, and other factors in determining filial behavior.

The working and nonworking women were providing roughly equal amounts of care to their dependent mothers. Substantial proportions of both groups were experiencing many of the various strains and mental health symptoms referred to above. But simply comparing all of the working women with all of the nonworking women obscured those who were under the most pressure.

We found that *28% of our sample of nonworking women had quit their jobs because of their elderly mothers' needs for care. They had been displaced from the work force. A similar proportion of the working women were conflicted: they were considering giving up their jobs for the same reason and some had already reduced the number of hours they worked.*

Women's capacities may indeed be elastic in accommodating many roles, as some researchers have observed. But ultimately, those data indicate, elastic snaps if stretched too thin. To illustrate—

Compared with the other working and nonworking women in the study, the women who had left their jobs were in the most difficult parent care situations and the ones who were considering doing so were very close behind. Both of those groups had more functionally dependent mothers. They experienced more interferences with their life styles and time for their husbands. They had been helping their mothers for longer periods of time and they tended to be the only ones providing that help. And they more often felt that parent care made them feel tied down and as though they had missed out on something in life.

The women who had already quit their jobs were older than any of the other women in the study and they had older mothers. They also had an additional set of problems: they more often shared their households with their mothers (a living arrangement which is a strong predictor of strain), they reported that parent care had resulted in more deterioration in their health and more of certain mental health symptoms, and they had the lowest family incomes. (See Brody et al., 1984 and Kleban et al., 1984 for detailed reports on these findings.)

Values and socioeconomic considerations also proved to be influential. Compared with the women who had quit their jobs, the women who were thinking of doing so were better educated, held higher level jobs and to a much greater extent viewed their work as part of a career rather than as "just a job." Within 2 years after the study, one-quarter of all the women in the study had changed their work status; some of the nonworkers entered the labor force (most because the money was needed—to send children to college, for example) and some of the working women had increased or decreased their working hours or were no longer working.

Obviously, patterns of parent care, work, and other role performance must be viewed as long-term processes. As yet, we have no data about this extraordinarily diverse and complex mosaic depicting responses to parent care over the individual and family life-course. Study of women's shifting work and family roles has focused on the earlier stages of their lives; the full story is yet to be written about the shifting of their roles later in life.

Virtually nothing is known about the processes by which different options are selected—processes which have profound implications for clinical approaches and social policy. Caregivers who were not part of our sample may have exercised other options such as nursing home placement of the parent or the redistribution of care in other ways along the informal and formal support systems. Other paths might have been taken by daughters who were not married or by sons.

Given the increasing diversity in women's life courses (cf. Lopata & Norr, 1980), we do not know what choices will be made by future cohorts of women as they move into the parent care years. We do not know how the old behavioral borders that have been measured by research will respond to lifestyle changes, to possible changes in family structure and size, to economic changes, or to changes in mobility patterns, for example.

And what of the myth? How did it fare in the views of the women we studied? To recapitulate the experiences of these "women-in-the middle"—

- They were the principal caregivers to their dependent mothers.
- They were in the middle of competing demands on their time and energy.
- They were experiencing many strains as a result of parent care.
- Their "empty nests" had been refilled—for some quite literally, and for all in terms of increased responsibilities.
- Care of their mothers was but one episode in time-extended "caregiving careers" to older relatives.
- Some had quit their jobs to care for their mothers and others were considering doing so or had cut back on the number of hours they worked.

Yet three-fifths of those very same women said that "somehow" they felt guilty about not doing enough for their mothers, and three-quarters of them agreed that nowadays children do not take care of their elderly parents as was the case in the good old days.

THE MYTH: A HYPOTHESIS

Why is that myth so tenacious in the face of the factual evidence that refutes it? It is important to understand the myth because of its power to inhibit constructive practice and policy approaches.

Many explanations have been advanced for the myth's apparent immortality and it is probable that each of them plays a role. For example—observation of increased mobility and the geographic distance of adult children from their parents; the proliferation of nursing homes and age segregated living arrangements; the visibility of concentrations of old people in places with favorable climates; the taxpayer's fear of the escalating costs of formal system care; the fact, as Shanas (1963) suggested, that those in the helping professions see only the problem situations; and the tendency to romanticize and idealize some vague time in the past.

A hypothesis suggested here is that one possible contributant to the myth's vitality lies at a deeper level and is related to the dependence/independence dialectic:

The myth does not die because at its heart is a fundamental truth.

At some level of awareness, members of all generations may harbor the expectation that the devotion and care given by the young parent to the infant and child—that total, primordial commitment which is the original paradigm for caregiving to those who are dependent— should be reciprocated and the indebtedness repaid in kind when the parent, having grown old, becomes dependent.

The "truth" to which the myth speaks is that adult children cannot and do not provide the same total care to their elderly parents that those parents gave to them in the good old days of their infancy and childhood. The roles of parent and child cannot be reversed in that sense. The good old days, then, may not be earlier periods in our social history (after all, the myth existed then too), but an earlier period in each individual's and family's history to which there can be no return.

The myth exists because of the disparity between standards and expectations on the one hand and the unavoidable realities on the other hand. The disparity leads to guilt. The myth persists because the guilt persists, reflecting a universal and deeply rooted human theme. That may be why we hear over and over again from adult children "I know I'm doing everything I can for my mother, but somehow I still feel guilty." The fantasy is that "somehow" one should do more. That may be one reason that so many adult children are overwhelmed with guilt when a parent enters a nursing home. It is experienced as the total surrender of the parent to the care of others—the ultimate failure to meet the parent's dependency needs as that parent met the child's needs in the good old days.

Guilt may be a reason that people assert that they and their own families behave responsibly in caring for their old, but that most people do not do so as was the case in the good old days. They need to defend against the guilt and to deny their own negative and unacceptable emotions (emotions such as resentment, anger, and the wish not to be burdened, which add another dimension to the guilt), by feeling that others do not behave as well. *"They* are *really* guilty; I am not."

In completing the feedback loop, by exacerbating the guilt the myth contributes to the strains of parent care. Not only does the myth persist because the guilt persists, but the guilt persists because the myth persists.

To quote Erma Bombeck, "Guilt is the gift that keeps on giving" (1984).

SOCIAL POLICY

Since the 1963 Symposium, social policy (which expresses the values of the time), has made some progress in applying knowledge about filial behavior. Medicare and Medicaid came into being (1965) and an income floor was established by Supplemental Security Income (SSI, 1974). Medicaid and SSI together eliminated compulsory financial support of the old by their adult children. With Social Security (1935) as a base, the proportion of older people who were wholly dependent on family for economic support dropped from about 50% in 1937 to 1.5% in 1979 (Upp, 1982). (Note that these figures do not speak to adequacy of income.) Those programs (together with savings, private pensions, etc.) enabled more of the aged to live as they prefer (close to, but not in the same household with their children) and to realize their wish not to depend on their children for income or the costs of catastrophic illness. There has been considerable development of services and living facilities, though many more are needed.

At present, however, in expressing current values, social policy echoes, uses, and perpetuates the myth, exerting psychological pressure on adult children, increasing their guilt, and adding to their strains by failing to provide services and facilities that are urgently needed to back up their efforts.

The myth is being invoked as a rationale for a philosophy that would shrink the formal support system and encourage its non-use to save public funds. The call to restore the good old days of family values is being operationalized in a variety of ways. For example—

- The States have been encouraged to reinstitute the archaic requirement that people in the grandparent generation be compelled to pay the costs of nursing home care for the great-grandparent generation.
- A variety of cost-containment efforts are limiting nursing home beds, frustrating efforts at quality care, and effectively closing nursing home doors to those who need them most—the "heavy care" Medicaid patients (U.S. GAO, 1983) such as those with Alzheimer's disease (Brody et al., in press). As a result, aging caregivers who have gone beyond the limits of endurance will have no relief. This, though scientists on both sides of the "compression of morbidity" controversy agree that the number of those in need of long-term chronic care will continue to increase, at least for the next few decades (e.g., see Fries, 1984; Schneider & Brody, J., 1983). And this, though it has been shown that community care is not cheaper than nursing home care for severely disabled older people (Comptroller General of the United States, 1977b; Fox & Clauser, 1980).
- Services that would relieve the unrelenting strains on families of non-institutionalized old people should be increasing but are being cut back. Family focused services—notably respite care and day care—are sparse, uneven regionally, and are not funded consistently.

The language used is revealing. The injunction issued is not to "supplant" family services, though research evidence indicates that services strengthen family caregiving (Horowitz, 1982; Zimmer & Sainer, 1978). There are suggestions for "incentives" for families to care, implying that they need to be induced, rather than helped, to do what they want to do and have been doing. Issues are framed artificially as competing propositions such as institutionalization *versus* community care, family (informal) care *versus* formal (government and agencies) care, even respite services to provide temporary relief for caregivers *versus* training programs to build their caregiving skills.

When a "family policy" means cheering the family on to increase its efforts, the effect is to undermine the very family the rhetoric purports to save. The call for filial responsibility masks social irresponsibility, disadvantaging the elderly and the young as well as the middle generation. Binstock (1983) has called attention to the scapegoating of the old. Many policies scapegoat their adult children.

In the future, there could be radical changes in demands for parent care and other long-term support services if bio-medical break-throughs result in prevention or cure of conditions causing chronic dependency—Alzheimer's disease, for example. But social policy cannot await such major advances. The informal system, which pro-tects the formal system from being overwhelmed, should be sup-ported, not weakened. Overburdening family members can increase the costs to the community of the mental and physical health prob-lems they experience as a result.

Since knowledge has not dispelled the myth, and if the hypothesis advanced here means that one of its aspects is relatively immutable, perhaps the realistic goal is not to slay the Hydra monster but to render it powerless to impede constructive clinical approaches and a sound social policy. As gerontologists, we provide facts which are correctives so that policy based on bias and myth does not go un-challenged.

In a paper presented by co-authors Steve Brody and Don Kent at the 1968 GSA meetings, they said "The union of social research and social action is a long way off, but there are at least signs that such a bridge can be built . . ." (Brody & Kent, 1968). We have made progress in building that bridge, and our efforts have been increas-ing. Since the 1963 Symposium, the membership of this organization has risen from 2,000 to 6,000, with an exponential increase in the amount of research.

We cannot do it all, of course. Adult children will continue to care for and about their elderly parents. They will continue to be con-cerned, to provide affection and emotional support, to do what they are able, and to arrange for the needed services that they cannot supply. (Perhaps those are the only appropriate norms for filial be-havior.) The strains families experience are not completely prevent-able or remediable. But policy should rest on knowledge rather than a myth if it is to create a dependable formal system that forges an effective partnership with the dependable family. Knowledge, properly used, can do much to prevent families from reaching the limits of endurance and can help us as a society to meet our collective filial responsibility.

REFERENCES

Archbold, P. (1978). Impact of caring for an ill elderly parent of the middle-aged or elderly offspring caregiver. Paper presented at the 31st Annual Meeting of the Gerontological Society, Dallas, TX, November.

Bengtson, V. L., & Treas, J. (1980). The changing context of mental health and aging. In J. E. Birren & R. B. Sloane (Eds.), *Handbook of mental health and aging.* Englewood Cliffs, NJ: Prentice-Hall.

Binstock, R. H. (1983). The aged as scapegoat. *The Gerontologist, 23,* 136–143.

Blenkner, M. (1965). Social work and family relationships in later life with some thoughts on filial maturity. In E. Shanas & G. F. Streib (Eds.), *Social structure and the family: Generational Relations.* Englewood Cliffs, NJ: Prentice-Hall.

Bombeck, Erma, quoted by Skow, John (1984). "Erma in Bomburgia," *Time,* July 2, p. 56.

Brody, E. M. (1981). "Women in the middle" and family help to older people. *The Gerontologist, 21,* 471–480.

Brody, E. M. (1979). Aged parents and aging children. In P. K. Ragan (Ed.), *Aging Parents.* Los Angeles, CA: University of Southern California Press.

Brody, E. M. (1978). The aging of the family. *The Annals of the American Academy of Political and Social Science, 438,* 13–27.

Brody, E. M. (1977). *Long-term care of older people: A practical guide.* New York: Human Sciences Press.

Brody, E. M. (1977a). Environmental factors in dependency. In A. N. Exton-Smith & J. G. Evans (Eds.), *Care of the Elderly: Meeting the Challenge of Dependency* (pp. 81–95). London: Academic Press; New York: Grune & Stratton.

Brody, E. M. (1969). Follow-up study of applicants and non-applicants to a voluntary home. *The Gerontologist, 9,* 187–196.

Brody, E. M. (1967a). Aging is a family affair. *Public Welfare,* 129–140.

Brody, E. M. (1967b). The mentally-impaired aged patient: A socio-medical problem. *Geriatrics Digest, 4,* 25–32.

Brody, E. M. (1966a). The impaired aged: A follow-up study of applicants rejected by a voluntary home. *Journal of the American Geriatrics Society, 14,* 414–420.

Brody, E. M. (1966b). The aging family. *The Gerontologist, 6,* 201–206.

Brody, E. M., & Gummer, B. (1967). Aged applicants and non-applicants to a voluntary home: An exploratory comparison. *The Gerontologist, 7,* 234–243.

Brody, E. M., Johnsen, P. T., & Fulcomer, M. C. (1984a). What should adult children do for elderly parents: Opinions and preferences of three generations of women. *Journal of Gerontology, 39,* 736–746.

Brody, E. M., Johnsen, P. T., Fulcomer, M. C., & Lang, A. (1982a). The Dependent Elderly and Women's Changing Roles. Final report on Administration on Aging Grant #90-A-1277.

Brody, E. M., Johnsen, P. T., & Fulcomer, M. C. (1982b). "Women in the middle" and care of the dependent elderly. Final Report on AoA Grant #90-AR-2174.

Brody, E. M., Johnsen, P. T., Fulcomer, M. C., & Lang, A. M. (1983). Women's changing roles and help to the elderly: Attitudes of three generations of women. *Journal of Gerontology, 38,* 597–607.

Brody, E. M., Kleban, M. H., & Johnsen, P. T. (1984). Women who provide parent care: Characteristics of those who work and those who do not. Paper presented at the 37th Annual Meeting of The Gerontological Society of America, San Antonio, TX, November.

Brody, E. M., Lawton, M. P., & Liebowitz, B. (1984). Senile dementia: Public policy and adequate institutional care. *American Journal of Public Health, 74,* 1381–1383.

Brody, E. M., & Spark, G. (1966). Institutionalization of the aged: A family crisis. *Family Process, 5,* 76–90.

Brody, S. J. (1973). Comprehensive health care of the elderly: An analysis. *The Gerontologist, 13,* 412–418.

Brody, S. J., & Kent, D. P. (1968). Social research and social policy in a public agency. Paper presented at the 21st Annual Meeting of the Gerontological Society, Denver, CO.

Brody, S. J., Poulshock, S. W., & Masciocchi, C. F. (1978). The family care unit: A major consideration in the long-term support system. *The Gerontologist, 18,* 556–561.

Cantor, M. H. (1983). Strain among caregivers: A study of experience in the United States. *The Gerontologist, 23,* 597–604.

Cantor, M. H. (1980). Caring for the frail elderly: Impact on family, friends and neighbors. Paper presented at 33rd Annual Meeting of The Gerontological Society of America, San Diego, CA.

Comptroller General of the United States (1977a). *The well-being of older people in Cleveland, Ohio,* U.S. General Accounting Office, #RD-77-70, Washington, DC, April 19.

Comptroller General of the United States (1977b). Report to Congress on Home Health—*The Need for a National Policy to Better Provide for the Elderly,* U.S. General Accounting Office, HRD-78-19, Washington, DC, December 30.

Danis, B. G. (1978). Stress in individuals caring for ill elderly relatives. Paper presented at 31st Annual Meeting of the Gerontological Society, Dallas, TX.

Fox, P. D., & Clauser, S. B. (1980). Trends in nursing home expenditures: Implications for aging policy. *Health Care Financing Review*, 65–70.

Frankfather, D., Smith, M. J., & Caro, F. G. (1981). *Family care of the elderly: Public initiatives and private obligations.* Lexington, MA: Lexington Books.

Friedan, B. (1963). *The feminine mystique.* New York: Dell.

Fries, J. F. (1984). The compression of morbidity: Miscellaneous comments about a theme. *The Gerontologist, 24,* 354–359.

George, L. K. (1980). *Role transitions in late life.* Monterey, CA: Brooks/Cole.

Goldfarb, A. I. (1965). Psychodynamics and the three-generation family. In E. Shanas & G. F. Streib (Eds.), *Social structure and the family: Generational relations* (pp. 10–45). Englewood Cliffs, NJ: Prentice-Hall.

Gruenberg, E. M. (1977). The failures of success. *Milbank Memorial Fund Quarterly*, Health and Society, 3–24.

Gurland, B., Dean, L., Gurland, R., & Cook, D. (1978). Personal time dependency in the elderly of New York City: Findings from the U.S.-U.K. cross-national geriatric community study. In *Dependency in the elderly of New York City.* New York: Community Council of Greater New York, 9–45.

Hareven, T. K. (1982). The life course and aging in historical perspective. In T. K. Hareven & K. J. Adams (Eds.), *Aging and life course transitions: An interdisciplinary perspective* (pp. 1–26). New York: Guilford Press.

Hoenig, J., & Hamilton, M. (1966). Elderly patients and the burden on the household. *Psychiatra et Neurologia,* Basel, *152,* 281–293.

Horowitz, A. (1982). The role of families in providing long-term care to the frail and chronically ill elderly living in the community. Final report submitted to the Health Care Financing Administration, DHHS, May.

Johnsen, P. T., & Fulcomer, M. C. (1984). "Culture's consequences" in attitudes, opinions, and preferences affecting family care of the elderly. Paper presented at the 37th Annual Meeting of The Gerontological Society of America, San Antonio, TX, November.

Katz, S., Branch, L. G., Branson, M. H., Papsidero, J. A., Beck, J. C., & Greer, D. S. (1983). Active life expectancy. *The New England Journal of Medicine, 309,* 1218–1224.

Kent, D. P. (1972). Social policy and program considerations in planning for the aging. In D. P. Kent, R. Kastenbaum, & S. Sherwood (Eds.), *Research planning and action for the elderly* (pp. 3–19). New York: Behavioral Publications.

Kent, D. P. (1965). Aging—fact or fancy. *The Gerontologist, 5,* 2.

Kleban, M. H., Brody, E. M., & Hoffman, C. (1984). Parent care and depression: Differences between working and nonworking adult daughters. Paper presented at the 37th Annual Meeting of The Gerontological Society of America, San Antonio, TX, November.

Lang, A., & Brody, E. M. (1983). Characteristics of middle-aged daughters and help to their elderly mothers. *Journal of Marriage and the Family, 45,* 193–202.

Lawton, M. P., & Brody, E. M. (1968). The social cost of care for the elderly. Final report, U.S.P.H.S. Grant #CD00137.

Lawton, M. P., & Lawton, F. (Eds.) (1965). *Mental impairment in the aged: Institute on the mentally impaired aged.* Philadelphia, PA: Philadelphia Geriatric Center.

Lopata, H. Z., & Norr, K. F. (1980). Changing commitments of American women to work and family roles. *Social Security Bulletin,* June, *43,* 3–14.

Lowenthal, M. F. (1964). *Lives in distress.* New York: Basic Books.

Mindel, C. H. (1979). Multigenerational family households: Recent trends and implications for the future. *The Gerontologist, 19,* 456–463.

Murray, J. (1973). Family structure in the preretirement years. *Social Security Bulletin,* October, *36,* 25–45.

Myllyuoma, J., & Soldo, B. J. (1980). Family caregivers to the elderly: Who are they? Paper presented at the 33rd Annual Meeting of the Gerontological Society, San Diego, CA.

Neugarten, B. L. (1974). Age groups in American society and the rise of the young-old. *The Annals of the American Academy of Political and Social Science, 415,* 187–198.

NRTA-AARP (National Retired Teachers Association-American Association of Retired Persons) (1981). National survey of older Americans.

Peck, R. C. (1968). Psychological developments in the second half of life. In B. L. Neugarten (Ed.), *Middle age and aging: A reader in social psychology* (pp. 88–92). Chicago, IL: University of Chicago Press.

Rosow, I. (1965). Intergenerational relationships: Problems and proposals. In E. Shanas & G. F. Streib (Eds.), *Social structure and the family: Generational relations* (pp. 341–378). Englewood Cliffs, NJ: Prentice-Hall.

Sainsbury, P., & Grad de Alercon, J. (1970). The effects of community care in the family of the geriatric patient. *Journal of Geriatric Psychiatry, 4,* 23–41.

Schneider, E. L., & Brody, J. A. (1983). Aging, natural death, and the compression of morbidity: Another view. *The New England Journal of Medicine, 309,* 854–856.

Schorr, A. L. (1960). *Filial responsibility in the modern American family.* Washington, DC: U.S. DHEW, Social Security Administration, Government Printing Office, June.

Shanas, E. (1979a). Social myth as hypothesis: The case of the family relations of old people. *The Gerontologist, 19,* 3–9.

Shanas, E. (1979b). The family as a social support system in old age. *The Gerontologist, 19,* 169–174.

Shanas, E. (1963). The unmarried old person in the United States: Living arrangements and care in illness, myth and fact. Paper presented at the International Social Science Research Seminar in Gerontology, Makaryd, Sweden, 1963.

Shanas, E., & Streib, G. F. (Eds.) (1965). *Social structure and the family: Generational relations.* Englewood Cliffs, NJ: Prentice-Hall.

Shanas, E., Townsend, P., Wedderburn, D., Friis, H., Milhøj, P., & Stehouwer, J. (Eds.) (1968). *Old people in three industrial societies.* New York: Atherton Press.

Soldo, B. J. (1980). The dependency squeeze on middle-aged women. Presented at Meeting of the Secretary's Advisory Committee on Rights and Responsibilities of Women, Department of Health and Human Services.

Soldo, B., & Myllyluoma, J. (1983). Caregivers who live with dependent elderly. *The Gerontologist, 23* (6), 605–611.

Spark, G., & Brody, E. M. (1970). The aged are family members. *Family Process, 9,* 195–210.

Streib, G. F., & Shanas, E. (1965). An introduction. In E. Shanas & G. F. Streib (Eds.), *Social structure and the family: Generational relations.* Englewood Cliffs, NJ: Prentice-Hall.

Sussman, M. (1979). Social and economic supports and family environment for the elderly. Final report to Administration on Aging, Grant #90-A-316, January.

Townsend, P. (1965). The effects of family structure on the likelihood of admission to an institution in old age: The application of a general theory. In E. Shanas & G. F. Streib (Eds.), *Social structure and the family: Generational relations* (pp. 163–187). Englewood Cliffs, NJ: Prentice-Hall.

Troll, L. E. (1971). The family of later life: A decade review. *Journal of Marriage and the Family, 33,* 263–290.

Uhlenberg, P. (1980). Death and the family. *Journal of Family History, 5,* 313–320.

U.S. Bureau of Labor Statistics (1984). *Employment and earnings,* Table 3, January.

U.S. General Accounting Office (1983). *Medicaid and nursing home care: Cost increases and the need for services are creating problems for the States and the elderly.* Washington, DC: U.S. General Accounting Office, October 21.

U.S. National Committee on Vital and Health Statistics (1978). *Long-term health care: Minimum data set.* Preliminary report of the Technical Consultant Panel on the Long-Term Health Care Data Set, NCHS, September 8.

Upp, M. (1982). A look at the economic status of the aged then and now. *Social Security Bulletin,* March, *45,* 16–22.

Zarit, S. H., Reever, K. E., & Bach-Peterson, J. (1980). Relatives of the impaired aged: Correlates of feelings of burden. *The Gerontologist, 20,* 649–655.

Zimmer, A. H., & Sainer, J. S. (1978). Strengthening the family as an informal support for their aged: Implications for social policy and planning. Paper presented at the 31st Annual Meeting of the Gerontological Society, Dallas, TX.

7

A Comparison of Helping Behavior to Elderly Parents of Adult Children with Intact and Disrupted Marriages*

Victor G. Cicirelli

Although controversy has arisen in recent decades over the extent to which the family provides for its elderly members, ample evidence indicates that adult children are providing at least some measure of support and services for their elderly parents at the present time and will continue to do so in the future (Brody et al., 1978; Cicirelli, 1979; Horowitz, 1978; Shanas, 1980). However, there may be limitations on the kinds and amounts of services that adult children can and will provide (Brody et al., 1978; Treas, 1977; Ward, 1978). In our changing society, fewer adult children are present to help elderly parents than in earlier times, the role of women has changed as more go to work and are less available to provide help, the increasing longevity of elderly parents is concomitant with increased age of their adult children who may be preoccupied with their own retirement and health problems, a rise in multi-generation families may lead to different priorities in allocating family resources (other than helping elderly parents), and so on.

*The Gerontologist, 23 (6) (1983), 619–625.

Research reported in this paper was supported by grants from the AARP Andrus Foundation. The assistance of R. Chaffee, L. Demian, T. Lavelle, C. Michaelson, R. Michaelson, B. Mosbacher, J. Nussbaum, and P. Sutton in the collection of data is gratefully acknowledged.

Another possible limitation on the help that adult children can provide for their elderly parents is the increase in marital disruption in the lives of the adult children of the elderly. Sussman (1977) has estimated that 42% of all family types in the United States in 1976 were composed of remarried adults; widowed, separated, or divorced adults; and single adults. Thus, the maritally disrupted constitute an important group for study in today's world, as the percentage of adult children with intact marriages has diminished considerably in comparison to earlier times.

We regard adult children with marital disruption as those who have had at least one divorce or widowhood or have remarried following divorce or widowhood. The common factor underlying all these conditions is the loss of the original spouse. Although there are obvious differences among the divorced, widowed, and remarried, there are also similarities in that all three groups have experienced the breaking of the original marital bond and share many common problems as a result of the marital disruption.

Members of these groups frequently face financial difficulties (Berardo, 1968; Troll et al., 1979), practical problems with duties of everyday living (Stevens-Long, 1979), and problems in interpersonal relationships with parents (Duberman, 1975; Johnson & Vinick, 1982; Mueller & Pope, 1977; Spanier & Hanson, 1982), the former spouse and "in-laws," and their own children, siblings, and other kin (Hunt & Hunt, 1976; Kalish & Visher, 1982; Weiss, 1975) as well as friends (Spanier & Casto, 1979). Such problems may limit the ability or willingness of adult children to provide help to their elderly parents.

Few studies in the existing literature deal with the relationship of widowed, divorced, and remarried adult children with elderly parents. What is known about divorce suggests that contact with parents and affection for parents do not decline after the marital disruption (Ahrons & Bowman, 1982; Anspach, 1976; Spicer & Hampe, 1975). Yet, many elderly parents view the marital disruption as a negative and traumatic life event (Johnson & Vinick, 1982; Mueller & Pope, 1977; Spanier & Hanson, 1982). Up to 10 years after the divorce, many parents still regard a divorce as traumatic and upsetting to them, using such adjectives as sad, disastrous, and so on (Barkas, 1980; Johnson, 1980; Johnson & Vinick, 1982). Consequently, many adult children with disrupted marriages experience strains in their relationships with elderly parents.

Although the relationship of family members with the elderly widow has been extensively studied, insufficient evidence has been gathered about family relationships of the middle-aged person who has lost a mate. Lopata (1979) has observed that little family support is extended to widows; this may indicate interpersonal distancing from the widowed individual rather than a drawing closer following the loss.

The relationship with elderly parents is also affected when remarriage follows a divorce or widowhood. Although acceptance of divorce and remarriage has increased in our culture, Duberman (1975) found a considerable amount of rejection of the new spouse by the adult child's parents. The new spouse may not be well-accepted by elderly parents, particularly if the first spouse was well-liked, often leading to strained relationships between adult child and elderly parent. Even with the best of intentions, the relationships of elderly parents to a new son- or daughter-in-law may never attain the closeness possible with the original spouse, who literally may have grown up like a son or daughter in the family. The elderly parent may never feel comfortable with the new spouse, and vice versa. These awkward feelings then make it more difficult for the adult child to spend time with the parent. (And when grandchildren are to be incorporated into a reconstituted family, the relationship of adult children and elderly parents may be further complicated.)

In short, the limited studies available indicate that contact with and affection for elderly parents may be maintained after the adult child's divorce, widowhood, or remarriage, but there is also evidence of adjustment problems and potential conflict that may strain the relationship or lead to mutual withdrawal or distancing. If the latter is true, less help may be provided to elderly parents, especially if the timing of critical events is such that the marital disruption occurs when parents' dependency is greatest.

Yet, no studies are available on how divorce, widowhood, and remarriage affect adult children's behavior toward elderly parents. The present study was undertaken in an effort to explore this question by comparing the amount of help provided to elderly parents by divorced, widowed, and remarried adult children and by comparing help provided by children with marital disruption with help provided by children with intact marriages.

METHOD

Data were gathered in 1980 and 1981 in two of a series of overlapping field studies of the elderly and their families carried out in a small midwestern city.

The first source of data consisted of 141 adult children in a small midwestern city who had experienced marital disruption and who had a living elderly parent over 60 years of age. Since adult children with marital disruption proved difficult to identify from known population lists, the sample was obtained from contacts with clubs, churches, and other community organizations. The sample included 48 men and 93 women, of whom 93 were divorced, 20 widowed, and 28 remarried. Ages ranged from 28 to 71, with a mean age of 45.14 years. Eighty-five respondents had living fathers and 127 had living mothers. Interviews were administered at home. Ninety-four percent of the men and 87% of the women were employed; clearly, marital disruption is associated with a high level of employment among women. Thirty-nine percent of study participants had been married more than once. On the average, these adult children had 2.7 children; two-thirds were still providing some form of support to their children.

The second source of data was a study of 164 adult children with intact marriages that measured many of the same variables (Cicirelli, 1981b). Thus, data from the two studies can be used to make comparisons between adult children who have experienced marital disruption and those who have not. The 1981 sample was selected through a block sampling procedure of residents in the same city and consisted of 75 men and 89 women ranging in age from 29 to 71 years. These adult children were also interviewed at home.

The two samples were compared to determine their similarity on various demographic criteria. In spite of the accidental nature of the sample of adult children with marital disruption, a comparison of the characteristics of this sample with the characteristics of the sample of adult children with intact marriages from the same community provides some basis for confidence in the nature of the sample. The study of adult children with intact marriages was based on a block sampling procedure and thus can be viewed as representative of middle-aged adults residing in the community. Table 7.1 presents several characteristics for the two samples, including age, educational and occupational levels (based on 7-point Hollingshead scales with 7 indicating the highest level), number of children, percentage employed, number of siblings, parental age, and parental health (rated on a 7-point scale). None of the t tests performed to test the difference between the two samples was statistically significant at the .05 level. In addition, no significant difference was found in the percentage of employed men, although the difference was significant in the case of employed women, $\chi^2(1) = 17.57$, $p < .05$. Thus, it is clear that, except for the percentage of women employed, the two groups did not differ

Table 7.1. Selected Demographic Characteristics of Adult Children with Disrupted and Intact Marriages

Variable	Disrupted (n = 141)		Intact (n = 164)		t
	Mean	SD	Mean	SD	
Age	45.14	9.38	46.38	8.74	−1.19
Educational level	5.40	1.20	5.18	1.21	+1.59
Occupational level	4.79	1.48	4.88	1.74	−0.49
Total number of children	2.73	1.70	2.81	1.62	−0.42
Number of living siblings	2.14	1.78	2.17	2.02	−0.14
Parents' age					
Fathers	72.91	8.47	74.14	7.60	−1.33
Mothers	72.46	9.60	74.07	8.23	−1.56
Rated parental health					
Fathers	5.06	1.36	4.94	1.31	+0.78
Mothers	4.90	1.34	4.75	1.41	+0.95
	%		%		
Employed					
Men	94		92		
Women	87		61		
Living siblings	85		88		

greatly on most of these characteristics. The percentage of women employed was much higher among those with disrupted marriages than among those with intact marriages, but this is not surprising in view of the economic pressures experienced by women who have lost their husbands. In other characteristics, the two groups can be regarded as generally representative of the same community. The adult children who participated in the study were whites of predominantly Northern European ancestry and were mostly of middle-class status. Although the study may suggest important ways in which the two groups differed in regard to provision of help to elderly parents, it is not argued that marital disruption is necessarily the cause of any such differences. However, the study can provide strong suggestive evidence that marital disruption is such a cause.

Adult children's help to elderly parents was assessed for 16 types of services to elderly. The services can be roughly classified according to a threefold scheme (Cicirelli, 1979): primary services (provided to all elderly for survival and daily maintenance in independent living), secondary services (needed for optimum contact, participation, and reality orientation to the community), and tertiary services (concerned with the enhancement of the individual on both the physical and psychological levels). The 16 types of help comprised 6 primary services (homemaking, housing, income, maintenance, personal care, home health care), 6 secondary services (transportation, psychological support, social and recreation activities, spiritual support, protection, and bureaucratic mediation), and 4 tertiary services (reading materials, career education, employment, and enrichment). The amount of present help that adult children gave to elderly parents for each of 16 types of services was reported on a 5-point scale ranging from "not at all" to "all of the time." Preliminary factor analysis (Cicirelli, 1981b) indicated the presence of only a single general factor; therefore, a total score was calculated by summing over the 16 types of services.

RESULTS

Preliminary Analysis

In the preliminary analysis of the help provided by adult children with marital disruption, the effects of type of marital disruption and sex on the amount of help were determined for the total score and for the specific services using analysis of variance. No significant effects appeared on the total child help score, but significant effects ($p < .05$) were found for 3 of the 16 service areas. A significant effect of marital status was found on help with income, with remarried adult children ($\overline{M} = 1.50$) giving more help than either divorced ($\overline{M} = 1.13$) or widowed ($\overline{M} = 1.15$) groups. A significant sex effect was found on psychological support, with women ($\overline{M} = 2.73$) giving more psychological support to their parents than men ($\overline{M} = 2.23$). A significant sex difference was also found for help with employment, with men ($\overline{M} = 1.21$) providing more help than women ($\overline{M} = 1.02$). In view of the fact that no sex or type of marital disruption effects were found for the total help score or for 13 of the 16 specific types of services and since very low amounts of help were given with income and employment, the subgroups were combined for the remaining analysis.

Percentages of Adult Children Giving Help

First, it may be of interest to examine descriptively the percentages of adult children who were providing some help to their parents. These were obtained by combining the four response alternatives indicating that some degree of help was provided. These percentages are presented in Table 7.2.

From Table 7.2, one can observe that the percentages of adult children with marital disruption providing some degree of help to elderly parents were significantly lower than the percentages of adult children with intact marriages for psychological support, maintenance, bureaucratic mediation, and transportation. The trend was in the same direction for protection, homemaking, social and recreational activities, spiritual support, personal care and reading material. Second, regardless of differences between the two groups, some degree of psychological support was provided by a very high percentage of adult children. Third, both groups show an extremely low percentage of adult children providing any help regarding employment or career education for elderly parents.

Overall, the mean percentage of adult children with marital disruption providing some degree of help with the 6 primary services was 20.5%, compared to 35.3% providing help for secondary services and

Table 7.2. Percentages of Adult Children with Disrupted and Intact Marriages Giving Some Degree of Help to Elderly Parents in 16 Service Areas

Service	Type[a]	Percentages		χ^2
		Disrupted	Intact	
Psychological support	S	76	91	8.17*
Protection	S	37	45	1.32
Maintenance	P	35	55	8.08*
Homemaking	P	35	46	2.51
Bureaucratic mediation	S	30	46	5.43*
Transportation	S	28	45	6.23*
Social and recreational activities	S	23	34	2.97
Enrichment	T	23	23	0.00
Spiritual support	S	19	30	3.27
Home health care	P	16	15	0.04
Personal care	P	15	16	0.04
Reading materials	T	12	20	2.38
Housing	P	11	13	0.19
Income	P	11	13	0.19
Employment	T	04	01	0.45
Career education	T	01	01	0.00

[a]P = primary services; S = secondary services; T = tertiary services.
*$p < .05$.

only 10.0% providing help with tertiary services. For adult children with intact marriages, the mean percentage for primary service was 26.5%, compared with 48.5% providing help with secondary services and 11.2% giving help with tertiary services.

Amount of Help to Elderly Parents

Means and standard deviations for the total help score and for each type of service are presented in Table 7.3 for the groups with disrupted and intact marriages, along with the results of t tests for the difference between the two groups. One can observe from Table 7.3 that adult children with marital disruption provided less total help to parents than did those with intact marriages, as well as less help with 12 of the 16 specific services. The t-test results indicated significant differences ($p < .05$) between the groups in total help and in help with

Table 7.3. Amount of Help from Adult Child with Disrupted and Intact Marriages to Elderly Parents in 16 Service Areas: Group Means and Standard Deviations

Type of service	Disrupted		Intact		
	Mean	SD	Mean	SD	t
Primary:					
Homemaking	1.52	0.92	1.79	1.10	–2.30*
Housing	1.26	0.84	1.45	1.22	–1.56
Income	1.21	0.67	1.10	0.50	+1.64
Maintenance	1.54	0.88	2.11	1.30	–4.41*
Personal care	1.22	0.59	1.26	0.72	–0.52
Home health care	1.24	0.68	1.27	0.78	–0.35
Secondary:					
Transportation	1.59	1.12	2.03	1.40	–3.00*
Psychological support	2.60	1.25	2.73	0.96	–1.03
Social and recreational activities	1.38	0.86	1.60	1.00	–2.04*
Spiritual support	1.28	0.68	1.54	0.99	–2.63*
Protection	1.70	1.14	1.88	1.18	–1.35
Bureaucratic mediation	1.64	1.17	1.92	1.29	–1.97*
Tertiary:					
Reading materials	1.28	0.76	1.48	0.96	–1.99*
Career education	1.02	0.28	1.01	0.11	+0.42
Enrichment	1.38	0.83	1.29	0.58	+1.11
Employment	1.08	0.51	1.03	0.32	+1.04
Total child help	22.93	7.91	27.55	8.83	–4.78*

*$p < .05$.

homemaking, maintenance, transportation, social and recreational activities, spiritual support, bureaucratic mediation, and reading materials services. It may be somewhat surprising that no significant difference was found between the two marital status groups in the amount of psychological support provided, since the two groups did differ in the percentages giving some degree of help in that area (Table 7.2). However, the fact that a relatively greater percentage of those with disrupted marriages provided lower levels of psychological support in comparison to those with intact marriages accounts for the lack of a significant difference in *amount* of help provided.

Further Comparisons

In an attempt to better understand some of the reasons why adult children with marital disruption provided less help to elderly parents than did those with intact marriages, we compared the two groups on three variables which have been found to be related to helping behavior (Bengtson et al., 1976; Cicirelli, 1981a): perceived need, filial obligation, and limitation on help.

Adult children's perceptions of elderly parents' need for each of the 16 types of services were reported on a 5-point scale ranging from "not at all" to "all of the time." A total score was calculated by summing for the 16 types of services. The adult children with marital disruption perceived the elderly parents' need for help as significantly less ($M = 24.60$, SD = 9.70) than did adult children with intact marriages ($M = 27.15$, SD = 9.18), $t (303) = -2.35$, $p < .05$.

A 5-item adaptation (Cicirelli, 1981b) of the Filial Expectancy Scale (Seelbach & Sauer, 1977) was used to measure the obligation which adult children felt toward elderly parents. Scores ranged from 50 to 25, with a high score indicating a greater sense of filial responsibility. The adult children with marital disruption ($M = 16.61$, SD = 3.57) showed significantly less filial obligation compared to adult children with intact marriages ($M = 18.14$, SD = 3.17), $t (303) = -3.95$, $p < .01$.

Both groups were asked at what point they could no longer continue to help their parents. Some 29% of the adult children with intact marriages but only 16% of those with marital disruption felt that they could continue to help their elderly parents under any circumstances. This difference was significant, $\chi^2(1) = 4.85$, $p < .05$. Among the group with marital disruption, job responsibilities were cited by the great majority as the main reason why their help to parents would have to be limited.

Again, the highest level of help, as well as the greatest number of significant differences between the two marital status groups, was found for secondary services, with lower levels of help for primary services and the least help for tertiary services.

DISCUSSION

In summary, adult children with disrupted marriages provided a lesser amount of help to their elderly parents than adult children with intact marriages (although the mean amounts of help were relatively low for both groups). Thus, the results do indicate that marital disruption affects help to elderly parents.

Perhaps this can be partially explained by these adult children's perceptions of their parents as having less need for help and by their lessened sense of obligation to help. Being preoccupied with their own problems of adjustment, they may be less sensitive to their elderly parents' needs or degree of dependency or have a weakened commitment or obligation to provide help. In any event, these factors are seen as important antecedents for helping behavior by many experts. Bengtson et al. (1976) proposed a model of intergenerational solidarity in which helping behavior was viewed as an aspect of intergenerational solidarity. Helping behavior was seen as a function of the dependency needs of the elderly, residential propinquity, filial responsibility, and sex linkage. According to such a model, more helping behavior would occur when the parent's dependency needs became greater and when the adult child felt a greater sense of filial responsibility (as well as when the adult child lived closer and when the adult child was a daughter).

In addition to Bengtson et al. (1976), concepts of filial obligation have been advanced by many, such as "irredeemable obligation" (Blau, 1973), family loyalty (Adams, 1968), and filial maturity (Blenkner, 1965), and are held to be responsible for much helping behavior. On a psychological level, Cicirelli (in press) has formulated an attachment model of helping behavior that includes filial obligation and dependency needs as predictors of helping behavior. Whether the lower filial obligation of those with marital disruption is a consequence of the marital disruption or merely reflects different family values of long standing is a question which was not investigated in the present study. It is possible that those with weaker family values would be more likely to divorce, but it is difficult to apply such reasoning to widowhood. Certainly this is a question which warrants further study.

The limits of helping are relevant as a possible explanatory variable as they constitute an aspect of cost of helping which fits in with equity theory (Walster et al., 1978). The latter may well be applied to the topic of adult children's helping behavior to elderly parents. When benefits or rewards from the relationship in comparison to costs become less than what the other party is perceived as gaining, the individual becomes discontented and seeks to restore equity to the relationship.

In applying notions of equity to the helping relationship, one can note first that considerable evidence exists that the balance of mutual aid between generations shifts as parents become older and more dependent, with more aid flowing from children to parents than vice versa (e.g., Aldous & Hill, 1965; Blau, 1973). Thus, as parents become more dependent, the balance of tangible mutual aid is no longer equitable, and at some point an adult child may feel that the cost of providing help is too high. In the present study, the limits of helping may be the threshold where the cost of helping is perceived as too high relative to benefits, and this threshold may be lower for adult children with marital disruption.

However, the present findings suggest that help to elderly parents from adult children with marital disruption, although significantly lower than that provided by children with intact marriages, is not *drastically* lower. In this sense, it is clear that adult children with marital disruption do attempt to meet their elderly parents' needs for help. Newer theoretical positions on the flexibility and adaptiveness of family systems (e.g., Duffy, 1982; Furstenberg, 1979, 1982) hold that family relationships evolve to meet the needs and promote the well-being of family members. Although there is evidence for such flexibility of family relationships following marital disruption, it is not yet clear just how well the needs of elderly parents are being met at this time.

Possibly adult children are merely more involved with their own problems and thereby less sensitive to parents' needs. Alternatively, they may simply have insufficient communication to become aware of parents' needs. Elderly parents may contribute to this lack of awareness by avoiding communication of their needs out of a desire not to burden their children.

Job responsibilities were cited by adult children with marital disruption as a main reason why help to parents would have to be limited. The level of employment among those with marital disruption, particularly divorced women, is quite high. In comparison to adult children with intact marriages, a greater proportion of the group with marital disruption felt that they could not continue to help parents if their job was threatened by doing so. Women who provide their own sole support and perhaps the support of their children are not in a position to jeopardize their livelihood by taking time off from work to help elderly parents. More women are now in the work force, and their attempt to juggle home, family, job, and care for parents may become highly stressful. Women in intact marriages have the option of stopping work to care for aging parents and there are indications that many do so when stresses become too great (Horowitz, 1982; Sherman et al., 1982). Those with marital disruption, however, may not have such an option (Cicirelli, 1981a). (Men, also, are under greater pressure to perform and achieve in order to maintain and advance in their jobs as economic conditions continue to change.) If help to parents cannot be accomplished within the limited amounts of free time available to these maritally disrupted adult children (especially divorced women), it may be very difficult indeed for them to take on any further responsibilities of parent care.

Psychological support, however, is one area which adult children with marital disruption see as especially important to their parents and which they could readily provide. Perhaps in the loss of their own spouses, whether by death or divorce, these adult children experienced a great deal of psychological trauma and learned the importance of psychological support from others. This kind of personal experience may make adult children with marital disruption particularly sensitive to their parents' needs for psychological support in facing the losses and vicissitudes of old age. It may also make them more appreciative of the value of such help.

The findings on psychological support are of particular importance since they fail to indicate that mutual withdrawal or distancing due to marital disruption is a major factor that might account for the lower amounts of help provided. Although some earlier studies have suggested a weakening of kinship ties following divorce (e.g., Anspach, 1976), such weakening occurred mainly in relation to the former spouse's kin. Strains in relationships with parents (Barkas, 1980; Hunt & Hunt, 1976; Spanier & Hanson, 1982) which may occur early in the adjustment period following divorce are apparently eased as time passes. Greater acceptance as divorce and remarriage become almost a cultural norm also tends to make withdrawal and distancing less likely.

Adult children in this study provided the most help with the secondary group of services (i.e., those that helped their parents maintain contact with and participation in the community). Help with primary services needed to survive and maintain daily life was given at a lower level. Although primary services are the most crucial needs of frail elderly, most of the elderly parents of the adult children of the study had reasonably good health and economic resources (Cicirelli, 1981b), and their needs for primary services were relatively low.

The tertiary services of employment, career education, and enrichment were viewed as the least important of the three types of services for elderly parents. Adult children with marital disruption, like those with intact marriages, do not appear to take seriously the possibility that older workers may need to reenter the job market (or to remain in it) in a time of increasing inflation and threats to Social Security and other government programs for the elderly. This is somewhat surprising in view of the importance which they attach to their own jobs. It may indicate the feeling that elderly parents are not capable of further training, either in relation to a job or career or in relation to areas of interest that could enrich their own living. At a time when older people are becoming more active and involved in a wide variety of interests, it seems paradoxical that their adult children appear to ascribe so little significance to it.

Assuming that in the future the number of elderly parents who need help will increase and simultaneously marital disruption among middle-aged adult children will become the norm, the interface of these critical life events for both groups is likely to lead to less help from children than parents desire or than children might wish to give. Before the problem becomes critical, more research is needed now to determine the capability and willingness of adult children with marital disruption to provide help to elderly parents.

From a practitioner's viewpoint, more emphasis should be given to encouraging communication between adult children with marital disruption and elderly parents who are frail and dependent so that both groups can better understand these critical events in their lives and know better what to expect of each other. Clearer definition of needs and better planning can result in more effective help to the parent with a limited amount of effort from the child. Finally, efforts should be made to make job demands more flexible when adult children with marital disruption are caring for elderly parents. This may well prove to be cheaper for employers in the long run than increased taxes to support formal services; it also enhances the productivity and satisfaction of workers.

REFERENCES

Adams, B. N. *Kinship in an urban setting*. Markham Publishing Co., Chicago, 1968.

Ahrons, C. R., & Bowman, M. E. Changes in family relationships following divorce of adult child: Grandmothers' perception. *Journal of Divorce*, 1982, *5*, 49–68.

Aldous, J., & Hill, R. Social cohesion, lineage type, and intergenerational transmission. *Social Forces*, 1965, *43*, 471–482.

Anspach, D. F. Kinship and divorce. *Journal of Marriage and the Family*, 1976, *38*, 323–330.

Barkas, J. L. *Single in America*. Atheneum, New York, 1980.

Bengtson, V., Olander, E. G., & Haddad, A. A. The generation gap and aging family members: Toward a conceptual model. In J. F. Gubrium (Ed.), *Time, roles, and self in old age*. Human Sciences Press, New York, 1976.

Berardo, F. M. Widowhood status in the United States: Perspective on a neglected aspect of the family life-cycle. *Family Coordinator*, 1968, *17*, 191–203.

Blau, Z. S. *Old age in a changing society*. Franklin Watts, New York, 1973.

Blenkner, M. Social work and family relationships in later life with some thoughts on filial maturity. In E. Shanas & G. F. Streib (Eds.), *Social structure and the family*. Prentice-Hall, Englewood Cliffs, NJ, 1965.

Brody, S. J., Poulshock, W., & Masciocchi, C. F. The family caring unit: A major consideration in the long-term support system. *The Gerontologist*, 1978, *18*, 556–561.

Cicirelli, V. G. *Social services for the elderly in relation to the kin network*. Report to NRTA-AARP Andrus Foundation, Washington, DC, 1979.

Cicirelli, V. G. *Effects of divorce, widowhood, and remarriage on adult children's relationship and services to elderly parents*. Final report to NRTA-AARP Andrus Foundation, Washington, DC, December 1981. (a)

Cicirelli, V. G. *Helping elderly parents: The role of adult children*. Auburn Publishing Co., Boston, 1981. (b)

Cicirelli, V. G. Adult children's attachment and helping behavior to elderly parents: A path model. *Journal of Marriage and the Family*, in press.

Duberman, L. *The reconstituted family*. Nelson-Hall, Chicago, 1975.

Duffy, M. Divorce and the dynamics of the family kinship system. *Journal of Divorce*, 1982, *5*, 3–18.

Furstenberg, F. F. Recycling the family: Perspective for a neglected family form. *Marriage and Family Review*, 1979, *2*, 1–22.

Furstenberg, F. F. Conjugal succession: Re-entering marriage after divorce. In P. B. Baltes & O. G. Brim (Eds.), *Life-span development and behavior* (Vol. 5). Academic Press, New York, 1982.

Horowitz, A. *Families who care: A study of natural support systems of the elderly*. Paper presented at the 31st Annual Scientific Meeting of the Gerontological Society, Dallas, November 1978.

Horowitz, A. *Predictors of caregiving involvement among adult children of the frail elderly.* Paper presented at the 34th Annual Scientific Meeting of the Gerontological Society of America, Boston, November 1982.

Hunt, M., & Hunt, B. The world of the formerly married. In S. Burden, P. Houston, T. Kripe, R. Simpson, & W. F. Stultz (Eds.), *The single parent family: Proceedings of the changing family conference V.* University of Iowa, Iowa City, 1976.

Johnson, E. S. *Older mothers' perceptions of their child's divorce.* Paper presented at the 33rd Annual Scientific Meeting of the Gerontological Society, San Diego, November 1980.

Johnson, E. S., & Vinick, B. H. Support of the parent when an adult son or daughter divorces. *Journal of Divorce,* 1982, *5,* 69–77.

Kalish, R. A., & Visher, E. Grandparents of divorce and remarriage. *Journal of Divorce,* 1982, *5,* 127–139.

Lopata, H. Z. *Women as widows: Support systems.* Elsevier, New York, 1979.

Mueller, C. W., & Pope, H. Marital instability: A study of its transmission between generations. *Journal of Marriage and the Family,* 1977, *39,* 83–92.

Seelbach, W., & Sauer, W. Filial responsibility expectations and morale among aged persons. *The Gerontologist,* 1977, *17,* 421–425.

Shanas, E. Older people and their families: The new pioneers. *Journal of Marriage and the Family,* 1980, *42,* 9–15.

Sherman, R. H., Horowitz, A., & Durmaskin, S. C. *Role overload or role management? The relationship between work and caregiving among daughters of aged parents.* Paper presented at the 34th Annual Scientific Meeting of the Gerontological Society, Boston, November 1982.

Spanier, G. B., & Casto, R. F. Adjustment to separation and divorce: A qualitative analysis. In G. Levinger & O. C. Moles (Eds.), *Divorce and separation.* Basic Books, New York, 1979.

Spanier, G. B., & Hanson, S. The role of extended kin in the adjustment to marital separation. *Journal of Divorce,* 1982, *5,* 33–48.

Spicer, J. W., & Hampe, G. D. Kinship interaction after divorce. *Journal of Marriage and the Family,* 1975, *37,* 113–119.

Stevens-Long, J. *Adult life: Developmental process.* Mayfield, Palo Alto, CA, 1979.

Sussman, M. B. The family of old people. In R. H. Binstock & E. Shanas (Eds.), *Handbook of aging and the social sciences.* Van Nostrand Reinhold, New York, 1977.

Treas, J. Family support systems for the aged: Some social and demographic considerations. *The Gerontologist,* 1977, *17,* 486–491.

Troll, L. E., Miller, S. J., & Atchley, R. C. *Families in late life.* Wadsworth, Belmont, CA, 1979.

Walster, E., Walster, G. W., & Berscheid, E. *Equity: Theory and research.* Allyn and Bacon, Boston, 1978.

Ward, R. A. Limitations of the family as a supporting institution in the lives of the aged. *Family Coordinator,* 1978, *27,* 749–756.

Weiss, R. S. *Marital separation.* Basic Books, New York, 1975.

Part IV

Caregiving

Two kinds of caregiving to older impaired persons have been described. One kind is the actual help or *providing* of care, such as nursing, shopping, laundry, and feeding. The other is arranging for others to perform these services, care *managing*. Archbold (1982) found, in an exploratory study in Oregon, that both are arduous and time-consuming. Care providers, usually spouses and daughters, must be involved in, to use Archbold's words, "daily management of problems like incontinence, diarrhea, constipation, rest, feeding, planning a well-balanced diet, bathing, getting the person from a bed to a chair, from a chair to the bathroom" (p. 21). Family providers usually have no training in the skills involved and must learn on the job as they improvise. They work around the clock, often at heavy physical labor. Care managers, meanwhile, are involved in finding and evaluating agencies and people, first; in supervising them and keeping them motivated and on the job, second; and in jumping into action for the frequent emergencies when they don't appear, third. Archbold, like most other writers on this topic (e.g., Brody, 1985; Part III of this volume) speaks of the need for services to help these family members, services like housekeepers and visiting nurses, guides or tutors to show them how to function, and respite care. Seltzer and Troll (1982) discuss the conflicting attitudes with respect to public policy on this issue. At one extreme is a belief that the government or community is responsible for all such services. At the other extreme is the equally firm belief that it is the family's responsibility, not the government's. On another plane, those interested in costs and financing find it strategic to emphasize the benefits of family care. There are some who have urged incentives for families to increase care, even though there is evidence that families are already strained to their limits.

As Shanas (1979; Part III of this volume) and others have demonstrated, when old people need care, this care comes mostly from their families—that is, from their wives for men and from their daughters for women. Brody (1985; Part III of this volume) notes that for every disabled person in a nursing home, there are two or more equally disabled living with and cared for by their families. Further, she says, adult children now provide more care and more difficult care over a much longer time than in the "good old days." The articles in this volume by Brody, Nydegger (1983), and Arling and McAuley (1983) review the evidence for these statements. Hickey and Douglass (1981) addresses the popular sensational notion of "elder abuse," the current version of the "neglected elder" myth. Even patients in nursing homes—three-quarters of a sample in Michigan who had family members within 25 miles—received help with shopping, etc. (York and Calsyn, 1977; this volume). In black families, there is more caregiving than in white families, but this is *down* the generation line, to children (Mutran, 1985; this volume). Older blacks do not get more help from their children than older whites unless they are poor and undereducated. Here we are talking about differences in need, not cultural values. Finally, Kivett and Atkinson's (1984; this volume) study of the effect of number of children on care shows the somewhat complex relationship between number of children and helping, at least among transitional rural families. The point was made in the previous section that national data do not show any difference attributable to having more children available to help. Another complex relationship with helping is that of marital status, as can be seen in Cicirelli's (1983a) article in Part III of this volume.

When Arling and McAuley (1983) surveyed the kinds of help given by families, they found that almost all families gave in at least one area, whether this was shopping, housekeeping, or personal care. A Massachusetts study (Branch and Jette, 1983) of community-living people over 70 years of age found that 80% of them were entirely self-sufficient in basic tasks like bathing, eating, and grooming, but that most used help with housekeeping, transportation, food preparation, shopping, and business.

When caregiving is by somebody living in the same household—but not a spouse—the burden on the caregiver can be intensified. Although this kind of situation is relatively rare, as has been noted earlier—5% of men over 65 and 14% of women (U.S. Bureau of the Census, 1975)—it is proportionately more prevalent. Stoller (1985) examined the consequences of such situations by means of a path analysis of variables affecting the quality of the caregiver/care-recipient relationship. Not surprisingly, the more help needed by the older person, the more negative the effect on the relationship, although it was the degree of disruption of the household rather than the actual quantity of help required that mattered. Curiously, attempts by the older person to help with household chores tended to harm rather than improve the relationship. Stoller suggests that these attempts were perceived as meddling and disruptive. Help from other family members improved the relationship, though.

Notice that most caregivers tend to be women, although men are not unknown in this role. Sex differences in the kind of care need to be examined, but so far little research has been done. In fact, so far, most research on caregiving has used global and diffuse variables. Caregivers, for example, are rarely differentiated except by relationship category, like spouse or child, and sometimes by household composition or family structure. What we could use information on is variation in quality of care as well as in the relation between quality of care and preexisting interpersonal relationships. So far, most research focuses on the mere fact of care or the quantity of care and rarely on family dynamics, particularly in the extended family.

A term used frequently is "the family." This family, however, often boils down to one person. While it is true that this one person is rarely isolated from other family members altogether, she (usually) has the overwhelming brunt of the daily work. Other family members give advice, participate in major decisions, or provide relief; or conversely, disagree with decisions, intrude competing demands, or fight with each other and the primary caregiver. When someone who has hitherto been the family's prime caregiver needs care, many long-lasting interpersonal balances can be upset, and many early rivalries and hostilities can be revived (Hess and Waring, 1978).

Recent studies have started to look at the stress experienced by caregivers, what makes it worse and what lightens it. For example, Brody (1985), in her article reprinted in this volume, speaks of caregiving daughters as "women in the middle" whose help varies from none at all to "round the clock." When their mothers live in the same household as they, the women give eight times more help than when they live separately. And most daughters try hard to respond to their mothers' needs, giving up their own freedom and relaxation in the process. Noelker and Poulshock (1982) report that many of the caregivers they talked with had been caretaking for over 6 years, that 6 years was the average length of time. They also found that the mother–daughter bond in the caregiving situation was an intense and exclusionary one—similar to the spousal caregiving bond described in Part I. The old mothers in Brody's investigation said that they wanted the affection and emotional support only women could give. Their daughters were their chief confidants, but they didn't want to burden them and expected help only when they really needed it.

Kuypers and Bengtson (1983) suggest that chronic illness and impairment are accepted in most families as a normative transition. Thus, even though they require adaptation and change, they are not necessarily accompanied by family dysfunction. After all, only 20% of the families surveyed by Noelker and Poulshock were severely burdened by their caregiving, while 18% reported only minimal burden. Note that perceptions of minimal burden can be accompanied by severe deprivation on the part of caregivers (Hooyman, Gonyea, & Montgomery, 1985; this volume). The caregivers seem to accept as given that they would have little time for themselves, little personal freedom, diminished personal energy, and few vacations or other social and recreational experiences. Maybe expecting to be burdened, as Kuypers and Bengtson suggest, makes women caregivers diminish the importance of their own needs so that they do not feel it necessary to mention their strain. It is interesting that Hooyman and her colleagues found that when the funding agency eliminated help with chore services there was no significant reduction in the extent of caregiving by the families—probably just more strain on the caregivers.

Scharlach and Scharlach (1985) went beyond asking caregivers how burdened they felt. They set up an experiment to see what kind of help might alleviate strain, on both caregivers and recipients. Thirty-seven caregiving daughters were assigned randomly to one of two workshop conditions or put on a waiting list for 6 weeks as a control. In one condition, the goal was to make the women's expectations more realistic. In the other, the goal was to increase their sense of obligation. Those women who had reported the highest strain in the caregiving situation, incidentally, were also more "burdened" and reported the poorest relationships with their mothers. They were also likely to be working full-time and had no siblings to share their burden. Their mothers were the loneliest and most unhappy. Changing expectations did result in less strain and better relationships, while heightening the sense of obligations only improved the relationships. Although this is a small sample, the differential results are worth noting: that role strain goes together with poor relationships. There was no effect on the women in the control group, by the way.

A few recent studies have looked particularly at which aspects of caregiving are the most burdensome or stressful. Poulshock and Deimling (1984; this volume) found that it was not physical impairment of the person being cared for, nor even cognitive incapacity, but rather deviant behavior—personality changes leading to unresponsiveness or unpredictability—that caused the caregivers' depression. At the same time, living arrangements that had fewest inconveniences went together with greater life satisfaction on the part of caregivers (Mindel & Wright, 1982). Perhaps this is why, in intrahousehold caregiving, spouses reported less strain than nonspouses, most of whom are children who may not have been living with their parent before the latter needed care (Soldo & Mylliluoma, 1983).

Exchange theory would predict that the more care receivers contribute to the household work, the less psychological stress they and their caregivers would feel. Remember that Walker and Thompson (1983) found this not to have a significant effect for older mother–daughter dyads. One study did find that this made the care receivers feel better (Dunkle, 1983), but not the caregivers. Johnson and Catalano (1983; this volume) talk about the downward spiral of comfort on the part of the caregivers; they use the term "cascade effect." Psychological distancing from the older person seems to be a frequent coping strategy, as does physical distancing, both seeing the person less and caring less. Yet this may not fully succeed. Brody (1985; this volume) wonders if the persistence of guilt in the face of heavy care and sacrifice may not refer to the feeling by the children that they can never do enough to make up for what their parents did for them when they were small. A poignant effect

8

Family Ties of the Aged in Cross-Cultural Perspective*

Corinne N. Nydegger

Anthropologists in multidisciplinary settings are likely to be "difficult." They offer dissenting evidence to comfortable generalizations through what has come to be known as the anthropological veto ("but not in New Guinea"), they debunk cherished myths about human nature and social systems, and they insist upon turning things upside down by questioning those very things we all take for granted. This paper follows that tradition. The value of bringing a cross-cultural perspective to bear on family ties of the elderly is not simply in the cataloguing of *other* societies' practices but in placing *our own* practices into the larger context which is generated by such studies. In so doing, we are forced to look at our institutions in a different light and may recognize aspects of family ties that we have neglected or preferred not to see.

True to still another anthropological tradition, this discussion focuses on myths—but not the intriguing totemic or creation tales of exotic cultures. Instead, it examines some of our own myths—ours as Americans and as gerontologists. Mythological systems are not mere assemblages of charming folk tales and cautionary morality plays; they are powerful unconscious shapers. By crystallizing ideology, they channel our thinking, often along unrealistic paths, which seriously hampers the effort to understand the world we live in. First, then, it is necessary to emphasize that most of our cherished beliefs

*The Gerontologist, 23 (1) (1983), 26–32.

about the treatment of the aged at other times and in other places are proving to be illusions. Second, our tendency to idealize late life family ties should be balanced by admitting the reverse side of the coin—*unpleasant* aspects of familial relations.

THREE MYTHS

A particular set of beliefs colors our view of aging worldwide. One common romance is that of a past Golden Age from which modern man has fallen, most often as a consequence of his own sinful acts. The historian Laslett (1965) has called this the "world we have lost" syndrome. A similar notion—the Golden Isles—displaces this paradise in space rather than time. It is to be found across the ocean, over the mountains, somewhere just out of reach. Here, as in the Golden Age of the past, are people without stain, a society without strain, and all who dwell therein are content. Interwoven through the fabric of these myths is the tenacious thread of the "natural" Rosy Family, a nuclear family with intergenerational extension, that provides strength, love, and sustenance to all its members.

It is reasonable to regard such tales as embodiments of cultural ideals, as visions of the perfect society, or as cautionary tales which foretell the pernicious consequences of moral lapses. But we all realize that it is not reasonable to regard such myths as history or as anthropology. At one level, these myths are on a par with the fabulous beasts found on old maps or those peculiar medieval hominids—one-footed or three-headed—reputed to dwell in distant lands.

However, Golden Ages or Golden Isles and their Rosy Families are more than merely fabulous constructs of the unknown: they embody many of our deepest desires and fears, and they are pointers to the way we believe things ought to be. They are crystallizations of our cultural concept of the good life. These images, in turn, are important forces shaping our attitude toward the world as it is. Although we are seldom fully aware of it, we often use these fables as ideal standards against which we judge reality. Not surprisingly, reality consistently fails to measure up.

Our society has elaborated subsets of these myths about the aged. They are identical to the generic Golden Age and Golden Isles fables, but these idyllic states are specific to the elderly. Because they are widely accepted as fact, these myths warrant an unsentimental scrutiny.

THE GOLDEN AGE

In a skillful exegesis, Laslett (1976) identified the following content of the Golden Age myth: (1) "there has been a *before* and an *after*" in the social consequences of aging and the transition has been uniform and is associated with moderization; (2) in the past, the aged "were both entitled to respect and were universally accorded it"; (3) "the aged had specified and valued economic and emotional roles"; and (4) aged persons normally resided in multigenerational households and were cared for by their kinsmen (pp. 89–90). In recent decades, a number of important contributions have been made to gerontology by historians who have developed techniques to make ingenious use of archival data. The evidence they have marshaled demolishes these mythic postulates for the dominant American ethnic streams.

Take the linchpin concept of the "typical" multigenerational household. Actuarial statistics long ago indicated that, because of high mortality throughout the life cycle, fewer parents attained old age and fewer children survived to adulthood. Therefore, the multigenerational household should have been the unusual case. Now a number of historians have confirmed that, in the English and American past, the multigenerational family is the least frequent form recorded (Anderson, 1971; Demos, 1965, 1968, 1978; Greven, 1966; Kobrin, 1976; Laslett, 1969, 1976; Lockridge, 1966; Pryor, 1972; Stearns, 1977). Brody, in her presidential message (1979), is the latest in a line of researchers to stress the fact that only in modernized nations with increased longevity can the multigenerational family occur with any real frequency.

Further, such data as are available indicate that, at least in colonial and nineteenth-century America and nineteenth-century England, the preferred residence for older persons was not with their children (Demos, 1978; Laslett, 1976; Seward, 1978). Coresidence, although more common, apparently was determined, as it still is, by economic conditions (Chudakoff & Hareven, 1978; Dahlin, 1980; Fischer, 1978). There is little question that the elderly and their children in our historic past valued the independence of separate residence as much as we do and that many elderly persons were not cared for by their families if other alternatives, such as institutions or hired help, were available (Laslett, 1976). When support was required, then—as now—the primary burden fell on the children, who received little help from the community. Certainly the total social burden in the past was lighter than that assumed now by our society. But for the individual families then involved in caretaking, the burden must have been even heavier than is presently the case, although we must keep in mind that they were spared catastrophic medical bills, for the acutely ill died more quickly in those days.

Evidence concerning respect for specific old age roles and for age itself is very scanty, but the few indices available suggest little community respect in the absence of wealth or prestige. Rather, historical studies agree that the pervasive view in Western Europe disvalued old age and was not tolerant of old people (Hendricks & Hendricks, 1977–78; Kastenbaum & Ross, 1975; Stearns, 1981). Stearns points out that "We can grant immense problems for the elderly at the present time, but we do not have to assume that their lot has ever been strikingly good in Western society" (1979, p. 40). So what remains of this Golden Age for the aged in our past? Only the possibility of valued roles reserved for the aged, based on wishful thinking and a dearth of hard evidence to the contrary—although this is slowly being rectified.

In passing, we should look at another much-touted indictment of modernization: that geographic mobility on its current scale results in more widely dispersed and, hence, less effectively supportive families. In terms of actual mileage, this may be true enough. But in terms of dependable, rapid communication and transportation, quite the opposite is true (Litwak, 1960). We forget that children in the past *did* leave their homes in very large numbers and that a sailor on a clipper ship out of Boston might not be heard of for two years, that what was then considered the West was a month or more away, that just getting a message to a child in the next county was no simple matter of direct dialing.

Rapid mobilization of all family members is much likelier today than has ever been the case. Thus, although the bulk of daily care must still rest on the proximate child, distant children and other family members can be more actively involved in decisions and support than was possible in the past. If the extensive work of Shanas and her associates (e.g., Shanas & Streib, 1965; Shanas & Sussman, 1976; Shanas et al., 1968) has documented anything in modern Western societies, it is precisely this kind of involvement of children in the support of their aged kin.

THE GOLDEN ISLES

If the lot of the aged has been overrated in our own past, is it not different some other place? Can we find the Golden Isles of the aged in ancestor-worshipping China or in small-scale, integrated societies?

Now that we are accumulating a body of ethnographic material specifically focused on aging, our picture of such societies is no longer as simple as it once was. Two issues are involved that are often confounded: the first is the question of relative power of the aged; the second is that of respect for age *qua* age. As to power, there is plenty of evidence that the control of resources or knowledge by elders compels respect, as specified by Rosow (1962). However, such control is seldom concentrated in the hands of the elderly in the rapidly changing societies of today (Cowgill, 1974; Cowgill & Holmes, 1972; Palmore & Manton, 1974). The critical question, then, is the degree to which such control by elders was *generally* high prior to modernization.

This issue is not yet settled and for many societies the necessary data are irretrievable, but critical inspection of the least modernized societies suggests that many claims are indigenous versions of the Golden Age. For example, true gerontocracy is the exception and, where it occurs, is associated with spectacular displays of intergenerational and intrafamilial competition and conflict (Baker, 1979; Foner & Kertzer, 1978; Levine, 1965; Shelton, 1972; Spencer, 1965). For these groups, modernization does indeed mean a rapid loss of power for the elderly, but we lack sufficient data and accurate indices to compare age distributions of power across a broad range of non-modernized societies. We do know it varies enormously; thus, under some conditions, modernization may have little effect (Holmes, 1972) and may even increase the resource base of the elderly (Amoss, 1981). At present, sweeping generalizations about the relative power of the aged in premodernized societies must be regarded as suspect.

With respect to general esteem for age *qua* age, claims based on selective readings of scriptural or moralistic literature (particularly popular in regard to the Orient) can be rejected out of hand: *all* societies provide quotable homilies about filial piety and respect for one's elders. Unfortunately, despite patient effort, the incidental data in archival collections are generally inadequate, and studies based on them may be misleading (Maxwell & Silverman, 1970; Sheehan, 1976). They cannot avoid confounding (1) professed attitudes with actual treatment of the aged (Glascock & Feinman, 1980) and "ritual deference" with "realistic appraisal" (Lipman, 1970), (2) respect for the aged per se with respect for the few powerful old, and (3) esteem of the aged in general with esteem for one's own aged kin (Nydegger, 1981). Simmons (1945), in the first cross-cultural study of aging, demonstrated a sensitivity to these issues wanting in many of his successors.

As early as 1964, Harlan drew attention to discrepancies between idealized reports of respect for old age and observed behavior, and Lipman (1970) pointed out that ritualistic deference was devoid of meaning. As anthropologists became more involved in gerontology, increasingly sophisticated ethnographies substantiated these warnings and lead us to conclude that the claim of other societies' general respect for the aged is yet another example of the "world we have lost" syndrome. They document again and again a point made by Simmons (1945): in no society do the aged constitute a homogeneous group. In all societies we must specify precisely which aged we are speaking of: the ill or the healthy, the chronologically ancient or only the generationally elder, male heads of households or family-less widows, wise leaders or village failures. The research by anthropological gerontologists proves that generalizations about "esteem of the aged" are generally as superficial and just plain wrong in other societies as in our own.

SOURCES OF VARIABILITY

We can hazard a few suggestions concerning sources of variability in the status of elderly persons within and among societies:

(1) In most cases, control of resources is incorrectly attributed to the aged as a group or age grade; rather, it is differentially exercised by various older individuals. All groups have members who are not respected and have little status or power at any age. Even in true age-grade societies, wherein entire age sets advance through hierarchical stages, not all age-peers are equal, and individuals compete for position at each stage (Baxter & Almagor, 1978).

(2) Where the elderly accumulate power, they do command respect, but it is due to their power, not their age (Press & McKool, 1972). The sole exception is the special case wherein increasing age augments supernatural power simply because one moves closer to its source (Lee & DeVore, 1968).

(3) We must draw a sharp distinction between reports of old individuals in relatively low-percentage elderly populations where only the sturdy survive and reports of age-grades in high-percentage elderly populations where many frail elderly survive (Isaacs, et al., 1972). They involve significantly different conditions of aging.

(4) At the individual level, in all societies, including our own, the ability to function is critical for the position of the elderly (Glascock & Feinman, 1980). Nowhere is decrepitude valued.

(5) The elderly sometimes contribute substantially to the economic well-being of the group, but the only generic role assigned to the aged is that of old women's babysitting and kitchen help. Although male ethnographers have assumed that this is a fulfilling role, nowhere does it have high social status.

(6) Cultural values about aging vary, and they make a difference in people's acceptance of and accommodation to aging processes in themselves and their kin (e.g., Clark & Anderson, 1967; Holmes, 1972; Osako, 1979).

(7) The final responsibility for the aged and for decisions about their fate invariably rests with their closest kin, typically children. Usually this does mean support, but even in societies where the aged are killed when they can no longer function, the sons must make the judgment and carry it out—it is one of their filial duties (Glascock & Feinman, 1980). However, sizable percentages of elderly individuals have no surviving children and have only marginal and unenforceable claims on more distant relatives. Without personal resources and in the absence of institutionalized aid, their position is generally wretched even in societies professing reverence for the aged (Delaney, 1981). With few exceptions, charity really does begin at home—and ends there.

THE "NATURAL" NUCLEAR FAMILY

Integrated with the myths of golden time and place is a persistent set of beliefs about families that warrant detailed attention. The first is the conviction that the nuclear family is strong "naturally" (which seems to mean in a "state of nature"—a myth in its own right) but that modernization has stripped this natural unit of its inherent functions.

For most of us, the term "family" conjures up our type, the separate nuclear family of a married couple with their children, which may be extended to include the parents of the couple; but this is by no means a universal arrangement. For cross-cultural use, "family" is an ambiguous term with hazy boundaries because it refers to the intersection of the two basic principles of social organization: kinship and residence. Despite their apparent simplicity, humankind has elaborated each of these principles with ingenuity; combining the two yields still more diversity. Although anthropologists take care to keep these principles analytically distinct, any discussion of families necessarily involves both.

Because the term "family" is altogether too imprecise for cross-cultural use, Fortes (1949) and Goody (1958) have encouraged the use of "domestic group," thus focusing specifically on the residential unit. At any given time, several types of family (e.g., extended matrilocal, nuclear, etc.) can be identified in most communities. In longitudinal perspective, these different "types" often represent different residential phases of a few family forms as they evolve over the life course. From this perspective, "residence patterns are the crystallizations, at a given time, of the developmental process" (Fortes, 1958, p. 3).

Parenthetically, this approach could be used to advantage in studies of our own society, for taking the nuclear family as the "natural" unit presses us to treat any other pattern as an aberration. The result is a Ptolemaic complexity of forms. If we begin instead with the distribution of domestic groups, we then can determine which types represent developmental phases and which are genuinely divergent. Thus, the co-residence of a widow and her sibling need not be startlingly misrepresented as a "multigenerational family" (Mindel, 1979); rather, it is one of a number of domestic groups which is now being documented as a common form in late life. This approach also may clarify those situations where domestic groups do not fit our dominant nuclear family pattern, as in many ethnic minorities and in the complex kingroupings now being produced by multiple remarriages (Furstenberg, 1980).

The nuclear family is the most widespread unit in marital terms, although it does not universally function as such (Fortes, 1949; Mair, 1965; Minturn & Hitchcock, 1966). Generally it is too small to be maximally efficient in other respects. Thus, the basic unit of social organization in most societies is the localized kin group, made up of a number of closely related, extended families. The basic residential unit generally includes a number of these kin groups, plus other more distantly related families.

In these settings, the typical nuclear family is not the independent unit we think of. Often such nuclear units are firmly embedded in the local kin group and their autonomy is quite limited. Autonomy varies, of course, with a host of factors such as type of economy, control of resources, residential arrangements, and marriage patterns, but it is far less than we generally take for granted. For example, major decisions are generally in the hands of kin group heads. They include not only questions of subsistence activities and social control but issues we regard as personal. For example, decisions about children's futures or transition events such as puberty rituals and marriage are undertaken only with their approval. But there are few truly personal matters because the individual is too interwoven into the social fabric of the group. The nuclear unit can be so completely submerged in the larger group that even its survival as a unit is of no great moment, and divorce is commonplace.

In short, the kin group guarantees its members continuity, security, and support throughout life and often beyond. The price is individual subordination to the group and limited autonomy of the nuclear family. The goal of socialization practices in such societies is to achieve the closest possible identification of self with the group (Benedict, 1946; Dyk, 1938; Levine, 1969, 1973; Nydegger & Nydegger, 1966; B. Whiting, 1963; J. Whiting, 1941). The nuclear family, then, cannot be said to be "naturally" strong.

As to its presumed loss of functions due to modernization, a better argument can be made that the once-strong kin group, not the dependent nuclear family, has lost the most. Indeed, in those situations wherein government can be depended upon to perform many of the kin group's functions, modernization is likely to increase the nuclear family's autonomy and its control over its own members. For example, among the Navajo of the American Southwest, the first consequence of urbanization was to strengthen nuclear family bonds—at the expense of the larger kin group (Nydegger, 1970; Sasaki, 1960). Newly independent nuclear families cherish their fresh autonomy. Those who romanticize the larger kin group do so because they never experienced the heavy hand of its authority.

Where kin groups dominate, the aged are favored since control traditionally is exercised by those who are mature and often old. This is one source of the Golden Isles notion, but it remains largely mythic, for such predominance is by no means universal. Even where the aged predominate, degree of control varies widely. Most importantly, as pointed out earlier, not all leaders are old and not all old men are leaders. *De jure* authority rests in the hands of the old as a group only in a small number of age-grade societies (Coult & Habenstein, 1965; Eisenstadt, 1956; Stewart, 1977) but de facto authority is *always* limited to a few regardless of age (Baxter & Almagor, 1978). Control by an elite of elderly men cannot be equated with high status for the elderly.

Do historical and anthropological studies, and the promise of more in the future, signal the end of the widespread myths of golden times and places for the aged? No, not for some time to come. These myths express what we feel ought to have been; because they crystallize our desires and anxieties, we want to believe them. We are not alone in this. Everywhere, in all periods, the claim is made that the old days were better, that the world is going to hell. This complaint is easy to understand: social change is often unsettling, and in nostalgic retrospect the past is simplified and regularized and its ambiguities are resolved. Past miseries cannot pierce us as do immediate misfortunes, and personal recollections tend to be gently washed in a rosy tint (Brim & Ryff, 1980; Field, 1979; Gigy, 1978; Yarrow et al., 1970). Thus, it is all too easy to project current wishes onto the past. Dull facts cannot effectively compete, so such myths have a remarkable lease on life.

THE NATURE OF FAMILY TIES

Americans also have established a set of Norman Rockwell idealizations about family ties, including some specific to the aged. Although they are not altogether fabulous, they are part-truths—the "good" part—and they share the golden glow of the myths just discussed. They portray the Rosy or Pollyanna family, but even a cursory glance at the ethnographic literature reveals the less photogenic side of family ties.

First, Americans have a culturally unique view of kinship as a set of personal relationships rather than formal relations (Schneider, 1968). In line with this perspective, and impelled by the best of motives, gerontologists have solidly documented supportive kin behavior and positive bonds, speaking most often of meeting needs and providing emotional support—the spectrum of tender, loving care. Acrimony is seldom mentioned; rather, they speak more blandly of children's lack of support, of not understanding, and occasionally of an older person being "difficult." The older parent, generally a mother, tends to be portrayed as a colorless, passive victim of her failing health and social disregard, whose only resource is, in Dowd's chilling phrase, "the humble capacity to comply" (1975, p. 587) with her children's wishes.

Anthropologists, on the other hand, tend to focus on the interlocking and competing sets of rights and obligations which make up adult kin-group life. They have been less concerned with qualities of relationships as such unless they reflect significant features of the kinship structure. In anthropological discussions, controls and strategies figure prominently, along with competition and hostility: a kind of kin cold war. Strife and antagonism are given their due.

It would be beneficial if we looked at each other's questions more often. Anthropological accounts undoubtedly have been guilty of overemphasizing the problems of formal family structures and of neglecting affectional ties and qualitative variation in relations among kin. Gerontologists have made the opposite error of treating conflicts induced by kin structures as individual psychological problems and of neglecting the way kin structures shape family ties and are used by the aged.

For example, family statuses impose obligations and confer rights on their members everywhere. These family systems can be maintained in two ways: (1) developing mechanisms of control which will ensure that obligations generally will be met, or (2) relying on the affection, goodwill, and enlightened self-interest of their members. No society, including our own, relies solely on the latter, although we come close to this. It is particularly dangerous for the aged to do so because their contribution to family welfare is likely to be declining and they may constitute a very real burden on resources or caretaking capacity. Structurally, they become dependent charity cases, as exchange theorists have pointed out. Consequently, they have a vested interest in the social control of obligations (Lozier & Althouse, 1974).

Mechanisms used by the aged to ensure support vary widely in number and effectiveness from society to society. They include threat by witchcraft or appeal to supernatural agencies, by rousing public opinion through gossip and public complaint, or through legal action where that is possible. At the other extreme, guilt is a common lever to pry a little extra from kin, and women favor this technique with children, especially sons. It is often the only tool they have at their disposal but, if initiated early in the child's life, it can be powerful when needed in old age. The new gerontological ethnographies are particularly rich in accounts of complex manipulative programs undertaken by women to ensure strong positions in old age (e.g., Cool & McCabe, 1981; Kerns, 1980; Wolf, 1972).

The major institutionalized mechanism, and the surest, is inheritance. Much of the strength of kinship lies in the fact that, everywhere, kinship is the predominant conduit of inheritance. It may amount to only a small cash bequest or a few personal belongings, but in most groups it includes permanent status advantages and often the very resources for survival. The consequences of inheritance patterns, for both the individual and the group, cannot be overestimated. As they play themselves out in the short and long term, they can produce fragmentation of land holdings or consolidation of property; they can create dramatic status differentials among siblings; they may determine when one is considered adult and if and when one marries. They are the primary social determinant of the economics of old age.

Individuals vary as to how strongly they cling to active control in old age. In pre-modernized societies, most remain active, dying well before physical disability is pronounced. Where the aged do relinquish authority or ownership of property, inheritance is their primary means of control over future resources and care (Nason, 1981; Streib, 1972). For example, although inheritance is essentially asymmetrical, promises of future support commonly are built explicitly into the conditions of property transfer, converting the transaction into an exchange. Threats of future disinheritance can be manipulated, often with a skill that amounts to tyranny.

The uncritical presumption has been that the use of this mechanism is limited for most Americans and that modern inheritance typically provides only an education and a small cash start in life. Parents, as good consumers, are expected to use up their savings so that estates after death will be small. (The impact of disinheritance, however, as Rosenfeld (1979) points out, even when largely symbolic, should not be underestimated.) This picture is exaggerated. For many Americans, inheritance remains a viable method of control; among some farmers, land is still "the whip" (Salamon & Lockhart, 1980). And why have we failed to study our wealthy aged, who have sizable estates to distribute? Their families are likely to have little in common with the customary gerontological picture. At the very least, we could judge to what extent the wealthy old curmudgeon, aware of his power and using it to control his family, is a literary invention or a fact of American family life.

The possibilities of control inherent in different kinship structures and the ways in which they are used at various stages of life are among the major determinants of the complex, evolving nature of lifelong family ties. Mutual recrimination, tyranny and manipulation, rejection and hate are certainly not unknown in family life, as attested to by reams of clinical literature. Nor does this picture change simply because the family members grow older; indeed, it is often exacerbated (Calkins, 1972; Cath, 1972; Isaacs et al., 1972; Robinson & Thurnher, 1979; Sainsbury & DeAlarcon, 1970; Savitsky & Sharkey, 1972; Stein, 1978). But negative relations are not necessarily expressions of individual pathology or personality characteristics; some kin-residence structures virtually guarantee difficult relations among family members.

This paper has deliberately emphasized the reverse side of our idealizations. In simple justice it must be pointed out that loving, supportive families can be found in all societies. So can their opposites. We must accept these negative aspects as natural outcomes and attempt to pinpoint those structural features that encourage conflict before we can fully understand the aged and their family ties. Especially in light of the current movement to push our aged into the bosom of the family, we should be able to assess realistically the cost to parents and to children of trying to live out a myth.

REFERENCES

Amoss, P. Religious participation as a route to prestige for the elderly. In C. Fry (Ed.), *Dimensions: Aging, culture, and health.* Bergin, Brooklyn, 1981.

Anderson, M. *Family structure in nineteenth-century Lancashire.* Cambridge University Press, New York, 1971.

Baker, H. *Chinese family and kinship.* Columbia University Press, New York, 1979.

Baxter, P., & Almagor, U. (Eds.) *Age, generation and time: Some features of East African age organizations.* Hurst & Co., London, 1978.

Benedict, R. *The chrysanthemum and the sword.* Houghton Mifflin, Boston, 1946.

Brim, O., & Ryff, C. On the properties of life events. In P. Baltes & O. Brim (Eds.), *Life-span development and behavior,* Vol. 3. Academic Press, New York, 1980.

Brody, E. Message from the president. *The Gerontologist,* 1979, *19,* 514–515.

Calkins, K. Shouldering a burden. *Omega,* 1972, *3,* 23–36.

Cath, S. The institutionalization of a parent—a nadir of life. *Journal of Geriatric Psychiatry,* 1972, *5,* 25–46.

Chudakoff, H., & Hareven, T. Family transitions into old age. In T. Hareven (Ed.), *Transitions: The family and the life course in historical perspective.* Academic Press, New York, 1978.

Clark, M., & Anderson, B. *Culture and aging.* Charles C Thomas, Springfield, IL, 1967.

Cool, L., & McCabe, J. The "Scheming Hag" and the "Dear Old Thing." In J. Sokolovsky (Ed.), *Growing older in different societies.* Wadsworth Press, New York, 1981.

Coult, A. D., & Habenstein, R. *Cross-tabulations of Murdock's world ethnographic sample.* University of Missouri Press, Columbia, MO, 1965.

Cowgill, D. Aging and modernization: a revision of the theory. In J. Gubrium (Ed.), *Late life: Communities and environmental policy.* Charles C Thomas, Springfield, IL, 1974.

Cowgill, D., & Holmes, L. (Eds.) *Aging and modernization.* Appleton-Century-Crofts, New York, 1972.

Dahlin, M. Perspectives on the family life of the elderly in 1900. *The Gerontologist,* 1980, *20,* 99–107.

Delaney, B. Is Uncle Sam insane? Pride, humor, and clique formation in a northern Thai home for the elderly. *International Journal of Aging and Human Development*, 1981, *13*, 137–150.

Demos, J. Notes on life in Plymouth Colony. *William and Mary Quarterly*, 1965, *22*, 264–286.

Demos, J. Families in colonial Bristol, Rhode Island: An exercise in historical demography. *William and Mary Quarterly*, 1968, *25*, 40–57.

Demos, J. Old age in early New England. In J. Demos & S. Boocock (Eds.), *Turning points: Historical and sociological essays on the family. American Journal of Sociology*, supplement to Vol. 84. University of Chicago Press, Chicago, 1978.

Dowd, J. Aging as exchange: A preface to theory. *Journal of Gerontology*, 1975, *30*, 584–594.

Dyk, W. (Ed.) *Son of Old Man Hat: A Navaho autobiography*. Harcourt Brace, New York, 1938.

Eisenstadt, S. N. *From generation to generation*. Free Press, New York, 1956.

Field, D. Retrospective reports of personal events in the lives of elderly people. Unpublished paper presented at the meeting of the International Society for the Study of Behavioral Development, Stockholm, 1979.

Fischer, D. H. *Growing old in America*. Oxford University Press, New York, 1978.

Foner, A., & Kertzer, D. Transitions over the life course: Lessons from age-set societies. *American Journal of Sociology*, 1978, *83*, 1081–1104.

Fortes, M. Time and social structure. In M. Fortes (Ed.), *Social structure*. Oxford University Press, Oxford, England, 1949.

Fortes, M. Introduction. In J. Goody (Ed.), *The developmental cycle in domestic groups*. Cambridge University Press, Cambridge, England, 1958.

Furstenberg, F., Jr. Reflections on remarriage. *Journal of Family Issues*, 1980, *1*, 443–453.

Gigy, L. Reconstruction of the personal past: differences in older women. Unpublished paper presented at the 31st Annual Scientific Meeting of the Gerontological Society, Dallas, 1978.

Glascock, T., & Feinman, S. A holocultural analysis of old age. *Comparative Social Research*, 1980, *3*.

Goody, J. (Ed.) *The developmental cycle in domestic groups*. Cambridge University Press, Cambridge, England, 1958.

Greven, P. J. Family structure in seventeenth-century Andover, Massachusetts. *William and Mary Quarterly*, 1966, *23*, 234–356.

Harlan, W. Social status of the aged in three Indian villages. *Vita Humana*, 1964, *7*, 239–252.

Hendricks, J., & Hendricks, C. The age-old question of old age: Was it really so much better back when? *International Journal of Aging and Human Development*, 1977–78, *8*, 139–154.

Holmes, L. The role and status of the aged in changing Samoa. In D. Cowgill & L. Holmes (Eds.), *Aging and modernization*. Appleton-Century-Crofts, New York, 1972.

Isaacs, B., Livingstone, T., & Neville, Y. *Survival of the unfittest*. Routledge & Kegan Paul, London, 1972.

Kastenbaum, R., & Ross, B. Historical perspectives on care. In J. G. Howell's (Ed.), *Modern perspectives in the psychiatry of old age*. Brunner/Mazel, New York, 1975.

Kerns, V. Aging and mutual support relations among the black Carib. In C. Fry (Ed.), *Aging in culture and society*. Bergin, Brooklyn, 1980.

Kobrin, F. The fall in household size and the rise of the primary individual in the United States. *Demography*, 1976, *13*, 127–138.

Laslett, P. *The world we have lost*. Methuen, London, 1965.

Laslett, P. Size and structure of the household in England over three centuries. *Population Studies*, 1969, *23*, 199–224.

Laslett, P. Societal development and aging. In R. Binstock & E. Shanas (Eds.), *Handbook of aging and the social sciences*. Van Nostrand, New York, 1976.

Lee, R., & DeVore, I. *Man the hunter*. Aldine, Chicago, 1968.

Levine, R. Intergenerational tensions and extended family structures in Africa. In E. Shanas & G. Streib (Eds.), *Social structure and the family: Generational relations*. Prentice-Hall, Englewood Cliffs, NJ, 1965.

Levine, R. Culture, personality, and socialization: An evolutionary view. In D. Goslin (Ed.), *Handbook of socialization theory and research*. Rand McNally, Chicago, 1969.

Levine, R. *Culture, behavior and personality*. Aldine, Chicago, 1973.

Lipman, A. Prestige of the aged in Portugal. *International Journal of Aging and Human Development*, 1970, *1*, 127–136.

Litwak, E. Geographic mobility and extended family cohesion. *American Sociological Review*, 1960, *25*, 385–394.

Lockridge, K. A. The population of Dedham, Massachusetts, 1636–1736. *Economic History Review*, 1966, *19*, 318–344.

Lozier, J., & Althouse, R. Social enforcement of behavior toward elders in an Appalachian mountain settlement. *The Gerontologist*, 1974, *14*, 69–80.

Mair, L. *An introduction to social anthropology*. Oxford University Press, Oxford, England, 1965.

Maxwell, R., & Silverman, P. Information and esteem: Cultural considerations in the treatment of the aged. *International Journal of Aging and Human Development*, 1970, *1*, 361–392.

Mindel, C. Multigenerational family households: Recent trends and implications for the future. *The Gerontologist*, 1979, *19*, 456–463.

Minturn, L., & Hitchcock, J. *The Rajputs of Khalapur, India*. Wiley, New York, 1966.

Nason, J. Respected elder or old person: Aging in a Micronesian community. In P. Amoss & S. Harrell (Eds.), *Other ways of growing old*. Stanford University Press, Stanford, CA, 1981.

Nydegger, C. Effects of structural changes on Navajo familial roles. Unpublished master's thesis, Cornell University, Ithaca, NY, 1970.

Nydegger, C. Gerontology and anthropology: Challenge and opportunity. In C. Fry (Ed.), *Dimensions: Aging, culture, and health*. Bergin, Brooklyn, 1981.

Nydegger, W., & Nydegger, C. *Tarong, an Ilocos barrio in the Philippines.* Wiley, New York, 1966.

Osako, M. Aging and the family among Japanese Americans. *The Gerontologist,* 1979, *19,* 448–455.

Palmore, E., & Manton, K. Modernization and status of the aged: International correlations. *Journal of Gerontology,* 1974, *29,* 205–210.

Press, I., & McKool, M., Jr. Social structure and status of the aged. *International Journal of Aging and Human Development,* 1972, *3,* 297–306.

Pryor, E. T., Jr. Rhode Island family structure: 1815 and 1960. In P. Laslett & R. Wall (Eds.), *Household and family in past time.* Cambridge University Press, Cambridge, England, 1972.

Robinson, B., & Thurnher, M. Taking care of aged parents: A family cycle transition. *The Gerontologist,* 1979, *19,* 586–593.

Rosenfeld, J. P. *The legacy of aging: Inheritance and disinheritance in social perspective.* Ablex Publishers, Norwood, NJ, 1979.

Rosow, I. Old age: One moral dilemma of an affluent society. *The Gerontologist,* 1962, *2,* 182–191.

Sainsbury, P., & DeAlarcon, J. The effects of community care on the family of the geriatric patient. *Journal of Geriatric Psychiatry,* 1970, *4,* 23–41.

Salamon, S., & Lockhart, V. Land ownership and the position of elderly in farm families. *Human Organization,* 1980, *39,* 324–331.

Sasaki, T. *Fruitland, New Mexico: A Navaho community in transition.* Cornell University Press, Ithaca, NY, 1960.

Savitsky, E., & Sharkey, H. Study of family interaction in the aged. *Journal of Geriatric Psychiatry,* 1972, *5,* 3–19.

Schneider, D. *American kinship: A cultural account.* Prentice-Hall, Englewood Cliffs, NJ, 1968.

Seward, R. *The American family: A demographic history.* Sage Library of Social Research, Vol. 70. Sage, Beverly Hills, CA, 1978.

Shanas, E., & Streib, G. (Eds.) *Social structure of the family: Generational relations.* Prentice-Hall, Englewood Cliffs, NJ, 1965.

Shanas, E., & Sussman, M. (Eds.) *Older people, family, and bureaucracy.* Duke University Press, Durham, NC, 1976.

Shanas, E., Townsend, P., Wedderburn, D., Friis, H., Mihoj, P., & Stehouwer, J. *Old people in three industrial societies.* Atherton, New York, 1968.

Sheehan, T. Senior esteem as a factor of socioeconomic complexity. *The Gerontologist,* 1976, *16,* 433–440.

Shelton, A. The aged and eldership among the Igbo. In D. Cowgill & L. Holmes (Eds.), *Aging and modernization.* Appleton-Century-Crofts, New York, 1972.

Simmons, L. *The role of the aged in primitive society.* Yale University Press, New Haven, CT, 1945.

Spencer, P. *The Samburu: A study of gerontocracy in a nomadic tribe.* University of California Press, Berkeley, 1965.

Stearns, P. *Old age in European society.* Holmes & Meier, New York, 1977.

Stearns, P. The evolution of traditional culture toward aging. In J. Hendricks & C. Hendricks (Eds.), *Dimensions of aging*. Winthrop, Cambridge, MA, 1979.

Stearns, P. The modernization of old age in France: Approaches through history. *International Journal of Aging and Human Development*, 1981, *13*, 297–315.

Stein, H. Aging and death among Slovak-Americans. *Journal of Psychological Anthropology*, 1978, *1*, 297–320.

Stewart, F. H. *Fundamentals of age-group systems*. Academic Press, New York, 1977.

Streib, G. Old age in Ireland. In D. Cowgill & L. Holmes (Eds.), *Aging and modernization*. Appleton-Century-Crofts, New York, 1972.

Whiting, B. (Ed.) *Six cultures: Studies of child rearing*. Wiley, New York, 1963.

Whiting, J. W. M. *Becoming a Kwoma*. Yale University Press, New Haven, CT, 1941.

Wolf, M. *Women and family in rural Taiwan*. Stanford University Press, Stanford, CA, 1972.

Yarrow, M., Campbell, J., & Burton, R. Recollections of childhood: A study of the retrospective method. Society for Research in Child Development, Washington, DC, Monograph No. 35, 1970.

9

The Feasibility of Public Payments for Family Caregiving*

Greg Arling
William J. McAuley

This chapter examines the feasibility of public financial payments as one method of encouraging or maintaining family support in long-term care of the impaired elderly. The feasibility of financial payments depends on several criteria: 1) impairment and long-term care can be operationally defined; 2) families are capable of and willing to provide care; 3) financial considerations are an important, if not the major, factor, in the family's decision to care for an impaired older person; and 4) financial assistance can be cost-effective in either avoiding or delaying more expensive forms of care, such as nursing home care.

This study began as a response to several legislative initiatives in the Virginia General Assembly. The state pays family members as service providers under contract through the state Department of Welfare. This policy was to be evaluated to determine its impact on the family. Furthermore, the General Assembly was considering the

The Gerontologist, 23 (3)(1983), 300–306.

Data used in this paper were derived from the *Statewide Survey of Older Virginians*, funded by the Virginia Department of Welfare and the Virginia office on Aging, and the *Study of the Virginia Nursing Home Pre-Admission Screening Program*, supported by the Administration on Aging, Grant No. 90-AR-2109101. The authors wish to express their appreciation for review and comments by Dr. Elizabeth Harkins, Project Director for the Study of the Virginia Nursing Home Pre-Admission Program.

possibility of expanding the current income tax deduction for adult dependent care, which parallels the federal income tax credit for dependent care.

At least two states, Idaho and Oregon, have enacted tax provisions for the care of older adults, and several other states were considering adoption of similar provisions by the end of 1981 (Virginia Department of Taxation, 1981). Maryland has had a small demonstration project to determine the feasibility of direct payments to families (Whitfield & Krompholz, 1981). Given the increasing interest in providing public payments for family caregiving to the elderly, attention should be directed to the feasibility and potential impact of such policies.

The data used for this paper are drawn from a statewide survey of the non-institutionalized older population (age 60+) and a specialized study of older people who have applied and been recommended for nursing home care. The studies were not explicitly designed to evaluate the impact of financial payments. Therefore, our findings are used to describe the characteristics of older people and caregivers, the forms of long-term care provided, and the nature of economic factors in the process of nursing home application. We will not deal directly with financial payments as a motivation for caregiving, the cost differential between financial payments and other public forms of support, or the quality of care provided by families in comparison to institutions or professional services.

LITERATURE REVIEW

Families are the major source of long-term care for the impaired elderly in the home. In a national survey Shanas (1979) found that at least as many, and possibly twice as many, sick and frail elderly are living in the community as in nursing homes. The vast majority are either living in the homes of family members or they are receiving regular visits and assistance such as housework, meal preparation, or personal care from family members. The U.S. General Accounting Office (1977) reports from a study of older people in Cleveland, Ohio, that family and friends provide over 90% of assistance with personal care, over 75% of homemaker assistance, and over 80% of transportation for older people needing these forms of help. Medical services are the only category of assistance where agencies or professionals are the majority of providers.

There is little doubt that available family care is a major factor in the decision to seek institutionalization. When impaired old people live alone, when family caregiving is unavailable, or when family members cannot give enough assistance, the likelihood of institutionalization is much greater (Brody et al., 1978; Greenberg & Ginn, 1979; Palmore, 1976; Townsend, 1965; Vicente et al., 1979; Wan & Weissert, 1981).

The role of financial factors in family caregiving has been studied primarily through attitudinal surveys. Sussman (1979) studied the expressed willingness of individuals to care for older people under a variety of hypothetical circumstances. He found that 80% of the people responding to surveys in Cleveland, Ohio, and Winston-Salem, North Carolina, would be willing to assume responsibility for an older person in at least a minimal way. Over 90% of those who would assume responsibility would be willing to participate in a government program to support caregiving. The respondents indicated that a monthly check of $200 to $400 would be the preferred form of support; medical care, tax credits, government loans, and social services were less preferred public sources of support.

The findings from Sussman's study should be highly qualified. He surveyed only a small number of people who were actually providing care for an older person; he used scenarios depicting different situations for care instead of real situations facing the respondents; and he found that older people, who might have the most realistic view of caregiving requirements, showed the least willingness to provide care and to participate in a governmental program. Without a clear idea of the specific requirements of caregiving and some estimate of the costs of care, it is unlikely that the respondents could make realistic choices regarding their capacity to provide care or the types of support that they might need from governmental programs.

Cantor (1980) studied participants in a home-care program in New York City. She concluded that financial considerations are not the primary motivating factors for family caregivers. Adult children and other family members in her study contributed some financial assistance, but they did not necessarily accept complete or even major financial responsibility. They felt that the government should provide income support and insurance for health care such as Social Security, Medicaid, and Medicare. They attributed their problems in caregiving to such factors as worry about the health of the older person, insufficient help from others, their emotional strain and, lastly, their financial situation. Only about one-third reported financial strain.

Cicirelli (1980) conducted a survey of family caregivers in a small midwestern city. He also discovered that financial factors were less likely to be a source of strain compared to emotional or physical exhaustion, the complaints of the impaired older person, and the amount of time that must be devoted to care.

Whitfield and Krompholz (1981) evaluated a family support demonstration program for families in Maryland. Sixty families were subsidized with monthly payments averaging $1,824 a year. Fifty-nine families receiving no payments but with older family members who had similar levels of disability, age, sex and caregiving arrangements, were used as a comparison sample. Although the public cost of care for the group receiving financial payments was considerably less than the cost of potential nursing home care, the groups did not differ significantly in rate of institutionalization. The families expressed a need for and received counseling and respite care in addition to financial payments. After receiving payments for one year, families reported some increase in their ability to cope and to give care. They were able to purchase medical appliances and supplies, and they obtained respite or nursing services. Although Whitfield and Kromphloz found that the comparison group had a slightly higher rate of mortality, they did not report either improvement or decline in the older person's quality of life with regard to functional status and morale.

In summary, previous research indicates a high level of informal caregiving for the impaired elderly in the community, and this informal support seems to delay or avoid institutionalization. Financial strain is generally not reported as a major factor in the caregiving situation. The few research projects that have been conducted have involved relatively small samples without carefully controlled experimental conditions. Only one study has used a quasi-experimental design (Whitfield & Krompholz, 1981), and this project has failed to demonstrate that financial payments reduce nursing home admissions or avoid other costly forms of care.

DATA SOURCES

Two studies were utilized for this paper. The first was the Statewide Survey of Older Virginians (SSOV), a household survey of 2,146 older people (age 60+) conducted in 1979. The survey was based upon a state-level area probability sample of non-institutionalized older people. The response rate for the study was 87% of those households screened and identified as having a resident 60 years of age or older. The study used the OARS multidimensional functional assessment instrument (Duke University Center for the Study of Aging and Human Development, 1978). The demographic characteristics of the sample corresponded very closely to the census characteristics of Virginia's older population. The sample was statistically weighted to correct for potential sampling bias. The OARS interviewer rating scales were used to categorize a subsample of approximately 10% of the respondents who were moderately to totally impaired in activities of daily living (ADL). They required assistance with a range of daily living tasks such as meal preparation, housekeeping, personal care, and other forms of assistance that could lead to institutionalization if care were not provided in the home.

The second source of data for this paper was the Study of the Virginia Nursing Home Pre-Admission Screening Program (PASS). The program screens nursing home applicants who are community residents at the point of application and who are receiving Medicaid or would be eligible for Medicaid within 90 days of nursing home admission. Local health department screening committees either recommend nursing home placement or recommend against Medicaid coverage for nursing home care. Those applicants who are not admitted to nursing homes are referred to community and in-home services, or they find some alternative placement such as an adult home.

The PASS study began in 1980 with a survey of 399 older people who were either nursing home applicants or at risk for institutionalization and a significant other (primary caregiver or closely related person) for most of these respondents. In this paper we are using data from a subsample of 113 nursing home applicants. Ninety-five were living in their homes or the homes of family members at the point of application, and 18 were residing in group homes or living with non-related persons. All were screened for admission and recommended for placement in a nursing home. Most were interviewed prior to nursing home admission, and in all cases the interview questions refer to the period of time prior to nursing home admission. The applicants were either Medicaid eligible or potentially eligible within 90 days of admission. The survey contained questions regarding physical and mental status, service use, and reasons for seeking nursing home admission. Data from 108 significant others were also used for this paper. Five older people either had no significant other or identified a significant other who could not be located.

The PASS sample is not representative of all nursing home applicants because many people apply directly from hospitals or do not qualify for Medicaid within 90 days of nursing home admission. However, the sample was drawn through random procedures from different regions in the state. It should be representative of the category of nursing home applicants who are most likely to receive public support for nursing home care, who will enter directly from a home setting, and who have been screened or evaluated to determine their physical or mental needs.

The findings from these studies are presented separately in order to examine the nature of caregiving for the SSOV subsample of community elderly with moderate to total impairment in activities of daily living, and the PASS sample of impaired older people who applied and were recommended for nursing home care. The former sample represents the broad range of impaired older people who could potentially receive financial assistance from public programs. The latter sample represents a much smaller population that was about to receive the full range of care in a nursing home at public expense. The characteristics of the sample are compared, and their reasons for nursing home application are examined to determine the role of financial factors in the decision-making process.

AVAILABILITY OF ASSISTANCE FROM FAMILY AND OTHER INFORMAL SOURCES

Among the SSOV subsample who were moderately to totally impaired in activities of daily living ($n = 219$), 95% had at least one major helper who regularly assisted with shopping, housekeeping, personal care, or other forms of care. Forty-four percent had two or more helpers. The spouse was the primary helper for married respondents, and an adult child or other family member was the primary helper for unmarried respondents. Only 11% of the married and 14% of the unmarried older people had an agency or paid source as a primary helper.

All of the respondents from the Nursing Home Pre-Admission Screening Study (PASS) received assistance in at least one activity of daily living. Ninety-five percent had a significant other who was also interviewed in the study. For 53% of the respondents, the significant other was an adult child; for 12%, a husband or wife; for 13%, a sibling; for 15%, another relative; and for 3%, a non-related person.

The level of informal support that both groups received was indicative of their living arrangements. Only 10% of the moderately to totally impaired individuals from the SSOV lived alone and only 19% of the PASS respondents lived alone. The remainder lived with a spouse, adult child, other relative, or non-relative.

USE AND SOURCES OF IN-HOME CARE

The level of use and the sources of in-home care are displayed in Table 9.1 and Table 9.2. Five activities were used to define in-home care: nursing care, or assistance with treatment or medications; personal care, or assistance with bathing, dressing, and feeding; homemaker/housekeeping or household chores; continuous supervision or companionship; and meal preparation.

The PASS respondents were heavy users of in-home care. Seventy-one percent had nursing care, 85% had personal care, 95% had homemaker/housekeeping assistance, 67% had continuous supervision, and 94% had meal preparation. The use of assistance for the impaired older people in the SSOV was somewhat lower. Thirty-one percent had nursing care, 50% had personal care, 82% had homemaker/housekeeping assistance, 48% had continuous supervision, and 80% had meal preparation.

The individuals in the PASS sample were more likely to use in-home services, but they were somewhat less likely to rely exclusively or primarily upon informal services. The percentages for the SSOV respondents in Table 9.2 are based upon informal caregivers as the primary source of care; that is, agency or paid sources may be secondary providers in a small number of cases. The percentages for the PASS sample represent informal caregivers as the exclusive sources of care. For the SSOV subsample of impaired elderly, informal caregivers were the primary sources for 78% of the nursing care, 83% of the personal care, 88% of the homemaker/housekeeping assistance, 94% of the continuous supervision, and 86% of the meal preparation.

Table 9.1. Percentage Receiving Each Type of In-Home Care

	Percentage Receiving Care	
Type of Care	SSOV Sample[a] (n = 219)	PASS Sample (n = 113)
Nursing care	31[b]	71[c]
Personal care	50	85
Homemaker housekeeping	82	95
Continuous supervision	48	67
Meal preparation	80	94

[a]Subsample of respondents with moderate to total impairment in activities of daily living.
[b]Refers to assistance being received at the time of the interview.
[c]Refers to assistance received within one month of the interview.

Table 9.2. Family, Friends or Other Non-Paid Persons as Sources of Care Among Those Receiving Care

| | Percentage Receiving Care Primarily or Exclusively from an Informal Source | | | |
| | SSOV Sample[a] | | PASS Sample | |
Type of Care	%	n	%	n
Nursing care	78	67[b]	73	80
Personal care	83	109	66	96
Homemaker housekeeping	88	180	79	107
Continuous supervision	94	105	69	75
Meal preparation	86	176	70	106

[a]Subsample of respondents with moderate to total impairment in activities of daily living.
[b]Total number receiving this type of care.

Among the PASS sample, informal sources were the sole providers for 73% of the nursing care, 66% of the personal care, 79% of the homemaker/housekeeping assistance, 69% of the continuous supervision, and 70% of the meal preparation.

The PASS respondents may have made greater use of agency or other paid sources for care either because they were more severely impaired or because their informal supports were less capable of giving a full range of care. In addition, since the PASS respondents were all potentially eligible for Medicaid, their access to Medicaid funded in-home services was probably greater than that among SSOV respondents. The differences between the samples should not, however, obscure the fact that both groups relied heavily upon family and other non-paid persons for their in-home care.

USE OF HEALTH SERVICES AND HEALTH INSURANCE

The moderately to totally impaired in ADL among the SSOV sample were relatively heavy users of health services. Eighty-one percent reported a visit to a physician within 6 months prior to the survey. Thirty-two percent reported being hospitalized in the 6 months before the interview, and 7% experienced hospital stays of more than 20 days. Eighty-two percent of the PASS respondents visited a physician as an outpatient in the 6 months before the interview. Fifty-six percent reported being hospitalized, and 31% were hospitalized for more than 20 days.

Most of the respondents in both studies had some form of health insurance or medical coverage. Fifty-seven percent of the PASS respondents had Medicaid, and, among the remainder without Medicaid coverage, 39% had Medicare and 5% had some other coverage such as veteran's benefits, Public Health Service medical care, and private insurance. For the moderately to totally impaired subsample from the SSOV, 27% had Medicaid (with or without Medicare), 66% had Medicare only, 6% had some other health care coverage, and 1% reported no insurance. These insurance plans or entitlements to health care have some inadequacies in coverage for medical and hospital care, but they meet the basic costs of visits to the physician and hospital services. Most older people are unlikely to face catastrophic medical costs which are not covered by Medicaid or Medicare. The prospect of long-term care, especially nursing home care, however, can be a major financial problem if the older person's income or assets are too great to meet Medicaid eligibility criteria.

ATTITUDES OF CAREGIVERS OR CLOSELY RELATED PERSONS

A significant other for each of the respondents in the PASS sample was interviewed to determine the nature of care provided to the older person and the factors that led to the decision to seek institutionalization. One set of questions involved the changes that had taken place in the life of the significant other during the 6 month period prior to nursing home application. The questions were asked in an open-ended manner and were later coded into response categories.

Table 9.3 presents the types of changes mentioned by the significant others. Only 10% of the respondents indicated that their finances had been strained by caregiving. In comparison, over 40% of the significant others had to consider the older person in planning activities with others, experienced less time to themselves, and felt mental anguish or worry as a result of caregiving. Thirty-one percent decreased their social or recreational activities, 28% spent less time with their spouses and/or children, and 11% experienced interference with work or had more family disagreements. Small percentages men-

Table 9.3. Changes in the Life of the Significant Other During the Six Months Prior to Application to a Nursing Home ($n = 108$)

Type of Change	Percentage[a]
Must consider older person in planning activities with others	43
Less time to self	42
Mental anguish or worry	41
Social or recreational activities decreased	31
Less time with spouse or children	28
More family disagreements	11
Interference with work	11
Finances strained	10
Decreased housework	10
Need to rearrange household	5
Caregiving has been an enriching experience	2
Other	25

Note. Responses based on interviews with significant others of nursing home applicants in the PASS study.
[a]Total percentages exceed 100 because multiple responses were allowed.

tioned other changes such as increased housework, the need to rearrange the household, and so on. One must remember that these impaired older people were receiving the majority of their in-home care directly from family members and not through agency or paid sources. The daily provision of care is an arduous responsibility, especially for an impaired older person who must be continuously supervised and requires assistance with bathing, dressing, getting in and out of bed, and other daily living activities.

Significant others were also asked to identify the most important and second most important reasons for the decision to seek institutional care. Table 9.4 shows that financial considerations were not mentioned by any of the significant others as the primary reason for deciding to seek institutional care; only 4% mentioned financial considerations as the second most important reason. Changes in the informal support system were mentioned as the most important reason by 20%, and 28% mentioned this factor as the second most important reason. A decline in the older person's health was reported as the primary reason by 68% and by 18% as the secondary reason. A physician's recommendation was mentioned as the most important reason by 7% and as the second most important reason by 11% of the significant others. Three percent reported that family concern about the older person's ability to live independently was the most important reason, and 19% cited this as the second most important reason.

Table 9.4.   Reasons Mentioned by Significant Other for Seeking Nursing Home Care ($n = 107$)

	Percentage Mentioning as:	
Reason	Most Important	Second Most Important
Decline in older person's health	68	18
Change in informal support system— reduced capacity for care	20	28
Strong recommendation from physician or service provider	7	11
Family concern about older person's ability to live independently	3	19
Change in finances of older person or family caregiver	0	4
Other reason	2	14
No second reason mentioned	—	7
Total	100	101[a]

Note. Response based on interviews with significant others of nursing home applicants in the PASS study.
[a]Total percentage exceeds 100 due to rounding.

The data in Tables 9.3 and 9.4 suggest that financial strain may be experienced by some significant others of the impaired, but it is not likely to be viewed as the main factor in the institutionalization decision. It should be noted that some significant others may be reluctant to report such factors as mental anguish and loss of time as the major reasons for institutionalization. This may partially explain the differences between changes experienced (Table 9.3) and major reasons for institutionalization decisions (Table 9.4). However, this does not alter the finding that financial problems were rarely mentioned in the PASS sample as either changes prior to institutionalization or as primary or secondary reasons for the decision to institutionalize the impaired person.

DISCUSSION

Several conclusions can be drawn from the findings in these studies. A relatively small proportion, about 10%, of older people (age 60 and older) living in community settings were substantially impaired and needed a range of daily living assistance. Ninety percent of the SSOV impaired elderly subsample lived with someone else in the household, and their daily living assistance or in-home care was most likely to come from a spouse if they were married or an adult child if they were unmarried. Families provided this assistance voluntarily, and only a minority relied upon agencies or other paid sources for in-home care.

The PASS sample, representing individuals who had applied, had been screened, and had been approved for nursing home admission, were more likely than the SSOV subsample to use in-home services. They relied somewhat more on formal sources, but the majority of care was provided by family members without payment. Both the PASS sample and the SSOV subsample used medical services, and their basic medical costs were covered by Medicare, Medicaid, or other health insurance.

Financial considerations in the decision to seek institutional care were mentioned by only a small minority of caregivers or closely related persons in the PASS sample. They experienced major changes in their lives, especially limitations on their time and emotional strain, and they sought nursing home care for the impaired older person because the individual's health had worsened or because the family was unable to continue providing care.

What is the role of a public financial payment system in caregiving by family members and in the decision to seek institutionalization? The findings from these studies do not offer direct answers to that question. They do, however, suggest several policy and programmatic issues.

1. Although only a small proportion (10%) of older people in the community have a need for major daily living assistance, they represent nearly three times as many individuals as are in nursing homes. A public financial payment system would have to target resources to only a small proportion of the impaired elderly if major new public costs were to be avoided. Most families and other informal providers are already caring for these impaired older people without public reimbursement. Some administrative mechanisms would have to be developed to determine need and regulate access to public payments so that substantial voluntary caregiving, which is already taking place, would not be reduced. This presents a sizable problem of eligibility determination in order to target payments to those informal supports who would not otherwise be able to give care.

2. A payment system based upon an accounting of the actual expenses associated with caregiving might be most cost-effective, but

the determination of actual costs is likely to be difficult. Much of the daily living assistance received by impaired older people is provided "in-kind" without cash expenditures. Payments based upon extent of involvement in helping would be difficult to monitor. A system which required documented expenditures would probably encourage greater use of formal providers in order for the family to qualify for payments. Even a flat grant system based upon a standard family budget would have to attach monetary value to informal caregiving. Such a valuation process could compound problems of eligibility determination and add to administrative overhead.

3. Non-financial factors, such as restrictions on personal time and emotional strain, weigh heavily on family caregivers and financial payments may not be effective in relieving these social and psychological pressures. Financial payments may reduce some of the anxiety or strain on caregivers, but financial relief alone may neither delay nor avoid the decision to seek institutional care. A carefully targeted and controlled system of payments would probably improve the quality of life for the older person and the caregiver. It is very difficult, however, to target public programs to those "at high risk" for institutional care, because institutionalization is often the consequence of idiosyncratic events such as an acute episode or the sudden loss of a family caregiver. Financial factors have, at best, a very complex role in the decision-making process for institutional care.

4. Informal care typically comes from several sources. Nearly half of the impaired elderly in the SSOV had two or more major helpers. The spouse, adult child, sibling, other relative, neighbor, or friend may share in the process of care. A financial payment system would have to be flexible in order to take into account the needs of individuals other than the primary caregiver. If a primary caregiver were given a financial payment, other caregivers might be reluctant to share responsibilities, feeling that they were not being adequately compensated.

5. The efficacy of financial payments as motivators in caregiving has not been established through systematic research. Should payments serve as *incentives* designed to encourage families to begin caregiving when the family would not have otherwise provided care? Should payments be *compensation* or *reimbursement* meant to help families deal with stress and expenses that threaten their ability to maintain care that they have voluntarily initiated? The use of payments as an incentive presents the danger that families might take on caregiving for economic gain when other factors, such as their coping skills and their sense of personal obligation, may not be sufficiently

strong to ensure high-quality care. Furthermore, even the most powerful incentives for family care are unlikely to be of benefit to those who live alone or who live with non-family. On the other hand, the promise of financial compensation might lead families to continue care beyond a tolerable level of stress. Informal caregivers may find themselves in a situation of conflicting motives: financial factors motivating them to continue care, and psychological and physical strain undermining their ability to give quality care or substantially reducing their own quality of life.

6. The effectiveness of financial payments has not been systematically compared with that of other methods of encouraging informal support. Family counseling, respite care, selected in-home services, voluntary support groups, adult day care, and other services might be more effective methods of dealing directly with family stress and time pressures.

7. Even though impaired older people are supposed to be the beneficiaries of programs to encourage informal caregiving, they are seldom considered as the recipients of financial payments for that purpose. A direct income supplement to the older person, to be used at his or her discretion, could increase the older person's autonomy and allow the individual to choose the method of care that he or she views as most appropriate. It might also reduce dependency upon family members and give the older person a major role in making decisions about the form of care to be employed. Payments made directly to families or other informal caregivers may detrimentally shift control and responsibility away from the impaired older person and increase the feeling of loss or helplessness associated with a disabling condition. In addition, direct income supplements to the impaired would increase the opportunity for those who live alone or who share their households with non-family to benefit from the program. To be most effective, direct payments should be made only to those impaired elderly who are mentally competent to handle their own finances, but the design and administration of competency tests would lead to ethical and practical problems as well as increased expense.

8. Policies for family support will have to determine a feasible *form* of payment. Should a public financial support system be administered through tax policies such as the provisions for child and dependent adult child care under the federal income tax? If so, should tax credits also be used to compensate caregivers who have little taxable income, such as many older people who rely primarily on Social Security? Should caregivers be required to be employed, there-

by eliminating incentives for retired persons? Can a system of financial support through tax policy be successfully monitored for appropriate need, eligibility, and reasonable expenses? If a direct grant is used as an alternative to tax policy, what governmental agencies will administer the grants, how will eligibility be determined, what is a reasonable range of expenses, and what percentage of program costs should be allocated to administration?

9. A financial payment system may change family values. Payment for care formalizes the family's obligations and its role in caregiving. Does this change the nature of care? Do family members feel more accountable and responsible, or do they become more detached or impersonal, separating their emotional commitment from their "duties" as paid caregivers?

10. Finally, a payment system will have to clearly define the financial responsibilities of the family and the older person. Although administration of the program would be simplified if no means test were employed, paying or compensating all families without regard to their economic means is not likely to be either practical or equitable. The simplest method of determining financial need is an income and assets ceiling. Financial eligibility limits are inherently arbitrary because some individuals inevitably fall barely above the maximum and are thus denied participation. Income and assets have a complex relationship to care because some assets, such as a home, cannot be feasibly liquidated, household costs vary widely by economic circumstances, and families have different standards of living. Families should not be expected to deny themselves food and shelter in order to contribute to care for the older person. Should they, however, defer college education for their children, limit their residential mobility, or substantially reduce the savings and investments which help ensure their own financial position in old age? Clearly, any effort to effectively sort out those families in greatest need of financial assistance should not be based upon simplistic criteria for establishing financial means. Criteria which take into account many different family circumstances often require complex procedures that may increase administrative costs.

REFERENCES

Brody, S. J., Poulshock, S. W., & Masciocchi, C. F. The family caring unit: A major consideration in the long-term care support system. *The Gerontologist*, 1978, *18*, 556–561.

Cantor, M. H. Caring for the frail elderly: Impact on family, friends, and neighbors. Paper presented at the 33rd Annual Scientific Meeting of the Gerontological Society of America, San Diego, 1980.

Cicirelli, V. G. Personal strains and negative feelings in adult children's relationships with elderly parents. Paper presented at the 33rd Annual Scientific Meeting of the Gerontological Society of America, San Diego, 1980.

Duke University Center for the Study of Aging and Human Development. Multidimensional functional assessment: The OARS methodology. Duke University, Durham, NC, 1978.

Greenberg, J. N., & Ginn, A. A multivariate analysis of the predictors of long-term care placement. *Home Health Care Services Quarterly*, 1979, *1*, 75–99.

Palmore, E. Total chance of institutionalization among the elderly. *The Gerontologist*, 1976, *16*, 504–507.

Shanas, E. The family as a social support system in old age. *The Gerontologist*, 1979, *19*, 169–174.

Sussman, M. B. Social and economic supports and family environments for the elderly: Final report to the Administration on Aging, Washington, DC, 1979.

Townsend, P. The effects of family structure on the likelihood of admission to an institution in old age: The application of a general theory. In E. Shanas & G. F. Streib (Eds.) *Social structure and the family: Generational relations*. Prentice-Hall, Englewood Cliffs, NJ, 1965.

U.S. General Accounting Office. The well-being of older people in Cleveland, Ohio. U.S. Government Printing Office, Washington, DC, 1977.

Vicente, L., Wiley, J. A., & Carrington, R. A. The risk of institutionalization before death. *The Gerontologist*, 1979, *19*, 361–367.

Virginia Department of Taxation. Design and revenue impact analysis of tax incentives for the care of elderly in the home. Report to the Virginia General Assembly, Richmond, 1981.

Wan, T. T., & Weissert, W. G. Social support networks, patient status, and institutionalization. *Research on Aging*, 1981, *3*, 240–256.

Whitfield, S., & Krompholz, B. Report to the General Assembly on the family support system demonstration program. State of Maryland Office on Aging, Baltimore, 1981.

10

Family Involvement in Nursing Homes*

Jonathan L. York
Robert J. Calsyn

Recent research into the quality of care and quality of life in America's nursing homes has revealed a dearth of resources available to both the patient and the nursing home itself. This lack of resources has been most obvious in the areas of quantity and quality of staffing (York, Calsyn, & Fergus, 1975); rehabilitative services (Brody, 1973; Gottesman & Bourestom, 1974); and physical plant (Butler & Lewis, 1973). At the same time that researchers and social planners lament this paucity of resources, a potentially powerful and inexpensive resource, the patient's family, lies fallow or, worse, works against the patient's well-being.

The present investigation was undertaken in order to study some of the factors that affect family involvement in nursing home care. Specifically, the interrelationships between the following categories of variables were examined:

(1) Family involvement prior to nursing home placement.

(2) Factors leading to the decision to place the patient in the nursing home.

(3) Quantity and quality of family visits to the patient after placement in the nursing home.

(4) Willingness of families to participate in various educational and therapeutic programs.

The Gerontologist, 17 (6) (1977), 500–505.

(5) Level of support families receive from physicians and nursing home staff.

(6) Mental and physical status of the patient.

The study was initiated under the auspices of a consultation program offered by a community mental health center to nursing homes. During consultation visits mental health center staff observed many nontherapeutic interactions between residents and their families. Thus, a major purpose of the study was to collect data which would be helpful in planning programs to improve resident-family interaction. Following the recommendations of Siegel, Attkisson, and Cohn (1974) regarding needs assessment studies, data were collected on (1) the extent of the problem (i.e., the quality of resident-family interactions), (2) availability and utilization of existing services, and (3) willingness of family members to use services that might be offered in the future. To get a more complete picture of family-resident interaction, data were also collected on family involvement prior to nursing home placement and level of support families received from various sources. We have dispensed with the usual review of the literature and instead will integrate the results of previous research into the presentation of our own findings.

SAMPLE AND MEASUREMENT TECHNIQUES

The participants in this study were all families of patients at three Lansing, Michigan, area nursing homes. The 76 patients and their families were a subset of a random sample of 116 patients assessed in a previous study on mental health intervention in nursing homes (York & Fergus, 1976); patients were excluded because of death or discharge from the home (n = 4), lack of family in the area (n = 17), refusal to participate (n = 10), or unavailability of family (n = 19). Thus, the final sample consisted of 76 patients and their families who lived within a 25-mile radius of the nursing home. The specific family member to be interviewed was defined as that person who was identified on the patients chart as "person to contact in an emergency." Of the 76 interviews conducted, all but 12 were with children of nursing home patients; these other 12 were spread among spouses, nieces and nephews, and brothers and sisters. Interviews were conducted in the place of the families' choosing by an experienced interviewer; average interview time was approximately 1 hour. Data concerning patient status were collected through ratings by charge nurses in nursing homes, as described further below.

Mean age of patients sampled was 81; 80% were female. Mean length of stay in the nursing home was almost 3 years. Sixty-three percent of the patients were paid for out of public funds; marital status included 78% who were widowed. These figures do not vary significantly from other studies of nursing home patients.

Level of patient functioning was assessed by two instruments created by the researchers for a previous study (Fergus, York, & Calsyn, 1977). The first of these, the Behavior of Older Patient's Checklist (BOP), is a nurse's observational rating scale of behavioral and psychological functioning; separate scales on this instrument measure cognitive functioning (sensorium), social interaction, verbal hostility, physical hostility, depression, psychotic behavior, and personal appearance. The second instrument, the Physical Capabilities Checklist (PCC) is also nurse-rated, and looks at level of functioning on four scales: self-care, sensory capability, ambulation, and activity level. Additional data, such as medication and demographic and historical information, were taken from the patient's chart.

The Family Interview was a 45- to 60-minute instrument composed of both open-ended and closed-ended questions. This instrument breaks down into seven separate areas of inquiry: family involvement before placement, problems leading to placement, nursing home choice process, family visiting, family support systems, and programmatic needs of the family.

PRE-PLACEMENT INVOLVEMENT OF FAMILY

A prevalent myth which seems to run through much of American culture, and indeed through much of the gerontological literature, can be termed the myth of family uninvolvement or, as it is called by Spark and Brody (1970), "the myth of segregation of the aged." Shanas (1963) has attacked this "alienation theory," which holds that old people who live alone or separate from their children are neglected by their children. She cites evidence that the ties between older people and their families continue (Shanas, 1960), and that families behave responsibly to their older member's needs (Shanas, 1968). In addition, she has found that families regularly perform household tasks for their older relatives and often house their relatives with them in time of crisis (Shanas, 1968). Townsend (1965) studied family structure and its effects on the likelihood of admission to a home for the aged; he found that over 45% of the older persons sampled had moved in with family until severe circumstances forced their institutionalization. Similarly Miller and Harris (1965) found that

Table 10.1. Percentage of Families Providing Help Before Placement in Areas of Need.

Help With:	% Providing Regular Help
Shopping	72
Laundry	69
Medical affairs	69
Heavy cleaning	69
Cooking	58
Light cleaning	42
Bathing	32
Dressing	21
Toileting	12
Transferring	10
Feeding	4

54% of the patients of a nursing home lived with their children or other relatives immediately prior to placement. As a World Health Organization report summarized the issue, "wherever careful studies have been carried out in the industrialized countries, the lasting devotion of children for their parents has been amply demonstrated" (WHO, 1959).

Our data reaffirmed the conclusion of previous researchers that families do not separate themselves from their older relative. As Table 10.1 indicates, a large proportion of families in our sample helped their older relative on a variety of tasks, from shopping to physical care. In addition 30% of the families took the older relative into their home before placement, and nearly all of the families maintained frequent telephone contact (X = 9 visits per month).

THE PLACEMENT DECISION

Although it is clear from the above data that families of the elderly do not ignore the plight of their older relatives, the study also revealed that families did not utilize alternatives to institutional care, even though many of the alternative services were known to a majority of the families (see Table 10.2 for percentages for each service).

Families were not very thorough or sophisticated in their search for a nursing home for their older relative. Fifty-one percent of the families did not even visit the home their relative was placed in prior to placement. Only 31% of the families visited three or more homes

Table 10.2.   Awareness and Utilization of Alternative Services.

Service	% of Families Aware of	% of Families Used
Visiting Nurses	93	20
Physical Therapy	78	12
Meals-on-Wheels	85	8
Transportation for Older Persons	71	5
Home Health Aides	40	5
Public Health Clinics	74	3
Mental Health Centers	75	3
Chore Services	34	1
Adult Day Care	28	0

before making their decision. Availability of a bed (75%) and location (62%) were the principal reasons given by families for choosing a particular home. Quality of staff (35%), quality of physical care (10%), quality of the activity program (12%), cleanliness (24%), and cost (15%) were much less influential in the choice of a nursing home. This lack of sophistication in choosing a nursing home is consistent with Linn and Gurel's (1969) finding that quality of meals was a highly significant factor in family judgments of the quality of a nursing home.

Since 59% of the patients came directly to the nursing home from the hospital, it is not surprising that physicians (83%) and hospital social workers (43%) were listed by the family as being important factors in the decision to place the patient in the nursing home. However, it is somewhat alarming that the inputs of others, e.g., nursing home staff (12%) and especially the patient himself (19%), had considerably less effect in the decision to place the patient.

The above statistics clearly point to the need to develop better information and referral services to assist families in making decisions regarding the placement of their relative in the nursing home. As our data indicated, families typically did not utilize alternatives to nursing home care. Furthermore, their choice of home was not guided by an assessment of the quality of the home, but rather by availability of a bed and geography. In addition, the failure of most families to involve the patient and the nursing home staff in the decision to place the patient would seem to increase the risk of future unhappiness on the part of the patient and subsequent management problems for the nursing home staff.

Careful attention should be given to when and how alternatives to nursing home care are presented to families, since only 33% of our sample indicated they would have liked or needed more information on alternatives to nursing homes before placement. This may be indicative of the fact that most families seemed to feel extremely frustrated and defeated at the time of placement and that no alternatives would have been acceptable at that late date. It seems reasonable to assume that simply delineating available alternatives to families would have little effect and that a more active approach is indicated.

Area Agencies on Aging would seem to be in an ideal position to coordinate and improve information and referral services for families who are in need of services for one of their older members. These agencies should be capable of coordinating a multidimensional assessment (cf. Pfeiffer, 1975) which would not only point out the varying areas of need and problems of the older person but also direct them and their families to appropriate treatment and support services. However, it would seem prudent for Area Agencies to first inform physicians and hospital social workers of alternatives to the nursing home and convince them of their utility before launching an information and referral service aimed at families who are potentially in need of a nursing home for their older relative. First, physicians and hospital personnel are the largest single source of referrals to nursing homes. Second, since physicians and hospital social workers seem to be the most influential people in the decision to place a relative in a nursing home, any information and referral service that ignores this influence process is probably doomed to failure. A majority of the families in the present study were unaware of the existence of information and referral services and went directly to the physician or hospital social worker for advice.

FAMILY VISITING AT NURSING HOMES

Contrary to the common belief that families abandon or "dump" their relative once placed in the nursing home, the families in this study stayed involved with their older relatives after placement. The mean number of visits per month was 12; only two families visited less than twice monthly. The amount of family involvement with the patient prior to placement was related to the number of visits after placement; number of nursing home visits correlated significantly with preplacement telephone contact ($r = .281$, $p < .01$). Although not extremely strong relationships, these imply that families tend to maintain patterns of involvement established before placement. Somewhat surprisingly the number of family visits was not related to the amount of patient impairment as measured by the seven BOP scales or the four PCC scales, indicating that families are willing to at least continue visiting their older relatives despite their physical or mental deterioration.

Although the data support the finding that families do not abandon their relatives in a nursing home, a much more significant and problematic issue is the quality and enjoyment of visits. Forty-two percent of the families reported enjoying less than half of their visits. Enjoyment of visits was not related to what was done on visits (i.e., activities versus just talking). However, enjoyment of visits was related to the amount of mental deterioration of the patient. Specifically, enjoyment of visits correlated significantly with the PCC self-care disability scale ($r = -.239$, $p < .05$), and with the impaired cognitive functioning ($r = -.242$, $p < .05$) and the poor personal appearance scale ($r = -.342$, $p < .01$) of the BOP. Families of those older people who were disheveled and/or confused thus seemed to have less enjoyable visits. However, enjoyment of visits was not significantly related to physical or sensory disabilities. Family members confirmed that they did have greater difficulty coping with mental deterioration (37%) than physical disabilities (15%). The relationship between resident mood disturbances and family members' enjoyment of visiting was less clear. While a large percentage of the families (30%) indicated that mood disturbances such as depression were the most upsetting aspects of their family member's illness, there were no significant correlations between enjoyment of visiting and the mood scales of the BOP (social isolation, depression, physical hostility, and verbal hostility).

WILLINGNESS TO PARTICIPATE IN PROGRAMS

While the above data indicate that families continue to stay involved with their older relatives after placement in a nursing home, the data and interviews also indicate that families need help in how to make their visits with their older relative more productive. In this respect, 83% of the families indicated they would want to take part in some sort of program that might be offered by the nursing home for their benefit. Over 2/3 wished to meet with staff; 51% indicated that they would attend classes on aging; and 47% expressed interest in getting advice on how to make their visiting more productive and enjoyable.

A lesser but still considerable amount, 30%, were interested in meeting with other families to share concerns and problems.

What becomes obvious then is that a large proportion of families feel a need to become more involved and knowledgeable in their relatives' care and see formalized programs as one method of attaining this goal. These programs can be structured in several different ways. The most traditional model would consist of classes concerning the aging process. Since families report the greatest difficulty in coping with mental deterioration and mood disturbances, specific attention should be devoted to organic brain syndrome and associated behavior changes. A second type of family program, possibly serving as a follow-up to the teaching oriented sessions, would be a training program in nursing home visiting. One of the major problems noted in the interviews was the lack of anything to do on visits; many families felt that they just sat and stared at their relative for an hour twice a week. Training families to visit more productively would be geared toward improving the quality and enjoyment of these visits for both parties and toward developing a therapeutic and constructive role for the family.

Another type of program would involve group meetings of families. These meetings would be intended to assist the relatives in gaining support from others in the same position and in being able to discuss their concerns about the nursing home. Combining this type of function with the two above would serve to provide specific information and techniques for the family and support in using these techniques. Examples of programs which have been developed to meet some of these needs include those of Manaster (1967), Shore (1964), and Safford (1976). Unfortunately, little data exists on the impact of these programs on family involvement, family satisfaction, and patient functioning.

SUPPORT MECHANISMS

The programs mentioned above all would serve to fill a gap revealed by this study—namely, the support families feel they receive in dealing with the physical and psychosocial problems of their relatives. In our sample of families very little support was forthcoming from the physician; less than one-third of the respondents felt that they received any help from their relative's physician in understanding psychological changes, and only half felt they received any help understanding the physical aspects of aging. This may be because the physicians felt that essentially their role ended after nursing home placement, or because the families were unclear in their demands and expectations of the physicians.

An encouraging sign was that the nursing home staff was somewhat filling this gap in supportive help for the family. Over 80% of the families felt that they received some support from the nurses in dealing with their relatives' physical problems and almost 50% received support in dealing with the emotional problems. Surprisingly, over 50% received support in understanding physical problems and 38% in dealing with emotional problems from the nurses aides, a group traditionally looked upon as the least knowledgeable and professional in a nursing home. Thus, it can be seen that for many families the channels of communication with nursing home staff are already opened. The task, then, is to facilitate the proper usage of these channels in order to improve the overall quality of nursing home treatment.

The willingness of families to be involved in programs to help them with their relatives is related in an interesting manner to the support systems used by the families. Those families who tended to use the physician were less willing to take part in programs ($r = -.397$, $p < .001$) than those who relied more on nursing home personnel ($r = .290$, $p < .05$). It could be argued that those families who feel they can get support from the physician are less in need of help with coping with their older relatives' impairment. However, if this were true, families who rely on the physician for support should enjoy their visits more than families who rely on nursing home staff; no such difference was found in the data. We do not feel that our data imply that physicians should be less involved with the families of their patients; on the contrary, the data underscore the need for greater cooperation between physicians and nursing home staff. If possible, physicians should be involved in programming efforts for family members. At the very least, physicians need to be informed of any programs for family members and asked to encourage the families of their patients to participate.

CONCLUSION

In summary, the research indicated that families did not separate themselves from their elderly relatives. Not only did they visit and talk frequently with their older relatives prior to placement in the nursing home, but they often assisted them with a variety of household tasks. However, when confronted with a crisis, families did not utilize alternatives to nursing home care and they were not very sophisticated in choosing a nursing home.

The data also revealed that families continued to visit their relatives after they were placed in the home; very often, however, they did not enjoy these visits. A great majority of the families expressed frustration, resentment, and guilt concerning their visits; very few actually said that they looked forward to visiting. In addition, it became apparent in the course of this study that much of this problem was related to the families' lack of knowledge concerning their relatives' situation and lack of skills in visiting. Thus, programs should be developed to help family members better cope with their older relatives' illness. Since mental deterioration of the patient was associated with less enjoyment of visits by family members, program interventions should include information about organic brain syndrome and confusion as well as suggestions for improving visits with mentally impaired patients. The data also indicated that families were already relying on nursing home personnel for emotional support and that they were willing, and often eager, to participate in a variety of programs that might be offered by the nursing home staff.

REFERENCES

Brody, E. M. A million procrustean beds. *Gerontologist*, 1973, *13*, 430–435.

Butler, R. N., & Lewis, M. I. *Aging and mental health*. C. V. Mosby, St. Louis, 1973.

Fergus, E., York, J., & Calsyn, R. Total mental health intervention in nursing homes, unpublished, 1977.

Gottesman, L. E., & Bourestom, N. C. Why nursing homes do what they do. *Gerontologist*, 1974, *14*, 501–506.

Linn, M., & Gurel, L. Wives' attitudes toward nursing homes. *Journal of Gerontology*, 1969, *24*, 368–372.

Manaster, A. The family group therapy program at Park View Home for the Aged. *Journal of American Geriatrics Society*, 1967, *15*, 302–306.

Miller, M. B., & Harris, A. Social factors and family contacts in a nursing home population. *Journal of American Geriatrics Society*, 1965, *13*, 845–851.

Pfeiffer, E., (Ed.), *Multidimensional functional assessment: The OARS methodology*. Center for the Study of Aging & Human Development, Duke University, Durham, 1975.

Safford, F. A training program for relatives of the mentally impaired aged. Paper presented at 29th Annual Meeting of the Gerontological Society, New York, Oct., 1976.

Shanas, E. The unmarried old person in the United States: Living arrangements and care in illness, myth and fact. Paper presented for the International Social Science Research Seminar in Gerontology, Markaryd, Sweden, Aug., 1963.

Shanas, E. Family responsibility and the health of older people. *Journal of Gerontology*, 1960, *15*, 408–411.

Shanas, E. *Old people in three industrial societies*. Atherton Press, New York, 1968.

Shore, H. Relatives of the resident. In M. Leeds & H. Shore (Eds.), *Geriatric institutional management*. G. P. Putnam's Sons, New York, 1964.

Siegel, L. M., Attkisson, C. C., & Cohn, A. H. Mental health needs assessment: Strategies and techniques. In W. A. Hargreaves, C. C. Attkisson, L. M. Sieget, & M. H. McIntyre (Eds.) *Resource materials for community mental health program evaluation: Part II.* Langley Porter Neuropsychiatric Institute, San Francisco, 1974.

Spark, G. M., & Brody, E. M. The aged are family members. *Family Process*, 1970, *9*, 195–210.

Townsend, P. The effects of family structure on the likelihood of admission to an institution in old age: The application of a general theory. In E. Shanas & G. F. Streib (Eds.), *Social structure and the family*. Prentice-Hall, Englewood Cliffs, NJ, 1965.

World Health Organization. *Mental health problems of the aging and the aged.* Technical Report Series, No. 171. World Health Organization, Geneva, 1959.

York, J. L., Calsyn, R. J., & Fergus, E. O. Training nursing home staff in mental health: The implication of staff attitudes. Paper presented at 28th Annual Meeting of Gerontological Society, Louisville, Oct., 1975.

York, J., & Fergus, E. CMHC consultation aids nursing homes. *Innovations*, 1976, *3*, 37–38.

11

Intergenerational Family Support among Blacks and Whites: Response to Culture or to Socioeconomic Differences*

Elizabeth Mutran

The presence of extensive intergenerational support networks is a well-documented finding (Adams, 1968; Hays & Mindel, 1973; Shanas, 1967; Sussman, 1959; Troll, 1971), and researchers no longer debate the issue of the isolation of the nuclear family. It is accepted that the family is a major source of support, both emotional and tangible in nature; however, a number of questions concerning racial differences in the way families respond to the needs of their elderly remain. It has been suggested that the extended family is more important among blacks than among whites (Hays & Mindel, 1973; Hill, 1971; Jackson, 1973; Rosow, 1962; Schorr, 1960; Seelbach & Sauer, 1977; Streib, 1976), and the cause of this difference is debated. Rosow (1962) spoke of a black subculture, whereas Jackson (1973) suggested socioeconomic reasons rather than race as the underlying cause for differences in the extended family contacts. Kent (1971, p. 27) simply stated that there is a need for studies that will "separate out the influence of the black experience as a cultural phenomenon."

To sort out the effects of race involves three analytical concerns. First, there is the question of the representativeness of the samples and, therefore, the generalizability of the findings. Studies examining

*Journal of Gerontology, 40 (3) (1985), 382–389.

race effects have often used specific types of samples, primarily studies of low income and urban populations (Cantor, 1979; Seelbach & Sauer, 1977); thus leaving open to question the effects of status in the general population. Second, race may interact with other variables that predict family support in such a way that any given variable may be a stronger predictor of support in one racial group vis-a-vis the other. Little attention has been given to these possible interaction effects, yet there is reason to suspect that interaction may exist. Dowd and Bengtson (1978) showed that minority aged adults are often doubly disadvantaged as a result of both their ethnic and age status. A decline in health or a loss of spouse might be a heavier burden for one racial group than the other, and the events that may initiate family helping behavior need not be the same among blacks as among whites. The double jeopardy that blacks face may cause a response to an event, such as widowhood, that is different than that found in a group more structurally integrated, and therefore the slopes between a given life crisis and family help may be of different magnitude across races.

A third research concern is whether there is a racial difference that can be attributed to culture. A cultural effect implies value differences and, in this instance, a value with respect to family life that might influence helping behavior to a greater or lesser degree in one racial group versus the other.

The literature on the black family strongly suggests the existence of mutual support activity between generations (Cantor, 1979; Hays & Mindel, 1973; Hill, 1971; Jackson, 1973, 1980). This support is attributed to a number of factors including greater poverty (Williams, 1980), poorer health (Dowd & Bengtson, 1978; Williams, 1980), and household composition. Sixty-seven percent of black women aged 60 or more are widowed compared with 50% whites (Williams, 1980). Consider also the striking difference in the proportion of young family members in households with elderly heads—31% of black families versus 14.8% of white families (Williams, 1980).

The differences in objective conditions are seen as a major explanation of the increased family support among blacks. Cantor (1979) in a study of New York's inner city elderly adults, found no real difference between blacks and whites with respect to the amount of help received from children or in the feeling of closeness to children. She suggested that measures of socioeconomic status are more stable and overriding predictors of both the span and comprehensiveness of the social support system than race. Seelbach (1978) reached a similar conclusion from a study of low income elderly adults in Philadelphia;

he found no racial difference in terms of filial help. He also argued that social class may be a more useful variable than race in explaining and understanding differences in family functioning.

The issue of cultural differences still persists, however. Cantor (1979) found racial differences in the flow of help from older to younger generation; blacks assisted their adult offspring to a greater extent than whites. Both the study conducted in New York and the one in Philadelphia exclusively dealt with low income, urban families. In addition to limiting their generalizability, the poverty of the sample may severely limit any voluntary or discretionary help. It may be asked if, under more moderate social conditions, racial differences would appear.

In a study comparing families of black manual workers to those of black nonmanual workers, Jackson (1973) reported higher status black parents receive more instrumental assistance from their children. Similarly, the children of such parents receive more help than lower status children. It is reasonable to think of the extension of instrumental aid as a function, at least in part, of the ability to give and not simply a response to absolute poverty.

Whether or not the ability to give leads to a racial difference, the alternative cultural interpretation seems most often to be a residual explanation. If racial differences remain after socioeconomic controls are exercised, this is assumed to be a cultural effect, but the factors that produced the racial differences remain unknown. It may be that beliefs or values also influence helping behavior, and these attitudes may be differentially held across races. An example of possible attitudinal differences are values that reflect the importance of and respect for each generation, attitudes that Wylie (1971) pointed out are more likely to be held by blacks. These measures have not been used generally, and if such measures are also related to socioeconomic status the effect of the latter may be overestimated. In addition, attitude measures may directly tap differences between blacks and whites in family exchange patterns that are independent of socioeconomic status.

A further question not addressed in past studies is whether the factors that predict family help are the same across racial groups. Perhaps the racial groups have adopted different coping strategies to given life crises. In one group the customary support for a particular crisis might come from the family whereas in another group that crisis would be met by other service providers. This raises the issue of interaction effects between the two groups.

In order to study the issue of cultural differences versus socioeconomic necessity as influences on intergenerational exchange within the family, several steps are necessary: (a) The data base should be a nationally representative sample versus one restricted to the elderly poor. (b) Possible interaction effects of race need to be examined as well as main effects. (c) A measure tapping value differences in attitudes toward the generations should be included. It is anticipated that black, lower status families and those with children under 18 in the home will be more involved in family helping behavior. Widowed parents, parents more advanced in years, and those in poor health will give less and receive more. Those who hold attitudes reflecting the importance of each generation will be involved in greater helping behavior.

DATA AND METHODS

The data are derived from a national survey conducted by Louis Harris and Associates for the National Council on Aging in 1974. The sample included an overrepresentation of persons over 65, in general, and of elderly blacks in particular. The sample for the present analysis comprises black and white elderly adults, 65 and over, who have adult children. This results in a subsample based on 194 blacks and 1,120 whites, of whom 58% were women, 44% widowed. The mean age was 72.7 years.

Variables

The dependent variables are the receiving and giving of help. Receiving help is a scale constructed by finding the principal component that explains the variance in a number of different types of support activities. The activities include such things as receiving aid when ill, having someone shop, running errands, chauffeuring, receiving gifts or money, fixing things around the house, and receiving advice on such things as life's problems, money matters, or job. The scale for giving aid consists of similar items, including gift giving, running errands, taking care of children or grandchildren when ill, and various forms of advice giving. The individual items were coded as 1 (having given to or received from any adult child that particular service), 0 otherwise. The items are weighted by the factor score coefficients obtained from the principal components analysis of the sample as a whole. The reliability of the scales is .83 for receiving help, as measured by Cronbach's alpha; for giving help, the comparable reliability is .75. The subgroup reliabilities for the scales were also high; .89 for receiving help and .83 for giving help for blacks, and .82 and .74, respectively, for whites. The two scales are composite measures of either receiving or giving help. They are meant to be indicators of underlying constructs of family helping behavior rather than measures of particular types of support.

The independent variables used in the analysis were selected to emphasize the major structural differences between black and white families. The effect of marital status is measured by two dummy variables, 1 = widowed and 1 = divorced or separated. Married persons are represented in the reference category. Age is measured in years, and education is indicated by a series of categories ranging from no formal schooling to postgraduate education. Income refers to household income and is measured by 11 categories ranging from under $1,000 to $25,000 and over. Health is a subjective evaluation of one's physical condition and is measured by responses to "How serious a problem is poor health for you personally these days—a very serious problem (high score), a somewhat serious problem, or hardly a problem at all?" As coded, the measure is one of health as problematic.

The potential for involvement in an extensive family network within the same household is measured by the number of children under 18 in the home. Finally, measures of attitudinal respect or appreciation across generations are included. The items are: "Generally speaking, do you feel that younger people get too much, too little, or just about the right amount of respect from older people these days?" and, alternatively, if older people get too much, too little, or just about the right amount of respect from younger people.

Methods of Analysis

The study examines the main effects of race by entering control variables in a series of steps using regression analysis. Race, sex, and age of parent were the first variables to be considered in explaining why some parents give aid and/or are assisted whereas others are not, and these variables were entered in the initial step. To test whether the influence of race is direct or whether it operates only through the status variables, household income and education were entered on the second step, followed by health, marital status, and number of children under 18 in the household. These latter variables were entered at a later stage to test whether it is socioeconomic status itself that is associated with different levels of family support or if helping behavior is the consequence of other measures also associated with status. Finally, to test for a value difference that may reflect cultural diversity, the attitude variables measuring generational respect were entered. The implied causal model is shown in Figure 11.1.

Interactions

In addition to the differences in family support activity between the races, which is reflected in the coefficient for race, a second strategy was used to analyze the interaction effects. Within racial groups, some of the independent variables may be more salient for whites than for blacks and have a greater effect on family support, and this too may indicate a cultural difference. Race might mitigate or buffer the effects of certain variables. Two methods were used to analyze interaction effects. First, a comparison of the covariance matrices was made to test for homogeneity. This was assessed by the use of the Box's M Test (Specht & Warren, 1976). Box's M, however, does not indicate which covariances are unequal; therefore cross-multiplicative terms were constructed for each of the independent variables and race. Each term was added to the regression equation after all other independent variables were in the equation (Kim & Kohout, 1975). The appropriate test for the significance of the multiplicative term was the hierarchical F test for the increment to R^2. Kim and Kohout state that use of multiplicative terms may result in multicollinearity that can affect the magnitude of the slope and the size of the standard error, therefore affecting the individual significance test for the multiplicative coefficient. This problem is avoided by the use of the hierarchical F test.

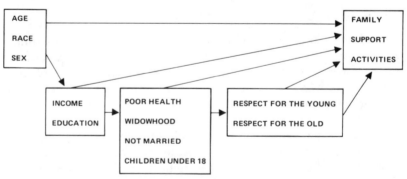

Figure 11.1.   Proposed causal model.

RESULTS

Racial Differences in Level of Exchanges

Initially there appears to be substantial evidence of a racial effect as indicated by the results in Tables 11.1 and 11.2. In the first step of the analysis, the slope for blacks on both dependent variables was significantly higher than for whites. The racial effect, however, is different across the two equations.

Racial differences persisted when the focus was on the older generation's contribution to the exchange network, that is, when they are the givers (see Table 11.1). Only a small fraction, approximately 7%, of the racial effect operated indirectly through the entire set of intervening variables; the major effect of race on the giving of help was direct, and race remained a strong predictor of parental help extended to children and grandchildren, although there are significant effects of age, education, number of children, and one of the attitude measures. After all controls were entered into the analysis, the slope for blacks was .439 higher than for comparable whites, as demonstrated by the size of the coefficient for the dummy variable.

A different pattern emerged when the dependent variable was the scale for receiving help (see Table 11.2). In this analysis, the direct effect of race was eliminated by controls for socioeconomic status. As a group, black elderly parents appear to receive more help from their children because on the average they also are less educated and have less income. Fifty percent of the total effect of race operated indirectly through education and income. Another 18% of the total effect operated through health, marital status, and children in the home. The difference by race in the final analysis was only .114, a nonsignificant difference. This direct effect was only 35% of the total effect. We are, therefore, able to explain 65% of the racial difference in the elderly parent's reception of family support by socioeconomic factors and differences in health, marital status, and number of young persons in the household (see Alwin & Hauser, 1975, for decomposition of effects).

Other Independent Effects

Race had the strongest effect on predicting help that flows from older to younger generations (Table 11.1), but the size of its standardized coefficient was followed closely by the number of children within the household and age of respondent. The number of children in the

Table 11.1. Regression Coefficients for Giving Help, Race Main Effects

Variable	Step 1	Step 2	Step 3	Step 4
Age	−.025*(.006) −.120	−.024*(.006) −.117	−.022*(.006) −.104	−.021*(.006) −.103
Race	.507*(.099) .140	.514*(.103) .141	.473*(.105) .130	.439*(.105) .121
Sex	−.163*(.071) −.062	−.137 (.072) −.052	−.085 (.081) −.032	−.085 (.081) −.033
Income		.032 (.018) .056	.016 (.018) .029	.019 (.018) .034
Education		−.032*(.018) −.052	−.033*(.018) −.054	−.038*(.019) −.062
Poor health			−.067 (.045) −.042	−.077 (.045) −.049
Widowhood			−.131*(.085) −.050	−.115 (.085) −.044
Not married			−.250 (.190) −.037	−.267 (.190) −.039
Children under 18			.225*(.057) .109	.231*(.056) .112
Respect for young				.074 (.060) .034
Respect for old				.026*(.068) .082
R^2	.040	.043	.057	.065

Note. Unstandardized coefficients are shown on the first line for each variable, standardized on the second line. Standard errors are in parentheses.
*$p < .05$.

same household is an obvious indicator of the availability of extended family members, and black families have greater opportunity for family exchange because more elderly black households contain children under 18 than white households. It can be expected that much of this help involves child care in some way. In such settings, the older generation appears to be actively involved in family support activities, and the older person is not a dependent member of the household.

The remaining significant factor was the attitudinal variable. Elderly persons who feel that the older generation deserves more respect are also the elderly persons more often involved in helping the other members of their family. The attitude expecting respect for elderly

Table 11.2. Regression Coefficients for Receiving Help, Race Main Effects

Variable	Step 1	Step 2	Step 3	Step 4
Age	.018*(.005) .098	.014*(.005) .077	.007 (.005) .039	.007 (.005) .040
Race	.327*(.085) .104	.163*(.088) .052	.104 (.088) .033	.114 (.089) .036
Sex	.412*(.061) .182	.371*(.061) .164	.272*(.068) .120	.264*(.068) .117
Income		−.049*(.015) −.100	−.040*(.015) −.080	−.040*(.015) −.081
Education		−.057*(.016) −.108	−.048*(.016) −.091	−.050*(.016) −.094
Poor health			.147*(.038) .107	.153*(.038) .110
Widowhood			.218*(.072) .097	.224*(.072) .100
Not married			−.307 (.160) −.052	−.304 (.160) −.051
Children under 18			.169*(.048) .095	.166*(.048) .093
Respect for young				.081 (.050) .043
Respect for old				−.052 (.057) −.024
R^2	.054	.080	.114	.118

Note. Unstandardized coefficients are shown on the first line for each variable, standardized on the second line. Standard errors are in parentheses.
*$p < .05$.

adults may indicate pride in themselves and their own familial importance. This attitude may also be derived from their past contributions.

Variables that predict whether elderly persons are themselves the receivers of help (Table 11.2) emphasize the vulnerability of elderly individuals. Those persons over 65 who possess fewer economic resources, including income and lower levels of education, receive more assistance. The sick, women, and those who are widowed are among the elderly persons who receive assistance from their families.

The present analysis shows aid that flows upward from the middle generation is a response to need. There is no evidence of a racial or ethnic difference once need is controlled, and there is no cultural difference in terms of attitudes. The behavior of both black and white middle generations appear to be similarly perceived by elderly parents.

Interaction Effects

The amount of statistical interaction appears to be minimal. The result of the Box's M test reveals that the two covariance matrices are not equal and, therefore, the structural parameters would not be equal (Specht & Warren, 1976). This omnibus test does not indicate which parameters are unequal. The addition, however, of the multiplicative terms to the regression equation made a significant increment to R^2 in only three instances: (a) race by attitudes of respect due the young, (b) race by number of children under 18 in the household and (c) race by widowhood status. The first two significantly affect the older person's giving of help and the latter significantly affects the older person's receiving of help.

Further, the correlations of two of the multiplicative terms with race were extremely high (.94 and .67). Their inclusion in the regression equations resulted in large standard errors and a change in the sign of the coefficient for race, indicating a problem with multicollinearity. Table 11.3 permits a comparison of all slopes across the two groups; only those slopes that significantly differ, as ascertained by the hierarchical F test, are discussed. The majority of variables influence blacks and whites in a similar manner with but few exceptions. Those few exceptions do give some credence to a cultural interpretation.

Two of the exceptions occur in the equation for giving help. Notably, the elderly adults' attitude toward young family members significantly influenced the giving of such help. Among blacks, the attitude that young individuals deserve more respect was significantly related to giving help, and the contrast with whites is striking, as reflected in the b of .302 compared with .021 (see Table 11.3). The measure of respect for the older generation was also much stronger in predicting support activity by older blacks (.479 compared with .166); however the difference in slopes was not significant. Also among blacks, the number of children in the household had almost three times the impact on the older generation's involvement in helping behavior than it did in the white sample (b = .441 compared with .159).

The remaining interaction occurred in the equation for receiving help. Widowhood was a significant and strong predictor of an elderly

Table 11.3. Analysis within Race of the Variables Affecting Family Support

Variable	Blacks		Whites	
	Giving	Receiving	Giving	Receiving
Age	−.015 (.018) −.063	.024* (.015) .115	−.022**(.006) −.114	.004 (.005) .024
Sex	−.060 (.249) −.020	.342* (.216) .130	−.100 (.085) −.040	.258**(.071) .118
Income	.015 (.061) .019	−.030 (.053) −.043	.022 (.019) .039	−.038**(.016) −.079
Education	.035 (.072) .037	−.098* (.063) −.124	−.045**(.019) −.078	−.046**(.016) −.090
Poor health	−.059 (.141) −.030	.005 (.123) .003	−.076 (.048) −.050	.177**(.040) .133
Widowhood	−.149 (.259) −.050	−.112 (.225) −.043	−.102 (.090) −.041	.282**(.075) .130
Not married	−.285 (.387) −.055	−.383 (.336) −.086	−.233 (.228) −.031	−.344* (.191) −.052

Table 11.3. (continued)

Variable	Blacks		Whites	
	Giving	Receiving	Giving	Receiving
Children under 18	.441**(.129)	.286**(.112)	.159**(.064)	.121**(.053)
	.245	.184	.074	.064
Respect for young	.302* (.162)	.213* (.141)	.021 (.064)	.053 (.054)
	.132	.108	.010	.028
Respect for old	.479**(.221)	.048 (.192)	.166**(.071)	−.062 (.059)
	.157	.018	.070	−.030
n	194		1120	
R^2	.12	.10	.04	.11

Note. Unstandardized coefficients are shown on the first line for each variable, standardized on the second line. Standard errors are in parentheses.
*$p < .10$; **$p < .05$.

white parent's receiving of help. It was equal in strength to poor health as a determining factor. Among blacks, widowhood does not act independently of the other variables.

DISCUSSION

The present study addresses the issues of racial differences in family helping behavior and whether the difference results from socioeconomic variables or cultural factors. It is asserted that a cultural interpretation should not rest on the residual variance explained by race but should be substantiated by value differences or relationships that varied within groups.

The answer to the first issue is relatively simple. Black families do appear to be more involved in exchanges of help across generations. The slope for blacks on both giving and receiving of help is significantly higher even considering differences in age and sex composition of the two groups.

The answer to the second question is not as simple. First, one can look at the elimination of a racial difference in the reception of help by older parents once controls for socioeconomic factors are included. This would argue that, at least in terms of the aid that flows from the younger generation to the older generation, socioeconomic factors, not culture, produce the observed racial difference. One could argue, however, that as a racial difference persists in the behavior of the older generation, there is evidence of a cultural effect. The lack of an effect of race on receiving help may be an example of the younger generation of a minority group accepting the culture of the dominant society, similar to the assimilation that occurs among the various ethnic groups that migrate to this country.

This interpretation has to be qualified, however, when one considers the variables that have been analyzed and those factors that could alter the conclusion. The racial difference in the giving of help from older to younger generation may exist because of the greater economic need of the black middle and younger generations for continued assistance, variables for which we have no information. Alternatively, perhaps the lack of a racial effect in predicting receiving help after controlling for parental socioeconomic status does not consider the ability or resources of the younger black family members in comparison with whites to help or assist their elderly parents. A second related caution is that the data report only the behavior of one generation. We do not know if the older generation is underreporting the help they have received, or, if underreporting occurs, does it occur more often among one racial group vis-a-vis the other. Thus we are not able to exclude either the cultural or socioeconomic interpretations. Certainly the data show that socioeconomic factors eliminate some of the difference in support behavior between the two racial groups, and even among blacks the more educated elderly are less dependent on younger family members for help.

Different factors distinguish the racial groups in producing family helping behavior, and these differences lend support to cultural interpretations. Most notably among these differences is the influence of attitudes on helping behavior. Among blacks the feeling that the younger generation deserve more respect influences the elderly person's extension of aid. Among whites, we see very little effect of either variable and, in particular, no influence of the variable respect for the young generation. This finding supports previous research which found that blacks are more likely than whites to regard elderly individuals with respect (Wylie, 1971).

In conclusion, it seems unwise to present the two interpretations in opposition to one another, that is to argue that the observed differences are due to socioeconomic status only or they are due to cultural differences only. There is supporting evidence for both. Caution should be exercised, however, when assessing the socioeconomic impact to take into account not only the status of one generation, but the status of the network involved. At the same time, a cultural explanation should not rest simply on the residual variation explained by racial categories but should begin to investigate what customs, beliefs, or attitudes bring about the difference. Further, it is necessary to investigate the reasons why certain variables (e.g., widowhood) should effect aid offered elderly adults in one population but have no effect in the other. One might speculate whether this distinction, too, is one of culture or of socioeconomic factors.

REFERENCES

Adams, B. N. (1968). The middle-class adult and his widowed or still married mother. *Social Problems, 16,* 58–59.
Alwin, D. F., & Hauser, R. M. (1975). The decomposition of effects in path analysis. *American Sociological Review, 40,* 37–47.
Cantor, M. (1979). The informal support system of New York's inner city elderly: Is ethnicity a factor? In D. E. Gelfand & A. J. Kutzik (Eds.), *Ethnicity and aging: Theory, research and policy.* Springer Publishing, New York.

Dowd, J. J., & Bengtson, V. L. (1978). Aging in minority populations: An examination of the double jeopardy hypothesis. *Journal of Gerontology, 33,* 338–355.

Hays, W. C., & Mindel, C. H. (1973). Extended kin relations in black and white families. *Journal of Marriage and the Family, 35,* 51–57.

Hill, R. B. (1971). *Minority aged in America.* Institute of Gerontology. The University of Michigan-Wayne State University, Detroit, MI.

Jackson, J. J. (1973). Family organization and technology. In K. S. Miller & R. M. Dreger (Eds.), *Comparative studies of blacks and whites in the United States.* Seminar Press, New York.

Jackson, J. J. (1980). *Minorities and aging.* Wadsworth, Belmont, CA.

Kent, D. P. (1971). The elderly in minority groups: Variant patterns of aging. *The Gerontologist, 11,* 26–29.

Kim, J., & Kohout, F. (1975). Multiple regression analysis: Subprogram regression. In N. H. Nie, C. Hull, J. Jenkins, K. Steinbrenner, & D. Bent (Eds.), *Statistical package for the social sciences.* McGraw Hill, New York.

Rosow, I. (1962). Old age: One moral dilemma of an affluent society. *The Gerontologist, 2,* 182–191.

Schorr, A. J. (1960). Filial responsibility in the modern American family. Social Security Administration, Division of Program Research, Washington, DC.

Seelbach, W. C. (1978). Correlates of aged parents' filial responsibility expectations and realizations. *The Family Coordinator, 22,* 341–350.

Seelbach, W. C., & Sauer, W. J. (1977). Filial responsibility expectations and morale among aged parents. *The Gerontologist, 17,* 492–499.

Shanas, E. (1967). Family help patterns and social class in three countries. *Journal of Marriage and the Family, 29,* 257–266.

Specht, D. A., & Warren, R. D. (1976). Comparing causal models. In D. R. Heise (Ed.), *Sociological methodology.* Jossey-Bass, San Francisco.

Streib, G. F. (1976). Social stratification and aging. In R. H. Binstock & E. Shanas (Eds.), *Handbook of aging and the social sciences.* Van Nostrand Reinhold, New York.

Sussman, M. B. (1959). The isolated nuclear family: Fact or fiction? *Social Problems, 6,* 330–340.

Troll, L. E. (1971). The family of later life: A decade review. *Journal of Marriage and the Family, 33,* 263–290.

Williams, B. S. (1980). Characteristics of the black elderly. (Publication #1 (OHDS) 80-26261) U.S. Department of Health, Education, and Welfare, Washington, DC.

Wylie, F. M. (1971). Attitudes toward aging and the aged among black Americans: Some historical perspectives. *Aging and Human Development, 2,* 66–70.

12

Filial Expectations, Association, and Helping as a Function of Number of Children among Older Rural-Transitional Parents*

Vira R. Kivett
Maxine P. Atkinson

Despite a growing body of research on intergenerational support (Adams, 1968; Bengtson et al., 1976; Lang & Brody, 1983; Lee, 1980; Shanas, 1979; Streib & Beck, 1980; Troll, 1971), little or no attention has been given to differences in patterns of association or assistance that may occur as a function of number of children (Beckman & Houser, 1982; Kivett & Learner, 1980). Historical trends toward smaller families, longer life spans, and increasingly high mobility of both young and old have important implications for children's potential as a primary resource in old age.

Information on the patterns of association and assistance of older adults with varying numbers of children and the factors impacting their relationships can provide useful directions for future research

Journal of Gerontology, 39, (4) (1984), 499–503.
This paper is No. 8920 of the Journal Series of the North Carolina Agricultural Research Service, Raleigh, NC 27650. It was presented at the annual meeting of the South Carolina Gerontological Society, Greenville, SC, October, 1983.

and policy. Data from areas of rural to urban transition where mobility of the second generation and employment of women is generally high are of special interest. The purpose of the present study was to compare older parents with regard to filial expectations and frequency of parent-child association and assistance according to number of children. Also considered were the differential effects of factors impacting upon expectations and interaction.

METHODS

Sample

This study was a secondary analysis of a data base of 321 adults aged 65 years and older living in a rural-transitional area in the southeastern United States. During the past three generations the county of location had undergone transition from an agriculturally based economy to an industrial one, centered on textile production. As a result, respondents represented, primarily, agricultural and skilled labor backgrounds. Compact cluster sampling procedures utilizing census tract data were used. Respondents for the present analysis ($N = 279$) comprised all adults in the original sample who had one or more living children. Approximately 38% of respondents were men. The majority of the sample, 94%, were white and married, 61%. Although 47% of older adults had not been born in the county of current residence, the average length of residence in the neighborhood of location was 35 years.

Parents having more than one child based their responses to a questionnaire on the child with whom there was the most contact (referent child). Children of most contact were as likely to be sons, 49%, as daughters. For comparative purposes, the sample was divided into three groups: parents with an only child (G_1), $n = 57$; parents with two or three children (G_2), $n = 139$; and parents with four or more children (G_3), $n = 83$.

Measures

Respondents were administered a 141-item questionnaire that included general demographic data; marital history; information on health, retirement, income, morale, social roles, and interaction with kin; helping patterns with kin; expectations for kin assistance; and feelings of affect toward kin. Data on kin were obtained for a relative of most contact for each of seven levels of consanguineous and affinal kin. Only data relative to children were used for the present analysis, and only those variables relative to the purposes of this study discussed.

Association was a composite measure of face-to-face contact and the frequency with which children telephoned and wrote to parents. The face-to-face component was measured by the frequency of interaction with children in 12 activities. These included commercial, home, and outdoor recreation; visits; vacations; family reunions; emergencies; working together; baby sitting; holidays; church; and shopping. Responses to each item were coded 1 to 9 according to one of nine levels of frequency ranging from never to daily. Similarly, frequency of writing and telephoning was recorded using the 9-point response scale.

Help received was measured by the frequency with which older parents received assistance in 11 categories of help from children. Categories included help with transportation, minor household repairs, housekeeping, shopping, yardwork, car care, illness, important decisions, legal aid, financial aid, and other help specified by the respondents. The same frequency of response schedule was used with this item as with the association measure.

Filial expectations were measured through responses to four scenarios depicting hypothetical situations of older parents who needed financial help, aid during illness, or who were lonely. Respondents indicated the degree of responsibility they felt children should assume in each situation. Responses were summed to obtain a composite score. Higher scores represented stronger feelings of responsibility.

Geographical proximity was a measure of how close respondents lived to the referent child: in the same household, 10 min away or less, 11 to 30 min away, 31 to 60 min away, over 60 min to less than a day away, and 1 day or more away. Responses were coded 1 to 6, respectively.

Health of the parent was measured by the Cantril ladder technique (Cantril, 1965). Respondents, after being shown a picture of a ladder with rungs numbered from 0 to 9, were asked to rate their health at the present time.

Recency with which respondents had seen referent children was determined through responses to the question, "When did you last see (child of most contact)?" Responses were: you live in the same household, today or yesterday, 2 to 7 days, 8 to 30 days, 31 days to a year, or not in the past year. Responses were coded 1 to 6, respectively.

Analyses

Stepwise multiple regression was used to determine the importance of income, sex, and health of parents and sex and proximity of children to frequency of association and help received from children. Analysis of covariance was used to observe the relationship between filial expectations and number of children, controlling for health of the parent. A number of demographic and parent-child characteristics were also compared using chi-square tests of independence, analyses of variance, and Scheffè's test for multiple mean contrasts.

RESULTS

Table 12.1 presents descriptive findings across groups. Tests of differences were also performed on some of these data. Several differences were observed through analyses of variance in the demographic characteristics of older parents when compared by number of children. Age varied, $F (2,274) = 6.89, p < .01$, and educational level varied, $F (2,268) = 5.64, p < .01$. Parents in both G_1 and G_2 were younger (73.0 and 73.4 years, respectively) than parents in G_3 (76.2 years) (Scheffè's test). G_2 parents had significantly higher educational levels than G_3 parents. No statistical differences were observed in the self-reported health status or income of parents in the three groups, and no age difference was found between the referent children of the three groups. Additional descriptive data showed that 56% of G_1, 55% of G_2, and 64% of G_3 lived within 30 min of their referent child. Chi-square analysis indicated that geographical proximity was not related to number of children. Frequencies on occupational data showed that 90% or more of the daughters of parents in each group were employed. Daughters in G_1 were most likely to be in white collar occupations (50%), as were sons (42%). Daughters and sons in G_2 were divided approximately equally between blue and white collar positions; 44% of daughters and 41% of sons were blue collar workers, and 49% of daughters and 44% of sons were white collar workers. Blue collar occupations were most characteristic of daughters and sons in G_3 (61% and 77%, respectively).

Results of the analysis of covariance showed that filial expectations did not differ by number of children when parents' health was controlled. Overall means for filial expectations showed moderately high expectations for all groups (Table 12.1). No relationship was observed between frequency of association and number of children; however,

Table 12.1. Ranges, Means, and Standard Deviations for Parent-Child Characteristics According to Number of Children

	Number of children								
	One ($n = 57$)			Two or three ($n = 139$)			Four or more ($n = 83$)		
Variables	Range	M	SD	Range	M	SD	Range	M	SD
Parents' income[a]	$138–2375	494.16	378.96	$90–1386	426.69	246.04	$115–1143	379.76	228.59
Health	1–9	5.9	2.2	1–9	5.9	2.3	0–9	5.6	2.2
Age	65–96	73.0	6.5	65–90	73.4	5.5	66–94	76.2	6.7
Education	0–19	9.7	3.7	0–193	9.9	3.3	0–19	8.3	3.6
Filial expectations	7–12	9.6	1.3	6–12	10.0	1.2	8–12	10.0	1.2
Association	18–63	36.9	12.2	17–80	36.6	10.8	22–60	38.7	8.8
Help received	9–42	17.9	9.8	9–81	22.9	13.9	9–66	25.4	13.8
Children age	21–75	43.5	8.6	22–65	44.3	8.6	23–65	45.6	9.4

[a]Monthly income.

differences were found in the recency with which the groups had seen a child, χ^2 (6, $n = 276$) = 16.42, $p < .01$. Parents of only children were less likely to have seen their child in the last day or two than other parents. Differences were also observed in amount of help received by parents according to number of children, F (2,265) = 5.17, $p < .01$. Parents in G_1 received less help than those in G_2 and G_3 ($p < .05$). In general, low levels of help were observed for each group (Table 12.1). Help received usually took the form of vital assistance such as transportation and help when ill. Chi-square tests showed no relationship between the resource (e.g., child, spouse, friend, doctor) that parents would call upon in a crisis and number of children. Other data showed a difference between groups with regard to transportation. Parents in G_3 were less likely to have their own car than others, χ^2 (2, $n = 279$) = 8.37, $p < .02$.

As seen in Table 12.2, more variance in association and help received could be explained for parents with an only child than for other parents. The variable most consistently related to association

Table 12.2. Regression of Association and Help Upon Income, Sex, and Health of the Older Parent and Sex and Geographic Proximity of the Adult Child

Independent variables	Number of children		
	One	Two or Three	Four or more
Association			
Income (parents)		9.28**	
Sex of parent		−3.21*	
Sex of child			−3.57*
Geographical proximity	−3.89***	−1.22*	
Health of parent			
R^2 (adjusted)	.36**	.08***	.04*
Help received			
Income (parents)	7.14*		
Sex of parent		−8.14**	
Sex of child			−7.35**
Geographical proximity	−2.86***	−2.01**	
Health of parent	−1.56**	−.96*	−1.47**
R^2 (adjusted)	.29***	.15**	.12**

Note. Entries are metric regression coefficients, with the exception of the last row in each section.
*$p < .05$; **$p < .01$; ***$p < .001$.

and help received was geographical proximity. Association and help increased with propinquity to child for every group except G_3. Each of the five independent variables was significantly related to amount of help received for at least one group of parents; however, the factors varied greatly in their influence depending upon number of children. Whereas income, geographical proximity, and health of the parent were important in G_1, proximity, health, and sex of the parent were significant in G_2; and health of parent and sex of the child were central to explaining the amount of help received by parents in G_3. Parents of an only child received more help if they (parents) were in poor health and if the child lived in close proximity. Help also increased with parents' income. Parents with two or three children received more help from the referent child if they (parents) were female and if the child lived close by. Assistance also increased with poor health. Parents with four or more children received more help from the referent child if the child was a daughter and if the parents' health was poor. Not only did the factors related to association and help vary by number of children, but so did the amount of variance explained.

DISCUSSION

The results of this research indicate that number of children is related to the recency with which older parents living in a rural-transitional area have seen a child, the amount of assistance that they receive, and the factors influencing their interaction with children. The data show that the current cohort of older parents with few children (an only child or two to three children) constitute a "young-old" group in contrast to parents with a larger number of children (four or more). This observation appears to be age-cohort related and can be traced to comparatively lower fertility rates among the age group 65 to 75 than earlier cohorts (Cutler, 1981).

Fewer age-related dependencies (e.g., health and transportation) would appear to account, in part, for the observation that parents of only children reported less recency of visits and help received. The overall low levels of help received by older adults in the study may have been related, in part, to the rural-transitional nature of the area (i.e., the majority of daughters, traditionally the kin-keepers, were employed). The critical life stage of middle-aged children and associated family and career demands and stresses may also have contributed to low helping behaviors.

Number of children would appear to have little implications for filial expectations. Parents of all family sizes had similar moderately high expectations for help and planned to call upon a child with equal frequency in a crisis situation. These data suggest that older parents expect children to assume an appreciable level of responsibility in meeting important health, economic, and emotional needs regardless of how many offspring there are to share in this assistance. It is also possible that older respondents, regardless of number of children, were aware of potential resources beyond the child level such as friends, neighbors, and other kin. Unpublished analyses of these same data showed, for example, amount of kin assistance to be related to number of children. Assistance from children-in-law, grandchildren, siblings and siblings-in-law, and nieces and nephews increased as number of children decreased. Shanas et al. (1968) also found elements of replacement in the helping network of older adults. The finding that situational factors such as income, geographical proximity, and health of parent more strongly influenced the help received by the one-child elderly parents than other groups was probably related to the fact that there were no other children to share in the assistance to the older parents. The availability of other children may have served to "level" the effects of variables on helping patterns for parents with more than one child as evidenced by the minimal variance explained.

The centrality of geographical propinquity to patterns of generational relationships has been discussed by others (Bengtson et al., 1976; Troll, 1971). Data from the present study show that geographical proximity is a more stable predictor of older parent-child interaction (across family sizes) than sex-linkage or the dependency needs (health) of the parent. This finding may be a function of the social character of the overall sample. That is, direct services, the primary mode of intergenerational exchange among the working class, might be expected to decrease as residential proximity decreases. This is in contrast to the middle class who may be seen to balance assistance by economic exchange or gifts when distance is great (Troll, 1971). Similarly, the economies of personal contact, either face to face or by telephone, would reduce association between older working class adults and children when distance is great.

The data supported, in part, number of children as a function of socioeconomic status, a finding with implications for family interactional patterns (Lee, 1980). The observed educational differences between parent groups along with sex differences in child assistance confirm earlier reports of class differences in sex effects on kin interaction. Streib and Beck (1980), in their comprehensive review of the literature on older families, cited the relationship between sex-segregated interaction and socioeconomic level. Similarly, in the present study, daughters who were primarily blue collar workers (G_3) were found to provide more assistance to older parents and to have more association with parents than corresponding sons. Contrary to the literature, data from the present research showed sex of child to have little influence on the amount of help received when there are few children (Bengtson et al., 1976; Troll, 1971).

Another socioeconomic indicator, income, was also salient in intergenerational interaction for some groups in the present study. Income appeared to be an "enabler" to greater contact with and assistance from children. The data showed that visiting and getting together with children increased as income of parents of moderate family size increased. Similarly, parents with an only child were likely to receive more help as their income increased. This finding suggested that economic resources may increase opportunities for reciprocity in helping among some parent-child groups, an important factor in mutual help patterns. Few factors in the present study explained differences in frequency of association between parents and children or in filial expectations when controlling for number of children. Differences that were explained in most cases were small (with the exception of parents of only children).

In conclusion, the results of this study indicate that intergenerational patterns of interaction vary considerably among older adults based upon number of adult children. Included here are patterns of association and assistance as well as the factors impacting these relationships. The amount of assistance expected by older parents, however, appears to be unrelated to number of offspring. The data suggest the need to control for family size in future investigations of intergenerational interaction and in particular, helping relationships. The observation that, despite the rural-transitional character of the area studied, older adults and children of most contact had remained residentially stable should be taken into consideration when generalizing the results of this research to other similar geographical areas.

REFERENCES

Adams, B. N. *Kinship in an urban setting.* Markham, Chicago, 1968.
Beckman, L. J., & Houser, B. B. The consequences of childlessness on the social-psychological well-being of older women. *Journal of Gerontology,* 1982, *37*, 243–250.

Bengtson, V. L., Olander, E. B., & Haddad, A. The "generation gap" and aging family members: Toward a conceptual model. In J. F. Gubrium (Ed.), *Time, roles, and self in old age*. Human Sciences Press, New York, 1976.

Cantril, H. *The pattern of human concerns*. Rutgers University Press, New Brunswick, NJ, 1965.

Cutler, N. E. The aging population and social policy. In R. H. Davis (Ed.), *Aging: Prospects and issues*. University of Southern California Press, Los Angeles, CA, 1981.

Kivett, V. R., & Learner, R. M. Perspectives on the childless rural elderly: A comparative analysis. *The Gerontologist*, 1980, 20, 708–714.

Lang, A. M., & Brody, E. M. Characteristics of middle-aged daughters and help to their elderly mothers. *Journal of Marriage and the Family*, 1983, 45, 193–202.

Lee, G. R. Kinship in the seventies: A decade review of research and theory. *Journal of Marriage and the Family*, 1980, 42, 923–934.

Shanas, E. The family as a social support in old age. *The Gerontologist*, 1979, 19, 169–174.

Shanas, E., Townsend, P., Wedderburn, D., Friis, H., Milhøj, P., & Stehouwer, J. *Old people in three industrial societies*. Atherton Press, New York, 1968.

Streib, G. F., & Beck, R. W. Older families—A decade review. *Journal of Marriage and the Family*, 1980, 42, 937–956.

Troll, L. E. The family of later life: A decade review. *Journal of Marriage and the Family*, 1971, 33, 263–290.

13

The Impact of In-Home Services Termination on Family Caregivers*

Nancy Hooyman
Judith Gonyea
Rhonda Montgomery

With the rapidly growing pressure for long-term care services in a time of declining public resources, policy-makers are increasingly advocating greater private responsibility in meeting the elderly's needs. In fact, as Brody notes (1981), the informal support system, under the policy rubric of "preserving family ties," is being heralded as the primary resource for the aged. Policy initiatives such as various state Family Responsibility Amendments to Medicaid exemplify how concern over spiraling costs has resulted in increased expectations on family caregivers to prevent or delay institutionalization of the elderly. At the same time, social and health professionals are concerned about the family's capability to provide long-term care and the consequences of caregiving for the informal support system (Maddox, 1975; Tobin & Kulys, 1981).

This issue of family caregiving responsibilities for the elderly has been conceptualized in terms of achieving a balance of responsibility between family and state. Litwak and Figueria (1968), for example, maintain that caregiving functions must be shared since families and bureaucracies are differentially effective in performing certain types

*The Gerontologist, 25 (2) (1985), 141–145.

of tasks. An "optimal sharing of functions" is achieved when families respond to their members' idiosyncratic, socio-emotional needs and bureaucracies deal with predictable or routine tasks.

Refining Litwak's model of "optimal fit," Nelson (1982) proposes that the state may compete with, complement, or substitute for the roles performed by the family system; he contends that more policies are needed which support the family's important role as a service delivery system for the aged. Moroney (1976) analyzes the relationship between the family and the state in terms of the level of transfer of responsibility. Three major dimensions are measured along a continuum: the extent of the transfer (partial to permanent), the duration of the transfer (temporary to permanent), and the intent of the transfer in relation to the family's role (supportive to substitutive).

Common to these three conceptual frameworks is the recognition that the social, economic, and emotional costs of caring for the elderly are too great for the informal system to bear alone and that policies and programs are needed to complement or support the family's caregiving efforts. In-home or chore services, for example, represent a partial-permanent transfer of care from the family to the state and are assumed to complement the family's caregiving functions. Through the provision of such services as meal preparation, laundry, house cleaning, and transportation, chore services are intended to minimize the elderly's daily needs for care from informal support systems and, in the long run, to prevent institutionalization. Accordingly, these conceptual frameworks suggest that, when such complementary services are reduced or eliminated, the burdens faced by families providing care will increase, resulting in negative consequences for both the informal caregiving system and the elderly.

The opportunity to test these assumptions about the loss of complementary services negatively affecting family caregivers arose when approximately 2,000 clients were terminated from the chore services program in Washington state. Whereas, during the previous biennium, income eligibility for chore services was set at 50% of the State Median Income (SMI), that figure was reduced to 30% of the SMI during the 1981–83 biennium. For persons between 30 and 40% of the SMI, some proportion of the authorized hours were provided based on their income. The public response to these reductions was immediate and widespread. Elderly clients, family members, professionals, and citizen advocacy groups all expressed concern that the chore service reductions would negatively affect both clients and family caregivers, and it was widely believed that some terminated clients would be prematurely or inappropriately institutionalized. In response, the Washington State Department of Social and Health Services (DSHS) mandated a study of the effects of chore service termination on older clients. It was also speculated that the absence of chore services could overburden family members, resulting in caregiver stress and institutionalization of their elderly relative. This study, which was initiated in response to such concerns and conducted separately from the state's study, was intended to determine how the reduction in chore services affected the family caregivers. Specifically, this research focused on whether chore service reductions were related to changes in family members' caregiving behaviors and perceptions of burden and stress.

METHODS

Sample

The data for this study were collected approximately 1 year after the chore policy change. Family members included in the study were identified as "emergency contacts" for chore service clients (both terminated and continued) who had previously participated in a state-conducted survey (Denton et al., 1982). The sample included 42 relatives of terminated clients and 38 relatives of continued clients.

The sample consisted of identified family members in four target counties who 1) were willing to be interviewed, 2) considered themselves to be the primary person providing assistance to their older relative, and 3) lived within a 1-hour driving distance from their relative. The demographic characteristics of the sample, presented in Table 13.1, were similar to those reported in other studies of caregivers (Brody, 1981; Cicirelli, 1981; Horowitz & Dobrof, 1982). The majority of the sample were adult children, including daughters (44%), sons (26%), and daughters-in-law (5%). The remaining 25% of the sample was made up of 8 siblings, 4 nieces and nephews, 1 wife, and 7 other relatives. The sample was predominantly Caucasian (89%) and married (71%). Over half (61%) of the caregivers were employed either full-time (45%) or part-time (16%), while 31 (39%) were keeping house, retired, or unemployed. The median income of the family caregivers was $20,000 and the median age was 56 years. Comparisons of the two groups of caregivers on *t*-tests revealed no significant differences between the groups on any of the demographic variables listed in Table 13.1.

Table 13.1. Demographic Characteristics of Caregivers

Characteristic	n	%
Sex		
Male	21	26.2
Female	59	73.7
Relationship to Elder		
Spouse	1	1.2
Child	60	75.0
Sibling	8	10.0
Niece/nephew	4	5.0
Other relative	7	8.7
Marital Status		
Married	57	71.2
Not married	23	28.8
Employment Status		
Full-time	36	45.0
Part-time	13	16.2
Not employed	31	38.7
Age (median/years)	56.0	
Family Income (median/dollars)	20,000	

Note. Percentages may not add to 100 due to rounding.

MEASURES

Structured interviews were conducted in the respondents' homes. The interviews averaged 45 minutes in length and elicited demographic data and information about caregiving behaviors, perception of burden, and stress.

The extent of caregiving and types of caregiving behaviors were assessed by showing respondents a list of 21 tasks and asking 1) whether they had assisted their elderly relative with each task in the past month; 2) how many hours per week, on the average, they spent performing each task during the preceding month; and 3) how long they had provided assistance with this task. Twenty-one types of assistance were grouped into four task areas: *personal care tasks* (bathing, dressing, feeding, toileting, care of appearance, medications, nursing care, wheelchair transfer, assistance with walking, and bed transfer), *household tasks* (yard care, laundry, meal preparation, housework, and telephone assistance), *community tasks* (transportation, shopping and errands, personal business, and handling money), and *psychosocial tasks* (telephone check-up and companionship).

Perceived burden was measured with the 14-item, 5-point inventory shown in Table 13.2. Respondents were asked to report the extent to which their caregiving behaviors had changed 14 areas of their lives, such as privacy, personal freedom, and relationships with family and friends. Previous research has identified these areas as the ones most frequently affected by the caregiving experience (Archbold, 1981; Cicirelli, 1981; Horowitz & Dobrof, 1982; Robinson & Thurnher, 1979; Zarit et al., 1980). Chronbach's alpha was used to test the reliability of the measure. The alpha was equal to .85.

Stress was measured using a single item. Family members were told that "Almost everyone feels some degree of stress from time to time. At times you may feel no problem with anything; at other times, things seem to pile up and you feel tense, angry, or afraid. Let's call all of that feeling 'under stress.' " Respondents rated on a 5-point scale the amount of stress they were feeling in relation to caring for their older relatives.

Table 13.2. Measurement of Burden

Number	Item
1.	The amount of time you have to yourself
2.	The amount of privacy you have
3.	The amount of money you have available to meet the rest of your expenses
4.	The amount of personal freedom you have
5.	The amount of energy you have
6.	The amount of time you spend in recreational and/or social activities
7.	The amount of time you spend in volunteer activities
8.	The amount of vacation activities and trips you take
9.	Your relationships with other family members
10.	Your relationships with friends
11.	Your health
12.	Your performance at work
13.	Your satisfaction with your own life
14.	Your ability to manage or control your daily schedule

Note. Respondents were asked to rate items 1–8 in terms of whether they had "a lot less, a little less, a little more, or a lot more of these aspects" in their lives than they had a year ago. They were asked to rate items 9–14 in terms of whether those aspects of their lives had "become a lot better, become a little better, remained the same, become a little worse, or become a lot worse" than they were a year ago.

FINDINGS

In contrast to the expectations of many interested parties, the presence or absence of chore services was not found to be associated with the extent of caregiving involvement. The family caregivers of terminated and continued chore clients did not differ significantly with regard to type, frequency, or duration of assistance to their older relatives, as shown in Table 13.3. Both groups primarily provided one or more psychosocial tasks (95% of all caregivers). Although the difference was not statistically significant, caregivers of current clients provided 12 more hours of care per month than caregivers of former clients. The average amount of care provided was 72 hours per month, with caregivers of terminated clients providing 69 hours and those of current clients providing 81 hours. Nor did the two groups of caregivers differ on the length of time assistance had been provided. Rather, length of time was related to the nature of the task, with psychosocial tasks being provided for the longest period of time and personal care tasks for the shortest time.

Table 13.3. Number of Caregivers*, Average Number of Hours Care Provided**, Average Number of Years Care Provided, by Task Grouping

	Task Groupings			
	Psycho-social	Com-munity	House-hold	Personal Care
Current Clients (*n* = 38)				
No. of Caregivers	36	35	25	25
Av. No. Hours Care Provided	38	20	14	9
Av. No. Years Care Provided	18.8	17.5	8.3	7.3
Former Clients (*n* = 42)				
No. of Caregivers	41	38	23	29
Av. No. Hours Care Provided	40	12	13	4
Av. No. Years Care Provided	20.0	12.3	9.3	6.4

*Caregivers who performed at least one task within a category were included in that category.
**The average number of hours tasks were provided in the preceding month.

Data analyses also indicated that the receipt or loss of chore services was not associated with the caregivers' perceptions of burden or with their level of stress. In general, the majority of caregivers felt that providing assistance to their older relative had not resulted in any changes in the areas identified to measure perceived burden (see Table 13.4). Very few respondents, however, felt that their personal lives had improved while caring for their relative. Life satisfaction was the one exception to this pattern of negative changes, with 27.3% of the respondents reporting an increase in life satisfaction during the past year as a result of caring for their older relative. Slightly over one-half of the total respondents reported that the present situation with their older relative had resulted in an increase in the amount of stress in their lives.

Table 13.4. Percent of Caregivers' Responses on Burden Scale Items (n = 79)

Item	A Lot More	A Little More	The Same	A Little Less	A Lot Less
1. Amount of time	2.6	1.3	46.2	28.2	21.8
2. Amount of privacy	1.3	1.3	68.4	22.8	6.3
3. Amount of money	5.1	0.0	73.1	15.4	6.4
4. Amount of freedom	2.6	1.3	52.6	28.2	15.4
5. Amount of energy	3.8	0.0	55.7	26.6	13.7
6. Amount of social and recreational activities	3.8	3.8	56.4	25.6	10.3
7. Amount of volunteer activities	0.0	0.0	89.5	7.0	3.5
8. Amount of vacation and trips	1.3	1.3	58.4	24.7	14.3

Item	A Lot Better	A Little Better	The Same	A Little Worse	A Lot Worse
9. Relationship with family	3.8	11.4	72.2	12.7	0.0
10. Relationships with friends	1.3	5.1	78.5	13.9	1.3
11. Health	0.0	0.0	72.5	23.8	3.7
12. Work performance	0.0	2.0	82.0	16.0	0.0
13. Life satisfaction	10.4	16.9	57.1	10.4	5.2
14. Control over daily schedule	0.0	2.5	66.7	25.6	5.1

In fact, on most items, a substantial proportion of all caregivers, ranging from approximately 30% to 50% of the total sample, felt that their personal lives had changed for the worse during the past year. The aspects of their personal lives that caregivers most often cited as changing in a negative direction were amount of time for themselves (50.0%), amount of personal freedom (43.6%), amount of personal energy (40.3%), amount of vacations and trips (39.4%), amount of social and recreational activities (35.9%), control over daily schedule (30.7%), and amount of privacy (29.1%).

Given this lack of significant relationship between the presence or absence of chore services and caregiver burden, a question was raised as to what factors contributed to a family caregiver's perception of burden. Because the various independent variables related to caregiving behaviors were intercorrelated, the use of stepwise multiple regression to explore further the correlates of objective burden was especially useful (see Table 13.5). The multiple regression suggested that types of tasks performed were better predictors of perception of burden than were the frequency or length of time that a family member provided care. Neither the frequency nor the length of time that families provided care remained significant after the performance of type of tasks was controlled for in the stepwise regression. Specifically, the performance of personal care or body contact tasks, such as bathing, feeding, and toileting, was strongly correlated with perceived burden. In contrast, the more impersonal tasks of shopping, laundry, and house cleaning, which help older persons to manage

Table 13.5. Analyses of Perceived Burden ($n = 80$)

	Correlations		
Variables	Perceived Burden	Stress	Personal Care
Perceived Burden	1.00	.65	.47
Stress		1.00	.27
Personal Care			1.00

	Regression on Perceived Burden			
Variable	Multiple R	R^2	F	Significance
Personal Care	.50	.25	26.25	.000

their environment and which have been traditionally provided by in-home programs, were not strongly correlated with families' perceptions of burden.

DISCUSSION

The finding that the presence or absence of chore services did not influence the extent of family caregiving involvement deserves some attention. The data reflect the findings of other studies that, even when formal services are utilized, the family remains extensively involved (Brody et al., 1978; Cantor, 1980; Cicirelli, 1981). In fact, the lack of difference in the extent of assistance by family caregivers of terminated and continued clients suggests that these families may already be providing all the support that they are able or willing to give.

The coordination of roles has been identified as a critical factor in how families and the state share responsibility for the elderly's care (Litwak & Figueria, 1968; Nelson, 1982). Because the chore services program focuses on household and community tasks for only a limited time period, it may not have achieved an "optimal sharing of functions" in relation to the family. Instead, the most frequent tasks chore services provide are housework (94% of clients), shopping (41% of clients), transportation (40% of clients), yard work (20% of clients), and help with meal preparation (20% of clients), not assistance with the personal care tasks that families find most burdensome. Furthermore, the amount of services provided to clients is fairly minimal, with 55% receiving chore services only 1 to 4 days per month and only 21% receiving chore services 4 to 8 days per month. Even for full-service clients, chore services provide 57% of all assistance, over three-fourths of household and laundry, just under half of meal preparation and transportation, and one-third of personal care assistance. For full-service clients, families are the other major source of help, providing 28% of the total assistance (Olson & Crews-Rankos, 1982). In other words, time-limited chore services do not address the conditions underlying perceived burden—the performance of personal care tasks—and therefore may not complement families by providing them with the type of help they need most.

One reason for the strong relationship of performance of personal care tasks to perceptions of burden may be that perceived burden is, in part, a function of the family's expectations and norms regarding their appropriate caregiving role. Although family members undoubtedly expect to assist their elderly relatives with household and community tasks or to provide emotional support, they are often unprepared to perform personal care tasks. Assisting an older relative with intimate bodily tasks may violate family norms about appropriate familial roles and interactions and may create feelings of role reversal. The family member performing personal care tasks thus may feel burdened, even when receiving government-sponsored services such as chore. Another consequence from chore services not complementing families around the most burdensome tasks may be that families become less effective at performing the social-emotional tasks for which they are best suited (Litwak & Figueria, 1968; Sussman, 1977). Performing such instrumental tasks may, over time, interfere with the family's expressive exchanges with their relative, thereby reducing the affective quality of their relationship.

Of greatest policy significance may be the relationship found between performing personal care tasks, perceptions of burden, and the detrimental effects of stress as a long-run consequence of providing personal care. One outcome of the stress of caregiving, extensively documented elsewhere, is inappropriate institutionalization of the older person (Brody et al., 1978; Kraus et al., 1976; Teresi et al., 1980). Interventions are clearly needed to reduce the stressful situation created by the increased burden of performing personal care tasks for elderly relatives.

CONSTRAINTS OF THE STUDY

In interpreting this study's findings, several limiting factors must be identified. The findings are based on data collected at only one point in time, approximately 1 year after the chore policy change, from a relatively small purposive sample group of 80 predominantly white family caregivers. Information is available only on the family member named as primary caregiver, not on other family members or other formal services (e.g., volunteers) that might also have been providing care. The extent to which clients' needs remain unmet is unknown. Lastly, an assessment of the impact of any single service, such as chore services, is not adequate without examining the overall context of services utilized. In-home services might better be evaluated as one component of a more comprehensive continuum of care.

FUTURE DIRECTIONS

Although previous work has suggested the importance of policies to complement or support the family in their caregiving efforts, there is a need to specify and refine the meaning of complementarity. This could include further examination of the factors associated with the caregivers' perception of burden, especially the types of tasks performed; the role of expectations regarding appropriate caregiving tasks for the family to perform; and the types of care tasks that may interfere with the family's ability to perform socio-emotional tasks.

From a practice perspective, comprehensive multiple services designed to share responsibilities with the family must coordinate with families around the personal care tasks that they find most burdensome. For example, educational/training programs for family members might provide opportunities for families to clarify their expectations about appropriate relationships with an older relative requiring personal care. Likewise, having personal care aides make regular visits to the home to bathe, dress, and perform special nursing care tasks could serve to reduce some of the burden of caregiving on families. The burden of personal care tasks could also be reduced by providing equipment and environmental supports to enable the older person to perform tasks such as bathing and toileting more independently. Unfortunately, although families with sufficient financial resources may be able to obtain such supports, families who depend upon Medicare or Medicaid benefits have fewer options since governmental funding of personal care services is limited (Newman, 1980). The findings of the study thus raise critical research and policy questions about the lack of availability of the type of services that appear to complement family caregivers and thereby reduce the burden created by personal care tasks.

REFERENCES

Archbold, P. G. (1981, July). *Impact of parent-caring on women.* Paper presented at the XII International Congress of Gerontology, Hamburg, West Germany.

Brody, E. (1981). Women in the middle and family help to older people. *The Gerontologist, 21,* 471–480.

Brody, S. J., Poulshock, S. W., & Masciocchi, C. F. (1978). The family caring unit: A major consideration in the long-term support system. *The Gerontologist, 18,* 556–561.

Cantor, M. (1980, November). *Caring for the frail elderly: Impact on family, friends, and neighbors.* Paper presented at the 33rd Annual Scientific Meeting of the Gerontological Society of America, San Diego, CA.

Cicirelli, V. G. (1981). *Helping elderly parents: The role of adult children.* Boston: Auburn House.

Denton, R., Richards, P., Olson, D., & Crews-Rankos, D. (1982). *An analysis and evaluation of chore services for the elderly of Washington State.* Olympia, WA: Department of Social and Health Services.

Horowitz, A., & Dobrof, R. (1982). *The role of families in providing long-term care to the frail and chronically ill elderly living in the community.* New York: Brookdale Center on Aging, Hunter College.

Kraus, A. S., Spasoff, R. A., Beattie, E. J., Holden, D. E. W., Lawson, J. S., Rodenburg, M., & Woodcock, G. M. (1976). Elderly application process: Placement and care needs. *Journal of the American Geriatrics Society, 24,* 117–125.

Litwak, E., & Figueria, J. (1968). Technological innovation and theoretical functions of primary groups and bureaucratic structures. *American Journal of Sociology,* 468–481.

Maddox, G. L. (1975). Families as a context and resource in chronic illness. In S. Sherwood (Ed.), *Long-term care: A handbook for researchers, planners and providers.* New York: Spectrum.

Moroney, R. M. (1976). *The family and the state: Considerations for social policy.* New York: Longmans.

Nelson, G. M. (1982). Support for the aged: Public and private responsibility. *Social Work, 27,* 137–143.

Newman, S. J. (1980). *Government policy and the relationship between adult children and their aging parents: Filial support, Medicare, and Medicaid.* Unpublished manuscript, Institute for Social Research, Ann Arbor, MI.

Olson, D., & Crews-Rankos, D. (1982). *Terminating chore services for selected clients: A report to the legislature.* Olympia, WA: Department of Social and Health Services.

Robinson, B., & Thurnher, M. (1979). Taking care of parents: A family-cycle transition. *The Gerontologist, 19,* 586–593.

Sussman, M. B. (1977). Family, bureaucracy, and elderly individuals: An organizational/linkage perspective. In E. Shanas & M. Sussman (Eds.), *Family, bureaucracy, and the elderly.* Durham, NC: Duke University Press.

Teresi, J., Toner, J., Bennett, R., & Wilder, D. (1980, November). *Factors related to family attitudes toward institutionalizing older relatives.* Presented at the 33rd Annual Scientific Meeting of the Gerontological Society, San Diego, CA.

Tobin, S. S., & Kulys, R. (1981). The family in the institutionalization of the elderly. *Journal of Social Issues, 37,* 145–157.

Zarit, S. H., Reever, K. E., & Bach-Peterson, J. (1980). Relatives of the impaired elderly: Correlates of feelings of burden. *The Gerontologist, 20,* 649–655.

14

Families Caring for Elders in Residence: Issues in the Measurement of Burden*

S. Walter Poulshock
Gary T. Deimling

Evidence continues to mount that families care for elderly relatives and that they do so in a variety of settings and contexts (Shanas, 1979; Shanas et al., 1968). Researchers report that elders who receive care from close kin exhibit substantial levels of physical and mental impairment and that their families experience a variety of effects (Litman, 1971; Morycz, 1980; Zarit et al., 1980). These effects are typically referred to as burdens.

The bulk of research on caregiving burdens is in the field of mental health (see Brown et al., 1972, and Thompson & Doll, 1982, for extensive reviews of the literature). Findings generally indicate that providing high levels of care to dependent relatives, whether they are chronically ill (Manjoney & McKegney, 1978) or acutely ill (Herz et al., 1976), mentally ill adults (Lefton et al., 1962) or retarded children (Fatheringham et al., 1972), produces difficulties for caregivers. These studies, however, define and measure burden in diverse ways making cross-study comparisons difficult.

Journal of Gerontology, 39 (2) (1984), 230–239.
This is a substantially revised version of a paper presented at the 35th Annual Meeting of the Gerontological Society of America, Boston, November 1982. Support was provided by Administration on Aging grant no. 90-AR-2112.

The purposes of this paper are to clarify the concept of caregiving burden, urge a multidimensional perspective, and suggest measurement techniques that will prove useful for other researchers in the field. The analysis underscores the need to apply the concept of burden to subjective interpretations by caregivers of problems that flow from elders' impairments. Concomitantly, a variety of less subjective effects or impacts are also important and measureable. The model, then, is one in which burden is a mediating force between elders' impairments and impact on caregivers. These issues are elaborated and illustrated utilizing data and findings from the Benjamin Rose Institute's (BRI) survey of 614 families in which impaired elders resided with and were provided care by family members.

Burden has been broadly defined and differentially measured. The definitions range from burden as emotional costs qua feelings of embarrassment and overload (Thompson & Doll, 1982) to specific changes in caregivers' day-to-day lives such as disruption of daily routine (Fatheringham et al., 1972). Other areas include financial difficulties, role strain, and physical health deterioration (Robinson, 1983; Zarit et al., 1980). As a result of the breadth of issues that have been subsumed under the general term, its use as a unified concept is questionable. Attempts to derive specific measures from a concept so broadly defined result in a lack of precision that leaves the research findings in doubt. A few investigators have recognized this problem and dealt with it by dividing the concept into two components labeled "subjective" and "objective" burden (Thompson & Doll, 1982). This approach has not proved to be a satisfactory solution, as a potpourri of items are subsumed within each category.

Thus, research either treats the variety of caregiving effects as unidimensional or inconsistently labels these effects as either objective or subjective burden. This is not to minimize the need to make distinctions between types of burden. One of the chief benefits of doing this is that it makes explicit the importance of caregivers' subjective perceptions and interpretations of the burdens they experience. Although the more concrete or instrumental effects families experience are of importance and will be touched on later, it is the subjective experience of caregivers that color or filter their reports of effects. As a result they must be included in any analysis of caregiving's impact.

The analytic model proposed here is based on the assumption that the burdens caregivers experience are the result of their highly personal and individualized responses to specific caregiving contexts.

These are defined largely by the types of impairment the elderly care recipient exhibits. Elders require care from family members as the result of physical dependence, mental impairment, or some combination of the two.

The data in the BRI study indicate that the linkage between impairment and impact is centered on the subjective view of caregivers that certain tasks performed and derived from the impairments were burdensome, or that certain deviant behaviors on the part of elders were perceived by caregivers to be extremely stress producing. On the other hand, some caregivers faced with similar types of tasks or disruptive behaviors did not subjectively view them as burdens and, therefore, measured extremely low on the impact scales. A study by Brown et al. (1972) utilized, with good results, this analytical approach of placing the emotional response of caregivers in a mediating role, in this example, between impairment derived from schizophrenia and relatively objective measures of caregiving effects.

In the case of outcome measures we urge that the term *caregiving impact* be utilized in place of *objective burden*. The reason for relabeling these more or less objective changes in caregivers' lives is that the term objective burden, like burden, has had a variety of referents in previous research. For precision, in this chapter, the measures utilized to operationalize the effects of caregiving will be referred to as impact. The items chosen to represent impact are constructed using relatively unidimensional elements that assess the impact caregiving has on various aspects of caregivers' daily lives. Many of the items utilized in previous research as objective measures of burden are suitable. These include the impact caregiving has on family relationships, social activities, health, or employment changes. The point is not which items are used to operationalize impact. Rather, the issue is the way in which they are combined. Correlational analysis and factor analytic models utilized in this paper demonstrate ways in which the unidimensionality and independence of the impact measures may be enhanced.

Beyond burden and impact, as they have been described, other concepts should be included in order to illuminate more fully the relationship between elder impairment, burden, and impact on caregivers. Certainly, the characteristics of the elder's incapacity affects the caregiver's perception of burden and the impact that caregiving has on her life. The caregiver's own mental and physical well-being, however, are implicated in this relationship as well. Caregivers with lower levels of mental and physical well-being may be limited in their capacity to respond to the rigors of caregiving. For this group the burdens they perceive, as well as the actual impact that caregiving has on them, may be accentuated.

One area of caregivers' mental health that is particularly salient in understanding their responses to caregiving is the amount of depression exhibited. As Lezak (1978) pointed out, virtually all caregivers experience some level of depression, and it may be associated with caregiving. As such, it constitutes an effect or impact that caregiving has on the individual. Depression may have an entirely different origin, however; that is, it may result from biological changes experienced by the caregiver or from difficulties with other family matters unrelated to caregiving. In these cases, depression would more likely be an antecedent variable. In either situation, it has significant potential for affecting caregiving's impact.

To summarize: the model that is being utilized is one in which burden plays a central role between the elder's impairment on the one hand and the impact that caregiving has on the life of the caregiver and the family on the other hand. Moreover, this framework incorporates an analytic design in which the meaning of burden as well as its measurement flows from a connectedness to the care recipient's impairment. This subjective filter, designated burden, then, is associated with the tasks affiliated with physical dependence and mental incapacity. In the remainder of this paper these issues are developed further using data derived from the BRI study of family members living with and caring for impaired elders.

METHOD

Sample

The principal study site was the Greater Cleveland metropolitan area and 10 adjacent nonmetropolitan counties. The 614 families were chosen from over 2,000 referrals from approximately 120 sources. They were selected using a purposive sampling strategy that stratified them into three major substrata: (a) geographic area of residence (40% urban, 40% suburban, 20% rural); (b) racial characteristics (25% black, 75% white); and (c) generational configuration (50% one-, 30% two-, and 20% three-generation households).

In addition to these sociodemographic sampling criteria the family also included an impaired elderly relative who received personal care assistance from a primary caregiver in the household. Approximately 50% of the caregivers in this study were the impaired elder's spouse, equally divided between men and women. The remaining one-half of the total sample were adult children and children-in-law: 83% daughters, 9% sons, and 8% daughters-in-law. The respondents (primary caregiver and elder in each family unit) were interviewed utilizing structured interview schedules.

Measures

The three conceptual categories and corresponding indicators were elder impairment, burden, and impact. All factor analytically derived indicators were weighted sums.

Elder Impairment

The elder impairment measures were dependency associated with physical illness and three measures of mental impairment. The former was represented by the number of Activities of Daily Living (ADL) with which the elder required assistance: bathing, dressing, toileting, mobility, incontinence, and eating. The ADL dependency indicator represents the variety and complexity of ADL impairment exhibited by the elder rather than the level of severity for each of the

Table 14.1. Description of Key Indicators for Caregiving Sample

Domain	Measure	Range	M	SD
Elder impairment	ADL impairment	0–6	3.05	1.82
	Sociability	0–4	3.04	1.01
	Disruptive behavior	0–4	1.02	0.93
	Cognitive incapacity	0–4	1.02	0.93
Burden	ADL impairment burden	0–3	1.68	1.15
	Sociability	1–3	1.96	0.75
	Disruptive behavior	1–3	1.97	0.67
	Cognitive incapacity	1–3	1.72	0.66
Impact	Negative impact on ECF relationships	0–4	1.05	0.90
	Caregivers social activity restrictions	0–3	1.05	0.91
Caregiver mental health	Zung standardized depression score	25–100	44.40	11.30

items. On average the elders were dependent in three of the six areas; approximately 30% of the sample were dependent in at least five areas (Table 14.1). This level of impairment signified that the primary caregivers had to provide substantial amounts of care.

Beyond physical impairment, the mental impairment of elders also has considerable potential for the creation of burden and impact on caregivers and their families. Three dimensions of mental impairment derived from 23 separate items in a factor analytic model with Varimax rotation were used (Table 14.2). The first factor, Sociability, contained eight items loading between .49 and .70, tapping the elder's level of cooperativeness, withdrawal, isolation. A low score on this indicator represented a lack of sociability. The second factor,

Table 14.2. Rotated (Varimax) Factor Structure for Mental Status Variables

Item	Factor 1	Factor 2	Factor 3
Elder is interesting to talk to	.70	−.07	−.27
Elder is enjoyable to be with	.68	−.28	−.18
Elder is friendly and sociable toward people	.66	−.08	−.00
Elder seems interested in things	.64	.06	−.29
Elder is cooperative	.64	−.42	−.05
Elder is clean or neat about self	.58	−.06	−.19
Elder is appreciative or grateful for help	.57	−.40	−.03
Elder is withdrawn or unresponsive	−.49	.08	.27
Elder complains or criticizes things	−.01	.69	.02
Elder interferes with caregiver and other household members	−.02	.60	.17
Elder fails to respect privacy	−.09	.55	.26
Elder yells or swears at people	−.14	.53	.18
Elder does embarrassing things	−.24	.49	.23
Elder disrupts meals or makes them unpleasant	−.22	.45	.19
Elder physically strikes out at people	−.28	.38	.25
Elder is confused	−.43	.05	.65
Elder is forgetful	−.38	.02	.60
Elder hears or sees things that are not there	−.07	.23	.58
Elder wanders inside the house	−.11	.26	.45
Elder has unrealistic fears	−.04	.35	.44
Elder talks or mumbles to self	−.30	.27	.43
Elder repeats self	−.04	.36	.42
Elder does things harmful to self and others	−.16	.18	.38

Disruptive Behavior, contained seven items loading between .38 and .69, and included areas focused on the elder's acting out, such as striking family members, swearing, and disrupting meals. The third factor, Cognitive Incapacity, contained eight items that loaded between .38 and .65. These measured the more traditionally assessed aspects of mental impairment such as forgetfulness and confusion. All three indicators were based on the caregiver's reports (i.e., at the time of the interview) of current behaviors or incapacities that the elder exhibited.

Because these weighted indicators are derived from factor scores, the absolute level of mental impairment as defined in this study is difficult to discern. Basic frequency tabulations are more helpful in this regard: 33% of elders exhibited two or more disruptive behaviors, 50% had three or more symptoms of cognitive incapacity, and approximately one-third demonstrated a consistent lack of sociability (three or more of eight items).

Burden

It was suggested earlier that the indicators of burden should correspond directly to the four indicators of impairment. The burden measure associated with ADL impairment incorporated caregiver responses to several questions on the tiring, difficult, or upsetting nature of caregiving tasks. Caregivers who indicated that these tasks were neither tiring, difficult, nor upsetting received the lowest score (0); those who indicated that tasks were tiring, difficult, and upsetting received the highest score (3); intermediate scores (1, 2) were based on other combinations of responses. Approximately one-third of the caregivers reported that the personal care tasks associated with the elder's physical impairment were difficult, tiring, and upsetting. Moreover, another 80 respondents indicated that they found the tasks they performed *either* difficult, tiring, or upsetting.

The burden measures associated with the three mental impairment indicators were derived from caregiver responses to questions about the degree to which the specific impairment upset them or created a problem for them: not at all (1), somewhat (2), or a great deal (3). Over 40% of caregivers reported that the elder's lack of sociability upset them somewhat or a great deal; 45% reported that the elder's disruptive behaviors upset them somewhat or a great deal. Over 20% reported that the elder's cognitive incapacity created a problem for them.

Impact

Two impact measures were developed from factor analysis of 34 separate items in which caregivers indicated that because of caregiving, or since caregiving began, specific aspects of family life were altered or affected. The 34 items covered a broad range of topics including job conflict, financial hardships, caregivers' physical/mental health, family relationships, and social, group and recreational activities. Many of the items were similar to those utilized by other researchers (e.g., Moos, 1974; Zarit et al., 1980). Based on this analysis, 19 items were selected for the factor solution shown in Table 14.3.

Factor 1 contained 11 items that loaded between .46 and .75 and reflect the negative changes in elder-caregiver/caregiver-family relationships (ECF) resulting from caregiving. Nine of the 11 items were

Table 14.3. Rotated (Varimax) Factor Structure for Impact Variables

Item	Factor 1	Factor 2
Caregiver feels angry toward elder	.75	−.01
Caregiver's relationship with elder makes caregiver depressed	.73	.13
Caregiver relationship with elder is strained	.73	.04
Caregiver feels resentful toward elder	.69	.01
Elder has negatively affected relationship with family members	.65	.17
Caregiver feels elder tries to manipulate caregiver	.63	.10
Caregiver wish elder and caregiver had better relationship	.60	.10
Caregiver relationship with elder gives pleasure	−.57	−.13
Caregiver feels elder makes more requests than necessary	.54	.17
Caregiver feels pressured between giving to elder and others in the family	.52	.25
Caregiver feels that elder can only depend on caregiver	.46	.19
Caregiver takes part in group/organized activities less	.07	.70
Caregiver takes part in theatre, concerts, shows less	.08	.64
Caregiver visits family/friends less	.13	.63
Caregiver takes part in volunteer activities less	.00	.62
Caregiver feels social life has suffered because of elder	.41	.60
Caregiver doesn't have enough time for self	.44	.56
Caregiver takes part in church related activities less	.04	.55
Caregiver takes part in other social activities less often	.14	.50

specific to the caregiver-elder relationship; the remaining two, which focused on other family members, demonstrated similarly strong loadings. The second factor that emerged contained eight items that loaded from .50 to .70; these represented the restrictions in caregivers' activities resulting from caregiving. Descriptive data indicated that 52% of caregivers reported two or more areas of negative impact on ECF relationships and 68% reported two or more restrictions in their activities.

As a result of their demonstrated importance in other studies, a number of additional variables were included in this analysis: e.g., the elder's age, the caregiver's age, socioeconomic status, physical health, and depression. Only the latter (as measured by the Zung Depression Scale, 1972) displayed any consistent relationship with the other measures on which this paper focuses.

RESULTS

Intercorrelation of Burden Measures

The first argument presented was that separate burden indicators should correspond to different types of impairment. This is based on the assumption that the caregiving context is highly differentiated and that caregivers delineate burden according to context. One test of this assumption is the degree to which the individual burden measures are associated with each other. The data displayed here document the independent nature of the different measures of burden (Table 14.4). Several items showed substantial correlation, most notably cognitive incapacity burden and sociability burden ($r = .46$). None, however, explained as much as 25% of the variance in each other. In general, the three burden measures that correspond to the three elder mental impairment variables were correlated most highly. In contrast, the weakest association was between the burden corresponding to the elder's ADL impairment and those corresponding to the elder's mental impairment. For example, in the case of the relationship between ADL impairment burden and the burden created by the elder's lack of sociability, the correlation was .15.

These data indicate that although the various measures of burden expressed by caregivers are correlated, they are not synonymous. Furthermore, the greatest independence among burden measures was demonstrated by the burden associated with the elder's ADL impairment and the burden associated with the elder's mental im-

Table 14.4. Zero-Order Correlation Matrix for Impairment, Burden, Impact Indicators, and Caregiver Depression

Indicator	1	2	3	4	5	6	7	8	9	10
Elder Impairment										
1. Sociability										
2. Disruptive behavior	−.38									
3. Cognitive incapacity	−.53	.45								
4. ADL impairment	−.23	.00	.20							
Burden										
5. Sociability	−.22	.30	.20	−.03						
6. Disruptive behavior	−.28	.35	.30	.02	.38					
7. Cognitive incapacity	−.34	.27	.44	.08	.46	.41				
8. ADL impairment	−.26	.23	.27	.46	.15	.24	.25			
Impact										
9. Negative impact on elder-caregiver family (ECF) relationships	−.48	.63	.42	.05	.37	.46	.36	.30		
10. Caregiver social activity restriction	−.25	.29	.32	.40	.23	.23	.29	.45	.31	
Caregiver mental health										
11. Zung depression score	−.27	.31	.27	.15	.18	.29	.23	.30	.40	.29

235

pairment. This independence provides support for examining the impact of mental and physical impairment as two versions of the measurement model proposed in this paper.

Burden and Impairment

The second argument was that burden should be linked to specific impairments of the elder. In order to examine this proposition empirically additional correlational data are presented in Table 14.4, including the four measures of impairment and the four corresponding burden measures. In every case there was a moderate association between elder impairment and the corresponding burden reported by caregivers.

Cognitive incapacity and ADL impairment demonstrated the strongest associations with their corresponding burdens. These correlations ($r = .44$ and $.46$, respectively) suggest that the elder's cognitive incapacity (forgetfulness, confusion and behavior harmful to self) translates quite directly into perceptions of burden. This is probably due to the perceived pervasiveness of the tasks required to care for a disoriented or physically impaired elder. Whereas it may be possible to ignore or avoid an elder who is withdrawn or isolated, the confused or incontinent elder requires constant surveillance or attention.

Overall, there was a moderate-to-strong empirical link between elder impairment characteristics and the corresponding perception of burden. The strength of the relationship, however, was not of such magnitude that it suggests that impairment and burden are synonymous. In no case did impairment explain as much as 25% of the variance in a corresponding burden measure. In the strongest correlational example ($r = .46$) the proportion of variance explained was 21%. Clearly, factors other than impairment are affecting the sense of burden.

Burden and Impact

The third argument was that the concept of burden was related to relatively objective changes in caregivers' lives, as well as in those of their families. Obviously, establishing the linkage between burden and impact is essential if the case is to be made for the former as intermediary between impairment and impact.

The two specific measures of impact used in this analysis are the caregivers' reports of negative changes in ECF relationships and restrictions in caregivers' social activities. The intercorrelations between the two impact and four burden measures are displayed in Table 14.4. Additionally, the correlational data concerning the elders impairment are provided to demonstrate the relationship of impairment to impact. With minor exception, all the measures of both impairment and burden were significantly correlated with the two impact measures. The single strongest correlation between any of the impairment indicators was the relationship between disruptive behaviors exhibited by elders and negative impact on ECF relationships ($r = .63$).

Moreover, the single strongest correlation among any of the burden measures and impact was between the burden associated with disruptive behavior and negative impact on ECF relationships ($r = .46$). As Vincent (1967) pointed out, the family has substantial adaptive capacity and can respond to serious challenges; however, behavior that is defined as deviant or bizarre on the part of a family member creates a great deal of strain on that adaptive capacity. The findings from the BRI study, moreover, indicate that an elder's deviant behavior is perceived as a severe burden and has serious implications for family relationships. In contrast, other research (Zarit et al., 1980), studying caregiving burden among families of elderly relatives with senile dementia, found little correlation between several measures of mental impairment, including behavioral problems and caregiving burden. That research, however, treated burden as a singular dimension, and it is possible that several underlying dimensions correlated in contrasting ways with mental impairment and thus were obscured.

From the data in Table 14.4 several patterns emerge. First; the mental impairment measures were more highly correlated with impact measures than with their corresponding burden measures. In contrast, the ADL impairment measure was less strongly correlated with the impact measures than with the corresponding burden measure. A second pattern is that both the impairment and burden measures related to the elder's mental health operate more closely to affect the nature of family relationships than do those related to ADL. ADL impairment and corresponding burden measures were more highly correlated with the restrictions caregivers experience in their activities. Recalling earlier comments concerning the adaptability of the family, family caregivers are apparently able to absorb considerable additional workload as a result of their elders' physical incapacities without experiencing a negative impact on elder-caregiver and other family relationships. The rigors of providing care to a physically disabled family member, however, have a substantial effect on both the perception of burden and, ultimately, on the social and group activities in which caregivers participate.

The final argument is that caregivers' feelings of depression have an important effect on the perception of burden and the impact on their lives. The correlations between caregivers' depression, measures of impairment, burden, and impact are also shown in Table 14.4. In general, there was a persistent relationship between the caregiver's depression score and burden as well as the impact measures. The strongest relationship was between the caregiver's depression score and negative impact on ECF relationships ($r = .40$). The pervasive nature of the effects of caregiver depression on the measures of concern in this study reinforces the need to consider these effects in a multivariate context. Whether depression is viewed as an *effect* of caregiving or as an *antecedent* influence, from the standpoint of measurement, it must be considered. If not, it may confound the interpretation of the relationships between other measures employed in the analysis.

To summarize the findings so far, the correlational analysis demonstrated that it is important to differentiate the varying dimensions of impairment, burden, and impact. Further, it is important to take into account the depression level of the caregiver as it affects measures of both burden and impact.

More specifically, the data indicate that the measures of elder mental impairment and the corresponding burden measures are substantially correlated with the negative impact on ECF relationships. Alternatively, the elders' ADL impairments and burdens are more highly correlated with restrictions in caregivers' activities. The data also indicate that, although the measures selected to operationalize impairment, burden, and impact exhibit substantial correlation, they clearly do not represent a single dimension. The correlational data, however, portray only the gross relationships between these variables. In order to understand more fully their relationship to one another and to examine the role of burden as an intermediary between impairment and impact, the independent and additive effects of these measures must be examined.

Impairment, Burden and Impact: Independent and Additive Effects

To identify the independent and additive contribution of impairment and burden to caregiving impact, as measured by ECF relationships and caregiver activities, an extensive series of regression equations was estimated. It is not possible within the scope of this paper to display all the equations and the models that they represent. For the sake of parsimony, the results from several of these analyses are depicted in the two diagrams shown in Figures 14.1 and 14.2. These are in the general form of a path diagram, and they demonstrate the relationship between elder impairment, burden, caregiver depression, and impact for those measures that show the strongest associations in the correlational analysis. Moreover, the two path diagrams were chosen for presentation because they demonstrate the measurement model in two different contexts. The first is defined by the elder's mental impairment, where the relationship between the elder's disruptive behavior, the associated burden, and the impact on ECF relationships is examined. The second context is defined by the elder's physical impairment, its effects on burden, and the caregiver's restrictions of activities.

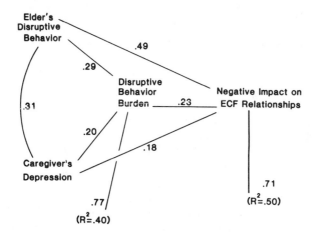

Variable	Direct Effects	Indirect Effects	Total Effects
Disruptive behaviors	.49	(.29 x .23).07	.56
Disruptive behavior burden	.23	—	.23
Caregiver depression	.18	(.20 x 23).04	.22

Note. All coefficients significant at .01 level

Figure 14.1. Path diagram of disruptive behavior variables as predictors of negative impact on ECF relationships.

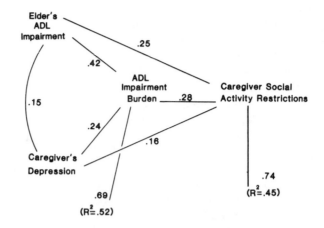

Variable	Direct Effects	Indirect Effects	Total Effects
ADL Impairment	.25	(.42 x .28=).12	.37
ADL Impairment burden	.28	—	.28
Caregiver depression	.16	(.24 x .28=).06	.22

Note. All coefficients significant at .01 level

Figure 14.2. Path diagram of ADL impairment variables as predictors of caregiver social activity restrictions.

Turning first to Figure 14.1, the independent and additive effects of the elders' disruptive behaviors and burden on ECF relationships are shown. Caregivers' depression scores are incorporated into the diagram because of their relationship to all of the other indicators. It should be noted that caregivers' depression is located on the left of the diagram along with impairment and burden. This location is intended to represent the fact that, whatever its source, the depression experienced by caregivers (which are their perceptions or reports) pervades the other measures in this study.

As a result of the substantial intercorrelation shown between the three predictors, it is important to determine what, if any, independent effect each of them has on the impact variable. Noting the path coefficient in Figure 14.1, it appears that all three measures—caregiver depression, disruptive behavior, and burden—have substantial independent effects on ECF relationships, with the strongest produced by the elder's disruptive behavior and corresponding subjective perception of burden (beta = .49 and .23, respectively). By far, the greater direct effect is produced by the elder's disruptive behaviors. Although the direct effect of the caregiver's depression is the smallest of any of the predictors (beta = .18), nevertheless, it is significant. Moreover, when this direct effect is added to the indirect effect of depression through burden, they combine to have an increased total effect of .22.

Because the direct effects of impairment in this instance are substantially greater than those of burden, the role that burden plays as an intermediary between impairment and impact is diminished. These relative differences notwithstanding, however, burden does have a statistically significant and substantially direct effect on impact. Although the intermediary role of burden in this case is diminished by the strong independent effect of the elder's disruptive behavior, in the next section, looking at physical impairment, we will see a somewhat different pattern.

The last issue to be examined in the mental impairment version of the model is the degree to which the three variables combine to explain the observed variance in impact on ECF relationships. The additive effects of the caregiver's depression, the elder's disruptive behavior, and burden are represented in the schematic by the error term associated with impact ($e = .71$; $R^2 = .50$). This indicates that the three predictors explain, in combination, 50% of the total variance in the impact on ECF relationships. The model, then, with only three independent variables is extremely parsimonious in that it explains half of the variance.

Once again the findings support the need to make the distinction between burden and impact inasmuch as the former has a substantial net effect on the latter and is correlated with both impairment and impact. The independent effects of impairment and burden, the latter measured as the subjective perceptions of the caregiver, are each important in explaining the impact that caregiving has on elder-caregiver and other family relationships.

As shown in the correlational analysis, the strongest correlates of caregiver activity restrictions were related to the elders' physical impairments, as measured by ADL dependencies and the corresponding ADL task burdens. In Figure 14.2 the independent and additive effects of those variables are examined. Caregivers' depression scores are included as before, because they were moderately correlated with both ADL burden and caregiver activity restrictions, and to test if, as in the previous diagram, the caregivers' depression has a persistent effect on the impact variable even after the effects of elder impairment and burden are removed.

Regarding the net relationship of the three measures to the impact on caregivers' social activity restrictions, all made a significant contribution. Unlike the pattern shown in Figure 14.1 where the burden measure had a significant but limited effect on the impact measure, the net effect of subjective burden is greater than the net effect of either elder impairment or caregiver depression. Focusing on the relationship between elder impairment and activity restrictions, the net effect of impairment (beta = .25) represents a substantial reduction from the zero-order correlation (r = .40) shown in Table 14.4. This indicates that burden plays an important role as an intermediary between elders' physical impairments and caregivers' social activities. As in the previous diagram where caregiver depression displayed a moderate but persistent net effect on ECF relationships (beta = .18), here again depression continues to have a moderate effect on caregivers' activity restrictions (beta = .16). In fact, the total of direct and indirect effects of depression were identical in both cases.

The total additive effects of caregiver depression, elder impairment and impairment burden on caregivers' social activity restrictions are represented by the error term (e = .74; R^2 = .45). Thus, 45% of the variance in caregivers' activities is explained. Here the combined effects of the three predictors are not quite as great as the additive effects of the disruptive behavior indicator on ECF relationships. In both cases, however, the three predictor variables make a significant independent contribution to the total explained variance.

Comparing the two diagrams some similarities and some differences are apparent. First, in both examples the three predictor variables explain a relatively large proportion of the total variance. In the first model, however, where the negative impact on ECF relationships is the focus, the net impact of elder's impairment is most important in that it shows the greatest net effect (beta = .49) and the greatest total of direct and indirect effects (.56). In the second instance, where the focus is on caregiver social activity restrictions, the burden measure, in this case ADL impairment burden, demonstrates a slightly greater independent effect than elder impairment (beta = .28 and .25, respectively).

A second point of comparison is the relative importance of the burden measure in terms of its independent effect on the impact measures. In the first case, the effects of disruptive behavior burden (beta = .23) show a substantial reduction from the zero-order correlation (r = .46) when the effects of elder disruptive behavior and caregiver depression are removed. This indicates that the correlation that burden has with impact is at least partly explained by the two other measures, elder impairment and caregiver depression.

In the second case, the net effect of the burden measure, ADL impairment burden (beta = .28), exhibits a similar but slightly smaller reduction from the zero-order coefficient (r = .45). This indicates that the relationship between burden and impact tends to be slightly less dependent on the combined effects of caregiver depression and elder ADL impairment. Also, ADL impairment burden demonstrated greater independence from the elder's impairment than did the disruptive behavior burden from the corresponding impairment.

These comparisons illustrate the complexity of the issues related to caregiver burden. The concept of burden has been shown to have both a mediating and independent influence on the impact that caregiving has on caregivers' lives. More importantly, the degree to which burden, defined here as the subjective perception of the caregiver specific to a particular type of elder impairment, operates independently or as a mediating measure is partly a function of the specific type of impairment and impact under investigation. The first diagram focused on the relationship between the elder's mental impairment, the corresponding burden, and the impact that caregiving has on elder-caregiver and other family relationships. In this case the effects that burden has on impact is overshadowed by the powerful influence of the elder's impairment. In contrast, the second diagram demonstrated that when the caregiver's activity restrictions are the focus, burden and impairment play nearly equal but somewhat independent roles. Thus, the data presented here show the interdependence of the various measures and, additionally, point to the uniqueness of their relationships depending on the caregiving context as defined by the elder's incapacity.

DISCUSSION

In most of the literature the concept of burden is synonymous with the effects of caregiving. The term is used to refer to a variety of phenomena related to caregiving, however. Moreover, the concept of burden has been measured or operationalized in a different manner in virtually every study of caregiving reviewed and, generally, has been treated as a unidimensional concept.

Tentative movement has taken place in that a few analysts have suggested dividing burden into subjective and objective components.

Even this distinction, however, is neither universally accepted nor consistently operationalized. We have suggested several alternatives. First, the concept of burden should be used to refer to the subjective perceptions of caregivers related to the degree of problems experienced in relation to elders' specific impairments. Further, these impairments should be differentiated in terms of the mental and physical capacities of the elder. Second, burden, as subjectively interpreted by caregivers, should be treated as an intervening measure between impairment and other more objective indicators of caregiving effects.

Third, like burden, impact is a multidimensional concept. A variety of aspects of caregivers' day-to-day lives are affected by the actual care elders require and the subjective perception of burden that these caregiving tasks create. These many aspects need to be redefined as a limited number of dimensions that recognize the different kinds of impacts that caregivers experience. In this paper, two measures were utilized: impact on elder-caregiver and other family relationships and impact on caregiver activities. They are relatively independent from one another in that they are not strongly correlated; moreover, they correlated quite differently with a variety of caregiving variables.

An important ancillary measurement issue is suggested by the fact that the caregiver's depression was associated with both burden and impact. The fact that the caregiver's state of mental health at the time of the interview, whatever the cause, is reflected in a modest but persistent way in all these measures argues for treating it as an antecedent or intervening variable. This is especially important where the survey data are obtained largely from the self-reports of caregivers.

The multivariate analysis portrayed here served to highlight further the complexity of the measurement issues when looking at the effects of caregiving. The precise nature of the relationships between elder impairment, caregiver perception of burden, and the report of impact is dependent on the specific types of impairment and impact that are focused upon.

It is clear from this analysis that caregivers do report feelings of burden and that they are linked both to the impairment that gives rise to them and to changes in objective conditions within the family. The task remains for social scientists who examine family caregiving to refine explicitly the measurement of burden and impact indicators so that a more complex and reality-oriented perspective on caregiving can inform further research in this important area.

REFERENCES

Brown, G., Birby, L., & Wing, J. Influence of family life on the course of schizophrenic disorders: A replicator. *British Journal of Psychiatry*, 1972, *121*, 241–258.

Fatheringham, J., Skelton, M., & Hoddinott, B. The effects on the families of the presence of a mentally retarded child. *Canadian Psychiatric Association Journal*, 1972, *17*, 283–289.

Herz, M., Endicott, J., & Spitzer, R. Brief versus standard hospitalization: The families. *American Journal of Psychiatry*, 1976, *133*, 795–801.

Lefton, M., August, S., Dimetz, S., & Pasamanick, B. Social class, expectations and performance of mental patients. *American Journal of Sociology*, 1962, *68*, 79–89.

Lezak, M. Living with the characteriologically altered brain injured patient. *Journal of Clinical Psychiatry*, 1978, *39*, 592–598.

Litman, T. Health care and the family: A three generation analysis. *Medical Care*, 1971, *9*, 67–81.

Manjoney, D., & McKegney, F. Individual and family coping with polycrystic kidney disease: The harvest of denial. *International Journal of Psychiatry in Medicine*, 1978, *9*, 19–31.

Moos, R. *Family work and group environment scores: A manual.* Consulting Psychologists Press, Palo Alto, CA, 1974.

Morycz, R. An exploration of senile dementia and family burden. *Clinical Social Work Journal*, 1980, *8*, 16–27.

Robinson, B. Validation of a caregiver strain index. *Journal of Gerontology*, 1983, *38*, 344–348.

Shanas, E. The family as social support systems in old age. *The Gerontologist*, 1979, *19*, 169–174.

Shanas, E., Townsend, P., Wedderburn, D., Friis, H., Milhøj, P., & Stehouwer, J. *Old people in three industrial societies.* Atherton Press, New York, 1968.

Thompson, E., & Doll, W. The burden of families coping with the mentally ill: An invisible crisis. *Family Relations*, 1982, *31*, 379–388.

Vincent, C. Mental health and the family. *Journal of Marriage and Family*, 1967, *29*, 18–39.

Zarit, S., Reever, K., & Bach-Peterson, J. Relatives of the impaired elderly: Correlates of feelings of burden. *The Gerontologist*, 1980, *20*, 649–655.

Zung, W. W. K. The depression status inventory: An adjunct to the self-rating depression scale. *Journal of Clinical Psychology*, 1972, *28*, 539–542.

15

Strain among Caregivers: A Study of Experience in the United States*

Marjorie H. Cantor

The past decade has seen the emergence of considerable research validating the role of family and other informal supports in the care of frail and chronically ill elderly. Contrary to prevailing stereotypes, the informal support system provides more assistance than do formal organizations, and without the care given by informal support networks many more elderly would probably be forced to leave their homes and enter institutions (Branch & Jette, 1983; E. Brody, 1978, 1981; S. Brody et al., 1978; Cantor, 1975, 1980 a, b; Comptroller General of the United States, 1977; Shanas 1979 a, b).

In our New York City studies of the nature of the informal support system of older people we expanded the concept to include not only kin but friends and neighbors as well (Cantor, 1979; Cantor & Johnson, 1978). In addition, we documented the hierarchical compensatory nature of the operation of this system, with kin—

*The Gerontologist, 23 (6) (1983), 597–604.

A revised version of a paper presented in part at a round table organized by the Gerontological Society of America for the first World Assembly on Aging, Vienna, Austria, July 1982; a preliminary version was presented at the symposium "Families Caring for Elderly: Key Findings from Four Studies" at the Joint Meeting of the Gerontological Society of America and the Canadian Gerontological Association, Toronto, November 1981. This research was supported by the Administration on Aging, DHHS, Grant No. 90-A-1329, "The Impact of the Entry of the Formal Organization on the Informal Support System of the Elderly."

particularly spouse and children—preferred as the cornerstone of the support system, followed in preference by friends, neighbors, and eventually formal organizations in a well-ordered hierarchical selection process (Cantor, 1980b).

Confirming the presence of informal supports, however, is only a first step. Attention is now being directed to the dynamics of the helping situation in an attempt to discover ways of strengthening informal caregiving capacities (Brody, 1981; Cantor, 1980a; Gibson, 1981; Horowitz & Dobrof, 1982; Mellor & Getzel, 1980; Poulshock & Noelker, 1982; Zarit et al., 1980).

In documenting the process whereby the informal support system acts to assist older people, researchers and policy-makers have tended either to group all care providers into a single category labeled "caregivers" or to make the equally erroneous assumption that informal caregivers are family members and primarily women. The homogenization of such crucial variables as type of relationship, sex, age, health, and work status of caregivers has resulted in obscuring the differences among various groups of caregivers and the types of stress each may be experiencing in the process of giving assistance. Only by decoupling the various groups of caregivers and examining their respective characteristics and strains can we provide intervention modalities which strengthen their individual capacities to assist the elderly in their care. The findings presented herein will attempt to shed light on the variety of informal caregivers of the frail elderly and how the caregiving experience affects their lives.

THE STUDY AND ITS POPULATION

Data are drawn from a larger study, "The Impact of the Entry of the Formal Organization on the Informal Support System of Older Americans." The study population consisted of elderly clients and their primary caregivers served by a major homemaker service funded by the New York City Department for the Aging under Title III of the Older Americans Act.

Geared specifically to the marginal income frail elderly, the program was mandated to provide 12 hours of service per week for 12 weeks. (In some cases the period could be extended by reducing the service hours per week). Marginal income elderly were persons above Medicaid eligibility whose yearly incomes did not exceed $6,323 in the case of a single person, or $8,315 for a couple. Asset limitations were placed at $6,000 per individual or $8,500 per couple. Homemaker services included housekeeping, shopping, escort, and personal care.

Because of the 12-week service limitation, it was anticipated that the client population would be biased toward persons who could benefit from time-limited services. In actuality, about half of the clients required assistance because of an acute medical episode (e.g., return home after heart attack, broken hip, surgery), while the other half turned to the agency because of a gradual deterioration in functional ability, suggesting chronic needs. The study design called for interviewing both clients and their caregivers at two points in time— shortly after the commencement of formal service and after termination of service.

All clients accepted for service during the period from June 1979 to March 1980 were eligible for inclusion in the study except those considered by agency and research staff to be aphasic or disoriented. A total of 178 elderly homemaker clients was interviewed at Time 1. During the course of the interview, the participants were asked who helped them with a series of tasks of daily living and whom they regarded as their primary source of help. Based upon these designations permission was requested to interview the named primary caregivers. Of the 148 elderly with informal caregivers, 136 agreed to allow the interview. After several attempts interviews were obtained with 111 of them, a response rate of 82%.

PRIMARY CAREGIVERS

Caregiving involves at least a two-person dyad, the person receiving assistance—the care-receiver—and the individual providing care— the caregiver. Care-receivers in the study were frail older persons (73.9% white, 23.4% black, 0.9% Hispanic) assessed by social workers utilizing a standardized city-wide form from the New York City Department for the Aging as in need of home care. Over half lived alone, and another one-third with a spouse; only 14% resided with a child or another adult relative or friend. The vast majority were women, most over age 60 and approximately half aged 75 and over. On the Townsend Index of Functional Incapacity, 73% were rated as severely impaired, 15% as seriously impaired, and 12% as suffering from some or mild impairment (Shanas, 1968).

The primary caregivers encompassed all four types of informal supports: 33% were spouses, 36% children, 19% other relatives, and 12% friends/neighbors. As can be seen in Table 15.1, the profiles of these four types reveal some striking differences which appear related to the subsequent data on strain and stress.

In many ways spouses appeared to be the highest risk group among the caregivers. Their household incomes were the lowest of all caregivers, and, as one would expect, they were more likely to be old themselves. Most were at least 60 years of age, and almost half were 75 or over. Increased age predisposed them to poor health, and 84% perceived their own health as fair or poor. Furthermore, contrary to the common stereotype that caregivers are usually female, slightly over half of the spouse caregivers were males. Yet spouses, more than any other type of caregivers, were involved in providing personal care, shopping, cooking, and housework. For many of the men, such duties represent a reversal of long-established roles and life patterns. In virtually all cases, the husband–wife dyads lived alone without a child at home, thereby increasing the potential for isolation and psychological stress.

By contrast, children were mainly married women with families. Sixty percent were working, compared with one-third or fewer in the case of other caregiving groups and only 11% among spouses. Children tended to be middle-aged, with more than half between the ages of 40 and 59; 10% were over 60. As a group, children had somewhat higher incomes and higher social status scores on the Hollingshead Two Factor Index of Social Class (Hollingshead, 1958), but three-fourths reported that they just barely managed to get by on current incomes, faced with the combined demands of their own families and financial assistance to their parents. (Some 45% of the children provided some regular financial assistance or gifts to parents, with the most usual dollar value estimated at between $1,000 and $2,000 per year). Two-thirds of the children resided in separate households from the parents whom they assisted, resulting in duplication of household responsibilities. Hence, children were truly a "generation in the middle" with the potential for considerable stress from situational as well as personal factors.

The majority of "other relative" caregivers (71%) were as old as those for whom they cared and resembled, demographically, elderly spouse caregivers for whom they were often substitutes. The few younger relatives who served as primary caregivers were more similar to caregiver children but for the most part did not appear to be as deeply involved, either emotionally or financially.

The final group of caregivers, friends and neighbors, were fewer in number, and almost all were women living in the neighborhood, divided fairly evenly between younger persons and those aged 60 and over (see Table 15.1).

Table 15.1. Major Demographic Characteristics of Caregivers (Percentages)

	Total (n = 111)	Spouse (n = 37)	Child (n = 40)	Other Relatives (n = 21)	Friends Neighbors (n = 13)
Age					
20–39	14.4	—	22.5	14.3	30.8
40–59	27.9	10.8	57.5	9.5	15.4
60–74	29.7	32.4	10.0	66.7	23.1
75+	19.8	48.6	—	4.8	23.1
Sex					
Male	29.7	51.4	25.0	14.3	7.7
Female	70.3	48.6	75.0	85.7	92.3
Ethnicity					
White	73.9	75.7	85.0	66.7	46.2
Black	23.4	18.9	12.5	33.3	53.8
Hispanic	.9	2.7	—	—	—
Religious affiliation					
Protestant	19.8	10.8	12.5	33.3	46.2
Catholic	21.6	21.6	25.0	14.3	23.1
Jewish	52.3	62.2	55.0	47.6	23.1
Other	2.7	—	7.5	—	—
Marital status					
Married	70.3	91.9	62.5	61.9	46.2
Widowed	11.7	—	12.5	14.3	38.5
Never married	7.2	—	15.0	9.5	—
Separated or divorced	5.4	16.7	5.0	14.3	—
Place of birth					
Mainland U.S.	76.6	59.5	95.0	81.0	61.5

Eastern Europe	10.8	18.9	2.5	14.3	7.7
Other	8.1	16.2	2.5	—	15.4
Primary language					
English	85.6	70.3	97.5	90.5	84.6
Yiddish	5.4	13.5	—	4.8	—
Other	.9	2.7	—	—	—
Level of education					
Twelfth grade or less	33.3	45.9	15.0	42.8	38.5
High School graduate	34.2	29.7	52.5	19.0	15.4
Some college	14.4	8.1	15.0	19.0	23.1
College graduate	6.3	2.7	5.0	9.5	15.4
Graduate school	6.3	2.7	12.5	4.8	7.7
Work status					
Working full/part time	35.1	10.8	60.0	33.3	30.8
Retired	39.6	64.9	7.5	57.1	38.5
Unemployed	7.2	8.1	12.5	—	—
Never worked	15.3	13.5	17.5	9.5	23.1
Social class[a]					
I & II	12.0	5.4	17.5	9.5	23.1
III	18.0	16.2	25.0	19.0	—
IV & V (working and lower class)	63.9	72.9	52.5	71.4	61.6
Perceived health					
Good	41.4	10.8	65.0	47.6	46.2
Fair	36.0	45.9	30.0	33.3	30.8
Poor	19.8	37.8	5.0	19.0	15.4
Level of happiness					
Very happy	23.4	8.1	20.0	28.6	69.2
Fairly happy	39.6	37.8	45.0	47.6	15.4
Not too happy	21.6	37.8	15.0	9.5	15.4
Not happy at all	9.9	10.8	15.0	4.8	—

Note. Percentages may not total 100 due to missing data.
[a]Social class was computed on the basis of the spouse's education and occupation for married/widowed female respondents.

251

THE QUALITY OF RELATIONSHIPS

Feeling close to the person one cares for is probably, in most cases, a precursor to assuming the task. Although data on past relationships were not available, caregivers were questioned on how well they' currently got along with their care-receivers. As expected, 70% or more of all four types of caregivers felt "very close" to their care-receivers (see Table 15.2).

Getting along well on a day-to-day basis, however, is another matter. An inverse correlation appeared between closeness of relationship and ability to get along well. Friends and neighbors as a group got along best (92%), followed by other relatives (86%). In the case of spouses, only 60% reported getting along very well with the person cared for, and among children the proportion dropped to 53%.

Furthermore, spouses and children were far more likely than other types of caregivers to feel that they understood and treated the person for whom they were caring better than they were treated in return. Among children the normal strains of caring for an ill older person seemed to be compounded by intergenerational differences. Only 48% of the children felt that they understood their sick parent well, and only 28% felt that they were understood in return. Only 20% of the children felt that they shared similar views on life with their parents.

In addition, all four caregiving groups reflected differences in expectations and realities between themselves and those whom they care for. In the case of spouses and children, however, differences were magnified by the closeness of the bonds and intergenerational differences.

STRAIN OF CARING FOR THE FRAIL ELDERLY

To learn more about the nature of stress, respondents were asked a series of questions about worry, strain, and the impact of caregiving in eight areas of private life (see Tables 15.3, 15.4, and 15.5). With respect to worry, caregivers indicated on a 4-point rating scale the extent to which they worried about the care-receiver in four aspects of life: health and physical condition, mood and state of mind, financial situation, and ability to obtain sufficient help for the care-receiver. In rank order the subjects of greatest concern were health (mean 3.83), obtaining sufficient assistance (mean 3.42), mood and state of mind

Table 15.2. Quality of Caregiver/Care-Receiver Relationship by Type of Caregiver

Quality of Relationship Item	Proportion of Respondents in Agreement (Percentages)				
	Total (n = 111)	Spouse (n = 37)	Child (n = 40)	Other Relatives (n = 21)	Friends/Neighbors (n = 13)
Client and caregiver get along very well	65.8	59.5	52.5	85.7	92.3
Caregiver understands client very well	65.8	75.5	47.5	81.0	69.2
Client understands caregiver very well	51.4	64.9	27.5	66.7	61.5
Caregiver treats client very well	77.5	81.1	72.5	71.4	92.5
Client treats caregiver very well	72.1	67.6	62.5	81.0	100.0
Caregiver and client have very similar views on life	31.5	40.5	20.0	33.3	38.5
Caregiver and client are very close	73.0	73.0	75.0	71.4	69.2

Note. Percentages may not total 100% due to missing data.

(mean 3.01), and financial status (mean 2.73) (see Table 15.3). On a companion 3-point measure of strain experienced in the areas of emotional, physical, and financial stress, financial strain again ranked lowest in importance and emotional strain ranked first (see Table 15.4).

Stress and strain are not uniform across areas of life, however, nor were they felt uniformly by all caregivers. The overriding worry of all groups was the health of the dependent person, but beyond that spouses were most concerned with finances and the care-receiver's morale. Children, on the other hand, worried about obtaining sufficient help while their anxiety about financial matters was less (see Table 15.3).

With regard to strain, spouses reported the greatest degree of physical and financial strain. Children and other relatives suffered less from physical strain, and their level of financial strain was even lower and decreased progressively with decreasing centrality of the relationship (see Table 15.4). Emotional strain presented a different picture. It appeared to be pervasive across all groups, except friends and neighbors, and children and other relatives were just as likely to be negatively affected as spouses. Throughout, friends/neighbors appeared to be the least involved and registered the least amount of strain in the role of primary caregiver (see Table 15.4).

REQUIRED CHANGES AND ADJUSTMENTS IN LIFE STYLES

Assisting frail homebound older people not only involves worry and strain but often requires changes and adjustments in lifestyle on the part of the person providing primary care. Respondents were asked about eight common areas of activity and the degree to which their lives had been affected by their caring role. (A 3-point scale was used; see Table 15.5 for areas covered and mean scores by groups). When impact was indicated, follow-up questions elicited the nature of the impact and adjustments made to cope with the situation. In all cases, respondents indicated that the impact was negative and involved doing without or giving up something. Again, the amount of impact varied by type of caregiver, and some aspects of caregivers' lives were more severely affected than others (see Table 15.5).

The extent of impact on the everyday life of the caregiver appeared to be clearly related to the closeness of kinship bond and the availability of the caregiver for continual involvement. The impact was most

Table 15.3. Degree to Which Caregiver Worries about Care-Receiver's Situation by Type of Caregiver (Means and One-Way Anova)

Group	Care-Receiver's Health	Care-Receiver's State of Mind	Care-Receiver's Financial Condition	Obtaining Sufficient Help for Care-Receiver
Spouse	3.92	3.25	3.32	2.57
Child	3.82	2.95	2.50	3.44
Relative	3.95	3.10	2.67	3.60
Friend/neighbor	3.42	2.28	1.44	2.50
Total group	3.83	3.01	2.73	3.42
Main effect-F	4.116*	2.150	8.846**	4.328*
df	3, 105	3, 104	3, 103	3, 102

*$p \leq .01$; **$p \leq .0001$.
Scale: 1-not at all, 2-rarely, 3-sometimes, 4-quite a lot.

Table 15.4. Degree of Strain Experienced by Caregiver Arising from Caring Role by Type of Caregiver (Means and One-Way Anova)

Group	Emotional	Physical	Financial
Spouse	1.76	1.76	1.41
Child	1.63	1.34	.85
Relative	1.57	1.19	.52
Friend/neighbor	.71	.94	.24
Total group	1.56	1.41	.91
Main effect-F	8.204*	6.313**	10.556**
df	3, 106	3, 106	3, 106

*$p \leq .01$; **$p \leq .001$
Scale: 0–2, no impact to great deal of impact.

severe in the case of the spouses, all of whom lived in the same house as the person in need. The lives of the caregiver children were next most severely affected, followed by other relatives. In the case of friends and neighbors, the reported dislocations were minimal with some slight interference noted in the ability to run their homes and carry out everyday chores.

The findings suggest that caregivers forced to adjust their lives to encompass the increased demands of a dependent older person were most likely to give up those things which had some elasticity and were more marginal to personal or family equilibrium and survival. Thus, the most severe impact was registered in areas such as free time for oneself and opportunities to socialize with friends, take vacations,

Table 15.5. Impact on Lives of Caregivers by Type of Caregiver (Means and One-Way Anova)

Group	Run house everyday chores	Time spent with children other family members	Opportunities to socialize with friends	Time to do things you like—movies, hobbies	Ability to keep job—function on job	Opportunity to take vacation	Free time without responsibility	Relationships with those close to—spouse, children
Spouse	1.46	1.26	1.49	1.35	.64	1.41	1.58	1.25
Child	1.23	.82	1.08	1.10	.70	1.15	1.15	.69
Relatives	1.05	.90	.90	.81	.38	.86	1.00	.62
Friend/ neighbor	.42	.33	.17	—	.04	—	.25	.08
Total group	1.19	.93	1.08	1.01	.55	1.06	1.17	.80
Main effect-F	5.438**	4.657**	7.941***	8.785***	2.927*	9.372***	9.114***	8.142***
df	3, 106	3, 106	3, 106	3, 106	3, 106	3, 106	3, 106	3, 106

*$p < .05$; **$p < .01$; ***$p < .001$.
Scale: 0–2, no impact to great deal of impact.

have leisure time pursuits, and run one's own house. The major adjustment in all cases was personally restrictive—giving up something to provide the time to care for or socialize with the homebound older person. In most cases, the expandable items involved discretionary activities. The only exception was the negative impact on running the household—here standards might be lowered, but tasks had to continue to be performed.

When one turns to the items involving work and family, the picture is somewhat different. The impact was reported as more minimal in these areas, and this effect held true both for the group as a whole and for each of the four subgroups of caregivers (see Table 15.5). For those who worked; the preservation of the ability to function on the job undoubtedly arose from necessity. On the other hand, maintaining positive relationships with one's immediate family and devoting enough time to them would appear to stem from the same familial value system as willingness to accept responsibility for the welfare of the elderly care-receiver.

The caregivers' responses to the impact question make clear the immense strain on the individual providing care. It is in the sphere of personal desires, individuality, and socialization that the greatest deprivation occurs. Most caregivers protect their families and work, but at considerable personal expense to themselves. It is not surprising, therefore, that the greatest strain experienced by caregivers of dependent elderly is in the emotional area.

FACTORS ASSOCIATED WITH STRAIN

The findings thus far have suggested a series of personal and situational factors which conceptually appear related to the presence or absence of strain and stress in the lives of caregivers. In an attempt to determine the extent to which such factors contribute to the presence of strain, two stepwise multiple regressions were performed. In the first, a composite strain score, including physical, emotional and financial strain, was employed as the dependent variable. The second regression focused specifically on the impact on the life of the person giving the care, and the dependent variable was a composite score derived from responses to the question about impact in eight areas of personal life (see preceding section).

In both cases, the same 14 demographic, situational, and attitudinal factors were employed as the independent variables. These included the following:

six demographic variables (age, sex, race, SES, marital status, and relationship to caregiver), *five situational variables* (health status of care-receiver, geographic proximity of caregiver to care-receiver, work status of caregiver, caregiver's ability to manage financially, and the amount of assistance provided by caregiver), and *three attitudinal variables* (degree of worry, compatibility of relationship between caregiver and receiver, and attitude of caregiver towards the importance and value of family).

These 14 variables accounted for 56% of the variance in the strain model and 48% of the variance in the impact on the life of caregiver model.

Although tests of significance are frequently used in reporting regression results, of greater interest is the magnitude of the relationships expressed as the variance of a dependent variable that can be accounted for by the independent variable. Based upon the sample size, variables contributing 3% or more to the total variance were considered nontrivial and noteworthy of discussion. In all cases the F values of such variables are significant at the $p \leq .05$ or $p \leq .01$ level, as shown in Tables 15.6 and 15.7.

Turning first to the question of strain, five variables are illuminating with respect to the presence of strain (see Table 15.6). By far the most important, accounting for 37% of the total variance, was the type of caregiver and his/her relationship to the care-receiver. The closer the bond, the greater the amount of strain. Spouses were the group at greatest risk, followed by child, other relatives, and friends and neighbors. Thus, the concept of centrality, both kinship and functional, clearly relates to the dimension of strain and stress in the caregiving situation.

Four other variables also made a noteworthy contribution of 3% or more to the variance in strain: the degree to which caregiver worries, attitudes about the role of the family, the sex of the caregiver, and the quality of the relationship between the parties to the caring situation. Because the majority of caregivers were women, except in the spouse category, strain was more likely to be associated with women and with persons who were worried about the caring situation. In addition, the quality of interpersonal relationships between supporter and supported was a noteworthy contributor to strain.

A particularly interesting variable is the attitude toward family and the role of family as measured by a familism scale (Leichter, 1967). The more caregivers feel that family members have a responsibility towards other family members and that involvement in and sense of family is a positive value, the more likely they are to feel strain. The

Table 15.6. Demographic, Situational, and Attitudinal Variables Contributing to the Amount of Strain Experienced by Caregivers (Stepwise Multiple Regression Model)

Independent variable	Proportion of variance accounted for	Cumulative R^2
Type of caregiver	.368**	.368
Amount of worry	.063**	.431
Attitude towards family	.030*	.461
Sex of caregiver	.027*	.488
Degree of compatibility between dyad	.025*	.513
Amount of assistance	.010	.523
Age of caregiver	.014	.537
Ability to manage financially	.009	.546
Client's health	.008	.553
Race	.004	.557
Proximity	.001	.558
Work status	.001	.558
Marital status	.001	.559

$$.559 = R^2$$
(total proportion of variance)

Note. SES, although entered into the regression, did not meet the default criteria of the SPSS regression program and therefore is not shown.
*F values significant at $p = .05$; **F values significant at $p = .01$.

importance of familism as a predictor of strain suggests that a sense of family and a belief in family cohesion is an underlying dimension in the caregiving situation. Those who feel committed to such values are more likely to become deeply involved in caring for an older person, even as a friend and neighbor, and are apparently more likely to experience pervasive strain.

Although impact on life and degree of strain are related ($r^2 = .58$), they are two separate dimensions of the caring picture. Some of the same predictor variables emerge in both regression models (see Table 15.7). Again, the single most important factor associated with impact on life was the type of caregiver, accounting for 28% of the total variance. The sex of the caregiver and feelings about family also contributed substantial variance, but in the case of impact on life the variable worry dropped in importance and was replaced by a new variable—the total amount of assistance given. Strain, as we have seen, is a very emotionally laden factor that appears to transcend the amount of direct involvement in the care of the person. However, the more time and effort the caregiver spends in giving assistance, the

Table 15.7. Demographic, Situational, and Attitudinal Variables Contributing to Impact on the Lives of Caregivers (Stepwise Multiple Regression Model)

Independent variable	Proportion of variance accounted for	Cumulative R^2
Type of caregiver	.279**	.279
Sex of caregiver	.055*	.335
Amount of assistance	.039*	.374
Attitude towards family	.026	.401
Marital status	.019	.420
Amount of worry	.021	.441
Race	.013	.455
Degree of compatibility between dyad	.009	.464
Proximity	.008	.473
Ability to manage financially	.004	.477
Health of care-receiver	.003	.480
Age of caregiver	.000	.481
Work status	.000	.481
	$.481 = R^2$ (total proportion of variance)	

Note. SES, although entered into the regression, did not meet the default criteria of the SPSS regression program and therefore is not shown.
*F values significant at $p = .05$; **F values significant at $p = .01$.

more likely a resultant disruption and negative impact on personal life are to occur.

One final word about the regressions. The 14 independent variables included in each model accounted for a relatively high proportion of variance, 56% in the case of strain and 48% for life impact. Yet the overriding importance of the type of caregiver in influencing the effect of caregiving is underscored by the fact that this one variable alone accounted for 36% of total variance in strain and 30% in life impact. Furthermore, no other variable accounted for more than 6% of the variance in either case (see Tables 15.6 and 15.7).

CONCLUSION AND IMPLICATIONS

The study findings suggest the extent of stress and dislocation involved in the role of primary caregiver for the frail elderly. However, the amount of stress and disruption of daily life is very different for different group of caregivers. The closer the bond, the more stressful the caregiving role, and spouse and children would appear to be priority targets for interventions to strengthen the capacity of informal supports to assist the frail elderly.

In addition, the amount of continual, day-to-day, involvement compounds the impact on the caregiver. This is particularly true in the case of spouses, where considerable personal care and housekeeping is involved and often causes role reversal.

Financial strain may be a factor for caregivers with lower incomes, such as represented by spouses in our sample, but it is not as pervasive an issue as might be expected. What emerges as the overriding problem for all groups of caregivers is the emotional strain of dealing with increased frailty in a person to whom one is close. Although strong familial ties and close bonds of affection are present, lack of mutual understanding and/or intergenerational differences are often reported. The caregivers in our study handled the dilemmas of conflicting demands and interpersonal strains not by denial of responsibility but through considerable personal sacrifices. One must ask how long caregivers can carry such heavy responsibilities and what can be done to ease the burden for their own and their families' good.

The data suggest several alternatives, depending on the type of caregivers involved. For spouses, probably the most high risk and yet overlooked group of caregivers, some form of direct financial assistance may be of value. The same is true for the few other older relatives who live together. But one must question the value of some of the proposed financial incentives such as tax rebates or family allowances. In most cases they do not apply to spouses and the sums involved are too small to provide "private for pay" home care, even if it is available. More important for elderly spouse-relatives, who are often in poor health themselves, are public or voluntary agency sponsored in-home and respite services at a cost that they can afford.

Furthermore, since many spouses are men, issues of role reversal deserve attention. Instruction in how to care for the sick, particularly personal care, is another critical need, as are counseling and case management. Spouses do not desire to relinquish the caring role, but they express a need for relief and respite in order to conserve their limited resources for the difficult task they carry.

Children and other younger relatives, on the other hand, characteristically suffer from a multiplicity of roles. Work per se does not seem to be a reason for relinquishing responsibilities to the elderly, but job performance may be affected by the emotional stress and time pressures involved in providing primary care to a frail older person.

Flexibility in the work place could ease that strain and at the same time positively affect employee productivity. Employers should be encouraged to consider flexible work schedules and compensatory time off both for the care of children and the care of an aged parent.

The overwhelming concern of children and younger relatives involved with the frail elderly is their ability to obtain necessary help. This concern is not, it would seem, primarily a question of money. More important is information on community resources and the availability of dependable, professionally supervised social services, including assessment, case management, and, above all, in-home services. We often speak of "single entry points" for older people, yet too often children seeking assistance for elderly parents are involved in time-consuming bureaucratic duplication of effort.

Lastly, friends and neighbors, who are often more peripherally involved, are also a source of help for homebound elderly. The basic service plan for a frail older person cannot realistically be built around neighbors, yet they can provide important secondary assistance. Their immediate proximity and availability make them ideal for performing time-limited, neighborhood-centered tasks such as shopping, escorting, and visiting as well as serving as "spotters" to alert family and community agencies of crisis or neglect. Friends and neighbors also need training and support in their efforts. Churches, unions, neighborhood groups would seem well suited to act as organizers and catalysts for non-related persons in the community who desire to assist the frailer elderly.

Above all, our data underscore the danger of global solutions. The issue is not simply financial incentives versus services but, rather, what combination of financial aid, counseling, in-home, and respite services is needed by which group of caregivers. Only through differential planning based upon known characteristics of need can we maximize the potential of spouses, children, relatives, and friends and neighbors in support of the frail elderly.

REFERENCES

Branch, L., & Jette, A. Elders' use of informal long-term care assistance. *The Gerontologist*, 1983, 23, 51–56.

Brody, E. The aging family. *Annals of the American Academy of Political and Social Science*, 1978, 438, 13–27.

Brody, E. Women in the middle and family help to older people. *The Gerontologist*, 1981, 21, 471–480.

Brody, S., Poulshock, W., & Masciocchi, C. The family caring unit: A major consideration in the long-term support system. *The Gerontologist*, 1978, *18*, 556–561.

Cantor, M. Life space and the social support system of the inner city elderly of New York. *The Gerontologist*, 1975, *15*, 23–27.

Cantor, M. Neighbors and friends: An overlooked resource in the informal support system. *Research on Aging*, 1979, *1*, 434–463.

Cantor, M. Caring for the frail elderly: Impact on family, friends, and neighbors. Paper presented at the 33rd Annual Scientific Meeting, Gerontological Society of America, San Diego, November 1980. (a)

Cantor, M. The informal support system: Its relevance in the lives of the elderly. In E. Borgotta & N. McCluskey (Eds.), *Aging and society*. Sage, Beverly Hills, CA, 1980. (b)

Cantor, M., & Johnson, J. *The informal support system of the familyless elderly: Who takes over?* Paper presented at the 31st Annual Scientific Meeting of the Gerontological Society, Dallas, November, 1978.

Comptroller General of the United States. *The well-being of older people in Cleveland, Ohio*. Publication No. HCD-77-70, U.S. General Accounting Office, Washington, DC, 1977.

Gibson, M. J. *Family support patterns, policies, and programs in developed nations*. Paper presented at the Joint Annual Meeting of the Gerontological Society of America and the Canadian Gerontological Association, Toronto, November 1981.

Hollingshead, A. The index of social position. In A. B. Hollingshead & F. C. Redlich (Eds.), *Social class and mental illness*. John Wiley, New York, 1958.

Horowitz, A., & Dobrof, R. *The role of families in providing long-term care to the frail and chronically-ill elderly living in the community*. Final report: Brookdale Center on Aging of Hunter College, New York, 1982.

Leichter, H. *Kinship and casework*. Russell Sage Foundation, New York, 1967.

Mellor, J., & Getzel, G. *Stress and service needs of those who care for the aged*. Paper presented at the 33rd Annual Scientific Meeting of the Gerontological Society of America, San Diego, November 1980.

Poulshock, W., & Noelker, N. *The effects on families of caring for impaired elderly in residence*. Final report. The Benjamin Rose Institute, Cleveland, October 1982.

Shanas, E. Health and incapacity in later life. In E. Shanas, P. Townsend, D. Wedderburn, H. Friis, P. Milhøj, & J. Stehouwer, *Old people in three industrial societies*. Atherton Press, New York, 1968.

Shanas, E. The family as a social support system in old age. *The Gerontologist*, 1979, *19*, 169–174. (a)

Shanas, E. Social myth as hypothesis: The case of the family relations of old people. *The Gerontologist*, 1979, *19*, 3–9. (b)

Zarit, S., Reever, K., & Bach-Peterson, J. Relatives of the impaired elderly: Correlates of feelings of burden. *The Gerontologist*, 1980, *20*, 649–655.

Part V

Living Arrangements

Earlier in this volume, three articles eloquently demonstrated that even in the "good old days" old family members did not live in the same households as their relatives (Brody, 1985; & Nydegger, 1983; Shanas, 1979) any more than they do now. This is contrary to our prevailing myths about their once having been enfolded in multigenerational nests in a warm glow of love and care. The fact that increasing numbers of older people now choose to—as well as manage to—have independent homes has been interpreted, according the prevailing mythical scenario, as a sign of declining family solidarity, even of declining national morality.

Mindel's (1979) article in this volume reports the changes in living arrangements since 1940, showing a decline in men living with "other relatives" from 15% to 4% over the last 45 years and women from 30% to 13%. At present, almost one-half of women over 65 and almost all men over 65 (92%) head their own households.

Our myths about the "good old days" err in other ways too (Dahlin, 1980). When old parents lived with their children in 1900, the home they inhabited was most likely to belong to them, the old parents, not to their children. Further, those old parents continued to work, and they also usually had young children still living at home.

As earlier articles in this volume as well as previous discussions here have mentioned, our myth of the "golden age" of multigeneration households is usually reinforced by our conviction that other cultures still maintain this supposedly ideal condition. A longitudinal study of two cultures in Israel (Weihl, 1985b) rebuts this belief. Over a period of 12 years, both rural Arabs and Jews of European origin moved from households containing their young children (two as well as three generations deep) to separate households. And the major factor for this change was the desire and ability of the *youngest* generation to establish their own homes, not the desire or needs of the oldest generation to move in for help. The meager 3% of the old respondents who did move in with children over the years of the study explained that it was a problem of their child—widowhood, separation, illness, or financial need—that was the reason. The older generation members were all over 70 at the third round of interviewing, incidentally.

The concept of dependent old family members, therefore, is more fantasy than reality. Cross-cultural and historical data consistently find that economic systems—agricultural versus urban, for example, or inheritance laws—are what really determine household composition (e.g., Beck and Beck, 1984; Sweetser, 1984).

Longitudinal data on changes in residence (Fillenbaum & Wallman, 1984; this volume) found that over a period of 30 months, from 1972 to 1974, about 28% of the survivors of a survey sample of 997 people over the age of 65 in North Carolina had changed household composition. Morgan, Dickinson, Dickinson, Benus, and Duncan (1974) found even more change over 5 years, 58%. The most frequent cause of change in the composition of homes was a change in marital status—presumably from being part of a married couple to becoming a surviving widow. Next to widowhood (or in some cases, remarriage), the next most powerful predictor of household change was the length of time they had been helped. Curiously, ability to handle the activities of daily living, or rather deterioration in this ability, did not lead to a household change per se. Not all people who might be thought to need help, in other words, turned to another living arrangement. Soldo, Sharma, and Campbell (1984) found in recent census figures that it is the 6% of older unmarried women who need frequent help—compared with the 85% who need no help and the 8% who need periodic or minimal help—who are more likely to live in the home of another person, relative or not. (A comprehensive analysis of Oklahoma residents by Morgan et al. (1984), which looked at a variety of "environmental press" factors, concluded that safety of the home and neighborhood, ability to move around the house and neighborhood, and ease of communicating with family and friends were related to adjustment but not, apparently, to living arrangements.)

In accord with earlier studies, current data show that older people today, when they do live with their children, are rarely in three-generation households. The grandchildren have moved out before the old parents and their middle-aged children moved in with each other (e.g., Soldo & Myllyuoma, 1983). Also, as noted above, moving in like this is usually associated with disability or poverty. In light of this, we would not expect high levels of morale when households have been combined. It is not clear, however, that the joint-living solution to care of older family members is necessarily productive of lowered morale. Four studies in the United States—one in rural North Carolina (Kivett & Learner, 1982), one in a Midwestern university city (Mindel & Wright, 1982), one national probability survey (Soldo & Myllyuoma, 1983), and one in northeastern New York State (Stoller, 1985)—all fail to find differences in morale attributable to joint living per se. Stoller did find that problems resulting from disruption of previous household functioning were more likely if the daughter in the combined household was married; but this kind of problem, supposedly related to "role overload" or "role conflict," could be as true when daughters were helping their parents who did not live with them. The other studies found the same effects. Kivett and Learner state that those who have made the decision to share are more likely to say this was a good idea, as one would expect from theories of cognitive dissonance.

Joint households are also likely to consist of older generations who are helping the younger ones financially more than the other way around, consistent with the conclusions noted in the previous section. In other words, we need to look for other reasons for family problems in relationships and feelings than living arrangements.

What about retirement communities? It is often assumed that most retired family members move away from their children to the "sunbelt," thus indicating weakening of family ties. While sunbelt migration has been documented by large-scale surveys such as the Retirement Migration Project (Flynn, Longino, Wiseman, & Biggar, 1985), what they show is shifting patterns over the past several decades. To begin with, these migrants are primarily middle-class, married, and retired individuals. Two or three decades ago the flow was from rural to urban areas, then it went from urban to rural a decade or so later, and more recently there has been evidence of return migration from the sunbelt to metropolitan areas (Collins, 1983). When people who have enough money and are in good health first retire, they move off in search of a better climate and "amenities." Later, when one of the couple dies or health deteriorates, they return to be near their children, those who are likely to help them. Krout (1983) found that "snowbirds," those who move to warmer climates during winter months and return north in the summer, are likely to be married and to have higher socioeconomic status. While Gober and Zonn (1983) found that retirees who moved to Sun City and its neighboring communities—one of the largest of such enclaves in the nation—were not likely to have children living nearby, and that only 15% of them said they had moved there because of friends or relatives (mostly siblings), a more delineated study of the same communities (Sullivan, 1985) analyzed the information about these residents in terms of how long they remained there each year and found clear evidence of family importance. In other words, there was a clear relation between having children and being part-time residents. Those who had children or other ties "back home" were more likely to remain in Arizona just for the winter months and go back home the rest of the year. Those who came from more urban communities with fewer long-lasting local ties, and who had no children, were much more likely to stay in Arizona the year around. Sullivan also found, as had others, that the sunbelt residents were usually in good health, married, and more highly educated than the general population of retirees. In other words, as Troll, Miller, and Atchley (1979) concluded, "When these findings [of migration studies largely involving younger adults] are pooled, one cannot escape a mounting conviction that disruptive effects on kinship ties are at most only temporary" (p. 103).

16

Multigenerational Family Households: Recent Trends and Implications for the Future*

Charles H. Mindel

This chapter concerns the living arrangements of elderly individuals, in particular, those elderly who share households with kin other than their spouse. In addition, it examines and challenges some current beliefs regarding the relationships of elderly and their families. Trends in the living arrangements of elderly in the 20th century will be examined through the use of data collected by the U.S. Census Bureau. Finally, some suggestions for policy will be presented.

One of the more prevalent myths about elderly people is that the elderly either live in institutions (i.e., rest homes, mental institutions, homes for the aged, nursing homes), or that they will eventually find their way there. The reality, of course, is that at any one time no more than 5% of older people are in such institutions (Butler & Lewis, 1977), although, as Kastenbaum and Candy (1973) point out, ultimately almost one-quarter of the elderly will reside in institutions before they die.

The 95% of the elderly *not* presently in institutions are either living by themselves or with their spouses, friends, or in multigenerational family households. In fact, the largest majority of the elderly men and women live either by themselves or with their spouse, with a smaller number in multigenerational family households. Recent data on the

*The Gerontologist, 19 (5) (1979), 456–463.

living arrangements of elderly present graphic evidence on this matter (cf. Fig. 16.1). Some fairly substantial differences between men and women emerge. A large majority of both males and females live alone or with their spouse. More than twice as many elderly men are presently married than elderly women and two and one-half times as many elderly women are living alone as elderly men. Only a slightly greater proportion of elderly women live in institutions or other group quarters than elderly men (U.S. Census Bureau, 1975). However, the rather sizable number of elderly women and the somewhat smaller number of elderly men who are living with someone other than their spouse indicates that this living arrangement is still quite important for many elderly people (this group includes sons, daughters, other relatives or non-relatives).

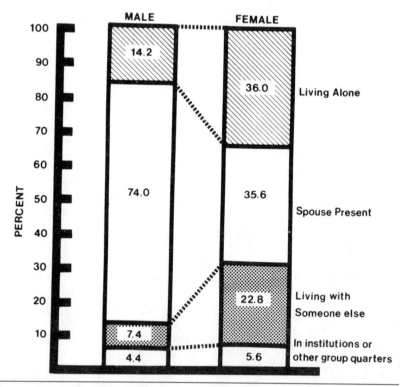

Figure 16.1.   Percent distribution of the male and female population 65 years old and over by living arrangements: 1975. (*Source:* U.S. Census Bureau, Current Population Reports, Special Studies. "Demographic Aspects of Aging and the Older Population in the U.S." Series P. 23, no. 59, 1975, fig. 6-2.)

Ultimately, the question being pursued in this paper concerns the changing nature of family and kinship relations in the U.S. and the status of elderly kin in the lives of family members. How have these relationships changed in recent years and what are the implications for social policy with respect to the place of the aged in American society?

MULTIGENERATIONAL HOUSEHOLDS

In this discussion the term multigenerational family household will include both families that have three or more generations living together under one roof and those two generational families in which the parent or parents of the head are present or in which a generation is missing (as for example, when a head of the household plus grandchildren live together). Also included as multigenerational families are those families in which elderly kin of the same generation live together, such as siblings or cousins. This latter group though not technically multigenerational are difficult to separate from truly multigenerational families given the nature of census data classification. In a sense, these distinctions are not that crucial in so far as the concern here is with the issue of elderly being cared for by family members within the same household. Whether or not there are two or three generations is not terribly crucial. Perhaps a better term for this type of family household is "expanded nuclear family" or more simply "expanded family."

Unlike many traditional societies in which multigenerational households might typically be the culturally prescribed form of family life, normatively and behaviorally the multigenerational household in the U.S. appears to be atypical and is an interruption in the usual family life cycle. As Beresford and Rivlin (1969) have stated, "there is no age at which multigenerational living is typical . . . nor is the life cycle concept helpful in analyzing multigenerational living." The multigenerational family tends to occur after children have formed their own nuclear families and their elderly parents or other relatives have grown quite old. It is at this point that the multigenerational family occurs and usually for a relatively short period of time. Though at any particular point in time this number is not very high relative to more independent living arrangements, the probability of a person living in a multigenerational family at some point early in his/her life and again later in life is high (Beresford & Rivlin, 1969).

In recent years social historians and others have rather convincingly put to rest the belief that at some time in the American past the American family was characterized by large, extended, family households (cf. Foner, 1978; Goode, 1963; Hareven, 1976; Riley & Foner, 1968; Shorter, 1975). The most recent positions claim that the dominant and central family unit has always been the nuclear family, not the extended family, and that for a variety of reasons, not the least of which is that relatively few individuals lived into old age, the multigenerational family household has been rather uncommon. Historical research by Beresford and Rivlin (1969), Pryor (1972) and Kobrin (1976) comparing family structure in the latter years of the nineteenth century with the recent past found the prevalence of multigenerational households relatively low, both then and now.

RECENT TRENDS

An example of a type of multigenerational household which has virtually ceased to exist in the U.S. is the household arrangement often described as the "doubling up" phenomenon (i.e., the household consisting of a married couple not maintaining its own household). Table 16.1 presents this phenomenon of a married couple continuing to live with one or the other sets of parents after marriage, an occurrence relatively infrequent in the 20th century. In fact, at the beginning of the century the proportion was lower than midway through the century. It was due only to the post-World War II hous-

Table 16.1. Married Couples Who Do Not Maintain Their Own Households ("Doubling Up") 1910–1978 (Selected Years).[1]

Year	Percent without Own Household
1910	5.4
1940	6.8
1945	4.8
1947	8.7
1950	5.6
1951	4.9
1955	3.5
1960	2.4
1965	1.9
1970	1.4
1975	1.3
1978	1.2

[1]Source: U.S. Bureau of the Census, Current Population Reports Series p-20, Nos. 56, 327.

ing shortage that significant numbers of married couples did not maintain their own household. The trend in the last 30 years has been steadily downward to a point where now 98.8% of all married couples maintain their own households. This data confirms dominance of the nuclear family in American society. If the extended family household exists it is only as an interruption of the normative family life cycle.

The above data probably comes as no surprise to anyone. The data clearly indicate this type of arrangement is virtually non-existent in American society at present and for significant numbers of years in the past. A much more common and potentially problematic living arrangement has been the case where elderly individuals live in the same household with their kin. In this case the elderly person is neither the head of the household nor the wife of the head of the household. Table 16.2 presents historical data describing the percent of persons 65 years or older living in households as an "other relative." The term "other relative" is a Census Bureau term used to

Table 16.2. Percent of Persons 65 Years or Older Living in Households as "Other Relative" (Neither Head nor Wife of Head) by Sex for Selected Years.[a]

Year	Males %	Females %
1940	15.0	30.2
1947	14.3	28.8
1953	10.2	24.7
1960	9.4	21.8
1965	9.4	20.0
1967	8.9	18.6
1968	7.7	14.9
1970	6.5	16.1
1971	7.0	15.0
1975	3.9	13.4

[a]Source: U.S. Bureau of the Census 1940 *Census of Population* Vol. IV, Part 1. U.S. Summary, "Characteristics by Age, Marital Status Relationship, Education and Citizenship" Table 11. U.S. Bureau of the Census, *Current Population Reports* Special Studies Series p-23, No. 59, "Demographic Aspects of Aging and the Older Population in the U.S." Table 6-3. Also *Current Population Reports* series p-20, Nos. 10, 50, 170.

describe a kin member who is neither the head of the household nor the wife of the head of the household and who is living in the household. This data also excludes those elderly not living in households (i.e., those in institutions or group quarters).

Table 16.2 illustrates three points: first, there are significantly more elderly living in households in which they are neither the head, nor wife of the head of a household than there are young married couples "doubled up" in households headed by elderly. Second, for females and to some extent for males, significant numbers of elderly are still living with their children or kin as opposed to being placed in institutions. Third, and perhaps most graphically illustrated, is the fact that there has been, at least over the last 35 years, a gradual but inexorable decline in the numbers of elderly who live in households with their children or other kin. In 1940, 15% of elderly men lived with their kin. In 1975 only about 4% did. The decline with respect to females has also been substantial, though the change has not been nearly as great with somewhat over a 50% decline in the last 35 years. Some of this change can be attributed to certain kinds of shifts in other household patterns. Table 16.3 indicates a large increase over the last 37 years in the proportion of elderly males and females who have been able to maintain themselves as heads of household. At present almost one-half of the elderly females and 92% of the elderly males head their own household. The proportion of elderly women who are wives of the head of the household has not increased sub-

Table 16.3. Individuals 65 Years or Over Who Were Heads of Households or Wives of Heads by Year (Numbers in Thousands).[a]

Year	Female Head of Household		Male Head of Household		Wife of Head of Household	
	N	%	N	%	N	%
1940	1509	40.0	3325	79.1	1373	30.9
1947	1717	32.7	3900	77.1	1681	30.4
1953	2426	35.3	5086	85.4	2444	35.5
1960	3225	38.2	5573	86.8	3005	35.6
1965	4196	43.2	6732	88.5	3386	34.9
1970	4938	45.2	7330	90.8	3867	35.4
1975	5991	48.3	8268	94.8	4664	37.5
1977	6436	49.6	8380	91.8	4797	37.0

[a]Source: U.S. Bureau of the Census, *Current Population Reports* Series P-20 Nos., 10, 50; U.S. Bureau of the Census, *1940 Census of Population* Vol IV, Part 1 U.S. Summary Table 11. U.S. Bureau of the Census, *1960 Census of Population* Subject Reports PC(2)-4A. U.S. Bureau of the Census *1970 Census of Population* Subject Reports PC(2)-4A.

stantially over the last 37 years. The major change has been the tendency for elderly women, mostly widows, to live alone. Likewise elderly men tend to either live alone or to remarry. (In 1975 2.5% of male family heads over 65 years of age were widowed whereas 86.9% of female family heads over 65 were widowed) (cf. *Current Population Reports*, 1975).

Elderly men tend to remarry and live with their spouses while elderly female widows live alone in their own independent households. Whether this indicates a reluctance on the part of children and kin to take care of their elderly, a reaffirmation of independent living norms on the part of the elderly, or greater financial well being due to the presence of Social Security and pension systems, is difficult to interpret from this data. If the main concern is the nature of family relationships between elderly and their children perhaps a more important population to examine are not those elderly who are presently living out their lives with their spouses in the normative American family pattern at its later stages, but rather those "single" elderly who are without a spouse. These would include the widowed, divorced or separated elderly, those who are or were married but whose spouse is not present, and those elderly who never married at all.

THE "SINGLE" ELDERLY

Table 16.4 presents the distribution of the elderly in the U.S. population in 1977. Considerably more men than women are living in families, reflecting the greater life expectancy of women and the typical disparity in age between spouses. Additionally, whereas one-fourth of the elderly men were single, almost two-thirds of the elderly females were single. Comparing those single elderly living in families who head their own households, and those single elderly living in families who do not head their own households, the latter group is more likely to be "dependent" elderly, while the former group is apt to be a more independent group of elderly individuals. Table 16.4 indicates that approximately one-third of both the single males and females are living in families, and for both males and females more of these single elderly, living in families are *not* heading their households. The data indicate that slightly more than 15% of the elderly population 65 and over are single and living in families. In 1977, almost two million elderly or about 9% of the total elderly population over 65 were single, living in families, and not heading their own household.

Table 16.4. Distribution of Elderly by Marital Status, Family Status, and
Sex: March 1977 (Numbers in Thousands).[a]

	Males		Females	
Elderly 65 or Over:	N	%	N	%
Total	9132	100.0	12968	100.0
Living in Families	7737	83.0	7496	57.8
"Single" Elderly	2354	25.8	8171	63.0
"Single" and Living in Families	796	33.8	2607	31.9
"Single," Living in Families, Head of Household	280	11.9	1144	14.0
"Single," Living in Families, Not Head of Household	516	21.9	1463	17.9

[a]Source: U.S. Bureau of the Census, *Current Population Reports* Series p-20, No. 323.

An examination of the trends over the last 30 years with respect to
where the single elderly were living, produces some rather meaningful trends. Table 16.5 presents the percentage of elderly single and
living in families for the years 1950 through 1977.

With respect to the single elderly males we find that during the
1970s there has been a slight though steady decline in the proportion
of single elderly men heading their own primary families. This is
particularly true among those elderly men between the ages 65 and
74. Those men 75 and over who were single and head of their own
primary family has remained quite stable since 1960.

Turning to those single elderly males living in families who do not
head their own household we find a substantial amount of fluctuation
in the data from year to year. These data for single males are not
easily interpreted. There appeared to be a tendency toward fewer
multigenerational households until the early 1970s, but since then
there has been a slow and at times fluctuating increase in the percentage of single elderly men living in this type of residence. These yearly
changes are apparently not due to sampling error since analysis of the
standard error of these estimates indicates, for example, that in 1976
and 1977 the standard error was approximately 1% with the chances
being 95 out of 100 that the estimate is within ± 2% of the actual
population figure (U.S. Bureau of the Census, 1978).

Overall it appears that there has been a decline in males heading
primary families though most of this decline has been with the
"young–old." However, there has recently been an increase in families in which the elderly person is not the head, especially among the
"old–old."

There has been a very steady and stable 16% of females aged 65 to 74 who head their own primary families. This is down from 24% in 1950 but since the early 60s this has been a relatively constant figure. With respect to those living with kin and not heading their own households those aged 65 to 74 indicate a definite downward movement from a high of almost 35% in 1950 to 11.8% in 1977, almost a two-thirds drop. What this probably represents is a continuation of maternal care by single elderly women when there are kin to be cared for but a general decline in the proportion of widows living as dependents of their children in this younger group.

With respect to those over 75 there has been a slight but definite downward trend away from living as a head of household at this age. However, for single elderly women over 75 years of age living in families but not heading households the percentage has stabilized at about 25% since the beginning of this decade, though it is down somewhat from the early 1960s. Compared to 1950 there has been almost a 50% decline. Overall the proportion of elderly women who are single and head their own primary family has remained relatively stable in recent years but there has been a definite decline with respect to those who are living in families and do not head their household, especially among the young-old. In fact, compared to the men there are proportionally fewer females living as members of a multigenerational household.

The data do appear to indicate that the multigenerational household is still a fairly common arrangement for older single elderly individuals. For those 75 years and older the percentage living in this form of residence has apparently stabilized at between 20 and 25% of the total. On the other hand for the younger elderly, especially the females (65 to 74) there has been a downward trend. The younger males appear to be responding to different kinds of environmental stimuli or forces in that the data appeared to fluctuate rather unexpectedly. Perhaps this group of men are responding to economic, political and/or health related events in a particularly volatile manner due to their relatively small number (in 1977 there were 2,354,000 single elderly men). This volatility is reflected in the population data. In any event, this population warrants further research.

CHANGING FAMILY STRUCTURE

Kobrin (1976) suggests that given the demographic changes over the last century (i.e., growth in the size of the elderly population), figures such as those cited by Pryor (1972) and Beresford and Rivlin (1969)

Table 16.5. Number and Percent of "Single" Elderly Living with Kin by Sex, Age, Head of Household Status, and Year.[a]

| Year | Total Single Elderly (in Thousands) | 65–74 | | 75 and Over | | 65 and Over | | Percentage 65 and Over of All Single Elderly Living with Kin % |
		Head of Primary Family %	In Family but not Head %	Head of Primary Family %	In Family but not Head %	Head of Primary Family %	In Family but not Head %	
Males								
1950	1848	22.7	22.7	20.2	35.5	21.7	27.9	49.6
1960	2039	18.3	20.9	16.4	30.5	17.5	25.1	42.6
1968	2457	15.9	15.4	10.6	27.8	13.1	19.4	32.5
1970	2643	10.9	20.9	13.4	24.2	12.1	22.5	34.6
1971	2530	12.3	18.0	11.9	21.8	12.1	19.9	32.0
1972	2069	16.7	14.2	17.4	20.3	17.0	17.0	34.0
1973	2150	15.6	16.4	14.2	20.3	14.9	18.2	33.1
1974	1982	16.2	9.1	13.8	15.7	15.0	12.3	27.3
1975	1982	13.2	10.6	13.7	18.0	13.4	13.1	26.5
1976	2099	14.8	9.8	13.5	21.6	14.2	15.4	29.6
1977	2354	10.8	24.0	13.5	19.0	11.9	21.9	33.8

Females

1950	4024	24.2	34.6	19.0	44.9	22.1	38.8	60.9
1960	5349	19.6	28.5	16.1	38.0	18.2	32.5	50.7
1968	7127	17.1	19.3	14.4	30.1	15.8	24.8	40.6
1970	7526	16.1	18.8	13.5	26.5	14.8	22.6	37.4
1971	7610	14.0	18.1	12.6	25.7	13.3	21.9	35.2
1972	7369	14.5	17.9	13.0	27.4	13.7	22.5	36.2
1973	7570	17.8	17.4	12.8	26.9	15.5	21.9	37.4
1974	7577	16.2	16.7	13.6	25.8	15.0	21.0	36.0
1975	7740	16.0	15.9	12.5	25.4	14.2	20.5	34.7
1976	8074	16.2	14.4	11.4	25.1	13.9	19.6	33.5
1977	8171	16.0	11.8	11.9	25.2	14.0	17.9	31.9

[a]Source: U.S. Bureau of the Census, *1950 Census of Population* Special Report P-E No. 2D, Table 1, *1960 Census of Population* Subject Reports PC (2)-1B Table 2, *Current Population Reports* Series P-20, Nos. 33, 103, 176, 218, 225, 242, 255, 271, 282, 296, 323.

suggesting little change in residential patterns in the last one hundred years, in fact, represent the occurrence of a major redefinition of the appropriate family group, away from the inclusion of non-nuclear members. Our evidence tends to confirm this in large measure, at least for the post World War II period. Virtually no married couples go to live with their family of orientation (i.e., married couples form their own independent nuclear households). There has been a decline in the overall number of multigenerational households reflecting the greater tendency of female widows to live by themselves and the equal tendency of males to remain married or remarry and maintain themselves as heads of their own households. Even with respect to the subgroup, "single elderly" this apparently inexorable trend is apparent. On the one hand, in 1950, almost 45% of single elderly females over the age of 75 lived with their relatives; in 1977 this figure has dropped to 25%, a 50% decline. The decline for males was roughly the same.

It would be a mistake however to assume that America's elderly are being abandoned and forced to live by themselves unaided by their kin. Brody (1978) refers to this as the "myth of abandonment." There is much literature and research on American kinship relations which has shown that there is a substantial kinship solidarity remaining in the American family system (cf. Adams, 1968; Litwak, 1969; Shanas, 1968; Sussman, 1965). It is generally agreed that normatively the American system is not multigenerational, at least in household terms. Attitudes studies have indicated that most individuals, both younger and older, prefer not to maintain this kind of living arrangement and that historically there have been strong norms in favor of independent living arrangements (Dinkel, 1944; Wake & Sporakowski, 1972). In spite of these norms it appears that the multigenerational household continues to be a viable alternative living arrangement for many elderly individuals and their families. Though the trend has certainly been on the decline there are still considerably more elderly living in multigenerational households than in institutions. For many families movement into a home of a relative is seen as an alternative to movement into an institution (cf. Newman, 1976). It has been noted by Brody (1976) and also by Habenstein and Biddle (1973) that living with a relative was often the antecedent residential location of the older person in the nursing home.

Living in a multigenerational household should be seen in the context of the mutual aid and help pattern of the American kinship system. Although elderly in increasing numbers are able to maintain themselves independently, the movement into a household with a child or other kin member can perhaps be seen as an intermediate step between independent living and institutionalization, being neither as satisfactory (to both generations) as independent living nor as threatening and guilt inducing as institutionalization. Since there are substantial numbers of individuals who choose this form of residential arrangement either because they think it is right and proper or due to circumstances beyond their control, it would appear that the support of multigenerational households under certain circumstances such as through government policies, programs, and services is a reasonable and appropriate direction to take. Certainly government at a minimum should not penalize the elderly or their families because of this. More positively, ways of supporting this potentially problematic family arrangement should be considered. As Brody (1978) states, "the absence of services can cause the family to exceed its tolerance for stress, to break down as a unit of service provision and emotional support, and can have reverberations down through the generations."

As an example of the ways in which the government might be penalizing elderly who live with their children or relatives we might consider the method by which Supplemental Security Income (SSI) payments are determined. For an elderly person living alone or in an institution, it is quite possible for SSI payments to be greater than for an elderly person living with a family (where there may be no payment at all). Or, eligibility for programs such as Meals on Wheels, Home Health Care or chore services might be denied if an elderly person is living with a family but not so to an elderly person who is living alone. There are several types of policies and programs that might be instituted which would encourage and ease some of the problems of adjustment to the multigenerational household. For example, if there was not enough room or there was crowding in the household due to an elderly person in the household perhaps a program which provides governmental subsidies or guarantees for loans to build onto houses or to add additional rooms to houses could be established. In addition, there is a whole range of potential modifications in the Internal Revenue Code that could be made to assist multigenerational household arrangements.

We know from some research (Habenstein & Biddle, 1973; Mindel, 1977; Newman, 1976) that elderly give up independent living due largely to their declining health and physical disability. It is often the inability, or unwillingness of family members to provide the constant and proper care to the elderly person that causes a move to an institution, often at great emotional cost to the various family members. In programmatic or service delivery terms it certainly would seem to be a useful step to develop programs, perhaps funded through Title XX, that would train family members or workers to provide certain kinds of medical care and services to elderly people living independently or in multigenerational families. The assumption underlying this recommendation is that many elderly people might be able to remain independent or in a family milieu, at less expense, and with greater psychological well being to them and their family if the provision of certain kinds of services were made available to them. At a minimum, though, policies toward the family which concern the elderly should visualize the elderly in the larger context of family, friends and community. It is only by recognizing the degree of integration between the elderly and their family and other groups that coherent and socially useful policies can be developed. Only then can appropriate and consistent programs relating to the elderly and their families be made.

REFERENCES

Adams, B. *Kinship in an urban setting*, Markham, Chicago, 1968.
Beresford, J. C., & Rivlin, A. M. The multigenerational family. In W. Donahue, J. Kornbluh & L. Powers (Eds.), *Living in the multigenerational family*, Inst. of Gerontology, Univ. of Michigan, 1969.
Brody, E. The aging of the family, *The Annals*, 1978, *438*, 13–27.
Butler, R. N., & Lewis, M. I. *Aging and mental health* (2nd ed.) C. V. Mosby, St. Louis, 1977.
Dinkel, R. Attitudes of children toward supporting aged parents, *American Sociological Review*, 1944, *9*, 370–379.
Foner, A. Age stratification and the changing family. *American Journal of Sociology*, 1978, *84*, S340–S365 (supplement, 1978).
Goode, W. J. *World revolution and family patterns*, Free Press, New York, 1963.
Harevan, T. K. The last stage: Historical adulthood and old age. *Daedalus*, 1976, *105*, 13–27.
Habenstein, R. W., & Biddle, E. Decisions to relocate the residence of aged persons. Final Report on NIMH grant #1 R03 MH22182-01, 1973.
Kastenbaum, R., & Candy, S. E. The 4% fallacy: A methodological and empirical critique of extended care facility population statistics. *Aging and Human Development*, 1973, *4*, 15–21.
Kobrin, F. The fall in household size and the rise of the primary individual in the United States. *Demography*, 1976, *13*, 127–138.
Litwak, E. Occupational mobility and extended family cohesion. *American Sociological Review*, 1969, *25*, 9–24.

Mindel, C. H. A multiple regression approach to satisfaction in multi-generational households. Paper presented at the 30th Annual Meeting of the Gerontological Society, San Francisco, 1977.

Newman, S. J. Housing adjustments of the disabled elderly. *The Gerontologist*, 1976, *16*, 312–316.

Pryor, E. T. Jr. Rhode Island family structure: 1815 and 1960. In P. Laslett & R. Wall (Eds.), *Household and family in past time*, Cambridge Univ. Press, Cambridge, England, 1972.

Riley, M. W., & Foner, A. Aging and society. Vol. I, *An inventory of research findings*, Russell Sage, New York, 1968.

Shanas, E., Townsend, P., Wedderburn, D., Friis, H., Milhøj, P., & Stehouwer, J. Old people in three industrial societies, Atherton Press, New York, 1968.

Shorter, E. *The making of the modern family*. Basic Books, New York, 1975.

Sussman, M. Relationships of adult children with their parents in the U.S. In E. Shanas & G. Streib (Eds.) *Social Structure and the Family: Generational Relations*, Prentice-Hall, Englewood Cliffs, 1965.

U.S. Bureau of the Census, *Current Population Reports*, Special Studies, Demographic Aspects of Aging and the Older Population in the U.S. Series P-23, No. 59, 1975.

U.S. Bureau of the Census, *Current Population Survey*, Marital Status and Living Arrangements, March 1977, Series P-20, No. 323, 1978.

Wake, S. B., & Sporokowski, M. An intergenerational comparison of attitudes supporting aged parents. *Journal of Marriage and the Family*, 1972, *34*, 42–47.

17

Change in Household Composition of the Elderly: A Preliminary Investigation*

Gerda G. Fillenbaum
Laurence M. Wallman

Because of the lack of longitudinal research (Streib & Beck, 1980; Troll, 1971), most available information about living arrangements and housing choice of elderly persons comes from three types of sources, all of which use cross-sectional data: anecdotal evidence, speculation that changes in certain environmental characteristics underly identified cross-sectional trends, and empirical studies that try to determine which characteristics distinguish elderly adults in one type of living arrangement from those in another (e.g., Chevan & Korson, 1975; Soldo & Lauriat, 1976; Soldo et al., in press; Troll, 1971). All three sources agree that elderly adults prefer to live independently and will try to do so if at all financially able. Living with kin is not a generally preferred alternative. This type of household arrangement may reflect a combination of earlier life cycle events such as marriage and having children (and so having kin); a problematic economic position, and need for help with personal care. Such demographic characteristics as race, sex, and age seem to make

Journal of Gerontology, 39 (3)(1984), 342–349.
  This research was partially supported by grant number 93-P-75172/4 from the U.S. Department of Health, Education and Welfare, Administration on Aging, Social and Rehabilitative Service and Health Resources Administration. Address reprint requests to the first author.

little independent contribution to explaining living arrangements, but health status may be important (Soldo & Lauriat, 1976). These findings suggest that both life cycle and environmental factors are important in explaining the living arrangement patterns identified in cross-sectional studies (e.g., Yee & Van Arsdol, 1977).

Living arrangements are not stationary. Households change over the life cycle (Burch, 1979). In looking at change in residential arrangements, information from cross-sectional studies suggests that change in residential arrangements may be occasioned by changes in the life cycle and in environmental circumstances. It is essential to be aware that we are dealing with two intersecting life cycles, that of the individual and that of the family (Burch, 1979; Hill & Mattessich, 1979). Each may be important and, so, should be identified separately, particularly because at a later age personal life cycle changes (e.g., deterioration of health) may place strains on the family life cycle (e.g., requiring help from mature offspring).

Because the longitudinal data presented here are based on a small sample ($N = 276$), we have restricted the variables included to those four that, in light of the theoretical framework proposed and on the basis of previous studies, are most relevant: economic status (representing environment circumstances), self-care capacity (representing an individual life cycle matter), marital status, and extent of help available from family and friends (representing family life cycle matters). Obviously there is overlap between the individual life cycle and the family life cycle, and one might question our assignment of marital status. We assigned it to the family life cycle because marriage (a) involves another person and (b) may largely determine the form of the family life cycle. We have excluded variables that seem to lack relevance (e.g., race) or which, like age and size of family, were proxies for health status and the availability of help in previous studies. Each of these four variables is considered individually. We recognize that they interact and take that into account during analysis.

Economic Status

Where financial matters are concerned, two main arguments seem to have been suggested to explain the living arrangements of elderly adults. One argument suggest that, if it is at all economically feasible, older persons prefer to live independently (e.g., Troll et al., 1979). The other argument asserts that older persons who have some income to contribute do not mind living with their financially strapped offspring, because they then feel that they are contributing (Anderson, 1977). Thus, a change in the economic status of an older person could affect residential arrangements. If income increases sufficiently, those previously living in the households of others might try to live independently. If income decreases, an independent living arrangement may no longer be financially feasible, and change might occur for this reason.

Self-care Capacity

Self-care capacity can range from total independence to total dependence. Reports indicate that, within the alternative types of community-based household composition, individuals representative of all the possible levels of impairment can be found (Lawton, 1980). Certain levels of impairment, however, are more common in certain types of living arrangements: Elderly persons living alone are more likely to be functioning independently; those living with kin and where the spouse is absent are the most functionally dependent (Shanas, 1962; Troll et al., 1979). It is more plausible that functional status determines residential arrangement than vice versa; thus, a marked change in self-care capacity may require a change in household composition, with improvement in self-care capacity facilitating living alone and deterioration requiring the presence of others who can provide help.

Marital Status

Whereas most classifications of household composition, including the one to be used here, reflect the presence or absence of kinship and marital ties among co-residents, almost by definition a change in marital status represents a change in household composition. Rarely, husband and wife may not live together because of personal preference, work requirements, health condition, or legal constraint.

In general, marital status is reported to mediate the effects of other factors that influence residential arrangements. In particular, evidence, which is largely anecdotal, suggests that elderly impaired couples compensate for each other's difficulties and, as long as each survives, can together maintain themselves independently. The death of one, however, may extinguish the independence of the other (e.g., Treas, 1977; Troll et al., 1979). So, conditions that might otherwise result in relocation or demand a change in household composition if the older person is to be cared for appropriately should be less likely to result in such a change when the older person has a spouse.

Availability of Help from Family and Friends

Information that indicates that severely impaired persons who live alone are more likely to enter an institution than are those who live with others (Comptroller General, 1977) and surveys that indicate that a disproportionate number of residents in institutions are childless or unmarried, entering because there is no one to take care of them (e.g., Brody, 1977), strongly suggest that the extent of availability of help may determine whether continued residence in the usual setting is feasible. Certainly we know that those who receive services, particularly more impaired elderly persons who receive extensive help, are more likely to receive that help from family and friends than from any other source (Comptroller General, 1977). Given the importance of this source, it is highly likely that the availability of such help may be crucial in maintaining the older person in his or her current household. Other matters being controlled, we would anticipate that the shorter the duration for which help would be available the greater the likelihood of a change in household composition, for certain types of household arrangements may only be feasible when help is assured.

We would expect specific changes within each independent variable and specific combinations of changes across independent variables to have specific effects on household composition. Because of the size of the sample, however, it was not feasible to test hypotheses developed at this level of detail. Our concern was, therefore, to determine whether change *per se* in economic status, self-care capacity, marital status, and extent of help available would explain change in type of household composition. Although our examination is limited, it is an essential first step in identifying those factors that determine change in household composition. Only when it has been determined which factors are important determinants of change in household composition are we justified in refining the examination and testing hypotheses on a sample of more adequate size.

A longitudinal study offers additional unique opportunities not available from cross-sectional data. Longitudinal data permit examination of the relative stability of different types of living arrangements (or, here, household composition), identification of the specific transitions that occur, and assessment of the amount of change in household composition. We examined the present data from these points of view also.

Our focus was twofold: to describe change in household composition for a sample of older persons who were all, initially, community residents and to see to what extent change in the household composition of these elderly persons can be explained in terms of the help available to them from family and friends, and the change in their economic status, personal self-care capacity, and marital status.

METHOD

Sample

In the absence of adequate nationally representative longitudinal data we turned to a locally representative study: the Duke Older Americans Resources and Services (OARS) survey of a random sample of community residents of Durham, North Carolina (Blazer, 1978).

In 1972 a 10% random sample of elderly residents were surveyed (N = 997, age 65 and over). A random third of this sample was recontacted 30 months later. Initial data from these 331 persons indicated that they were representative of the total sample of 997. Their mean age was 72 (SD = 5), their race and sex composition being 20% white men, 10% black men, 45% white women, and 26% black women.

On the first occasion information was obtained in personal interviews using the OARS Community Survey questionnaire. On the second occasion an abbreviated version of this questionnaire was administered by telephone. The OARS questionnaire is designed to assess personal functional status on each of five dimensions: social, economic, mental health, physical health, and self-care capacity. Multiple questions are asked in each area. Responses permit a valid and reliable summary assessment to be made separately for each dimension on a 6-point scale, with 1 denoting an excellent level of functioning and 6 total impairment (Fillenbaum & Smyer, 1981). Several of the questions are appropriate to the present study, namely specifics of household composition, economic status, detailed inquiry into eight instrumental and six physical activities of daily living, marital status, and extent of availability of help.

Measures Used

Household Composition

Over 30 different types of household composition were represented in the initial sample of 997 participants. These were classified into the following five types: living alone; living only with spouse;

living with spouse and kin; living with kin, no spouse present; other (e.g., a boarder, a housekeeper). Other did not include institutional residence on the first round, because only community residents were surveyed. Institutions were included under other on the second round, however, because by that time some members of the sample had entered institutions.

Change in Economic Status

Information on economic status was obtained initially and 30 months later. On each occasion summary ratings were made on a 6-point scale. Any difference in the ratings received on the two occasions was scored as a change in economic status. Of this sample 59% experienced a change in economic status (a deterioration for 39%, an improvement for 19%).

Change in Self-care Capacity

Both initially and 30 months later participants were asked to what extent (unaided, only with some help, not at all) they could carry out eight instrumental activities of daily living (use telephone, shop, cook, do housework, do laundry, travel, take own medicine, handle personal finances) and six physical activities of daily living (feed self, dress, groom, walk, bathe, remain continent). Any change in ability to perform any of these activities was rated as a change in self-care capacity. Change in self-care capacity was reported by 57% (deterioration, 36%; improvement, 9%; mixed, 12%).

Change in Marital Status

On both rounds participants were asked whether they were single (i.e., never married), married, widowed, divorced, or separated. Any change in self-reported marital status was coded as a change, except for widowed persons who later said they were divorced or separated and those who initially said they were divorced or separated but later said they were widowed. Because there seemed to be semantic confusion here, all such persons were coded as though they had experienced no change in marital status within the past 30 months. None had changed their living arrangements.

Based on these considerations, the marital status of 16 persons (6% of this sample) changed over the period of 30 months; 14 initially married persons became widowed, and two who were initially widowed had remarried.

Extent and Availability of Help

Only information obtained on the initial occasion is relevant, because that may determine the continued feasibility of the initial household composition. The questionnaire asked whether help was available from family or friends, and if available its duration (occasional, short term, extended care). This was dichotomized into extended care versus the rest. Seventy-two percent reported that extensive care was available to them.

RESULTS

Of the 331 persons selected for follow-up, 50 had died in the 30 months following initial contact. An additional five survivors were unavailable or refused to participate, so that information on change in household composition was available for 276, or 98% of the 281 survivors.

Overall Change in Household Composition

Household composition was divided into five types. Table 17.1 shows the distribution of the total sample ($N = 331$), the contacted survivors initially and 30 months later ($N = 276$), and the initial household composition of the 50 decedents. The initial household arrangements of the contacted survivors were very similar to that of the total group, but the distribution changed somewhat over the 30 months. The apparent amount and direction of change are indicated in the change column. Summing, these changes would seem to indicate that 12% of the survivors experienced a change in household composition.

This figure is misleading, however. The amount of change is considerably greater than these cross-sectionally derived summary percentages would suggest. Of the 276 participants 28% experienced some change in their households, which for 18% ($n = 49$) resulted in a change in type of household composition. Table 17.2 provides a cross-tabulation of initial by later household composition. It is notable that transfers seemed to occur from any household composition to almost any other household composition. Only 5 of the 25 cells registered no transfers. With a larger sample transfers to these might have been found.

Certain household compositions were more stable than others. Specifically, very little change was found among those who initially

Table 17.1. Household Composition Initially and after 30 Months: Cross-sectional view (percentages)

Category	Total sample		Contacted survivors[a]		Change of contacted survivors
	Initial	Decedents	Initial	30 months later	
Alone	25	18	26	30	+4
Married couple only	36	34	36	35	−1
Married couple and kin	9	12	9	6	−3
With kin, no spouse	25	32	23	21	−2
Other	6	4	6	8	+2
N	331	50	276	276	

[a]Information on five survivors was unavailable.

Table 17.2. Change in Type of Household Composition over a 30-month Period

Initial type	Type of household composition 30 months later						
	Alone	Married couple only	Married couple and kin	With kin, no spouse	Other	n	Percent of total
Alone	89	1	0	1	8	72	26
Married couple only	8	87	1	2	2	100	36
Married couple and kin	0	25	63	13	0	24	9
With kin, no spouse	9	2	0	81	8	64	23
Other	31	6	0	6	56	16	6
n	83	96	16	59	22	276	
Percentage of total	30	35	6	21	8		

Note. Entries are percentages based on initial type of household composition.

lived alone; lived only with their spouse; or lived with kin, a spouse being absent; 89%, 87%, and 81%, respectively, maintained their household composition over a period of 30 months. Married couple and kin, and other, were the least stable (they also had the fewest members). In the married couple and kin group one-quarter had lost kin (probably children), and 13% had lost a spouse (probably by death). Of those initially in other, 31% lived alone later.

Factors Determining Change in Household Composition

Four determinants of change in household composition were considered: change in economic status, change in self-care capacity, change in marital status, and the extent of availability of help when initially seen. Complete information was available for 254 of the 276 participants. Household composition changed for 44 of the 254. Chi-square analysis (Table 17.3) indicates that change in marital status and the duration of available help were related to change in household composition, with the latter being important even among those whose marital status remained stable (Table 17.3). Neither change in economic status nor in self-care capacity, however, seemed to be related significantly to change in household composition.

In order to assess better the relevance of these four factors in explaining change in household composition, a loglinear approach was chosen. Loglinear models are particularly appropriate for hypothesis testing in situations such as the present one where a multivariate approach is needed to examine categorical data. In the present case we wished to determine whether change in living arrangement was related to change in economic status, self-care capacity, marital status, was attributable to the amount of help available, or was related to some combination of these. Because we were concerned to explain only change, and not type of change, each variable has only two levels (i.e., change vs. no change, or, for amount of help available, extensive vs. nonextensive). Thus the data can be displayed in a table containing $2 \times 2 \times 2 \times 2 \times 2 = 32$ cells. Given the size of the sample on which full information is available ($n = 254$), a finer breakdown would not be appropriate. Too many cells would be empty simply because of the small size of the sample (sampling zeroes), and, although there are ways of handling this problem, the results might be biased. In any case, finer breakdown was unnecessary for testing the current hypotheses.

Our concern was to determine what minimum amount of information best explains the findings. Put simply, in a loglinear approach

Table 17.3. Change in Household Composition by Change in Four Independent Variables

Independent variables	All respondents (N = 254)			Stable marital status (n = 238)		
	No change	Change	$\chi^2(1)$	No change	Change	$\chi^2(1)$
Economic status						
No change	85	22		85	16	
Change	125	22	1.35	124	13	2.19
Self-care capacity						
No change	91	17		91	9	
Change	119	27	.33	118	20	1.63
Marital status						
No change	209	29		209	29	
Change	1	15	69.67***			
Help available						
Extensive	157	26		156	15	
Limited	53	18	4.44*	53	14	4.92*

*$p < .05$; ***$p < .001$.

this is done by disaggregating the summary table in specified ways (e.g., in terms of change in marital status when that is hypothesized to explain change in household composition). The expected cell frequencies obtained under the hypothesized model are then compared with the observed frequencies by means of a likelihood ratio chi-square test. Because the aim is to obtain a good fit for the data, if the hypothesized model is to be accepted the expected frequencies should not differ significantly from the observed frequencies as measured by a goodness-of-fit test (i.e., the chi square should be nonsignificant).

Each variable can be examined separately (i.e., first-order effects) or the table may be broken up in specified ways so that two (second-order effects) or more (higher-order effects) variables, in specified combinations, can be examined. The entire table can, of course, be reproduced exactly if all the variables considered are entered. Our intent, however, was to determine what minimum amount of information best explains the findings. For a technical discussion of hypothesis testing using loglinear models the reader is referred to Davis (1974) and Fienberg (1977).

The results of the loglinear analysis are displayed in Table 17.4. Baseline models that assume equiprobability of living arrangement

Table 17.4. Results of a Loglinear Analysis of Selected Variables

Model[a]	χ^2_{LR}	Degrees of freedom	p
Entire sample			
1 [EAMH]	168.96	16	.0000
2 [EAMH][L]	59.24	15	.00001
3 [EAMH][LE]	57.81	14	.00001
4 [EAMH][LA]	59.07	14	.00000
5 [EAMH][LM]	13.17	14	.52
6 [EAMH][LH]	54.21	14	.00001
7 [EAMH][LM][LH]	7.87	13	.85
No change in marital status			
8 [EAH]	158.42	8	.000
9 [EAH][L]	11.34	7	.125
10 [EAH][LE]	9.17	6	.164
11 [EAH][LA]	10.06	6	.122
12 [EAH][LH]	4.73	6	.58

[a]Abbreviations represent the following variables: L, living arrangements; E, economic status change; A, self-care capacity change; M, marital status change; H, help available (extensive/not extensive). The brackets indicate the different terms (effects) fit for a particular model.

changes were fit for both the entire sample (Model 1 [EAMH]), as well as for only those whose marital status remained stable (Model 8 [EAH]). This isolates the effects of the independent variables on the dependent from the known associations between the set of independent variables.

For the entire sample our baseline model [EAMH] did not fit, $\chi^2(1)_{LR} = 168.96$. Model 2 ([EAMH][L]) was fit under the hypothesis that change in household composition is not equiprobable. The brackets indicate the different terms (effects) fit for a particular model. When we compare the reduction in $\chi^2(1)_{LR}$ between the baseline model and Model 2 (168.96 − 59.24 = 109.72), the null hypothesis of equiprobability was rejected. Model 2, however, does not fit the data well, and additional explanatory variables must be considered.

We next checked whether, in order, change in marital status [LM] or change in economic status [LE] or amount of help initially available [LH] or change in self-care capacity [LA] could adequately explain the change in household composition (Table 17.4, Models 3 to 6). Of these, Model 5 [LM] provides an adequate fit (i.e., change in household composition can be explained adequately by change in marital status). Considered alone, the amount of help available does not adequately explain change in household composition (i.e., Model 6 does not fit the data adequately). If we take into account both change in marital status and amount of help available (Model 7, [LM][LH]), however, there appears to be a further improvement in fit.

This improvement seems to reflect the difference present between Models 2 and 6. If we compare Model 2 ([EAMH][L]) and Model 6 ([EAMH][LH]) we get a reduction in $\chi^2(1)_{LR}$ of 59.24 − 54.21 = 5.03. Comparison of Models 5 ([EAMH][LM]) and 7 ([EAMH][LM][LH]) yield a similar reduction in $\chi^2(1)_{LR}(13.7 - 7.87 = 5.30)$. The improvement in fit attributable to the additional parameter is statistically significant and fairly constant in magnitude, though small.

For both Models 6 and 7 the standardized loglinear parameter estimate for [LH] is approximately equal to −1.25, and the estimate of the multiplicative parameter (tau) for [LH] is equal to .81. This indicates that change in household composition is less likely for those who perceive that extensive help is available.

The analysis suggests that the best and most parsimonious model for the entire sample is Model 5 ([EAMH][LM]), with a χ^2_{LR} almost equal to its degrees of freedom (the expected value of χ^2_{LR} under the null hypothesis). There is evidence, however, that extent of help available may have some importance.

Those whose marital status changed represented only a minority (roughly a third) of those whose household composition changed. In order to determine more closely which factors may be important in explaining change in household composition for those whose marital status remains constant, the loglinear analysis was repeated for those persons. The relevant raw data are given in Table 17.3, and the results of loglinear analysis in the lower section of Table 17.4 (Models 8 to 12). As in the analysis for the entire sample, a comparison of the baseline model (Model 8 [EAH]), which assumes equiprobability of change in household composition, with Model 9 ([EAH][L]), which does not, indicates that the hypothesis of equiprobability should be rejected. Although Models 9 to 12 fit the data, Model 12 ([EAH][LH]) is preferred, because the χ^2_{LR} is closest to the degrees of freedom and the p value is about .5. For Model 12 the estimate of the multiplicative parameter (tau) for [LH] is .78. When marital status remains stable, if extensive help is available change in household composition is unlikely, but when, at best, only limited help is available, change in household composition is more likely to occur.

DISCUSSION

It is evident from the present data that cross-sectional information underestimates the actual amount of change in household composition that occurs among elderly people and may do so by a substantial amount. Treating the present data as two cross-sectional waves suggests that 12% of this sample experienced a change. In fact, the number of changes that occurred were at least 50% greater than this. We have ignored changes within a particular type of household composition. Including these brings the total changes between the two occasions to 28%, a figure in close accord with the 58% change found over a period of 5 years in the Five Thousand Families Study (Morgan et al., 1974). We have also ignored changes within the 30-month time period which, at the end of the period, left the respondent in the same type of living situation as was present at the beginning. Finally, we did not include those who made the most extreme and irreversible change, the 15% of the initial sample who died. Thus, the amount of change in household composition that occurs is substantial.

In trying to understand the reasons underlying change in household composition, we examined environmental circumstances (represented by change in economic status) and life cycle circumstances (represented by change in self-care capacity at the individual level and change in marital status and the extent of availability of help at the family level). Our data clearly show that, of these four variables, only the two family life cycle variables are important in determining change in household composition.

In our sample married couples almost invariably lived together. Only 1.6% of these husbands and wives lived apart. Our classification of household composition (indeed all the more usual classifications) reflected whether the respondent was or was not married; any change in that status, for instance the death of the spouse, was reflected as a change in household composition. Such a change in household composition is, obviously, not occasioned by a change in the personal status of the respondent but rather by a change in the status of another person to whom the respondent is attached legally.

The other main factor determining stability or change in household composition is the extent of availability of help from family and friends. When help was reported as being available for an extensive period of time, change in household composition was unlikely, but, when help was available for a maximum of 6 months, change in household composition was much more likely. We do not know the exact relationship of the helper; other studies, however, indicate that the family is the main source of help, friends being the primary helper for less than 8% of elderly adults (e.g., Comptroller General, 1977). These findings support suggestions that events occurring earlier in the life cycle and, specifically, events in the family life cycle, influence later household composition (e.g., Chevan & Korson, 1976).

Of the four factors examined, two had no apparent relationship to change in household composition. These were change in economic status and change in self-care capacity. Although economic status seems to be related to type of household composition, (e.g., Newman, 1976; Soldo et al., in press), there may be at least two reasons why it did not explain change in household composition among this sample of elderly adults. First, we may have had a problem of measurement, of assessing how big a difference should be considered a change. The size of change we accepted may have been inadequate to influence a change in household composition. Second, we did not relate change in economic status to income adequacy. Possibly only a change that results in crossing a border between adequate and inadequate income results in a change in household composition, whereas movement within each category has little effect.

Although there is evidence that the health status of persons in different types of household composition varies, there is also evidence that persons of almost any health status can be found and be cared for adequately in all the different types of household compositions examined (e.g., Lawton, 1980). This suggests that each type of household composition has a certain amount of flexibility regarding the condition of the persons who can be maintained. Given this, it is not surprising that change in self-care capacity had little effect on household composition. Thus, these data help to confirm the flexibility of residential arrangements and suggest that capacity to remain in a particular setting may depend less on the individual's personal capabilities than on the supportive services available, services that may but do not have to be provided by another resident.

Too often we focus almost exclusively on characteristics of the older person in trying to explain and understand his or her residential arrangements. We do not emphasize sufficiently the impact of events earlier in the life cycle—of marriage, the number of children born, the ages of the parents at the time, and the capabilities of these offspring. Such events may determine what housing and resources the older person can call on and what housing and resources he or she may have to continue to provide. Although there is clear awareness that changes in the status of other residents of the household and other members of the immediate family may determine the situation of the older person, we have not always integrated such information into our studies of household composition. Closer attention needs to be paid to the interconnections among the life cycles of the different members of the family. The present study suggests that change in household composition is primarily due to either an extreme event, the respondent's death, or change in status of other members of the family, such as the death of the spouse and the departure of kin, whereas stability of household composition rests less with stability of personal status than with the amount of help available from the family. Thus, for survivors, both change in and stability of household composition rest more on others, whose presence has been determined many years previously, than on the self.

REFERENCES

Anderson, M. The impact on the family relationships of the elderly of changes since Victorian times in government income-maintenance provision. In E. Shanas & M. B. Sussman (Eds.), *Family, bureacracy, and the elderly.* Duke University Press, Durham, NC, 1977.

Blazer, D. The OARS Durham surveys: Description and application. In Duke OARS *Multidimensional Functional Assessment: The OARS Methodology* (2nd ed.). Center for the Study of Aging and Human Development. Duke University, Durham, NC, 1978.

Brody, E. M. *Long-term care of older people.* Human Sciences Press, New York, 1977.

Burch, T. K. Household and family demography: A bibliographic essay. *Population Index*, 1979, *45*, 173–195.

Chevan, A., & Korson, J. H. Living arrangement of widows in the U.S. and Israel, 1960 and 1961. *Demography*, 1975, *12*, 505–518.

Comptroller General of the United States. *Home health—The need for a national policy to better provide for the elderly.* Report to Congress (HRD-78-19). U.S. General Accounting Office, Washington, DC, December 30, 1977.

Davis, J. A. Heirarchical models for significance tests in multi-variate contingency tables: An exegesis of Goodman's recent papers. In H. Costner (Ed.), *Sociological methodology, 1973–1974.* Jossey-Bass, San Francisco, 1974.

Fienberg, S. E. *The analysis of cross-classified categorical data.* MIT Press, Cambridge, MA, 1977.

Fillenbaum, G. G., & Symer, M. The development, validity and reliability of the OARS multidimensional functional assessment questionnaire. *Journal of Gerontology*, 1981, *36*, 428–434.

Hill, R., & Mattessich, P. Family development theory and life-span development. In P. B. Baltes & O. G. Brim, Jr. (Eds.), *Life-span development and behavior* (Vol. 2). Academic Press, New York, 1979.

Lawton, M. P. *Environment and aging.* Wadsworth-Brooks/Cole, Monterey, CA, 1980.

Morgan, J. N., Dickinson, K., Dickinson, J., Benus, J., & Duncan, G. *Five thousand American families-patterns of economic progress* (Vol. 1). Survey Research Center, Institute for Social Research, University of Michigan, Ann Arbor, MI, 1974.

Newman, S. J. Housing adjustment of the disabled elderly. *The Gerontologist*, 1976, *16*, 312–317.

Shanas, E. *The health of older people. A social survey.* Harvard University Press, Cambridge, MA, 1962.

Soldo, B. J., & Lauriat, P. Living arrangement among the elderly in the United States: A log-linear approach. *Journal of Comparative Family Studies*, 1976, *7*, 351–366.

Soldo, B. J., Sharma, M., & Campbell, R. Determinants of the community living arrangements of older, unmarried women. *Journal of Gerontology*, 1984. (in press)

Streib, G. F., & Beck, R. W. Older families: A decade review. *Journal of Marriage and the Family*, 1980, *42*, 937–956.

Treas, J. Family support systems for the aged: Some social and demographic considerations. *The Gerontologist*, 1977, *17*, 486–491.

Troll, L. E. The family of later life: A decade review. *Journal of Marriage and the Family*, 1971, *33*, 263–290.

Troll, L. E., Miller, S. J., & Atchley, R. C. *Families in later life.* Wadsworth Publishing, Belmont, CA, 1979.

Yee, W., & Van Arsdol, M. D., Jr. Residential mobility, age, and the life cycle. *Journal of Gerontology*, 1977, *32*, 211–221.

Part VI

Kinship Networks

Most thinking and research on family relations in later life has been concerned with categories of relatives (like adult children) rather than with larger family groups, even when terms like "the family" are used. In their classic survey of family relations of older people in five industrialized countries, Shanas et al. (1968) concluded that relatives other than spouses and children could be a reservoir from which substitutes for missing primary kin would be obtained. This proposition has not been tested directly, however. The emphasis on categories or specific dyads emerged from the realities of caretaking for the frail and needy. Usually only one family member—a spouse or child— takes on the caregiving role, as noted in the earlier section on this topic.

Three thin streams of research are exceptions to this generalization. One is concerned with what is usually called "networks." Another focuses on two "non-primary" categories, siblings and grandchildren. The third, and least explored, considers the family as a system that involves all of its members to some extent. The present section addresses these three streams.

NETWORKS

A network usually implies a loose affiliation of people surrounding a designated central person. They are generally assumed to include both kin and non-kin like friends, neighbors, and even professional helpers like nurses and social workers. In identifying a particular person's network, both structural and functional questions are asked. When target

respondents are asked whom they would nominate as important in their life, their answers can be used to assess size of
networks, which in turn can be associated with the age and sex
of the respondents (e.g., Stueve & Fischer, 1978). When they
are asked about their feelings about the people named, their
answers can suggest the quality of relationships. When they
are asked who does what with whom, functional answers can
be obtained, such as caretaking.

Similar to the construct of networks are two other heuristic
concepts, that of "convoys" (Antonucci & Akiyama, 1985; Kahn
and Antonucci, 1980) and that of "consociates" proposed by
Plath (1980). Both of these terms add a time component to
networks. They refer to the people with whom we move
through our lives, our fellow travelers, so to speak. So far,
research based upon these approaches has been no different
from network research.

One of the earliest network studies was that of Rosow (1967)
who examined contacts of older people as a function of neighborhood composition—specifically, the density of older people
living nearby. Not surprisingly, the more older people living
near them, the more contact or social integration. Using a
concentric circle technique, Antonucci and Akiyama (1985) analyzed the responses of those subjects in a national sample who
were over 50 years of age. All subjects had been asked to name
people who would belong in one of three circles in order of felt
importance. They found that the older the respondents (65–74
and 75–95, compared with 50–64), the smaller their networks.
They also found that members of networks of older people
were themselves older and included more women than men.
Older respondents also reported that they had known their
network members longer than younger respondents had, that
they lived closer to them, and that they had more contact with
them. With respect to functional characteristics, members of
the inner circle were more likely to exchange all types of support, while members of the outer circle exchanged more cir-
cumscribed functions. Network size varied around an average
of nine members. It is of interest here that 82% of all network
members were kin, that they ranged in age from 18 to 96, with
an average of 49, and that inner-circle nominees were younger
than outer-circle ones because they included grandchildren.

Hays (1984) used an ingenious way of finding availability of
relatives by looking in obituary columns for names of survivors

of people who died over the age of 45. She found that most (81%) were survived by at least one child; 67% by at least one sibling; 47% by a spouse; and 10% by a parent. When the decedents were categorized by age, however, 19% of those between 45 and 64 had neither children nor sibling living in the area and more (25%) of those over 65 had neither. Snow and Crapo (1982) looked at the psychological consequences of emotional bondedness to network members. Essentially, they found, it was not quantity of contacts with the important people in your life that made you feel good but the nature of your relationship with them.

One article is included in this volume that is related to the network approach: Mitchell and Register (1984). Mitchell and Register were looking not at age but at black–white differences. As noted earlier, in the national survey of older people conducted by Louis Harris and Associates (1975) the major difference between blacks and whites was not in help for older people but in help given by older people to younger kin. Consistent with the studies reviewed in the earlier section on caregiving, blacks were more likely to take children and grandchildren into their homes than whites, but the real cause was socioeconomic conditions rather than race.

It is a popular belief that people are basically gregarious and need the companionship of other humans. Self-help groups are based upon the assumption that providing companions will provide necessary social support and allay many problems, particularly in old age. Yet recent research is reemphasizing the original findings of Fiske (Lowenthal & Haven, 1968) that it is a special kind of relationship that makes a difference, not gregariousness per se. Longitudinal data show increasing purposefulness in relationships from early to middle adolescence onward (Troll, 1985b). Bankoff (1983b) found that social support per se had no effect on widows' psychological well-being; it depended who provided the support. In their case, mothers and other friends who had been widowed themselves were the most effective.

An English study (Argyle and Furnham, 1983), looking at positive and negative feelings in relationships, found that older respondents got more satisfaction from their relationships with their spouse, sibs, neighbors, and children, in that order. They were not as likely as younger people to derive both positive and negative feelings from the same relationships, however.

Further, the friends of older people tend to be long-lasting friends, and a possible consequence of long-lasting relationships is their having developed high levels of attachment, marked by emotional security and loyalty rather than by initial attraction, marked by passion and a mixture of both positive and negative affect (Troll, 1982a). This is also noted by Traupmann, Eckels, and Hatfield (1982). Satisfaction with intimate relationships is highly correlated with overall life satisfaction (.74), and it is not merely the existence of an intimate relationship that counts but the quality of that relationship.

SIBLINGS

Since most American families over the past century had more than one child, 80% of all older Americans today have at least one brother or sister (Harris and Associates, 1975), about the same proportion as have at least one child. Gerontological studies have looked at availability of siblings—whether there are any, how many, and how near they live to each other; whether they are turned to for help, material or emotional; the relation between sibling contact and mental and physical well-being; and the effect of losses like widowhood upon sib relations. In Hays' (1984) study described above, there were more siblings than spouses among survivors but not as many as children. Since the number of children per family has been dropping steadily over the years, younger cohorts may have fewer living siblings, however.

Youmans (1963) and Adams (1968a) reported that contact with siblings was intermediate in frequency between contact with children and friends. On the other hand, there is evidence that they do keep in touch with each other. In a cross-national study, Shanas (1979) found that about 40% of people over 65 years of age had seen a sibling within the past week. This varies by age; older people are less in touch than younger (Rosenberg & Anspach, 1973; Rosenthal & Marshall, 1985). In Rosenberg and Anspach's Philadelphia study, of those between 45 and 54 years of age, 68% had seen a sibling during the preceding week; of those between 55 and 64, 58%; and of those over 65 years, 47%. Also, keeping in contact with siblings is contingent upon having no "closer" relatives available. Old people who had never married or had children were more likely to turn to siblings (Shanas et al., 1968). Residential proximity also seems to be more important for maintaining sibling ties than for parent–child ties. In the southwestern United States, Scott (1983) found that siblings within 1 hour's distance had the most contact. Further, some writers concluded that sibling relationships become attenuated when their parents die (Adams, 1968a; Johnson, 1982; Young & Willmott, 1962), particularly among older urban working class people (Rosenberg & Anspach, 1973).

Cross-ethnic data show variations. When Johnson (1982) compared Italian Catholics and Protestants in Boston, the Italian Catholics were more likely to have a sibling in the city. But then, about four-fifths of the Protestants did too. Daily contact with their siblings was much higher among Italian Catholics, particularly those who were married to other Italians (63% for "in married" Italians, 32% for "out-married," and 12% for Protestants).

Researchers interested in resources for helping and caring point to the lesser likelihood of finding such help among siblings than among spouse and children. Only if they are the only relatives available are they likely to be the caregivers. Lopata (1973), for instance, describes the ephemeral nature of sibling help when a woman becomes widowed. They are there for the emergency but not for the long run. Yet some studies of widows indicate that sibling relationships are sometimes continuous, lifelong relationships which vary with the particular histories of the people involved (Morgan, 1984).

More recent studies which have looked at more psychological issues suggest that it is not how often one sees family members—or, for that matter, nonfamily—but how "emotionally bonded" one is with them that is important in contributing to emotional well-being (Reiss & Oliveri, 1983; Snow & Crapo, 1982). For one thing, family culture and personality— how family members shape their social world—determines how many family members and who are recognized as significant. Two studies (Lee & Ihinger-Tallman, 1980; McGhee, 1985) found that close ties with siblings in old age were not significantly related to morale or life satisfaction. McGhee concludes that siblings belong with other kin so far as feelings of obligation are concerned. Even though they are age peers like friends, association with them may not be as voluntary in nature. On the other hand, when Bedford (1985) looked at three different indices of relationship—affiliation, conflict, and separation—she found that affiliation was the most predominant, not only for women (with respect to sisters) but also for men (with respect to brothers). She used a projective measure, Thematic Apperception Test (TAT), rather than the usual questionnaire self-report so that part of the discrepancy between her findings and those of others could be attributable to difference in "level" of feeling. For example, she found that the three indices were unrelated to each other; one could feel affiliated to a sibling, experience conflict, and desire separation all at the same time. This is similar to the findings of Argyle and Furnham (1983), noted earlier. Also, men may retain strong feelings for their brothers even though they do not see them as much as women do their sisters nor report that they "feel close" as frequently. The more traditional approach used by Lenny (1985) did find sex differences in sibling attachment, affiliation, and autonomy. Because she studied all four possible sibling dyads, she could report that sister pairs were highest in affiliation, brother–sister pairs lowest if the brother was older. Brother pairs were highest in autonomy, while sister pairs and brother–sister pairs were lowest. The older pairs (age range 25–50) tended to be higher on affiliation and identification, but lack of comparability in ages (Bedford's older subjects were older than 50) makes a direct comparison between studies impossible. Bedford found more affiliation fantasies among younger, child-rearing men and women than among empty-nest respondents.

GRANDPARENTS

More people living out their life span and closer spacing of children over the first two-thirds of this century have made grandparents suddenly visible in American families. Within the past decade, articles and research on grandparents have multiplied in geometric proportion. The fact that a majority of people now become grandparents in middle age and with less competition from their own young children still at home (at least for grandmothers) has contributed to changing the image of grandparents from that of an ample lap in a rocking chair to a companion in fun and active family member.

As noted earlier, Troll (1983) labeled grandparents "family watchdogs" because although they often play an important role in family dynamics, they are customarily less central to those dynamics than parents, their behaviors are much more diverse than those of parents, and they seem to like it that way. They prefer to be monitors on the sidelines prepared to jump into action if needed when something goes wrong, but they like it better when nothing goes wrong and they can "play with their own friends." Evidence from studies of grandparents' role in divorce and teenage parenting shows their beneficial influence in those situations, however.

Both the sex and ages of the grandparents and the grandchildren affect their relationship. Studies repeatedly find that grandmothers, particularly maternal grandmothers, are the most important (Burton & Bengtson, 1985; Cherlin & Furstenberg, 1985; Hagestad, 1984; Hartshorne & Manaster, 1982; Lehr, 1982). Paternal grandfather–grandson dyads may be an exception to this rule, but unfortunately, such dyads occur much less frequently than the other three because men die younger than women, men become grandparents older than women, and paternal grandparents are more likely to become distanced from grandchildren following divorce of their son.

As for age, younger grandparents are usually more active in the lives of their grandchildren than are older grandparents, particularly when their grandchildren are young themselves (Bengtson, 1985; Cherlin & Furstenberg, 1985). In a unique videotaped observational study, however, Tinsley and Parke (1984) found all four grandparents highly involved with their infant grandchild.

Children's perceptions of their grandparents and what they enjoy about their grandparents follows a path of progressive cognitive development (Baranowski, 1982; Kahana & Kahana, 1970). Several studies of adolescents and their grandparents (e.g., Cherlin & Furstenberg, 1985) and of adults and theirs (e.g., Hagestad, 1984) show the continuing influence of grandparents. Different generations bring, respectively, the past to the young and the present to the old. On the other hand, while young-adult grandchildren say they are ready to take care of their grandparents if needed (see Brody, 1985; Part III of this volume), they are better considered reservoirs of kin for this function. Thus, most observers see grandparents as serving an extended-family function more than a specific child-rearing one. Their relation to their grandchildren is particularistic rather than general (Matthews & Sprey, 1985). They stabilize the family when it rocks, particularly by supporting the mother of the child-rearing unit (Abernathy, 1973; Hagestad, 1985). They have been found important in the transition to parenthood (Belsky & Rovine, 1984). They deflate the intensity of nuclear family interactions (Hagestad, 1985). They serve as confidants to adolescents (Konopka, 1976) and they buffer stress (Pearlin & Schooler, 1978). They stand as symbols of family continuity (Johnson, 1985a).

Today's grandmothers follow norms of middle age and of women's liberation, however, believing they should "do their own thing," not interfere in their children's lives, and not be judgmental. While all grandparents interviewed by Johnson (1985a) believed in these principles, the younger grandmothers, who belonged to the cohort of the liberated woman, found them easier to follow than the older ones.

Hagestad's Chicago data (1984) and Rosenthal and Marshall's Canadian data (1985) show that the grandparental roles differ for men and women. Grandfathers are heads of the family and grandmothers kinkeepers and "ministers of the interior," to use Hagestad's term. Older grandparents tend to be more formal and distant in performing these functions, though (Cherlin & Furstenberg, 1985; Neugarten & Weinstein, 1964). The middlewestern, middle-aged Catholic couples interviewed by Aldous (1985), furthermore, were most involved with their divorced daughters who had children (and their never-married children). It was their remarried, previously divorced children, incidentally, who gave *them* the most help.

Kivnick (1982) illustrates one of the several attempts to capture the variable of the meaning of grandparenthood to older Americans. Like the earlier investigations of Neugarten and Weinsten (1964) and Wood and Robertson (1976), Kivnick's data show enormous variability. When she asked grandparents about what being a grandparent meant to them, she found five general themes running through their answers: the degree of centrality of the role in their lives, the degree of significance of being a "valued elder," their feeling of deriving immortality through their descendants, their reliving of their own personal past, and the opportunity to be indulgent. While Kivnick (1985) acknowledges that grandparents do not choose whether or when they will become grandparents, they do have some control over their interactions with their grandchildren, and their satisfaction with being grandparents varies. Troll (1985a) makes the point that grandparenting is clearly different from parenting and that few grandparents want to become parents a second time around. Yet, they do have what Bengtson (1985) calls a "stake" in the outcome of their grandchildren's lives.

When Cherlin and Furstenberg (1985) interviewed a large sample of grandparents of teenagers, they found much diversity in relationships. Not only did the grandparents differ from one another, but each grandparent had a different relationship with each grandchild. Some were "detached" (20%); some were "passive" (29%); but many more were "active" (49%). The active grandparent–grandchild relationship was characterized by being supportive, authoritarian (parent-like), or influential (both parent-like and supportive).

Troll (1980a) termed the grandparental relationship "contingent" because it is mediated by the intervening middle generation. It is the relationship with their child that determines the amount of contact with that child's children, and the amount of contact in turn affects the feelings of "closeness" on the part of the grandchildren (Matthews & Sprey, 1985).

Finally, there appear to be significant ethnic variations. Mexican-American grandparents not only had more grandchildren than black and white (Anglo) grandparents (Bengtson, 1985), but they were more satisfied with being grandparents. On the other hand, the black grandparents in this Los Angeles study had more "fictive kin" (children they raised who were not blood kin). Sixty-six percent of the Mexican-American grandparents said they would like to live near grandchildren, and 33% of the black grandparents said they would, but only 20% of the whites. Cherlin and Furstenberg (1985) in their sample found that the black grandparents were more authoritative and influential than the whites.

Divorce is discussed in the next section, but its prevalence today has led to widespread concern about the legal rights of grandparents whose grandchildren may be "lost" to them (Wilson & DeShane, 1982). As noted earlier, these are more likely to be paternal grandparents whose son has not been granted custody.

FAMILY SYSTEM

Anthropologists remind us that family systems vary. At one end of the continuum are systems that encompass all of the life activities of their members, and at the other end are those that are loose, include few activities and feelings, and are voluntaristic—we can choose whom we wish to consider our kin or treat as our kin. Our mainline Western systems tend to be at the loose and voluntaristic end of the continuum, but we should not assume that this means that extended kin are not important to our lives. Furthermore, there are ethnic variations. Litwak (1960b), when he presented evidence that neither geographic nor occupational mobility removes extended family ties, called our system a "modified extended family." Thurnher (1982) describes the continuum of structures and functions present today in the United States, from the Japanese-Americans at the close end, through Mexican-Americans, blacks, and whites. We have earlier referred to Johnson (1982) who noted that Boston Italian Catholics are more family-connected than Boston Protestants.

Hagestad and Neugarten (1985) stress the embeddedness of individuals, not only in historical time but also in family time, suggesting that individual developmental transitions should be seen as family affairs because they impinge upon the lives of all members of the family system. Klein, Jorgenson, and Miller (1979) speak of "developmental reciprocities." The aging of older family members has repercussions for all younger members to some extent. Troll and Stapely (1986) found that ill health reported by grandmothers or grandfathers was associated not only with their own lowered happiness but also with increased distress in the middle-generation daughters as well as with changes in the salience of different family members for each other. Hagestad and Dixon (1980) refer to "career contingencies, countertransitions, and shared life chances." Parents' expectations for their childrens' life course are interwoven with their own life expectation (Seltzer & Troll, 1986), affecting feelings of being "on time" or "off time." Marriage of one family member produces in-laws for others. Parenthood creates grandparenthood. Divorce has "family ripple effects" (Hagestad, 1982).

Rosenthal and Marshall (1985), for example, found some interesting extended family comparisons when they looked at important family "occasions" and get-togethers. Having a parent alive increased the likelihood of wider family get-togethers among adults, particularly if there were also young children. Hagestad (1984) found a three-generational chain of mutual influence and family themes, albeit with important sex differences, particularly among the older generations. Grandfathers were most intent on influencing their grandsons, and in more or less traditional "masculine" areas of career and money. Grandmothers, reciprocally, were more intent on affecting interpersonal family relationships. They also did not differentiate so much between granddaughters and grandsons. The younger generations, as one might expect, were less sex-stereotyped, although not necessarily less interested in socializing their grandparents than their grandparents were in socializing them.

An elaborated examination of psychological correlates of family bondedness (Reiss & Oliveri, 1983) found two independent antecedents of preferred family network size. One line of influence on family system structure was the actual size of the mother's family (participants were adolescents and their parents). The other line of influence was the subjects' joint assumption about what the world was like: whether it could be trusted, how much agreement and shared pacing they used in solving problems, and how much flexibility in the light of new information they showed.

The importance of the mother's or female side of the family, or of female linkage altogether, has emerged repeatedly in this volume. Twenty years ago, Sweetser (1963) reported that if a nuclear family kept heirlooms and old photos, it was more likely to come from the mother's side and that family rituals like dinnertime practices and holiday celebrations were more like those of the mother's kin than the father's.

18

An Exploration of Family Interaction with the Elderly by Race, Socioeconomic Status, and Residence*

Jim Mitchell
Jasper C. Register

The role of family members in the lives of elderly people has been an area of research focus in gerontology (e.g. Larson, 1978; Lee, 1979; Shanas, 1979). Many researchers have been concerned more specifically with the contribution made by the frequency of contact with children to a sense of well-being among elderly people. Some have concluded that little or no relationship exists between these variables (Conner et al., 1979; Lee, 1979) while others have pointed to a need to consider the importance of contact by telephone or letter in cases involving physical separation (Troll et al., 1979).

Although studies have included black subsamples, relatively little attention has been given to potential black-white differences in family interaction and support. Shanas (1979) found the family to be important in the social support of the elderly but she used gender, not race, as a control variable. Seelbach and Sauer (1977) included racial comparisons in their study of morale among aged parents but their

*The Gerontologist, 24 (1) (1984), 48–54.
 The data utilized in this study were made available by the Inter-University Consortium for Political and Social Research and Duke University Medical Center. The data were collected by Louis Harris and Associates, Inc. for the National Council on Aging.

analysis was limited to urban, low-income persons. Dowd and Bengt-son (1978), using a probability sample of Los Angeles County residents from 45 to 74 years of age, found minority respondents (Mexican-American and black) interacted more frequently with family members than whites. This paper deals with an unresolved and important issue in the study of the black family—its extendedness. A data source is used that is more representative of blacks in the U.S. than those employed by most similar studies.

RACIAL DIFFERENCES IN FAMILY INTERACTION AND SUPPORT

A review of the literature concerning the black aging experience raises as many questions as it answers. Due to limited research and conflicting conclusions, "existing descriptive information and methodologies are generally insufficient for developing a valid and reliable body of theory about minority aging" (Jackson, 1980, p. 11).

Confusion is fueled by two conflicting descriptions of the family support system of aged blacks. In one orientation (Billingsley, 1968; Huling, 1978; Jackson, 1980; Kennedy, 1980), elderly blacks are viewed as adjusting to a family system changing from one with traditional roles for elderly people to a middle class orientation characterized by what Huling (1978) sees as "losses in interaction between current black generations" (p. 27). While Huling emphasizes the separation and increasing institutionalization of elderly blacks, Jackson (1980) concentrates upon the heterogeneity and resiliency of the elderly black population. She asserts that the black aged are not all poor, illiterate, dependent, in ill health, and in an extended family. Both Huling (1978) and Kennedy (1980) contend that the black family structure reflects an emphasis upon practical solutions to meeting needs. Blood links are clouded by an emphasis upon the function a person fulfills for the family.

In the other orientation in the literature (Baum & Baum, 1980; Hill, 1978; Jackson, 1972a, 1972b), the black aged are viewed as being at the center of an extended family network providing social and material support. The black extended family is described as a tool for survival during long periods of slavery and discrimination. According to Wylie (1976), "The sharing of bondage surely provided some glue for familial and other social relationships" (p. 280), and affectional ties were strengthened rather than weakened by common suffering.

The purpose of this paper is to clarify the position of the aged in the black family by exploring black–white differences in intergenerational interaction. Accordingly, the following hypotheses are offered under the assumption that black elderly people are more likely than whites to be part of an extended family:

1. Aged blacks see their children and grandchildren more often than aged whites.
2. Aged blacks receive help from their children and grandchildren more often than aged whites.
3. Aged blacks help their children and grandchildren more often than aged whites.
4. Aged blacks take grandchildren, nieces, or nephews into their homes to live with them more often than aged whites.

Following the recommendation of Bengtson et al. (1977) to include relevant control variables in aging research, both socioeconomic status (SES) and area of residence (rural or urban) will be introduced as control variables. Socioeconomic differentials between elderly blacks and whites have been documented (Hill, 1978; Kitagawa & Hauser, 1973) and the importance of SES as a control variable is underscored by Siegel (1980), who contends that mortality differentials between blacks and whites may be due primarily to socioeconomic factors. The possible effect of socioeconomic differentials between aged blacks and whites upon family interaction patterns has not been thoroughly explored by gerontological researchers, nor has the effect of residential pattern upon intergenerational interaction involving elderly people been extensively researched. Hassinger (1978) points out that "kinship ties beyond the nuclear family are usually much more extensive in rural communities than in cities" (p. 153). Consequently, the question of whether a more extended family pattern is more characteristic of blacks or more common among rural residents remains.

METHODOLOGY

The Sample

The data utilized in this study were drawn from a national survey published in 1975 by Louis Harris and Associates, Inc. The sample was restricted to 334 blacks and 1,813 whites aged 65 and over who had living children. The age range of respondents was from 65 to 96 years. The median age for whites was 71.8 years and that for black elderly respondents was 70.9 years. The median age of all of the individuals in the sample was 70 years. The household income of whites was higher, overall. Approximately 10% (181) of the 1,813 white elderly respondents had annual incomes of less than $1,000; the proportion for the 334 black respondents was 33%. Approximately 17.5% (318) of the whites had incomes in excess of $4,000 per year compared to only 3.5% (12) of the blacks. The educational differential was similar to that of income; 18.8% (342) of the whites completed high school compared to 5.3% (17) of the black respondents. One hundred nineteen (35.8%) black elderly respondents considered their health to be a very serious problem as opposed to 398 whites (21.9%). Approximately 50% (897) of the whites were married and 46% (836) were widowed. Fewer of the black respondents were married (129 or 38.7%) and slightly more (175 or 52.8%) were widowed. In sum, the characteristics of the aged people in the sample resemble racial differentials discussed elsewhere (Jackson, 1980).

Operationalization of Concepts

Three composite measures were constructed from responses to items in the Harris survey. These are (1) 6 items designed to determine whether elderly respondents receive help from children or grandchildren, (2) 9 items to ascertain whether elderly people gave help to children or grandchildren, and (3) a measure of socioeconomic status. A discussion of the operationalization of each concept follows.

The items used to measure whether respondents received help from or gave help to their children and grandchildren are shown in Table 18.1. The table includes means and standard deviations describing the patterns of responses to the items for subsamples of black and white respondents as well as the total.

The means describing responses to the items measuring whether respondents received help from their children and grandchildren indicate differences in the pattern of help received by race. The upper portion of Table 18.1 indicates that both whites and blacks tended to receive help to a greater extent when they were ill. Beyond this similarity, however, differences in the order of the means indicate some variation by race in help received. Blacks were less likely to receive help in shopping or running errands whereas whites were less likely to receive help in the form of advice on job or business matters.

The average inter-item correlation among the six items used to measure help received is .27, resulting in a Nunnaly's (1978) reliability coefficient of .85. The comparable correlation and reliability figures

Table 18.1. Means and Standard Deviations of Responses to Items in the Indexes of Receiving Help from and Giving Help to Children and Grandchildren by Race

Type of Help	Totals		Blacks		Whites	
	x̄	sd	x̄	sd	x̄	sd
Receiving Help						
Help out when someone is ill	1.74	.44	1.72	.45	1.75	.43
Give advice on running your home	1.27	.44	1.43	.50	1.23	.42
Shop or run errands for you	1.36	.48	1.31	.46	1.37	.48
Help out with money	1.46	.50	1.37	.48	1.48	.50
Give advice on job or business matters	1.22	.42	1.34	.48	1.20	.40
Give advice on how to deal with some of life's problems	1.45	.50	1.60	.49	1.42	.49
Reliability coefficient	.85		.89		.84	
Giving Help						
Help out when someone is ill	1.82	.37	1.76	.43	1.83	.37
Give advice on money matters	1.29	.45	1.40	.49	1.26	.44
Shop or run errands for them	1.74	.44	1.70	.46	1.75	.43
Help fix things around the house or keep house for them	1.61	.49	1.55	.50	1.63	.48
Help out with money	1.31	.46	1.47	.50	1.28	.45
Take them places such as the doctor, shopping, or church	1.67	.47	1.63	.48	1.68	.46
Give advice on running their home	1.18	.38	1.30	.46	1.15	.36
Give advice on job or business matters	1.18	.38	1.25	.44	1.16	.37
Give general advice on how to deal with some of life's problems	1.28	.45	1.36	.48	1.26	.44
Reliability coefficient	.95		.97		.94	

Note. The response continuum for the items in each index is (1) Don't do, and (2) Do.

for the subsample of white respondents are .26 and .84, respectively, and those for blacks are .35 and .89. These figures seem reasonable, although lower than what would be optimally desired, given the variability in the nature of the six kinds of help received.

The means in the lower portion of Table 18.1 indicate that both blacks and whites were more likely to give help to children or grandchildren in the event of illness, to run errands for them, and to take them places. They were less likely to give advice, whether related to business, money matters, or life's problems.

Agreement among responses to the nine items used to measure whether elderly people, regardless of race, gave help to children and grandchildren is supported by an average inter-item correlation of .34. The inter-item reliability among the items for the total sample is represented by a Nunnaly's (1978) coefficient of .95. When sub-samples of blacks and whites are considered, the correlation and reliability coefficients are .32 and .94, respectively, for whites and .46 and .97 for blacks. These values support the use of these items from the secondary data source as composite measures of receiving and giving help.

Socioeconomic status, the final composite measure, was estimated using a modified version of Hollingshead's Index of Social Position (1958). Indicators of the three measures in the original Index were not available but income and education were included in the survey. Because persons with little education may have ample income and those with smaller incomes may have a prestigious job, income and education were combined as a general indicator of socioeconomic status. Responses to each measure were categorized on a 7-point response continuum. After the weighting scheme used in the 3-factor form of the Index, education was given a weight of 5 and income a weight of 3. The two weighted values were summed as a composite measure of SES for each respondent. This technique was used by Register (1981) in his analysis of racial differences in attitudes toward the elderly and life satisfaction levels. Due to restrictively small numbers of black elderly respondents in the upper socioeconomic range—threatening the utility of SES as a control variable—and for consistency and ease in data presentation, the SES scores were dichotomized at the median for purposes of analysis.

Area of residence, a second control variable, was measured using a single item. Four response categories (rural, town, suburban, central city) were reduced to a dichotomy of rural and urban for ease and consistency in data presentation.

Remaining variables are (1) when respondents last saw children and grandchildren and (2) whether respondents took grandchildren, nieces, or nephews into their homes to live with them. These variables were operationalized using single questions.

Statistical techniques used in the analysis include chi-square (χ^2) in comparing categories of nominal and ordinal variables and, in cases with two or more nominal independent variables, analysis of variance. Measures of association accompanying chi-square are phi (ϕ) for two dichotomous variables and, when tables have more than 4 cells, the contingency coefficient.

FINDINGS

Contact with Children and Grandchildren

Hypothesis 1 tests the proposition that black aged see their children and grandchildren more often than white people. Items in the Harris survey did not permit the more desirable consideration of quality, rather than quantity, of contact. Table 18.2 presents separate frequency distributions for having seen children and grandchildren. Only respondents with grandchildren are included in this portion of the

Table 18.2. Frequency Distribution of When the Respondent Last Saw Children or Grandchildren by Race

When Last Saw	Totals		Blacks		Whites	
	n	%	n	%	n	%
Children						
Live with them	124	5.8	27	8.1	97	5.4
Last day or two	1,065	49.6	161	48.2	904	49.9
Last week or two	537	25.0	69	20.7	468	25.8
Month ago	165	7.7	24	7.2	141	7.8
2–3 months ago	81	3.8	10	3.0	71	3.9
Longer than that	175	8.1	43	12.9	132	7.3
Total	2,147	100.0	334	100.0	1,813	100.0
$\chi^2 = 18.39$, $p < .01$ Contingency Coefficient = .09						
Grandchildren						
Live with them	52	2.7	18	5.9	334	2.1
Last day or two	846	43.4	128	42.2	718	43.6
Last week or two	538	27.6	75	24.8	463	28.1
Month ago	188	9.6	21	6.9	167	10.1
2–3 months ago	104	5.3	14	4.6	90	5.5
Longer than that	221	11.3	47	15.5	174	10.6
Total[a]	1,949	100.0	303	100.0	1,646	100.0
$\chi^2 = 24.16$, $p < .001$ contingency Coefficient = .11						

Note. Totals may not equal 100% due to rounding.
[a]These totals include only those respondents with grandchildren.

analysis; consequently, the number totals in each part of the table may vary.

Over two-thirds (77% of the blacks and 81% of the whites) of the respondents had seen their children within the last 2 weeks. The frequency of seeing grandchildren was very similar among blacks and whites with 72.9% and 73.8%, respectively, seeing their grandchildren within the last 2 weeks. The only discernible difference between blacks and whites in seeing their children and grandchildren was a slightly greater tendency for blacks to either live with them or, if living apart, to see them infrequently (longer than 2–3 months ago). The tendency for blacks to live with children may be due to economic necessity. Overall, however, the pattern is very similar for both races. The chi-square values are large, but the weak measures of association suggest that this is a result of the relatively large sample size.

The distribution in Table 18.2 was analyzed while controlling for dichotomized categories of both SES and area of residence (copies of the table are available from the authors). In the present sample, black aged persons were more likely to be in the lower SES category than whites ($\chi^2 = 135.63$, $p < .000$ and $\phi = .26$). The contingency coefficients describing the relationships between race and seeing both children and grandchildren in Table 18.2 tend to be reproduced among respondents in the higher socioeconomic category. Among those in the lower socioeconomic category, however, the relationship between race and seeing children (.15) and grandchildren (.14) is slightly more pronounced, although differences are still minimal. Both blacks and whites in the lower SES category were less likely to live with their children and grandchildren. Those in the upper SES category were more likely to live with children and grandchildren although the differences, again, are minimal. This finding questions the previous assumption of economic necessity as a major consideration and suggests that those with more resources are more likely to be able to help others. In sum, although contingency coefficient and chi-square values suggest that the relationship between race and contact with children and grandchildren is stronger among older people in the lower SES category, examining the frequencies results in no substantive change from the original patterns found in Table 18.2.

The use of area of residence as a control variable does little to alter the pattern of contact in Table 18.2. Whether the elderly respondents lived in a rural or an urban area, blacks and whites saw their children and grandchildren quite frequently (approximately two-thirds had seen them in the last 2 weeks). Regardless of area of residence, however, a slight tendency was observed for blacks in the lower socioeconomic category to be overrepresented among elderly people who had seen their children and grandchildren more than 2–3 months ago. The findings in general do not support acceptance of Hypothesis 1.

Receiving Help from Family Members

Hypothesis 2 tests the proposition that elderly blacks receive more help from family members than whites. Data presented in Table 18.3 illustrate that respondents both gave and received large amounts of help from family members. The upper section indicates that a significant amount of variation in responses to the composite measure of receiving help from family members is explained by the three independent variables. The explained variation figure, however, is small compared to the residual or error variation remaining. The information presented indicates a significant interaction effect between race and SES and, additionally, between SES and area of residence. Significant interaction could, according to Mueller et al. (1977) lead to a more conservative test through a tendency to "overlook differences between population means that actually exist" (p. 479). Logically, one would speculate that race works through SES and, subsequently, leads to mean differences in amounts of help received. In any case, the bulk of the explained variation is a result of the effect of race and SES. The *uncontrolled* mean values in the first column of Table 18.3 indicate that black elderly (8.77) and those in the higher socioeconomic category (8.61) received more help than whites (8.38) and people in the lower socioeconomic category (8.35). The pattern can be further defined when the mean differences in help received are examined while the remaining independent variables are controlled. When SES and area of residence are controlled, black elderly in the upper socioeconomic category living in a rural area received the most help ($\bar{X} = 9.52$). The mean values reflect that blacks in the lower SES category (8.50) received more help than white elderly in a like position (8.29). Similarly, upper SES blacks received considerably more help (9.52) than upper SES white elderly people (8.54). The weak influence of area of residence in Table 18.3 is reinforced by the finding that upper SES rural blacks (9.57) received only slightly more help than their urban counterparts (9.30). Upper SES whites' mean level of help received (8.54) was higher than that for whites in the lower SES category (8.29). Black aged people, regardless of SES, tended to receive more help than whites. This is supported by

Table 18.3.   Analysis of Variance for Giving and Receiving Help by Race, Socioeconomic Status, and Area of Residence

Source of Variation	x̄	sd	Sums of Squares	df	F	p<
Receiving Help						
Race			47.55	1	15.96	.000
White	8.38[a]	1.81				
Black	8.77	1.95				
SES			41.94	1	14.08	.000
High	8.61	1.80				
Low	8.35	1.79				
Area of Residence			7.74	1	2.59	.107
Rural	8.40	1.80				
Urban	8.50	1.88				
3-way interaction			37.00	1	.12	.72
2-way interactions						
Race—SES			17.10	1	5.74	.02
Race—Area			9.97	1	3.35	.07
SES—Area			20.24	1	6.80	.01
Explained			128.44	7	6.16	.000
Residual			2019.74	678		
Total			2148.18	685		
Giving Help						
Race			6.34	1	.76	.382
White	12.90[b]	2.65				
Black	13.36	3.11				
SES			103.49	1	12.47	.000
High	12.61	2.65				
Low	13.32	2.66				
Area of Residence			16.10	1	1.94	.164
Rural	12.98	2.86				
Urban	12.98	2.63				
3-way interaction			26.23	1	3.16	.08
2-way interactions						
Race—SES			2.77	1	.33	.56
Race—Area			.13	1	.02	.90
SES—Area			.22	1	.03	.87
Explained			168.57	7	2.90	.005
Residual			9485.08	1143		
Total			9653.64	1150		

[a]Values range from a low of 6 to a high of 12.
[b]Values range from a low of 9 to a high of 18.

the finding that, although people in the upper SES category in general received more help, lower SES blacks received approximately as much help (8.50) as upper SES whites (8.54). The possibility exists that the comparatively high level of help received by upper SES elderly blacks skews the distribution of help received by both blacks and whites toward the high end of the scale.

Examination of standardized partial regression coefficients from multiple classification analysis reveals, however, that race, SES, and area of residence cumulatively explain little variation in help received. The coefficients are equal to .16, .14, and .06 for race, SES, and area of residence, respectively. Cognizant of these coefficient values and the mean differences, the data suggest that Hypothesis 2 is confirmed.

Giving Help to Family Members

Hypothesis 3 tests the proposition that black elderly people give more help to family members than whites. The results of again controlling SES and area of residence are presented in an analysis of variance format in the lower portion of Table 18.3. The bulk of the small amount of variation in giving help to family members explained by the three independent variables is due to the influence of SES. This differs markedly from the results of the analysis of receiving help. When giving help is the dependent variable, the effect of race is not particularly pronounced over that of SES In a simple analysis of variance format, race explains some of the variation in help given ($F =$ 5.08, $p < .02$). It can be seen in Table 18.3, however, that, when SES and area of residence are controlled, the variation explained is greatly reduced. This supports a contention that the original difference in help given by race was due to the dominating influence of SES. The means representing respondents' levels of giving help by SES—not controlling the effects of race and area of residence—indicate that respondents in the lower socioeconomic category were more likely to give help to family members (13.32) than those in the upper socioeconomic category (12.61).

In any case, it should be emphasized that standardized partial regression coefficients from a multiple classification analysis indicate that race, SES, and area of residence explain a very small amount of the variation in giving help. The regression coefficients for race, SES, and area of residence are equal to .03, .11, and .04, respectively. Hypothesis 3 is not confirmed by the findings presented in the lower portion of Table 18.3.

Taking Children into the Home

The rationale for Hypothesis 4 is a logical extension and elaboration of Hypothesis 1. Previous results (see Table 18.2) indicate a tendency for black elderly to live with children and grandchildren more often than whites. It is not clear, however, whether the children live in the home of the elderly person or vice versa. Consequently, Hypothesis 4 directly addresses the question of whether black elderly people are more likely to take grandchildren, nieces, or nephews into their home as a form of aid to family members. Data testing Hypothesis 4 are shown in Table 18.4. The percentages indicate that blacks were more likely (31.5%) than white elderly (20.0%) to take children into the home. Although the chi-square value at the top of Table 18.4 indicates a significant difference, the value for phi is not particularly pronounced. It could again be argued that this apparent relationship is actually due to the socioeconomic resources of the elderly person or more likely to be the "norm" in the area where they live. The percentages in Table 18.4 do demonstrate a tendency for people with more resources to take children into their home more often, regardless of race. The strength of the association, however, is not markedly different from the original relationship when SES is not considered.

Area of residence, like SES, does not appear to alter the original relationship. The predominant pattern is that blacks, regardless of

Table 18.4. Percentage of Respondents Taking Children (Grandchildren, Nieces, or Nephews) into Their Home to Live with Them by Race, with SES and Area of Residence Controlled

Total, SES, and Residence	Totals		Blacks		Whites		χ^2	$p<$	ϕ
	n	%	n	%	n	%			
Total	362	21.8	178	31.5	280	20.0	16.4	.001	.10
SES									
Low	164[a]	21.7	57	29.2	107	18.1	10.4	.001	.12
High	188[a]	23.9	24	41.4	164	22.6	9.44	.01	.11
Residence									
Rural	178	22.0	47	32.4	131	19.8	10.4	.001	.12
Urban	184	21.6	35	30.4	149	20.2	5.54	.05	.08

Note. Only respondents who took children into their homes are included; consequently, the totals are less than those in Table 18.2.
[a]The combined total for low and high SES is less than 362 due to missing values.

where they live, were more likely to take children into their homes to live with them. The results of the analysis lend support to the acceptance of Hypothesis 4.

DISCUSSION

The findings of this study offer limited support for the extended family hypothesis of black aging suggested by Hill (1978) and others. Results of the analysis support a contention that aged blacks were more likely to receive help from their children and grandchildren. It could be argued that this is a result of the need for help. When socioeconomic status as an indicator of the need for economic help is controlled, however, results indicate that blacks continued to receive more help than elderly whites.

An extended family hypothesis is additionally supported by the finding that elderly blacks were more likely than whites to take grandchildren, nieces, and nephews into their homes to live, regardless of SES or whether the respondent lived in a rural or urban area.

Other findings, however, cast doubt on the relevance of race as a differentiating factor in intergenerational relationships. In contrast to previous findings by Dowd and Bengtson (1978), it was found that elderly whites, considering all of the categories of visitation, tended to see their children and grandchildren more frequently than blacks. Even though black elderly were more likely to live with their children, among those living apart they were also more likely to see them rarely (less often than every 3 months). Perhaps outward migration of younger blacks looking for jobs has had an adverse effect upon contact with elderly people. This speculation is reinforced by the finding that the above relationship tends to be more applicable to elderly people in the lower socioeconomic category.

The salience of racial differences in the extended family hypothesis is questioned by some of the findings. The reader should be cognizant that only slight differences, even when statistically significant, were found between blacks and whites. In addition, results suggest that SES is more influential than race in explaining whether elderly people give help to their children and grandchildren. It appears, contrary to what would be expected, that those without resources tend to share more often what they have with children and grandchildren. Perhaps the need for help is the primary factor in demonstrated patterns of giving help. Persons in the upper socioeconomic category are more likely to have children in a like position and less in need of help. Similarly, elderly people in the upper socioeconomic category tend to receive more help, perhaps due to the ability of their offspring to furnish assistance. With those in the lower socioeconomic category, however, the need for help from elderly people may be more acute among children and grandchildren. Perhaps economic realities as well as the extent to which family members need help of all kinds have a leveling effect for all elderly, regardless of race.

IMPLICATIONS

This paper deals with an unresolved and important issue in the study of the black family—its extendedness. The data source used, despite the alteration of the sample design, is more representative of blacks in the U.S. than the majority of similar studies. The results of the analyses point to a need for policy makers and practitioners to focus upon the needs of individuals and disregard stereotyped views of black family structure. Hypotheses emphasizing the extendedness of black family relationships with the elderly were not uniformly accepted and racial differences were minimal. Although black elderly were more likely to receive help from family members and also to take children into the home to live with them, this could be due to a more pronounced need for help among black elderly people and a tendency for black elderly to help family members who are working elsewhere by caring for their children. Further research incorporating economic factors with intergenerational relationships could help to clarify whether these findings are a result of immediate need rather than a more all-encompassing extended family orientation rooted in emotional ties.

Kennedy (1980) concluded that, among the black families he observed, who is or is not considered part of the family is often based upon the function the person fulfills for family members. Perhaps practicality in the form of need fulfillment overshadows, in many instances, a stereotyped extended family pattern based upon emotional attachment. The finding that white elderly see their children and grandchildren more often, on the average, than black elderly certainly questions the assumption of a more extended family pattern among blacks. Frequency of contact, however, is variable and does not allow for strong emotional ties despite geographic separation. Consequently, future research should explore possible differences in the perceived quality, rather than quantity, of interaction. For the present, however, the findings of this study point to a need to drop the assumption of a more extended family among blacks and, rather, focus upon apparent differences in need among black and white elderly persons.

Finally, the results of this study have implications for further research. Among these are the following: (1) a need to clarify the importance of the type of help provided by and to elderly people; different kinds of help, or acts, obviously require different levels of motivation on the part of the helper and the expressed needs of those being helped. (2) Exploration of the possible mediating effect of the presence of a spouse upon family interaction and support. (3) A longitudinal, multi-generational study to clarify differences in family interaction patterns by race identified by cross-sectional research.

REFERENCES

Baum, M., & Baum, A. C. *Growing old: A societal perspective.* Prentice-Hall, Inc. Englewood Cliffs, NJ, 1980.

Bengtson, V. L., Cuellar, J., & Ragan, P. K. Stratum contrasts and similarities in attitudes toward death. *Journal of Gerontology,* 1977, *32,* 76–88.

Billingsley, A. *Black families in white America.* Prentice-Hall, Inc., Englewood Cliffs, NJ, 1968.

Conner, K. A., Powers, E. A., & Bultena, G. L. Social interaction and life satisfaction: An empirical assessment of late life patterns. *Journal of Gerontology,* 1979, *34,* 116–121.

Dowd, J. J., & Bengtson, V. L. Aging in minority populations: An examination of the double jeopardy hypothesis. *Journal of Gerontology,* 1978, *33,* 427–436.

Hassinger, E. W. *The rural component of American society.* Interstate, Danville, IL, 1978.

Hill, R. B. A demographic profile of the black elderly, *Aging,* 1978, Nos. 287–288, 2–9.

Hollingshead, A. A. *Social class and mental health.* John Wiley & Sons, Inc., New York, 1958.

Huling, W. E. Evolving family roles for the black elderly. *Aging,* 1978, Nos. 287–288, 21–27.

Jackson, J. J. The blacklands of gerontology. *Aging and Human Development,* 1971, *7,* 168–178.

Jackson, J. J. Comparative life styles and family-friend relationships among older black women. *The Family Coordinator,* 1972, *21,* 477–485. (a)

Jackson, J. J. Marital life among aging blacks. *The Family Coordinator,* 1972, *21,* 21–27. (b)

Jackson, J. J. *Minorities and aging.* Wadsworth Publishing, Belmont, CA, 1980.

Kennedy, T. R. *You gotta deal with it: Black family relations in a southern community.* Oxford University Press, New York, 1980.

Kitagawa, E. M., & Hauser, P. M. *Differential mortality in the United States: A study in socioeconomic epidemiology.* Harvard University Press, Cambridge, MA, 1973.

Larson, R. Thirty years of research on the subjective well-being of older Americans. *Journal of Gerontology,* 1978, *33,* 109–125.

Lee, G. R. Children and the elderly: Interaction and morale. *Research on Aging,* 1979, *1,* 335–360.

Mueller, J. H., Schuessler, K. F., & Costner, H. L. *Statistical reasoning in sociology.* Houghton Mifflin, Boston, 1977.

Nunnaly, J. C. *Psychometric theory.* McGraw-Hill, New York, 1978.

Register, J. Aging and race: A black-white comparative analysis. *The Gerontologist,* 1981, *21,* 438–443.

Seelbach, W., & Sauer, W. Filial responsibility expectations and morale among aged parents. *The Gerontologist,* 1977, *17,* 492–499.

Shanas, E. The family as a support system in old age. *The Gerontologist,* 1979, *19,* 169–174.

Siegel, J. S. On the demography of aging. *Demography,* 1980, *17,* 345–364.

Troll, L. E., Miller, S. J., & Atchley, R. C. *Families in later life.* Wadsworth Publishing Company, Belmont, CA, 1979.

Wylie, F. M. Attitudes toward aging and the aged among black Americans: Some historical perspectives. In R. C. Atchley & M. M. Seltzer (Eds.) *The sociology of aging: Selected readings.* Wadsworth Publishing Company, Belmont, CA, 1976.

Part VII

Childlessness and Divorce

It may be counterintuitive that so many older people not only have close kin to care for them when they need help but actually are cared for by these kin more than by other resource people like professionals or friends. But if we turn this finding around, we are left with a still significant number of old people who are childless, are currently not married, and have no acknowledged family members around. About 20% of older people in the Western world are childless. While the incidence of divorce is highest among young couples, it has risen across the age span and there are many divorced women—and some men—who do not have either spouse or children. In fact, if we add in older women who are widowed and not remarried, we are left with a substantial number of older women without family resources. An interest in this population has led to the recent studies of social networks or friendship networks reviewed in the previous section.

CHILDLESSNESS

Johnson and Catalano (1981) report that there are 5 million childless Americans over the age of 65. In their San Francisco study of older people newly discharged from an acute-care hospital, 28 out of 167 (17%) had no children, and 18 of these were not married. As noted in earlier sections, the married childless couples turn to each other with intensity greater than that of other older couples, often ending up in social isolation. One-fifth of those who were not married among these childless had substituted other kin for children such as siblings or children of siblings (nieces and nephews). They were also more involved with friends and neighbors than the others in that sample. A Los Angeles study (Beckman & Houser, 1982; this volume) compares the psychological well-being of childless women and mothers between the ages of 60 and 75. All were widows whose husbands had died between 1 and 5 years previously. The major finding was that widows had poorer general well-being ratings than did married women, and beyond that those widows who had no living children were lower in general well-being and more lonely and dissatisfied than those who had children. The married women who were childless, on the other hand, did not differ from married women who had children. This is consistent with earlier discussions of the primary relationships of older people, men turning to their wives and women to daughters in times of need. Large-scale survey data (Glenn & McLanahan, 1981, 1982) conclude that having had children contributes little to the psychological well-being of older couples, just as it has a negative effect on couples whose children are still residing at home. It does have a positive effect, however, on unmarried older white women.

DIVORCE

Although only 1% of divorces occur to people over the age of 65 and only about 5% of people now over 65 are divorced or separated—and not remarried, that is (Uhlenberg & Meyers, 1981; this volume), Hagestad (1982) points out that older people are nevertheless affected by the rise in divorce rates. She uses the term "the family ripple effect" to designate the impact divorce in their children and siblings usually has upon older people. As mentioned earlier, grandparents are important in the case of divorces of their children (Hetherington, Cox, & Cox, 1982; Tinsley & Parke, 1984). Maternal grandparents are particularly likely to be affected, partly because their daughters often come home for economic help and also for help with child rearing. Sons do too sometimes, but they are more likely to look for help from housekeepers and professional services— they usually have more money than their ex-wives, for one thing. Hagestad finds that contact may increase between maternal grandparents and their grandchildren following divorce.

The concern with divorce among gerontologists is indicated by the growing number of studies on the subject. Chiriboga (1982), whose San Francisco sample included men and women of varying ages, found that older divorced people were lower in morale than younger, and that men were significantly less happy than women. Women, however, were more highly distressed and had more symptoms of disturbance. Two other reports on divorce are included in this volume: Uhlenberg and Myers (1981), and Cicirelli (1983b). Uhlenberg and Myers looked at national demographic data, pointing to the negative consequences for older divorced men and women, who are less satisfied with their financial situation and have higher death rates than the married (men 33% higher and women 7% higher).

Cicirelli's (1983b) article is included in the earlier section on parent–child relations. He looked at the differences in helping behavior of children with intact and disrupted marriages. Much of the difference he found—in awareness of parents' needs and in financial and psychological support—showed little overall relationship to the children's marital status. Remarried children, however, helped more with financial matters than did divorced and widowed children, while those with disrupted marriages tended to be less aware of their parents' plights. Aldous (1985) had noted this same phenomenon. Obviously, remarried people have greater economic resources than singles, and people who are themselves distressed may be less likely to be "tuned in" to the distress of others. Remember, though, the finding that widowed women were comforted best by their widowed mothers (Bankoff, 1983a). Undoubtedly, there is a time factor involved. Tragedy, when it strikes, is felt acutely, but the emotional crisis lessens over time. Further, as Hagestad and Smyer (1982) and Hennon (1983) noted, the timing of divorce is important in its impact. This was also noted in most studies of widowhood (cf. Lopata, 1973) and of grandparenting (e.g., Hagestad, 1985). Hennon's comparison between widows and divorcees showed that some divorcees find the ending of their marriage leading to a reordering of priorities, a new sense of freedom, and a chance to realize unfulfilled potential. Others, though, find their lives shattered, particularly if they are already vulnerable because of poor health and low income.

19

The Consequences of Childlessness on the Social-Psychological Well-Being of Older Women*

Linda J. Beckman
Betsy Bosak Houser

It has frequently been contended that low fertility, and particularly childlessness, has negative psychological, economic, and social effects for women. Despite societal perceptions of childless women as less satisfied and more unhappy than women with children (Franzwa, 1974; Veevers, 1973), recent research finds no evidence that the involuntarily or the intentionally childless are more dissatisfied with their lot than are others. Several recent studies examining life satisfaction have found married couples without children to have significantly higher life satisfaction than those with children (Feldman, 1974; Van Keep, 1975). This finding has been upheld both for large-scale survey results (e.g., Campbell et al., 1976; Feldman, 1974) and for matched group or case-study designs (e.g., Houseknecht, 1979; Van Keep, 1975).

Journal of Gerontology, 37 (2) (1982), 243–250.

This research was supported by National Institute of Mental Health grant MH-29201 and a Research Scientist Development Award to the senior author. The authors would like to thank Tom Day for his invaluable suggestions regarding data analysis. Requests for reprints should be addressed to Dr. Beckman at the Department of Psychiatry, School of Medicine, University of California at Los Angeles, 760 Westwood Plaza, Los Angeles, CA 90024.

The overwhelming majority of this research, however, has concentrated on relatively young women who are in or recently beyond their childbearing years. It can be argued that lack of children should have its greatest negative effect on persons when they are elderly. The crux of this contention is that grown children satisfy their elderly parents' objective and subjective needs and that the type of social support offered by children is not readily available from other sources (Lopata, 1978). Therefore, older women without children will have lower life satisfaction and social-psychological well-being.

Evidence from social gerontology, however, finds little support for the view that childless women are less satisfied or have lower well-being than others. For instance, social contact with family members appears to have little effect on older persons' social-psychological well-being (Arling, 1976; Pihlblad & Adams, 1972). Although elderly childless persons tend to be more socially isolated, they appear no more likely to report that they are lonely than are older persons with children (Tunstall, 1966). These studies, however, were not designed specifically to study the effects of children on the well-being of elderly persons, and contradictory evidence also can be found. In a study of married and widowed older males and females residing in small towns in Missouri (Pihlblad & Adams, 1972), a small subsample of childless women widowed 1 to 4 years was lower than all other female groups on life satisfaction.

Given the limited evidence on the effects of parity on the life adjustment and satisfaction of the aged, this study's purpose was to examine the effects of childlessness on the social-psychological well-being of married and widowed women aged 60 to 75 years. The study was limited to women because women are greatly over-represented in this age group; in 1975 there were 69 men per 100 women aged 65 years and over (United States Bureau of the Census, 1976).

Social-psychological well-being is here defined as a multidimensional concept composed of a number of nonorthogonal dimensions such as depression and life satisfaction. It measures general affective experience in terms of a positive-negative continuum. It has been contended (see Larson, 1978) that there is good empirical justification for grouping the components of well-being into one general construct when studying the elderly. Studies using different conceptualizations and measures of well-being usually have yielded parallel results, and high intercorrelations typically have been found between scales measuring different components (Larson, 1978; Lohmann, 1977).

Our major hypothesis was that the relationship between parity and well-being would be moderated by variables such as marital status, financial status, and health. Only under conditions such as widowhood, low income, or poor health would childlessness have a significant negative effect on well-being. For those who are married, financially secure, or healthy, childlessness should have minimal effects on well-being.

Another prediction was that well-being would be related to whether or not an individual's reported fertility preferences have been achieved. For older women fertility preferences can be measured by asking, "if you could have had as many children as you liked, how many would you have had?" Christensen's (1968) notion of value-behavior discrepancy, defined in terms of the difference between a person's desires regarding number of children and that person's actual number of living children, predicts that persons who have a discrepancy between fertility desires and fertility outcomes will have lower well-being than will those without such a discrepancy.

This difference in well-being may also extend to the voluntariness of fertility status. Women for whom a parity was involuntary (e.g., they could not achieve desired parity because of sterility or subfecundity) may show lower well-being than women who voluntarily chose their number of children. The effects of voluntariness of fertility outcome status on well-being should be greatest among childless women because the differences between having or not having children should be perceived as much greater than the differences between having different numbers of children.

METHOD

Design

Personal interviews were conducted during 1978 and 1979 with 719 Anglo Los Angeles County women between the ages of 60 and 75 years. Half of the women were widows, and the other half were currently married and living with spouse. For each marital status group, the sample was further stratified so that approximately half of the women selected were *currently* childless and half had living children. All interviewers were women more than 45 years old.

Sample Selection

Because of screening problems involved in selecting persons in a limited age range with a relatively rare trait (i.e., childlessness), a relatively unusual combination of sampling methods was utilized. First, a sample of 7,400 death certificates of men who had died in Los Angeles County between 1973 and 1978 (and who would have been between the ages of 63 and 78 years if currently living) was selected randomly. The widows of all of these men were sent letters at their last known addresses explaining the purpose of the study and requesting completion of a short screening questionnaire to determine eligibility. Those who did not return the questionnaire were contacted by telephone whenever possible. These techniques resulted in location of 64% of the widows of men whose death certificates were selected. All of these women had been widowed between 1 and 5 years, and the parents and childless women did not significantly differ in the amount of time they had been widowed (parents, M = 2.5; childless, M = 2.2).

The second stage of sampling involved a modified "snowballing" procedure wherein married women were identified by the widows. All widows were asked to nominate neighbors between the ages of 60 and 75 years who were married and living with their husbands. Neighbors rather than friends were preferred for the married sample in order to limit the usual tendency to nominate "sociometric stars" while at the same time ensuring that the married and widowed samples be fairly similar in terms of sociodemographic characteristics. (However, it was not determined whether the neighbors nominated were also friends.) The names of 2,258 women, 94% of whom were located, were referred through these snowballing procedures. Married women were contacted through the same location procedures used for widows.

Criteria for Sample Selection

Eligible respondents had to be Anglo married or widowed women between 60 and 75 years of age who resided in Los Angeles County and were English speaking. Respondents were required to be capable of the activities of daily living such as dressing themselves, shopping, and keeping house, and they could *not* be living with a child or in an institution.

All individuals were screened for eligibility and willingness to volunteer to participate in the study. Respondents were then randomly selected from the four separate subsample pools of eligible women. Forty-nine percent of the widowed group and 37% of the married group did not meet the eligibility criteria for the study. The higher eligibility rate of the married group was expected since they had been identified because they might be eligible.

Actual refusal rates for each of the four groups are impossible to determine because most women refused to participate *before* their eligibility could be determined. However, approximately 70% of those refusals for whom eligibility could be determined were ineligible for participation. Conservative estimates of the overall refusal rate indicate that 44% of subjects refused to participate in the study. Although this percentage is relatively high, the subject matter of the present survey was sensitive and women in the studied age group were suspicious about allowing anyone into their homes.

Characteristics of the Sample

The demographic characteristics of the sample are presented in Table 19.1. These data show that the widowed women are less educated, $F(1, 714) = 6.57, p < .01$; lower in SES $F(1, 690) = 14.18, p < .01$; have lower present incomes $F(1, 640) = 169.56, p < .01$, and are more likely to be employed than are married women ($\chi^2 = 7.66, p < .01$). Childless women do not differ significantly from women with children.

Instruments

The interview schedule and self-administered forms included items regarding demographic characteristics, social interaction, health, fertility history, ideal family size, satisfaction with family size, perceived rewards and costs of children and of childlessness, relationship with children, proximity to children, and social-psychological well-being.

The major dependent variable, well-being, was measured along five major dimensions that primarily assess negative well-being rather than positive. Three dimensions were assessed through use of the Lawton Revised Philadelphia Geriatric Center Morale Scale (1975). This widely used 17-item scale has three subscales that have been found to have a high degree of internal consistency (Lawton, 1975). They are entitled attitude toward own aging (i.e., the belief that life gets worse as one gets older), agitation (i.e., worrying excessively, taking things hard, getting angry and upset), and lonely/dissatisfaction. Depression was assessed through use of Zung's Self-

Table 19.1. Demographic Characteristics of Older Women Sample

	Group			
	Married childless[a]	Widowed childless[a]	Married parent	Widowed parent
N	189	154	194	182
Years of education (M)	13.28	12.98	13.07	12.33
Age (M years)	68.87	68.73	67.65	68.95
Duncan socioeconomic index (M)	53.68	49.30	52.04	45.85
Income (M)[b]	13.99	9.01	13.73	8.42
Currently employed (%)	16.4	25.3	16.5	24.7
Religion (%)[c]				
Catholic	11.9	20.0	9.6	19.7
Protestant	70.0	60.7	68.3	58.6
Jewish	18.1	19.3	22.2	21.6

[a]Childless women are currently childless. The childless group contains a few women who had children who are no longer living.
[b]Income is coded in equal $1,000 intervals through $14,999 (e.g., 6 = $6,000 to $6,999); income categories for $15,000 and above included greater intervals. Therefore, mean values are somewhat deflated.
[c]The few respondents who listed religion as other or none are not included.

Rating Depression Scale (1967, 1973). The 20-item scale operationally defines depression in terms of four major symptoms: (a) mood disturbance, (b) physiological symptoms, (c) psychomotor disturbance, and (d) psychological disturbance. Social isolation was measured via the 9-item Dean Social Isolation Scale (1961). Those high on social isolation perceive other people as unfriendly and disinterested and their own position as characterized by anonymity and aloneness.

These particular instruments were chosen because they had previously been developed or at least used with elderly populations, they represented different facets of the construct social-psychological well-being, and, given the choices available, they appeared to have reasonable reliability and validity. It should be noted that no universally accepted operational definition of well-being exists. Indeed, it is not even agreed that it is multidimensional in nature. Therefore, the results found may to some extent depend on the particular measurement techniques used.

Important sociodemographic and background variables included age, education, socioeconomic status as measured by the Duncan socioeconomic index (SEI) (1961), income, religion, number of sisters and brothers, and current employment status. Measures of current status included physical capacity (based on a summary score of the degree of difficulty in performing seven daily activities), health (i.e., the presence/absence of a serious illness in the last year), and religiosity (i.e., how religious the woman considered herself to be, rated on a 5-point scale).

Measures of social contact included strength of support network (i.e., how many persons the respondent feels she can always count on in times of need), number of confidants (i.e., "persons close enough to talk to about the things that really bother me"), total quantity of social interaction (based on a *sum* of interaction with children, grandchildren, confidants, friends, neighbors, and other relatives, each rated on a 5-point scale from 1, less than once a month, to 5, daily), and satisfaction with the quality of social contact (based on an *average* of ratings of satisfaction with the quality of social contact with children, grandchildren, friends, neighbors, and other relatives, rated on a 5-point scale from 1, very dissatisfied, to 5, very satisfied). Finally, fertility-related measures included number of living children, satisfaction with family size (rated on a 5-point scale), desired family size, pregnancy history, and reasons for childlessness.

RESULTS

The Well-Being Dimensions

It is our contention that social-psychological well-being is a multi-dimensional concept. This view is supported by the correlations among the five scales, which ranged from .38 between social/isolation and depression to .52 between attitude toward own aging and lonely/dissatisfaction. These moderate intercorrelations support the notion that, although the scales share common variance, they do not measure identical dimensions.

When a factor analysis using the individual items from all five scales was computed, the first factor had an eigenvalue three to four times the size of the other eigenvalues, indicating the presence of a general factor. To obtain a general measure of well-being, the first principal component (i.e., the unrotated factor with the greatest eigenvalue) was extracted. Items involving dissatisfaction, unhappiness, and loneliness had the strongest loadings on this overall well-being factor.

Although the Dean Social Isolation Scale generally did not load as highly as the other scales on general well-being, two of its items had relatively high loadings (−.59 and −.50). All of its other items had loadings below −.35. The fact that some of the social isolation items contribute to the general well-being factor may raise interpretation problems since some of the independent variables (those dealing with number of confidants, number of people one can count on, and quality and quantity of contact) appear to tap a similar domain to that of social isolation. However, the Dean scale measures feelings regarding the world and people in general, whether humanity is perceived as friendly or as uncaring, unfriendly and isolated, whereas the social contact measures are specific to the respondent's actual social relationships.

Effects of Parity and Marital Status on Well-Being

The effects of parity and marital status on the five well-being dimensions and on the overall well-being index were first examined using analysis of variance and covariance (see Table 19.2). The 13 covariates were: age, years of education, income (under vs. over $10,000), religion (coded as three dummy variables), number of living sisters, current employment status (working vs. not working), physical capacity, presence of serious illness in last year, religiosity, strength of support network, presence of at least one confidant, total quantity of social contact, and mean satisfaction with social contact.

Analysis of variance on the unadjusted means (shown in Table 19.2) revealed that widows evidenced poorer general well-being than did married women; widows also scored lower on four of the five individual dimensions of well-being. Widows were more depressed, socially isolated, dissatisfied and lonely, and had a more negative attitude toward their own aging (all $ps < .01$).

Differences between childless women and women with children were more subtle. An important difference was between widows who were childless and widows with children. As indicated by significant parity by marital status interactions ($p < .05$), widowed women who were childless were lower in general well-being and more lonely and dissatisfied (as indicated by that subscale of the Philadelphia Geriatric Center Morale Scale) than widowed mothers. Married women in the two parity groups did not differ in well-being, although they had higher scores than either of the widowed groups.

Main effects for parity disappeared, but all other differences described previously remained stable when the effects of 13 de-

Table 19.2. Effects of Parity and Marital Status on Well-Being Dimensions

Dimension	Unadjusted means				ANOVA					
					Parent status		Marital status		Interaction	
	Childless married	Childless widowed	Parent married	Parent widowed	$p<$	ω^{2b}	$p<$	ω^{2b}	$p<$	ω^{2b}
General well-being factor	0.34	−0.55	0.32	−0.14	.05	.01	.01	.11	.05	.01
Agitation[a]	4.63	4.69	4.74	4.79			.01	.05		
Attitude toward own aging[a]	3.54	2.70	3.44	2.92						
Lonely/dissatisfaction[a]	5.43	4.44	5.43	4.96	.01	.01	.01	.07	.05	.01
Social isolation	22.61	24.51	22.17	23.22	.05	.01	.01	.02		
Depression	33.77	36.32	34.05	35.96			.01	.03		

Dimension	Adjusted means				ANCOVA					
					Parent status		Marital status		Interaction	
	Childless married	Childless widowed	Parent married	Parent widowed	$p<$	ω^{2b}	$p<$	ω^{2b}	$p<$	ω^{2b}
General well-being factor	0.36	−0.38	0.21	−0.18			.01	.10	.01	.01
Agitation[a]	4.62	4.85	4.63	4.79			.01	.03		
Attitude toward own aging[a]	3.55	2.91	3.30	2.89						
Lonely/dissatisfaction[a]	5.44	4.61	5.34	4.91			.01	.06	.05	.01
Social isolation	22.23	23.54	22.96	23.61			.01	.01		
Depression	33.45	35.58	34.67	36.26			.01	.02		

[a] On the Philadelphia Geriatric Center Morale Scale high scores indicate low agitation, more favorable attitude toward own aging, and low loneliness/dissatisfaction.

[b] ω^2 is the partial ω^2 statistic (Keren & Lewis, 1979). This was used to measure effect size because it partials out effects other than the one under consideration and most of the analyses are two-way ANOVAs and ANCOVAs.

mographic, current situational, and social interaction variables were controlled through analysis of covariance (see bottom halves of Table 2). However, significant F values ($p < .01$) for equality of slope on both the general well-being factor and the lonely/dissatisfaction scale indicated that at least some of the covariates did not show the *same* degree of relationship to the dependent variable for all of the four groups. Thus, strictly speaking, the assumptions of analysis of covariance were violated and additional analyses were required. These additional analyses were done only for the general well-being factor.

Effects of the Covariates on General Well-Being

The inequality of slopes in the analyses of covariance indicated that at least some of these covariates had differential effects on well-being for the four different marital status/parity groups. To pinpoint these differences separate regression analyses were conducted for each of the four groups. The hierarchical regression model used for each of the four analyses assumed that the set of variables first affecting the general well-being index are demographic/background variables (i.e., age, education, religion, income, and current employment status). The second set of variables entered sequentially in the regression model reflect current situation and beliefs (i.e., religiosity, presence/absence of serious illness, current physical capacity). The final set of variables, assumed to be affected by (but not to affect) prior variables, are measures of social contact and interaction (presence of a confidant, number of people who can be counted on, total quality of social contact, and satisfaction with quality of social interaction). Results of these sequential analyses, presented in Table 19.3, reveal that a greater portion of the variance (52%) in general well-being is explained in the widowed childless than in the other groups (33 to 41%). Among the background variables for all four groups, religion was the most consistent predictor of well-being. When religion was examined in a separate analysis, Protestants had significantly higher well-being than did Catholics, who, in turn, had significantly higher well-being than did Jews, $F(2, 510) = 33.63$, $p < .01$, $\omega^2 = .12$.

The effects of current situational variables were considered independently of the background variables. The major impact of this variable set was evident among the widowed childless group, in which these three variables explained a quarter of the variance even after the effects of background variables were controlled. This occurs because physical capacity had a particularly strong negative relationship to general well-being only for the widowed childless and religiosity showed a positive relationship to well-being only for the widowed women. For the married parents these variables had no impact on R^2, and for the childless married and widowed parents the effects were quite small (.04 and .06, respectively).

All four groups showed significant increases in the percentage of variance explained when the four social interaction measures were added to the regression equations (after the background and situational variables had been partialled out). These increases range from 13% for the widowed parents to 20% for the married childless. In all cases perceived quality of social contact was the social interaction variable most strongly related to well-being.

Discrepancies Between Fertility Desires and Outcomes

It was predicted that the presence of a discrepancy between fertility desires and actual number of children would be related to general well-being. Fertility desires were measured by asking women how many children they would have had if they could have had as many as they liked. Childless women were more likely to show a greater discrepancy between fertility desires and outcomes than were women with children, $F(1, 580) = 52.08$, $p < .01$, $\omega^2 = .08$. The sample on the average would have liked to have had 1.67 more children than they actually had. For childless women the mean discrepancy was over 2 and for women with children it was over 1. However, when parity was not controlled, the presence of a discrepancy itself had a very small negative effect on overall socialpsychological well-being, $t(582) = 1.66$, $p < .05$ one-tailed, $\omega^2 = .005$.

A more subjective measure of fertility outcomes is satisfaction with family size. When the relationship of satisfaction with family size on general well-being was examined through a two (parity) by three (satisfied, dissatisfied, or neutral regarding current family size) analysis of variance, it was found that satisfaction with family size had a highly significant main effect, $F(2, 585) = 18.80$, $p < .001$, $\omega^2 = .06$. However, a significant parity by satisfaction with family size interaction, $F(2, 585) = 4.51$, $p < .01$, $\omega^2 = .02$, also was present. Therefore, simple main effects (Winer, 1962, p. 237) were examined. Satisfied parents did not differ from satisfied nonparents on well-being. However, parents who reported neutrality were somewhat lower in reported well-being than were neutral childless women, $F(1, 95) = 4.02$, $p < .05$, $\omega^2 = .01$, whereas dissatisfied parents were somewhat higher on well-being than were dissatisfied childless women, $F(1, 55) = 4.88$, $p < .05$, $\omega^2 = .01$.

Table 19.3. Hierarchical Multiple Regression of General Well-Being on Background, Current Situational, and Social Contact Variables for Parity and Marital Status Subgroups

	Group			
	Childless married (n = 156) β^a	Childless widowed (n = 114) β^a	Parent married (n = 155) β^a	Parent widowed (n = 138) β^a
Level 1: Background				
Jewish	−.222*	−.083	−.062	−.156
Protestant	.045	.286	.251*	.374**
Catholic	.014	.114	.060	.110
Work status	−.192*	−.018	−.003	.069
Number of sisters	.087	.114	.022	.177*
Age	.063	.064	.029	.153
Education	−.063	−.031	.263**	−.022
Income	.048	.136	.056	.094
Increase in R^2	$R^2 = .12$ $F(8, 147) = 2.55*$	$R^2 = .11$ $F(8, 105) = 1.65$	$R^2 = .18$ $F(8, 146) = 3.96**$	$R^2 = .22$ $F(8, 129) = 4.67**$
Level 2: Current situation				
Physical capacity	−.061	−.438**	−.125	.056
Illness	−.173*	−.030	.033	−.172*
Religiosity	.013	.267**	−.013	.217*
Increase in R^2	$R\Delta^2 = .04$ $F(3, 144) = 2.01$	$R\Delta^2 = .25$ $F(3, 102) = 13.28**$	$R\Delta^2 = .01$ $F(3, 143) = .59$	$R\Delta^2 = .06$ $F(3, 126) = 3.49*$

344

Level 3: Social contact				
Quality of social interaction	.358**	.237**	.321**	−.309**
Person to count on	.159*	.151	.063	−.088
Confidant	.131	.075	.104	.110
Quantity of social interaction	.041	.063	.120	.084
Increase in R^2	$R\Delta^2 = .20$ $F(4, 140) = 10.43$**	$R\Delta^2 = .16$ $F(4, 98) = 10.89$**	$R\Delta^2 = .14$ $F(4, 139) = 7.26$**	$R\Delta^2 = .13$ $F(4, 122) = 6.72$**
Total R^2	$R^2 = .36$ $F(15, 140) = 5.15$**	$R^2 = .52$ $F(15, 98) = 7.05$**	$R^2 = .33$ $F(4, 139) = 4.50$**	$R^2 = .41$ $F(15, 122) = 5.60$**

[a]Standardized partial regression coefficient (β) at the step when all variables for that level and preceding levels have been entered.
*$p < .05$; **$p < .01$.

Voluntariness of Status

It was predicted that those who had chosen their fertility outcome voluntarily would have higher well-being than those confined to a fertility outcome involuntarily, and this effect should be particularly potent among childless women. The discrepancy between current fertility desires and outcomes may provide indirect information about the voluntariness of a fertility outcome; fertility desires, however, may have changed as a result of raising children or other life cycle events. Although a more direct measure of voluntariness of status was not obtained for women with children, an index of whether the absence of children was voluntary or involuntary was derived for childless women. This index was based on answers to questions regarding reasons for not having children and fertility history. Any childless women who stated one or more of the following reasons for not having children was considered involuntarily childless: (a) it was physically impossible for her or her husband to have children, (b) she had problems getting pregnant or carrying a pregnancy to term, (c) she married too late or was too old at age of marriage to have children, (d) she did not use contraception but never became pregnant, or (e) she tried (or wanted) to adopt a child but was unable to do so. Women who stated that they (or they and their husbands) did not want children, that they had other competing interests, or were too busy to have children were classified as voluntarily childless. A third group that emerged in the process of coding the data (and who gave neither voluntary nor involuntary reasons) was called semivoluntary; these were women who indicated they had no children because of health reasons, lack of money, their husbands' desires, or that they simply didn't know why they never had children.

Results suggest that voluntariness has limited effects on the well-being of childless women. Although results were in the predicted direction on general well-being, $F(2, 215) = 2.08$, $p > .05$, they did not reach significance. Voluntariness also appeared to have minimal effects on specific measures of the dimensions of well-being.

DISCUSSION

These results support the prediction that childlessness has a greater effect on well-being for widowed than for married women. Even when the effects of background, current status, and social interaction variables were controlled, childless widows had lower overall well-being and were more lonely and dissatisfied with their lives than were widows with grown children. The magnitude of these differences (indicated by ω^2), however, was small, explaining only 1% of the variance in general well-being for this sample. Thus, childlessness had very minimal effects on well-being. In contrast, the magnitude of the effects of marital status, religion, and social interaction was much greater, with each separately explaining over 10% of the variance in general well-being. The greater predicted effects of childlessness on well-being among those who are poor or in ill health were not directly supported by these results. However, the significant regression coefficient for physical capacity only in the widowed childless group suggests that physical capacity is predictive of well-being only when a woman does not have either children or spouse to provide assistance. Thus, it appears that it is the inability to perform daily activities and the absence of children *or* spouse that moderate the effects of poor health on well-being. Lopata's (1978) finding that children rather than other kin satisfy widowed parents' needs, thus, is indirectly supported.

As hypothesized, when desires regarding family size agreed with fertility outcomes or when women were satisfied with their family size, women had somewhat better well-being, but the very small size of this effect indicates that it is trivial. Also, involuntarily childless women did not report lower well-being than did voluntarily childless women as had been predicted. This contrary finding may reflect the fact that an outcome was characterized as voluntary or involuntary based on events that occurred many years previously. Women initially dissatisfied with their childlessness may have become reconciled to it over this lengthy period. Therefore, well-being was more closely related to *current* satisfaction with fertility outcome than to voluntariness of status some 30 to 40 years previously.

Also of interest are the effects of the covariates on general well-being and their interaction with childlessness. Religiosity was significantly positively related to well-being only for the widowed group. Since the effects of *both* religiosity and physical capacity are important only for the widowed childless group, in the multiple regressions presented in Table 19.3 more of the total variance (R^2) is explained for this group than for the other three groups. To be old, alone, without children or husband, and physically incapacitated is (almost by definition) to have a poor quality of life.

As found in previous research (Pihlblad & Adams, 1972), widows had much lower well-being than did currently married women. The effects of religion on well-being, however, were quite unexpected and, perhaps, can be explained by cultural differences among the three religious groups. The importance of quality of social interaction and strength of social support network in promoting positive well-being is clear from these data. As suggested by past research (Conner et al., 1979) perceived quality of interaction appears far more important than quantity of interaction in predicting well-being. More efforts should be made to explore the relationship between the qualitative and dynamic aspects of social support networks and well-being in the elderly. Also, those providing services to the elderly must be made aware that it is not the scope of an elderly woman's social network but rather the quality of her social relationships that most influences her well-being.

In conclusion, although results from this cohort of women born between 1902 and 1918 may not generalize to more recent birth cohorts, the present results suggest that women who are widowed, childless, Jewish, nonreligious, and without social support or satisfying social interactions are likely to evidence low social-psychological well-being. Women who represent combinations of such risk factors should be targeted for intervention strategies that can improve the quality of their lives.

REFERENCES

Arling, G. The elderly widow and her family, neighbors and friends. *Journal of Marriage and the Family.* 1976, *38*, 757–768.

Campbell, A., Converse, P., & Rodgers, W. *The quality of American life.* Russel Sage Foundation, New York, 1976.

Christensen, H. T. Children in the family: Relationship of number and spacing to marital success. *Journal of Marriage and the Family,* 1968, *30*, 283–289.

Conner, K. A., Powers, E. A., & Bultena, G. L. Social interaction and life satisfaction: An empirical assessment of late-life patterns. *Journal of Gerontology,* 1979, *34*, 116–121.

Dean, D. G. Alienation: Its meaning and measurement. *American Sociological Review,* 1961, *26*, 753–758.

Duncan, O. D. A socioeconomic index for all occupations. In A. J. Reiss (Ed.), *Occupations and social status.* New York, Free Press of Glencoe, 1961.

Feldman, H. Changes in marriage and parenthood: A methodological design. In E. Peck & J. Senderowitz (Eds.), *Pronatalism.* Thomas Y. Crowell, New York, 1974.

Franzwa, H. H. Pronatalism in women's magazine fiction. In E. Peck & J. Senderowitz (Eds.), *Pronatalism.* Thomas Y. Crowell, New York, 1974.

Houseknecht, S. Childlessness and marital ádjustment. *Journal of Marriage and the Family*, 1979, *41*, 259–265.

Keren, G., & Charles, L. Partial omega squared for ANOVA designs. *Educational and Psychological Measurement*, 1979, *39*, 119–128.

Larson, R. Thirty years of research on the subjective well-being of older Americans. *Journal of Gerontology*, 1978, *33*, 109–125.

Lawton, M. P. The Philadelphia Geriatric Center Morale Scale: A revision. *Journal of Gerontology*, 1975, *30*, 85–89.

Lohmann, N. Correlates of life satisfaction, morale and adjustment measures. *Journal of Gerontology*, 1977, *32*, 73–75.

Lopata, H. Z. Contribution of extended families to the support systems of metropolitan area widows: Limitations of the modified kin network. *Journal of Marriage and the Family*, 1978, *40*, 355–364.

Pihlblad, C. T., & Adams, D. L. Widowhood, social participation and life satisfaction. *Aging and Human Development*, 1972, *3*, 323–330.

Tunstall, J. *Old and alone*. Routledge & K. Paul, London. 1966.

United States Bureau of the Census. *Demographic aspects of aging and the older population in the United States*. Current Population Report Series PC-23, No. 59. U.S. Government Printing Office, Washington, DC, 1976.

Van Keep, P. A. Childfree cheer. *Human Behavior*, 1975, *4*, 44.

Veevers, J. E. The social meanings of parenthood. *Psychiatry*, 1973, *36*, 297–301.

Winer, B. J. *Statistical principles in experimental design*. McGraw-Hill, New York, 1962.

Zung, W. W. K. Depression in the normal aged. *Psychometrics*, 1967, *8*, 287–292.

Zung, W. W. K. From art to science. *Archives of General Psychiatry*, 1973, *29*, 328–337.

20

Divorce and the Elderly*

Peter Uhlenberg
Mary Anne P. Myers

The dramatic increase in divorce in the decade following 1964 and the sustained rate at an unprecedented high level in subsequent years are unquestionably of great social significance. In recent years there has been one divorce for every two marriages, and cohort projections indicate that a continuation of current rates would lead to 40% of recent marriages ending in divorce (Glick & Norton, 1977). Since the divorce rate is highest for the age group 20 to 24, and since the largest increase in the divorce rate in recent years has been among those age 25 to 39, divorce research has focused upon young adults. But it is not only young and middle-aged men and women who are affected by the changing divorce patterns. Current divorce trends have important implications for the social and economic well-being of the elderly. This paper examines the level of divorce among the elderly, suggests how it is likely to change in coming years, and discusses implications of these changes.

THE CURRENT DIVORCE EXPERIENCE OF THE ELDERLY

An overview of the current divorce experience of the elderly can be gained by answering three questions: How many get divorced after reaching age 65? How many of the elderly are currently divorced? How many have had their first marriage terminated by divorce?

*The Gerontologist, 21 (3) (1981), 276–282.

To answer these questions several different sources of data on divorce must be used. The number currently divorced can be calculated directly from the decennial censuses and the annual March Current Population Reports, which give marital status by age. Calculating the rate of divorce for those over age 65 requires two sources of data. The number obtaining a divorce during a year (the numerator) comes from the annual vital statistics reports, while the population at risk of a divorce (the denominator) comes from the census and current population reports data on the number currently married. Finally, there are two methods for estimating the proportion over 65 who have terminated a first marriage by divorce. One source is from the census, which asks those who are in a second or higher order marriage whether or not their marriage ended by the death of their spouse. It is assumed that if it was not terminated by death, it must have ended in divorce. Adding together those who are currently divorced and those who are married but experienced an earlier divorce, we have an estimate of how many have ever divorced. The other method involves tracing the experience of marriage cohorts, using vital statistics series. For a fuller discussion of these methods and possible errors in them (see Preston & McDonald (1979) and Carlson (1979)).

The main problem with the Census and the survey data comes from misreporting of current marital status. Because of social stigma attached to the divorced status it is likely that there is underreporting of being divorced. The problem with vital statistics is that a number of states still do not report divorces to the National Center for Health Statistics. Hence, national divorce rates must be estimated from the experience in those states which do supply divorce statistics. Because of these weaknesses in the data, the figures reported below should not be considered to be precise. On the other hand, they provide the best information available and can be used with some confidence to indicate general trends occurring over the past several decades.

The annual divorce rate for women over age 65 (i.e., divorces per 1000 married women in this age category) changed little during the 1960s, but then nearly doubled from 1.2 in 1970 to 2.2 in 1975 (Carlson, 1979). While this is a substantial percentage increase over a short time period, the rate of divorce by the elderly remains far below that of younger married adults (e.g., the divorce rate for those aged 20 to 29 in 1975 was about 40). Given the relatively low rate of divorce by the elderly and the smaller size of the older population compared to the younger, only 1% of all divorces in 1975 were to individuals aged 65 and over.

The second question concerns the distribution of the older population by marital status. Without regard to when the divorce occurred,
what percentage of older persons are currently divorced? In 1979
3.3% of both males and females over age 65 reported their marital
status as divorced (see Table 20.1). The 1979 figures show more than a
doubling since 1960 in the proportion of the elderly who are divorced,
and the proportion divorced among those age 65 to 74 is almost
double that of those aged 75 and older. Nevertheless, it is also
apparent from these data that being divorced in old age is still a
relatively uncommon experience in the United States. If we add those
who are separated from their spouses to those who are legally divorced, the proportion of older persons divorced or separated is only
slightly over 5%. Another way to measure the prevalence of the
divorced status is to compute the number of divorced persons per
1000 married with spouse present. These figures show the same trend
of increasing frequency of divorced over time, but in addition call
attention to the much higher frequency of older men than older

Table 20.1.   Marital Status of the Older Population by Age and Sex: United
States, 1979.

Sex and Marital Status	Age			
	65–74		75+	
	Total (in '000s)	%	Total (in '000s)	%
Male	6,385	100.0	3,162	100.0
Single	358	5.6	154	4.9
Married, wife present	5,006	78.4	2,115	66.9
Married, wife absent	182	2.9	63	2.0
Widowed	591	9.3	759	24.0
Divorced	248	3.9	71	2.2
Female	8,382	100.0	5,245	100.0
Single	504	6.0	324	6.2
Married, husband present	3,927	46.9	1,096	20.9
Married, husband absent	163	1.9	54	1.0
Widowed	3,454	41.2	3,656	69.7
Divorced	335	4.0	113	2.2

Source: U.S. Bureau of The Census, *Current Population Reports,* Series P-20, No. 349,
"Marital Status and Living Arrangements: March 1979."

women being currently married. For every divorced man there are 22 married men, while for every divorced woman there are only 11 married women.

Of course the proportion of older persons who have ever experienced a divorce is considerably larger than the proportion who are currently divorced, since many divorced individuals remarry. There are two methods for estimating the proportion of older persons who have had a marriage end in divorce, and they yield somewhat different figures. The first comes from the U.S. Census, which reports the number of persons who have ended their first and/or last marriage by divorce. According to the 1970 Census (U.S. Bureau of the Census, 1972), 10.2% of the population over age 65 had ever divorced. The proportion was highest for the age group 65 to 69 (13.6% for males and 12.3% for females), and declined for each successively older age category.

A second method of estimating the frequency of divorce is to cumulate the annual divorce rates for marriage cohorts from vital statistics records. Preston and McDonald (1979) have used this method to calculate the incidence of divorce for marriage cohorts since 1915, and their estimated proportion of older persons who have ever divorced is about 25% higher than the census reports. Several possible reasons for this discrepancy are suggested, but the most important one is probably the failure of some older persons to report an earlier divorce in the census. Using the census as a lower limit and the vital statistics as an upper limit, it appears that the proportion of the elderly population that has experienced a divorce is in the range of 10 to 13%.

Given the relatively low incidence and prevalence of divorce among the aged, as indicated by the above data, there may be some justification for the lack of attention given to this topic. However, if one is concerned about the *future* marital and familial experience of the elderly, it is important to inquire into how this situation is likely to change in coming years.

THE COMING RISE IN DIVORCE AMONG THE ELDERLY

Recent increases in divorce imply a very different divorce experience for the future elderly. Most certain is the change in the proportion who will have been ever-divorced. Based upon divorce rates in the years just prior to 1975, the Census Bureau projects that 38% of the women and 34% of the men born 1945 to 1949 who ever marry will end their first marriage in divorce. Since about 95% of these men and women will marry at some time, we can anticipate that over one-third of those reaching age 65 between 2010 and 2014 will have been divorced. Actually, the proportion experiencing a divorce could rise much higher than that for subsequent cohorts. If the marital-duration-specific divorce rates of recent years remain unchanged, 50% of those marrying now (and entering old age around 2020) will experience a divorce (Plateris, 1979). Between now and that time, the proportion who have divorced will continuously increase.

While a doubling or tripling over the next 40 years in the proportion of older persons who have been divorced is certain to occur, the frequency of divorce by the aged in the future is an open question. However, there are at least five reasons for expecting that the divorce rate for those over age 65 will also rise substantially.

First, as already noted, the annual divorce rate for the population 65 and older has increased rapidly in recent years. A simple projection of this trend into the future implies future increases.

Second, the big increase in the proportion of the elderly who will be in second or higher order marriages should lead to an increase in the divorce rate. Divorce at an earlier stage of the life course is generally followed by remarriage, but these remarriages are more prone to end in divorce than are first marriages. Among the married population over age 65 in 1970, 22.6% of the males and 19.2% of the females were in second or higher order marriages. However, among those over 65 who divorced in 1970, 73.5% of the males and 78.8% of the females had been married more than once (Plateris, 1978). This means that among the married population over age 65 the divorce rate was at least 10 times greater for those who had been married more than once than for those in first marriages. Thus, the steady increase in higher order marriages among the elderly implies a steady increase in the frequency of divorce.

Third, cohorts entering old age in the future are likely to be much more accepting of divorce as a solution to an unpleasant marriage. Not only will more have experienced divorce themselves, but all members of these cohorts will have witnessed the common occurrence of divorce among their age-peers. The changing frequency of divorce along with the liberalization of divorce laws in recent years suggest that expectations regarding the permanence of marriage is changing for cohorts now in the earlier stages of the life course. Stressors upon marriage (illness, lowered income, etc.) are not uncommon in old age, so increasing acceptability of divorce may be expected to lead to its greater use as a solution.

Fourth, increasing economic independence of women may encourage higher divorce rates. As cohorts enter old age in the future, an increasing proportion of the women will have been in the labor force, and the average length of time worked will increase. Therefore a larger proportion of women will have access to social security and pensions resulting from their own labor force experience. Also, increasing interest in problems of displaced homemakers is leading to legal changes which will enable divorced women to share the social security and pension benefits earned by their former husbands while they provided unpaid services in the home. Thus in coming years the economic constraints for older people to remain in unhappy marriages should be greatly reduced.

Finally, the reduction in mortality rates at earlier ages means that fewer marriages will be terminated by death prior to old age. With the resulting increased exposure to the risk of divorce after reaching old age, any given rate of divorce will result in a larger number of actual divorces. While this is not likely to be a major factor (e.g., see Preston & McDonald, 1979), it will exert some upward pressure upon the frequency of older persons experiencing divorce.

While these five arguments all indicate that the divorce rate among the elderly will increase in coming years, there is little basis for predicting precisely how high it might rise. Since the inverse relationship between marital duration and probability of divorce seems to be a very strongly established pattern, it is likely that divorce rates for the older population will always remain well below those for younger adults. Nevertheless, the number of older persons with an earlier divorce, the number whose marital status is "divorced," and the number who experience a divorce in old age can all be expected to increase rapidly in coming years. Therefore an interest in the future welfare and lifestyles of the elderly necessitates that attention be directed toward implications of divorce for the elderly.

DIVORCE AND THE WELFARE OF THE ELDERLY

Being divorced in old age (as in other ages) may negatively affect an individual's economic position and may increase his or her demands for social welfare support. Financial security for an elderly person is often precariously based upon ownership of house and basic consumer durables. The division of this property in a divorce settlement can result in both persons in the divorce experiencing a substantial decline in their economic well-being. Evidence to support this conclu-

Table 20.2.   Level of Satisfaction with Financial Situation, by Marital Status
and Sex: U.S. Population Aged 60 and Over, 1974–1978.

Sex and Level of Satisfaction	Marital Status			
	Married %	Widowed %	Single %	Divorced/ Separated %
Males (N)	(458)	(79)	(28)	(36)
Satisfied	45.4	41.8	46.4	38.9
More or Less Sat.	39.1	34.2	39.3	22.2
Not at all Sat.	15.5	24.1	14.3	38.9
Females (N)	(313)	(349)	(39)	(64)
Satisfied	49.2	43.7	48.7	28.1
More or Less Sat.	37.4	40.8	38.5	48.4
Not at all Sat.	13.4	15.5	12.8	23.4

Source: Computed from the combined 1972–78 Samples of The General Social Surveys
undertaken by The National Opinion Research Center at The University of Chicago,
James A. Davis, Principal Investigator: See footnote 1 for additional information.

sion of an adverse economic effect of divorce comes from two
sources.

First, some fairly direct information on this issue is available from
data collected in the General Social Surveys conducted by the National Opinion Research Center at the University of Chicago. National
samples for the years 1974, 1975, 1977 and 1978 can be combined since
the same questions were included, and we derive a national sample
of 1366 persons over the age of 60.[1] In each of these surveys, respondents were asked how satisfied they were with their financial situation. The distribution of older respondents on this variable, by sex
and marital status, is given in Table 20.2. While there is relatively little
difference between married, widowed, and never-married persons in
their subjective level of financial satisfaction, the divorced and separated older persons stand out as much less satisfied. A larger sample
of divorced and separated persons would be required to pursue a
more rigorous analysis of the casual relationship. Nevertheless, this
finding is supportive of the reasonable expectation that divorce will
damage the economic position of older persons.

[1] Each of these four surveys was drawn independently from the non-institutional
English-speaking population of the continental United States. A more detailed descrip-
tion of the sampling design can be found in the "General Social Surveys, 1972–78.
Cumulative Codebook," July, 1978, distributed by Roper Public Opinion Research
Center. Edward L. Kain provided computer assistance to obtain the data for Tables 2
and 3.

The second source of supporting evidence is studies of the economic consequences of divorce generally (i.e., not specific with respect to age). In his examination of these studies, Espenshade (1979) finds strong evidence that divorce is associated with a deterioration in the standard of living for wives, although it seems to have little effect upon husbands. For example, the Michigan Panel Study of Income Dynamics data allows a comparison of women who became divorced and did not remarry between 1967 and 1973 with women who were continuously married over this interval. Starting with "non-poor" women in 1967, 33% of the divorced women were classified as "poor" in 1973, compared to only 6% of the continuously married women. The major explanation suggested for the economic disadvantage of divorced women is simply the loss of economics of scale. Divorce leads to the establishment of separate living arrangements, with a subsequent loss in benefits derived from sharing fixed cost items (e.g., housing) of a common residence. There is no reason to expect that the economic impact upon older persons would be less than for those at other ages.

A second area of life potentially affected by divorce is the family and kinship relationships of the elderly. The myth that the elderly are abandoned by their adult children has been persuasively countered by the empirical research of several gerontologists (e.g., see Brody, 1978; Shanas, 1979). The Louis Harris 1974 study of aging found only 8% of those over 65 with children who had not visited with a child in the past 3 months, and 4 out of 5 had visited within the "last week or two" (Harris, 1975). These adult children offer important social relationships and they provide a wide range of services, such as health care, help with shopping and household chores, companionship on trips, and assistance in working through bureaucratic procedures. Based upon a 1975 national survey of the aged, Shanas reports, "the immediate family of the old person, husbands, wives, and children, is the major social support of the elderly in time of illness" (1979). No one who has carefully examined the evidence now doubts the importance of family and kinship in the lives of the elderly.

A picture of how individuals are enmeshed in social networks is presented by Kahn when he writes,

> each person can be thought of as moving through life surrounded by a set of significant other people to whom that person is related by giving or receiving of social support . . . The adequacy of social support is a determinant of individual well-being, of performance in the major social roles, and of success in managing life-changes and transitions (1979).

What happens to a person's social support network when there is a divorce? Surely divorce will frequently disrupt family and kinship ties which form critical links in the support system. But research on this topic is lacking. Probably because divorce among the elderly has in the past been so uncommon, as noted earlier, attention has not been given to its implications for their social well-being. Thus we are left with little but speculation regarding possible consequences.

Rates of remarriage after divorce are quite high, so a majority of divorced persons reestablish nuclear family relationships. But many do not remarry, and the remarriage rate has been declining since 1967. Therefore the high rate of divorce among young and middle-aged adults points to substantial increases in the proportion of elderly whose marital status will be "divorced." If divorce after reaching old age also becomes more common, as predicted above, the proportion who are divorced will increase even more. An immediate consequence of this change will be a smaller proportion of the elderly having a spouse to provide emotional and physical support.

Data from the NORC General Social Surveys mentioned above give evidence that divorced and separated older persons do in fact have lower satisfaction with some major areas of life. Table 20.3 compares levels of satisfaction with family life, friendships, and non-working activities (hobbies) for persons with differing marital statuses. Not surprisingly, the married report much higher levels of satisfaction with family life than do those with other marital statuses. Both males and females who are divorced or separated, however, express much less satisfaction than do other non-married categories (i.e., widowed and single). Likewise divorced and separated males report less satisfaction with friendships and with non-working activities than do those in any other marital status category. For females, marital status is essentially unrelated to level of satisfaction with areas of life other than the family.

Additional evidence of negative social welfare aspects of being divorced comes from studies of the relationship between marital status and mortality and mental illness. Kitagawa and Hauser (1973) have conducted the best U.S. study of marital status differentials in mortality. They found that for the population over age 65 around 1960, death rates for divorced males were 33% higher than for married males and 7% higher for divorced females than for married females. Thus, on the most basic measure of life chances, the divorced are seen to be disadvantaged. Likewise, studies of the relationship between marital status and mental health consistently find higher rates of mental illness for the divorced and separated than

Table 20.3. Level of Satisfaction with Family Life, Friendships, and Non-working Activities, by Marital Status and Sex: U.S. Population Aged 60 and Over, 1974–78.

Sex and Level of Satisfaction	Marital Status			
	Married %	Widowed %	Single %	Divorced/ Separated %
Males				
Satisfaction with family life				
High	93.2	61.0	61.5	42.4
Low	6.8	39.0	38.5	57.6
Satisfaction with friendships				
High	85.5	78.5	77.8	65.7
Low	14.2	21.5	22.2	34.3
Satisfaction with non-working activities				
High	69.5	68.0	70.4	62.9
Low	30.5	32.0	29.6	37.1
Females				
Satisfaction with family life				
High	92.0	78.2	76.9	70.8
Low	8.0	21.8	23.1	29.2
Satisfaction with friendships				
High	87.8	86.0	89.7	87.7
Low	12.2	14.0	10.3	12.3
Satisfaction with non-working activities				
High	76.9	75.9	76.9	80.0
Low	23.1	24.1	23.1	20.0

Source: Same as Table 20.2.

for the married population (e.g., see Gove, 1979). The lower satisfaction with relationships, the higher mortality rates, and the higher rates of mental illness for the divorced and separated population are all consequences that would be predicted to result from an inadequate social support network.

So far our attention has focused upon implications of being divorced in old age. However, in the future it is likely that, compared to the number who are divorced, a much larger number of the elderly will be divorced and remarried. What effect does a divorce earlier in life have upon the social relationships and support that older parents receive from their adult children? If contact with children is minimal for the parent who does not have custody, as frequently is the case, will there be reduced familial support for the elderly? What responsibility will adult children assume for their elderly step-parents? At this time we have no answers to these and related questions about the long-term consequences of divorce over the life course.

Another set of questions involves the effect of divorce in the middle-generation for relationships between older persons and their grandchildren. The Louis Harris survey found that 75% of the population over age 65 have grandchildren, and 74% of these grandparents had visited with a grandchild within the "last week or two." With smaller families and increasing frequency of divorce by both older persons and by their adult children, there is a potential sharp reduction coming in frequency of interaction between grandparents and their biological grandchildren. So little is known about interaction between the elderly and their grandchildren that it is difficult to even speculate on the significance of this possible change.

CONCLUSION

After surveying existing data to determine the contemporary older population's experience with divorce, this paper moved to an exploration of what might be expected in the future. Obviously the foundation for such speculation is not very firm, which means that this is an area badly in need of serious empirical research. The questions raised have great significance for the future welfare of the elderly since familial relationships are important in the lives of most older persons.

The proportion of the elderly who will be divorced or formerly divorced is going to increase quite rapidly over the next several decades. Reasons for expecting this change to produce a deterioration in the economic and social welfare of the elderly have been suggested. Perhaps other changes can also be anticipated. The experience of an earlier divorce may be a benefit when dealing with widowhood. Coping skills learned through the divorce and the assurance that survival is possible after a marital relationship ends could ease confrontation with the death of a spouse in old age. Another possibility is that an increase in the percentage of unattached men in the post-65 population could lead to increased non-marital sexual activity among the elderly. The speculation of possible changes could be continued, but starting some solid research into the implications of rising divorce among the elderly would be a far more constructive activity.

REFERENCES

Brody, E. M. The aging of the family. *Annals AAPSS*, 1978, *438*, 13–27.

Carlson, E. Divorce rate fluctuation as a cohort phenomenon. *Population Studies*, 1979, *33*, 523–536.

Espenshade, T. J. The economic consequences of divorce. *Journal of Marriage and the Family*, 1979, *41*, 615–625.

Glick, P. C., & Norton, A. N. Marrying, divorcing, and living together in the U.S. today. *Population Bulletin*, Vol. 32, No. 5. Population Reference Bureau, Inc., Washington, DC, 1977.

Gove, W. R. Sex, marital status, and psychiatric treatment: A research note. *Social Forces*, 1979, *58*, 89–93.

Harris, L. and Associates. *The myth and reality of aging in America*. The National Council on the Aging, Inc., Washington, DC, 1975.

Kahn, R. L. Aging and social support. In M. W. Riley (Ed.), *Aging from birth to death*. Westview Press, Boulder, CO, 1979.

Kitagawa, E. M., & Hauser, P. M. *Differential mortality in the United States: A study in socioeconomic epidemiology*. Harvard Univ. Press, Cambridge, MA, 1973.

Plateris, A. *Divorce and divorce rates: United States*. Series 21, No. 29. Vital and Health Statistics. National Ctr. for Health Statistics, Rockville, MD, 1978.

Plateris, A. *Divorce by marriage cohort*. Series 21, No. 34. Vital Health Statistics. National Ctr. for Health Statistics, Rockville, MD, 1979.

Preston, S. H., & McDonald, J. The incidence of divorce within cohorts of American marriages contracted since the Civil War. *Demography*, 1979, *16*, 1–25.

Shanas, E. The family as a social support system in old age. *Gerontologist*, 1979, *19*, 169–174.

U.S. Bureau of The Census, *Census of population: 1970*. PC(2)-4C, Marital Status. USGPO, Washington, DC, 1972.

References

Abernathy, V. (1973). Social network and response to the maternal role. *International Journal of Sociology and the Family, 3*(1), 86–92.

Adams, B. (1968a). *Kinship in an urban setting.* Chicago: Markham.

Adams, B. (1968b). The middle-class adult and his widowed or still married mother. *Social Problems, 16,* 51–59.

Albrecht, S. L., Bahr, H. M., & Chadwick, B. A. (1979). Changing family and sex roles: An assessment of age differences. *Journal of Marriage and the Family, 41*(1), 41–57.

Aldous, J. (1985). Parent-child relations as affected by the grandparent status. In V. L. Bengtson & J. F. Robertson (Eds.), *Grandparenthood* (pp. 117–132). Beverly Hills, CA: Sage.

Antonucci, T. C., & Akiyama, H. (1985, August). *A preliminary examination of the convoy concept.* Paper presented at the annual meeting of the American Psychological Association, Los Angeles.

Archbold, P. G. (1982). All-consuming activity: The family as caregiver. *Generations: The Journal of the Western Gerontological Society, 7*(2), 12–13.

Argyle, M., & Furnham, A. (1983). Sources of satisfaction and conflict in long-term relationships. *Journal of Marriage and the Family, 45*(3), 481–493.

Arling, G. (1976). The elderly widow and her family, neighbors, and friends. *Journal of Marriage and the Family, 38*(3), 757–768.

Arling, G., & McAuley, W. (1983). The feasibility of public payments for family caregiving. *The Gerontologist, 23*(3), 300–306.

Atchley, R., & Miller, S. (1983). Types of elderly couples. In T. H. Brubaker, (Ed.), *Family relationships in later life* (pp. 77–90). Beverly Hills, CA: Sage.

Atchley, R., Pignatiello, L., & Shaw, E. (1975). *The effect of marital status on social interaction patterns of older women.* Oxford, OH: Scripps Foundation.

Ballweg, J. A. (1967). Resolution of conjugal role adjustment after retirement. *Journal of Marriage and the Family, 29*(2), 277–281.

Bankoff, E. A. (1983a). Aged parents and their widowed daughters: A support relationship. *Journal of Gerontology, 38*(2), 226–230.

Bankoff, E. A. (1983b). Social support and adaptation to widowhood. *Journal of Marriage and the Family, 45*(4), 827–839.

Baranowski, M. D. (1982). Grandparent-adolescent relations: Beyond the nuclear family. *Adolescence, 17*(67), 575–585.

Baruch, G., & Barnett, R. C. (1983). Adult daughters' relationships with their mothers. *Journal of Marriage and the Family, 45*(3), 601–606.

Beck, S. H., & Beck, R. W. (1984). The formation of extended family households during middle age. *Journal of Marriage and the Family, 46*(2), 277–287.

Beckman, L. J., & Houser, B. B. (1982). The consequences of childlessness on the social and psychological well-being of older women. *Journal of Gerontology, 37*(2), 243–250.

Bedford, V. (1985). *Sibling themes among child-rearing and empty-nest adults.* Unpublished doctoral dissertation, Rutgers University.

Belsky, J., & Rovine, M. (1984). Social-network contact, family support, and the transition to parenthood. *Journal of Marriage and the Family, 46*(2), 455–462.

Bengtson, V. L. (1985). Diversity and symbolism in grandparental roles. In V. L. Bengtson & J. F. Robertson (Eds.), *Grandparenthood* (pp. 11–26). Beverly Hills, CA: Sage.

Bengtson, V. L., & Black, K. D. (1973, October). *Solidarity between parents and children.* Paper presented at the annual meeting of the National Council on Family Relations, Toronto.

Bengtson, V. L., Olander, E., & Haddad, E. (1976). The generation gap and aging family members: Towards a conceptual model. In J. F. Gubrium (Ed.), *Time, roles, and self in old age* (pp. 237–263). New York: Human Sciences Press.

Bengtson, V. L., & Robertson, J. F. (Eds.). (1985). *Grandparenthood.* Beverly Hills, CA: Sage.

Berardo, F. (1970). Survivorship and social isolation: The case of the aged widower. *Family Coordinator, 19*(1), 11–25.

Bernard, J. (1973). *The future of marriage.* New York: World Press (Bantam Books).

Blau, Z. (1961). Structural constraints on friendships in old age. *American Sociological Review, 26*(3), 429–439.

Branch, L. G., & Jette, A. M. (1983). Elders use of informal long-term care assistance. *The Gerontologist, 23*(1), 51–56.

Brody, E. (1985). Parent care as a normative family stress. *The Gerontologist, 25*(1), 19–29.

Brubaker, T. H. (Ed.). (1983). *Family relationships in later life.* Beverly Hills, CA: Sage.

Brubaker, T. H., & Hennon, C. B. (1982). Responsibility for household tasks: Comparing dual-earner and dual-retired marriages. In M. Szinovacz (Ed.), *Women's retirement: Policy implications of recent research* (pp. 205–219). Beverly Hills, CA: Sage.

Burgess, E. W., & Wallin, P. (1953). *Engagement and marriage.* Philadelphia: Lippincott.

Burton, L., M., & Bengtson, V. L. (1985). Black grandmothers: Issues of timing and continuity of roles. In V. L. Bengtson and J. F. Robertson (Eds.), *Grandparenthood* (pp. 61–78). Beverly Hills, CA: Sage.

Cheal, D. (1983). Intergenerational family transfers. *Journal of Marriage and the Family, 45*(4), 805–813.

Cherlin, A., & Furstenberg, F. F. (1985). Styles and strategies of grandparenting. In V. L. Bengtson & J. F. Robertson (Eds.), *Grandparenthood* (pp. 97–116). Beverly Hills, CA: Sage.

Chiriboga, D. A. (1982). Adaptation to marital separation in later and earlier life. *Journal of Gerontology, 37*(1), 109–114.

Chodorow, N. (1978). *The reproduction of mothering: Psychoanalysis and the sociology of gender.* Berkeley, CA: University of California Press.

Cicirelli, V. (1981). *Helping elderly parents: Role of adult children.* Boston: Auburn House.

Cicirelli, V. G. (1983a). Adult children and their elderly parents. In T. Brubaker (Ed.), *Family relationships in later life.* Beverly Hills, CA: Sage.

Cicirelli, V. (1983b). A comparison of helping behavior to elderly parents of adult children with intact and disrupted marriages. *The Gerontologist, 23*(6), 619–625.

Clark, M., & Anderson, B. G. (1967). *Culture and aging.* Springfield, IL: Charles C. Thomas.

Cleveland, W. P., & Gianturco, D. T. (1976). Remarriage probability after widowhood: A retrospective method. *Journal of Gerontology, 31*(1), 99–103.

Collins, G. (1983, December 9). Many more of elderly migrate to new states. *New York Times,* p. A20.

Cuber, J. F., & Harroff, P. B. (1963). The more total view: Relationships among men and women of the upper middle class. *Marriage and Family Living, 25*(May), 140–145.

Dahlin, M. (1980). Perspectives on family life of the elderly in 1900. *The Gerontologist, 20*(1), 99–107.

Dunkle, R. (1983). The effect of elders' household contributions on their depression. *Journal of Gerontology, 38*(6), 732–737.

Edwards, J. N., & Klemmack, D. L. (1973). Correlates of life satisfaction: A re-examination. *Journal of Gerontology, 28,* 497–502.

Feldman, H. (1964). *Development of the husband-wife relationship.* Ithaca, NY: Cornell University.

Feldman, H. (1981). A comparison of intentional parents and intentionally childless couples. *Journal of Marriage and the Family, 43*(3), 593–600.

Fengler, A. P. (1973). The effects of age and education on marital ideology. *Journal of Marriage and the Family, 35*(May), 264–271.

Fillenbaum, G. G., & Wallman, L. M. (1984). Change in household composition of the elderly: A preliminary investigation. *Journal of Gerontology, 39*(3), 342–349.

Fischer, L. R. (1981). Transitions in the mother-daughter relationship. *Journal of Marriage and the Family, 43*(3), 613–622.

Flynn, C. B., Longino, C. F., Jr., Wiseman, R. F., & Biggar, J. C. (1985). The redistribution of America's older population: Major national migration patterns for three census decades, 1960–1980. *The Gerontologist, 25*(3), 292–296.

Foster, D., Klinger-Vartabedian, L., & Wispe, L. (1984). Male longevity and age differences between spouses. *Journal of Gerontology, 39*(1), 117–120.

Freud, S. (1933). Femininity. In J. Strachey (Trans. and Ed.), *New introductory lectures on psychoanalysis.* New York: Norton.

Gallagher, D. E., Breckinridge, J. N., Thompson, L. W., & Peterson, J. A. (1983). Effects of bereavement on indicators of mental health in elderly widows and widowers. *Journal of Gerontology, 38*(5), 565–571.

Gilford, R., & Bengtson, V. (1979). Measuring marital satisfaction in three generations: Positive and negative dimensions. *Journal of Marriage and the Family, 41*(2), 15–50.

Glenn, N. D., & McLanahan, S. (1981). The effects of offspring on the psychological well-being of older adults. *Journal of Marriage and the Family, 43*(2), 409–422.

Glenn, N. D., & McLanahan, S. (1982). Children and marital happiness: A further specification of the relationship. *Journal of Marriage and the Family, 44*(1), 63–72.

Glick, P. (1980). Remarriage: Some recent changes and variations. *Journal of Family Issues, 1*(4), 455–478.

Gober, P., & Zonn, L. (1983). Kin and elderly amenity migration. *The Gerontologist, 23*(3), 288–294.

Goldman, N., & Lord, G. (1983). Sex differences in life cycle measures of widowhood. *Demography, 20,* 177–195.

Gutmann, D. (1975). Parenthood: Key to the comparative psychology of the life cycle. In N. Datan & L. Ginsberg (Eds.), *Developmental psychology: Normative life crises* (pp. 167–184). New York: Academic Press.

Hagestad, G. O. (1977). *Role change in adulthood: The transition to the empty nest.* Unpublished manuscript.

Hagestad, G. (1982). Divorce: The family ripple effect. *Generations, 7*(2), 24–25.

Hagestad, G. (1984). The continuous bond: A dynamic, multigenerational perspective on parent-child relations between adults. In M. Perlmutter (Ed.), *Minnesota Symposium on Child Psychology.* Hillside, NJ: Erlbaum.

Hagestad, G. O. (1985). Continuity and connectedness. In V. L. Bengtson & J. F. Robertson (Eds.), *Grandparenthood* (pp. 31–48). Beverly Hills, CA: Sage.

Hagestad, G. O., & Dixon, R. (1980). *Lineages as units of analysis: New avenues for the study of individual and family careers.* Paper presented at the NCFR Theory Construction and Research Methodology Workshop, Portland, OR.

Hagestad, G., & Neugarten, B. (1985). Age and the life course. In R. Binstock & E. Shanas (Eds.), *Handbook of aging and the social sciences* (pp. 35–61). New York: Van Nostrand Reinhold.

Hagestad, G. O., & Smyer, M. A. (1982). Dissolving long-term relationships: Patterns of divorcing in middle age. In S. Duck (Ed.), *Personal rela-*

tionships. 4. Dissolving personal relationships (pp. 155–196). New York: Academic Press.

Hagestad, G., Smyer, M., & Stierman, K. (1984). The impact of divorce in middle age. In R. S. Cohen, B. J. Cohler, & S. H. Weissman (Eds.), *Parenthood: A psychodynamic perspective* (pp. 247–262). New York: Guilford.

Haller, O. (1982). *An investigation of the perceptions of attachment in the mother–adult child dyad*. Unpublished doctoral dissertation, New York University.

Harris, L., and Associates, Inc. (1975). *The myth and reality of aging in America*. Washington, DC: National Council on Aging.

Hartshorne, T. S., & Manaster, G. (1982). The relationship with grandparents: Contact, importance, role conception. *International Journal of Aging and Human Development, 15*(3), 233–245.

Hays, J. A. (1984). Aging and family resources: Availability and proximity of kin. *The Gerontologist, 24*(2), 149–153.

Helsing, K. L., & Szklo, M. (1981). Mortality after bereavement. *American Journal of Epidemiology, 114*(1), 41–52.

Hennon, C. B. (1983). Divorce and the elderly: A neglected area of research. In T. Brubaker (Ed.), *Family relationships in later life* (pp. 149–172). Beverly Hills, CA: Sage.

Hess, B., & Waring, J. M. (1978). Parent and child in later life: Rethinking the relationship. In R. Lerner & G. Spanier (Eds.), *Child influences on marital and family interaction* (pp. 241–273). New York: Academic Press.

Hetherington, E. M., Cox, M., & Cox, R. (1982). Divorced fathers. *Family Coordinator, 25,* 417–428.

Hickey, T., & Douglass, R. L. (1981). Neglect and abuse of older family members: Professional perspectives and case experiences. *The Gerontologist, 21*(2), 171–176.

Hill, R. (1965). Decision-making and the family life cycle. In E. Shanas & G. Streib (Eds.), *Social structure and the family: Generational relations*. Englewood Cliffs, NJ: Prentice-Hall.

Holahan, C. K. (1984). Marital attitudes over 40 years: A longitudinal cohort analysis. *Journal of Gerontology, 39*(1), 49–57.

Hooyman, N., Gonyea, J., & Montgomery, R. (1985). The impact of in-home services termination on family caregivers. *The Gerontologist, 25*(2), 141–145.

Huyck, M.. H., & Hoyer, W. (1982). *Adult development and aging*. Belmont, CA: Wadsworth.

Johnson, C. L. (1982). Sibling solidarity: Its origin and functioning in Italian-American families. *Journal of Marriage and the Family, 44*(1), 155–168.

Johnson, C. L. (1985a). Grandparenting options in divorcing families: An anthropological perspective. In V. L. Bengtson & J. F. Robertson (Eds.). *Grandparenthood* (pp. 81–96). Beverly Hills, CA: Sage.

Johnson, C. L. (1985b). The impact of illness on late life marriages. *Journal of Marriage and the Family, 47*(1), 165–172.

Johnson, C. L., & Catalano, D. (1981). Childless elderly and their family supports. *The Gerontologist, 21*(6), 610–618.

Johnson, E. S. (1978). "Good" relationships between older mothers and their daughters: A causal model. *The Gerontologist, 18*(3), 90–96.

Johnson, E. S., & Bursk, B. (1977). Relationships between the elderly and their adult children. *The Gerontologist, 17*(1), 90–96.

Kahana, B., & Kahana, E. (1970). Grandparenthood from the perspective of the developing grandchild. *Developmental Psychology, 3*(1), 98–105.

Kahn, R. L., & Antonucci, T. (1980). Convoys over the life course: Attachment, roles, and social supports. In P. B. Baltes & O. G. Brim (Eds.), *Life-span development and behavior* (Vol. 3, pp. 253–286). New York: Academic Press.

Keating, N. C., & Cole, P. (1980). What do I do with him 24 hours a day? Changes in the housewife role after retirement. *The Gerontologist, 20*(1), 84–89.

Kivett, V. R., & Atkinson, M. P. (1984). Filial expectations, association, and helping as a function of number of children among older rural transitional parents. *The Gerontologist, 39*(4), 499–503.

Kivett, V. R., & Learner, R. M. (1982). Situational influences on the morale of older rural adults in child-shared housing: A comparative analysis. *The Gerontologist, 22*(1), 100–106.

Kivnick, H. Q. (1982). Grandparenthood: An overview of meaning and mental health. *The Gerontologist, 22*(1), 59–66.

Kivnick, H. Q. (1985). Grandparenthood and mental health: Meaning, behavior, and satisfaction. In V. L. Bengtson & J. F. Robertson (Eds.), *Grandparenthood* (pp. 151–158). Beverly Hills, CA: Sage.

Klein, D. M., Jorgensen, S. R., & Miller, B. (1979). Research methods and developmental reciprocity in families. In R. M. Lerner & G. B. Spanier (Eds.), *Child influences on marital and family interaction: A life-span perspective* (pp. 107–136). New York: Academic Press.

Konopka, G. (1976). *Young girls: A portrait of adolescence.* Englewood Cliffs, NJ: Prentice-Hall.

Krout, J. (1983). Second migration of the elderly. *The Gerontologist, 23*(3), 295–299.

Kuypers, J. A., & Bengtson, V. L. (1983). Toward competence in the older family. In T. Brubaker (Ed.), *Family relationship in later life* (pp. 211–228). Beverly Hills, CA: Sage.

Lamb, M. E., & Lamb, J. E. (1976). The nature and importance of the father-infant relationship. *Family Coordinator, 25,* 388–579.

Lee, G. R., & Ellithorpe, E. (1982). Intergenerational exchange and subjective well-being among the elderly. *Journal of Marriage and the Family, 44*(1), 217–224.

Lee, G. R., & Ihinger-Tallman, M. (1980). Sibling interaction and morale: The effects of family relations on older people. *Research on Aging, 2*(3), 367–391.

Lehr, U. (1982). Hat die Grosz familie heute noch eine chance? *Der Deutsche Arzt, 18.* Sonderdruck.

Leigh, G. K. (1982). Kinship interaction over the family life span. *Journal of Marriage and the Family, 44*(1), 197–208.

Lenny, B. K. (1985, August). *An investigation of the perception of attachment-relationships of siblings in adult life.* Paper presented at the annual meeting of the American Psychological Association, Los Angeles.

Lipman, A. (1961). Role conceptions and morale of couples in retirement. *Journal of Gerontology, 16,* 267–271.

Litwak, E. (1960a). Geographic mobility and extended family cohesion. *American Sociological Review, 25,* 385–394.

Litwak, E. (1960b). Occupational mobility and extended family cohesion. *American Sociological Review, 25,* 9–21.

Lopata, H. Z. (1973). *Widowhood in an American city.* Cambridge, MA: Schenkman.

Lopata, H. Z. (1979). *Women as widows: Support systems.* New York: Elsevier.

Lowenthal, M. F., & Haven, C. (1968). Interaction and adaptation: Intimacy as a critical variable. *American Sociological Review, 33*(1), 20–30.

Lowenthal, M. F., Thurnher, M. T., & Chiriboga, D. (1975). *Four stages of life.* San Francisco: Jossey-Bass.

Marshall, V. W. (1975). Age and awareness of finitude in developmental gerontology. *Omega, 6*(2), 113–127.

Masters, W. H., & Johnson, V. E. (1966). *Human sexual response.* Boston: Little, Brown.

Matthews, S. H., & Sprey, J. (1984). The impact of divorce on grandparenthood: An exploratory study. *The Gerontologist, 24*(1), 41–47.

Matthews, S. H., & Sprey, J. (1985). Adolescents' relationships with grandparents: An empirical contribution to conceptual clarification. *Journal of Gerontology, 40*(5), 621–626.

McGhee, J. (1985). The effects of siblings on the life satisfaction of the rural elderly. *Journal of Marriage and the family, 47*(1), 85–91.

Medley, M. L. (1976). Satisfaction with life among persons 65 years and older: A causal model. *Journal of Gerontology, 31*(4), 448–455.

Mindel, C. H. (1979). Multigenerational family households: Recent trends and implications for the future. *The Gerontologist, 19*(5), 456–463.

Mindel, C. (1983). The elderly in minority families. In T. Brubaker (Ed.), *Family relationships in later life* (pp. 193–208). Beverly Hills, CA: Sage.

Mindel, C. H., & Wright, R. J. (1982). Satisfaction in multigenerational households: *Journal of Gerontology, 37*(4), 483–489.

Mitchell, J., & Register, J. C. (1984). An exploration of family interaction with the elderly by race, socioeconomic status and residence. *The Gerontologist, 24*(1), 48–54.

Morgan, J. N., Dickinson, K., Dickinson, V., Benus, J., & Duncan, G. (1974). *Five thousand American families—patterns of economic progress* (Vol. 1). Survey Research Center, Institute for Social Research, University of Michigan, Ann Arbor, MI.

Morgan, L. (1984). Changes in family interaction following widowhood. *Journal of Marriage and the Family, 46*(2), 323–331.

Morgan, T. J., Hansson, R. O., Indart, M., Austin, D. M., Crutcher, M. M., Hampton, P. W., Oppegard, K. M., & O'Daffer, V. (1984). Old age and environmental docility: The roles of health, support, and personality. *Journal of Gerontology, 39*(2), 240–242.

Neugarten, B. L., & Weinstein, K. K. (1964). The changing American grandparent. *Journal of Marriage and the Family, 26,* 199–204.

Noelker, L. S., & Poulshock, S. W. (1982). *The effects on families of caring for impaired elderly in residence. Final report to the Administration on Aging.* Cleveland, OH: The Benjamin Rose Institute.

Nydegger, C. (1983). Family ties of the aged in cross-cultural perspective. *The Gerontologist, 23*(1), 26–32.

Nydegger, C. N., & Mitteness, L. (1982). Transitions in fatherhood. *Generations, 7*(2), 14–15.

Palmore, E., & Luikart, C. (1972). Health and social factors related to life satisfaction. *Journal of Health and Social Behavior, 13* (March), 68–80.

Parkes, C. M., Benjamin, B., & Fitzgerald, R. G. (1969). Broken heart: A statistical study of increased mortality among widowers. *British Medical Journal, 1,* 740–743.

Parron, E. (1979). *Relationships among black and white golden wedding couples.* Unpublished doctoral dissertation, Rutgers University.

Parsons, T. (1955). The organization of personality as a system of action. In T. Parson & R. F. Bales (Eds.), *Family: Socialization and interaction process* (pp. 135–186). Glencoe, IL: The Free Press.

Pearlin, L. I., & Schooler, C. (1978). The structure of coping. *Journal of Health and Social Behavior, 19,* 2–21.

Pineo, P. C. (1961). Disenchantment in the later years of marriage. *Marriage and Family Living, 23,* 1–12.

Plath, D. W. (1980). Contours of consociation: Lessons from a Japanese narrative. In P. B. Baltes & O. G. Brim, Jr. (Eds.), *Life-span development and behavior* (Vol. 3) (pp. 287–307). New York: Academic Press.

Quinn, W. H. (1983). Personal and family adjustment in later life. *Journal of Marriage and the Family, 45*(1), 57–73.

Raush, H. L., Barry, W. A., Hertel, R. H., & Swain, M. A. (1974). *Communication, conflict, and marriage.* San Francisco: Jossey-Bass.

Reedy, M. N. (1977). *Age and sex differences in personal needs and the nature of love: A study of happily married young, middle-aged, and older adult couples.* Unpublished doctoral dissertation, University of Southern California.

Reiss, D., & Oliveri, M. E. (1983). The family's construction of social reality and its ties to its kin network: An exploration of causal direction. *Journal of Marriage and the Family, 45*(1), 81–92.

Rempel, J. (1985). Childless elderly: What are they missing? *Journal of Marriage and the Family, 47*(2), 343–348.

Rosenberg, G. L., & Anspach, D. F. (1973). Sibling solidarity in the working class. *Journal of Marriage and the Family, 35,* 108–113.

Rosenthal, C., & Marshall, V. (1985, July). *Aging and multigenerational ritual occasions.* Paper presented at the International Association of Gerontology, New York City.

Rosow, I. (1967). *Social integration of the aged.* New York: The Free Press.

Rothbart, M. K., & Maccoby, E. E. (1966). Parents' differential reactions to sons and daughters. *Journal of Personality and Social Psychology, 4,* 237–243.

Scanzoni, J. (1975). *Sex roles, life styles, and childbearing.* New York: Macmillan.

Scharlach, A. E., & Scharlach, I. C. (1985, August). *The impact of role strain on late-life filial relationships.* Paper presented at American Psychological Association Annual Meeting, Los Angeles.

Scott, J. P. (1983). Siblings and other kin. In T. Brubaker (Ed.), *Family relationships in later life* (pp. 47–62). Beverly Hills, CA: Sage.

Seltzer, M. M., & Troll, L. E. (1982). Conflicting public attitudes towards filial responsibility. In L. E. Troll (Ed.), *Elders and their families. Generations, 7*(2). San Francisco: Western Gerontological Society.

Seltzer, M. M., & Troll, L. E. (1985, July). *Expected life history: A model in nonlinear time.* Paper presented at the International Association of Gerontology, New York City.

Shanas, E. (1979). The family as a social support system in old age. *The Gerontologist, 19*(2), 169–174.

Shanas, E., & Streib, G. F. (Eds.). (1965). *Social structure and the family: Generational relations.* Englewood Cliffs, NJ: Prentice-Hall.

Shanas, E., Townsend, P., Wedderburn, D., Fries, H., Milhhoj, P., & Stehouver, J. (1968). *Older people in three industrial societies.* New York: Atherton.

Shepherd-Look, D. L. (1982). Sex differentiation and the development of sex roles. In B. B. Wolman, (Ed.), *Handbook of developmental psychology* (pp. 405–433). Englewood Cliffs, NJ: Prentice-Hall.

Skolnick, A. (1981). Married lives: Longitudinal perspectives on marriage. In D. Eichorn, J. Clausen, N. Haan, M. Honzik, & P. Mussen (Eds.), *Present and past in middle age* (pp. 270–300). New York: Academic Press.

Smith, D. S. (1979). Historical change in the household structure of the elderly in economically developed societies. In R. W. Fogel, E. Hatfield, S. B. Kiesler, & E. Shanas (Eds.), *Aging: Stability and change in the family.* New York: Academic Press.

Snow, R., & Crapo, L. (1982). Emotional bondedness, subjective well-being and health in elderly medicare patients. *Journal of Gerontology, 37*(5), 609–615.

Soldo, B., J., & Myllyuoma, J. (1983). Caregivers who live with dependent elderly. *The Gerontologist, 23*(6), 605–611.

Soldo, B. J., Sharma, M., & Campbell, R. T. (1984). Determinants of the community living arrangements of older unmarried women. *Journal of Gerontology, 39*(4), 492–498.

Sternberg, R. (1985). *Love through the life span.* Paper presented at the meeting of the American Psychological Association, Los Angeles.

Stoller, E. P. (1985). Elder-caregiver relationships in shared households. *Research in Aging, 7*(2), 175–194.

Streib, G. (1965). Intergenerational relations: Perspectives of the two generations on the older parent. *Journal of Marriage and the Family, 27,* 469–476.

Stueve, A., & Fisher, C. S. (1978, September). Social networks and older women. Paper presented at Workshop on Older Women, Washington, DC.

Sullivan, D. A. (1985). The ties that bind. *Research on Aging, 7*(2), 235–250.

Sweetser, D. A. (1963). Asymmetry in intergenerational family relationships. *Social Forces, 41*, 346–352.

Sweetser, D. A. (1984). Love and work: Intergenerational household composition in the U.S. in 1900. *Journal of Marriage and the Family, 46*(2), 289–293.

Swenson, C., H., Eskew, R. W., & Kohlhepp, K. A. (1981). Stage of the family life cycle, ego development, and the marriage relationship. *Journal of Marriage and the Family, 43*(4), 841–853.

Szinovacz, M. (1980). Female retirement: Effects on spousal roles and marital adjustment. *Journal of Family Issues, 1*, 423–440.

Thomas, L. E. (1982). Sexuality and aging: Essential vitamin or popcorn. *The Gerontologist, 22*(3), 240–243.

Thompson, L., & Walker, A. (1984). Mothers and daughters: Aid patterns and attachment. *Journal of Marriage and the Family, 46*(2), 313–322.

Thurnher, M. (1976). Midlife marriage: Sex differences in evaluation and perspective. *International Journal of Aging and Human Development, 7*(2), 129–135.

Thurnher, M. (1982). Family patterns vary among U.S. ethnic groups. *Generations: Journal of the Western Gerontological Society, 7*(2), 8–9.

Tinsley, B. R., & Parke, R. D. (1984). Grandparents as support and socialization agents. In M. Lewis (Ed.), *Beyond the dyad* (pp. 161–194). New York: Plenum Press.

Traupmann, J., Eckels, E., & Hatfield, E. (1982). Intimacy in older women's lives. *The Gerontologist, 22*(6), 493–498.

Troll, L. E. (1972). Is parent-child conflict what we mean by the generation gap? *Family Coordinator, 21*, 347–349.

Troll, L. (1980b). Grandparenting. In L. Poon (Ed.), *Aging in the 1980's* (pp. 475–481). Washington, DC: American Psychological Association.

Troll, L. E. (1980b). Intergenerational relations in later life: A family system approach. In N. Datan & N. Lohmann (Eds.), *Transitions of aging* (pp. 75–91). New York: Academic Press.

Troll, L. E. (1982a). *Continuations: Adult development and aging.* Monterey, CA: Brooks/Cole.

Troll, L. E. (Ed.), (1982b). Elders and their families. *Generations: Journal of the Western Gerontological Society, 1*(2).

Troll, L. (1983). Grandparents: The family watchdogs. In T. Brubaker, (Ed.), *Family relationships in later life* (pp. 63–74). Beverly Hills, CA: Sage.

Troll, L. E. (1985a). *Early and middle adulthood* (2nd ed.). Monterey, CA: Brooks/Cole.

Troll, L. E., & Bengtson, V. L. (1979). Generations in the family. In W. Burr, G. Nye, R. Hill, & I. Reiss (Eds.), *Contemporary theories about the family* (pp. 127–161). New York: Free Press.

Troll, L. E., Miller, S., & Atchley, R. (1979). *Families of later life.* Belmont, CA: Wadsworth.

Troll, L. E., & Seltzer, M. M. (1985, August). Older women and poverty. Paper presented at the annual meeting of the American Psychological Association, Los Angeles. August.

Troll, L. E., & Stapley, J. (1986). Elders and the extended family system: Health, family salience, and affect. In J. M. A. Munnich, (Ed.), *Life span and change in a gerontological perspective.* New York: Academic Press.

Turner, B. F., & Huyck, M. H. (1982). Gerontologists and their parents: It's not any easier. In L. E. Troll (Ed.), Elders and their families. *Generations: Journal of the Western Gerontological Association, 7*(2), 32–34.

Uhlenberg, P., & Myers, M. A. (1981). Divorce and the elderly. *The Gerontologist, 21*(3), 276–282.

U.S. Bureau of the Census. (1975). Social and economic characteristics of the older population. *Current population reports,* Service P-23, No. 57, Washington, DC: Government Printing Office.

U.S. Bureau of the Census. (1982, January). *Census Population Reports.* Washington, DC: U.S. Government Printing Office.

Walker, A., & Thompson, L. (1983). Intimacy and intergenerational aid and contact among mothers and daughters. *Journal of Marriage and the Family, 45*(4), 841–850.

Walker, K. (1970, June). Time spent by husbands in household work. *Family Economics Review,* 8–11. Washington, DC: U.S. Department of Agriculture.

Weihl, H. (1985b, July). *Household development of aged persons over a period of twelve years.* Paper presented at the International Association of Gerontology, New York City.

Weishaus, S. S. (1978). *Determinants of affect of middle-aged women towards their aging mothers.* Unpublished doctoral dissertation, University of Southern California.

Wilson, K. B., & DeShane, M. (1982). The legal rights of grandparents. A preliminary discussion. *The Gerontologist, 22*(1), 67–71.

Wood, V., & Robertson, J. F. (1976). The significance of grandparenthood. In J. Gubrium (Ed.), *Time, roles, and self in old age* (pp. 278–304). New York: Human Sciences Press.

√ York, J. L., & Calsyn, R. J. (1977). Family involvement in nursing home. *The Gerontologist, 17*(1), 500–505.

Youmans, G. (1963). *Aging patterns in a rural and urban area of Kentucky.* Lexington, KY: University of Kentucky Agricultural Experiment Station.

Young, M., Benjamin, B., & Wallis, C. (1963). The mortality of widowers. *Lancet, 2,* 454–456.

Young, M., & Willmott, P. (1962). *Family and kinship in East London* (rev. ed.). Harmondworth, UK: Penguin.

Zarit, S. H., Reever, K. E., & Bach-Peteron, J. (1980). Relatives of the impaired elderly: Correlates of feelings of burden. *The Gerontologist, 20*(6), 649–655.

INDEX